Bayley - Journals?

Steinberg -

Will Monhon

Is there anything not only from mental?

Maybe Sampson +

— Brt & US either of
neil + Bell Jar

CW01499003

SYLVIA PLATH IN CONTEXT

Sylvia Plath in Context brings together an exciting combination of established and emerging thinkers from a range of disciplines. The book reveals Plath's responses to the writers she reads, her interventions in the literary techniques and forms she encounters, and the wide range of cultural, personal, artistic, political, historical and geographical influences that shaped her work. Many of these essays confront the specific challenges of reading Sylvia Plath today. Others evaluate her legacy to the writers who followed her. Reaching well beyond any simple equation in which biographical cause results in literary effect, all of them argue for a body of work that emerges from Plath's deep involvement in the world she inhabits. Situating Plath's writing within a wide frame of references that reach beyond any single notion of self, this book will be a vital resource for students, scholars, instructors and researchers of Sylvia Plath.

TRACY BRAIN is Reader in English Literature and Creative Writing at Bath Spa University, where she runs the PhD in Creative Writing programme. She is the author of *The Other Sylvia Plath* (2001) and co-editor of *Representing Sylvia Plath* (2011). She has published numerous essays on Plath's work. Her interests are wide-ranging – from an essay on sewing in *Jane Eyre* to a book about pregnancy and birth in the eighteenth- and nineteenth-century novel.

SYLVIA PLATH IN CONTEXT

EDITED BY

TRACY BRAIN

Bath Spa University

CAMBRIDGE
UNIVERSITY PRESS

CAMBRIDGE
UNIVERSITY PRESS

University Printing House, Cambridge CB2 8BS, United Kingdom

One Liberty Plaza, 20th Floor, New York, NY 10006, USA

477 Williamstown Road, Port Melbourne, VIC 3207, Australia

314–321, 3rd Floor, Plot 3, Splendor Forum, Jasola District Centre,
New Delhi – 110025, India

79 Anson Road, #06–04/06, Singapore 079906

Cambridge University Press is part of the University of Cambridge.

It furthers the University's mission by disseminating knowledge in the pursuit of
education, learning, and research at the highest international levels of excellence.

www.cambridge.org
Information on this title: www.cambridge.org/9781108470131
DOI: 10.1017/9781108556200

© Cambridge University Press 2019

First published 2019

Printed and bound in Great Britain by Clays Ltd, Elcograf S.p.A.

A catalogue record for this publication is available from the British Library.

Library of Congress Cataloging-in-Publication Data
NAMES: Brain, Tracy, editor.
TITLE: Sylvia Plath in context / edited by Tracy Brain.
DESCRIPTION: Cambridge, United Kingdom ; New York, NY : Cambridge University Press,
2019. | Includes bibliographical references and index.
IDENTIFIERS: LCCN 2019011493 | ISBN 9781108470131 (Hardback : alk. paper)
SUBJECTS: LCSH: Plath, Sylvia – Criticism and interpretation.
CLASSIFICATION: LCC PS3566.L27 Z9156 2019 | DDC 811/.54 [B]–dc23
LC record available at https://lccn.loc.gov/2019011493

ISBN 978-1-108-47013-1 Hardback

Contents

Notes on Contributors

SALLY BAYLEY is a Teaching and Research Fellow at Oxford University's Rothermere American Institute and a Lecturer in English, Lady Margaret Hall. She has co-edited two editions of essays on Plath: *Eye Rhymes: Sylvia Plath's Art of the Visual* (2007) and *Representing Sylvia Plath* (Cambridge University Press, 2011). She has completed a cross-disciplinary study of the American home, *Home on the Horizon: America's Search for Space* (2010), and a mixed-genre book on the diary as a coming of age story, *The Private Life of the Diary: From Pepys to Tweets* (2016). Her memoir *Girl with Dove: A Life Built by Books* was published in 2018.

LYNDA K. BUNDTZEN is Herbert H. Lehman Professor of English emerita and currently an Oakley Center Fellow at Williams College, Williamstown, Massachusetts. She is the author of *Plath's Incarnations: Woman and the Creative Process* (1983), winner of the Alice and Edith Hamilton Prize from University of Michigan Press, and *The Other Ariel* (2001). She has published widely on major film directors, including Ingmar Bergman, Bernardo Bertolucci, Werner Herzog, David Lynch and Ridley Scott. Essays on Ted Hughes include 'Mourning Eurydice: Ted Hughes as Orpheus in *Birthday Letters*', 'Confession, Contrition, and Concealment: Evoking Sylvia Plath in *Howls and Whispers*' and 'Traumatic Repetition in *Capriccio*'.

HEATHER CLARK is Visiting Professor at the University of Huddersfield and Visiting Research Scholar at the Graduate Center, City University of New York. She received a 2017–18 NEH Public Scholar Fellowship and a 2016–17 Biography Fellowship at the Leon Levy Center for Biography, City University of New York, and has recently been a Visiting Scholar at the Oxford Centre for Life-Writing and a Visiting US Fellow at the Eccles Centre for American Studies at the British Library. She is the author of two prizewinning monographs: *The*

Grief of Influence: Sylvia Plath and Ted Hughes (2010) and *The Ulster Renaissance: Poetry in Belfast 1962–1972* (2006). She is currently completing a literary biography of Sylvia Plath and *Sylvia Plath: A Very Short Introduction*. Her book reviews have appeared in the *Times Literary Supplement*, *PN Review* and the *Harvard Review*.

SARAH CORBETT is a poet and Lecturer in Creative Writing at Lancaster University. Her fifth collection of poems, *A Perfect Mirror* (2018), includes a number of poems addressed to Sylvia Plath. Her previous collections of poetry are: *The Red Wardrobe* (1998), awarded an Eric Gregory Award and shortlisted for the T. S. Eliot Prize and the Forward Prize for Best First Collection, *The Witch Bag* (2002), *Other Beasts* (2008) and *And She Was: A Verse-Novel* (2015). She has written on the verse novel and intimacy in contemporary women's poetry and is currently writing her first novel.

GAIL CROWTHER has held lectureships in Religion, Culture and Society and Sociology. She currently teaches Social Science at the Open University. She has published several papers and chapters on Plath, such as 'These Ghostly Archives' in *Plath Profiles* (2009–13), 'Haunting Places in the Poems of Plath' in *Critical Insights* (2013) and 'The Unquiet Graves of Ian Curtis and Sylvia Plath' in *Joy Devotion* (2016). She is the author of *The Haunted Reader and Sylvia Plath* (2016) and has co-authored two other books: *Sylvia Plath in Devon: A Year's Turning* (2014) and *These Ghostly Archives* (2017).

JONATHAN ELLIS is Reader in American Literature at Sheffield University. He is the author of *Art and Memory in the Work of Elizabeth Bishop* (2006), co-editor (with Angus Cleghorn) of *The Cambridge Companion to Elizabeth Bishop* (2014) and editor of *Letter Writing Among Poets: From William Wordsworth to Elizabeth Bishop* (2015). His essays and reviews have appeared in *English*, *Mosaic*, *PN Review*, *The Times Literary Supplement* and other journals. He is currently writing a short book on letter writing.

GARETH FARMER is Lecturer in English Literature at the University of Bedfordshire. He works on modern and contemporary poetry, poetics, experimental literature and critical theory. He is the Senior Academic Consultant to the Veronica Forrest-Thomson Archive at Girton College, Cambridge, and has worked on several projects relating to her work. He has edited and republished Forrest-Thomson's *Poetic Artifice: A Theory of Twentieth-Century Poetry*, and has recently published a monograph on her poetry and critical writing entitled, *Veronica Forrest-Thomson: Poet on the Periphery* (2017). He is also editing Forrest-Thomson's collected and uncollected writings. He has published essays, articles and reviews on a range of modern and contemporary poetry and experimental writing and is also a poet.

ELAINE FEINSTEIN is a prize-winning poet, novelist, biographer, radio dramatist and translator. She has taught at the University of Cambridge and the University of Essex. She has written for *The Times*, *The Telegraph*, *The New York Review of Books* and many others. In 1981 she was made a Fellow of the Royal Society of Literature. Her published books are too numerous to list. Her first novel, *The Circle* (1970), was longlisted for the Man Booker Prize and won the Betty Miller Prize for Fiction. Her novel *Mother's Girl* (1988) was shortlisted for *The Los Angeles Times* Fiction Prize. Her five biographies include *Ted Hughes: The Life of a Poet* (2001), which was shortlisted for the Marsh Biography Prize.

AMANDA GOLDEN is Assistant Professor of English at the New York Institute of Technology. She previously held the Post-Doctoral Fellowship in Poetics at Emory University's Fox Center for Humanistic Inquiry and a Marion L. Brittain Postdoctoral Fellowship at the Georgia Institute of Technology. She is the author of *Annotating Modernism: Marginalia and Pedagogy from Virginia Woolf to the Confessional Poets* (forthcoming) and editor of *This Business of Words: Reassessing Anne Sexton* (2016). She has published in *Modernism/modernity*, *The Woolf Studies Annual* and *The Ted Hughes Society Journal*.

KATE HARDING is a feminist writer, speaker and scholar. She is the author of *Asking for It: The Alarming Rise of Rape Culture – and What We Can Do About It* (2015), which was a finalist for the Minnesota Book Award, and co-editor of *Nasty Women: Feminism, Resistance, and Revolution in Trump's America* (2017). Co-author of two other books and a contributor to numerous anthologies, including *Yes Means Yes: Visions of Female Sexual Power and a World Without Rape* (2008), she holds an MFA in writing fiction, and is currently at work on a doctorate in nonfiction.

JANE HEDLEY is K. Laurence Stapleton Emeritus Professor of English at Bryn Mawr College. She is the author of *Power in Verse: Metaphor and Metonymy in the Renaissance Lyric* (1988) and *'I Made You to Find Me': The Coming of Age of the Woman Poet and the Politics of Poetic Address*

(2009), which includes a chapter on Sylvia Plath. Her most recent book, *Modern Marriage and the Lyric Sequence* (2018), includes discussion of Ted Hughes's marriage sequence, *Birthday Letters*. Hedley has also co-edited *In the Frame: Women's Ekphrastic Poetry from Marianne Moore to Susan Wheeler* (2009).

ANITA HELLE is Professor of English at Oregon State University, where she has served as Director of the School of Writing, Literature and Film. Her research interests include modern and contemporary American poetry, postmodern fiction, feminist and gender theory and illness narrative. She is editor of *The Unraveling Archive: Essays on Sylvia Plath* (2007) and has published widely on Plath and twentieth-century poetry, including in *Representing Sylvia Plath* (Cambridge University Press, 2011) and *The Oxford Handbook of the Elegy* (2010). She is currently working on a monograph on modern poetry and photographic portraiture.

BEATRICE HITCHMAN is a writer and is Lecturer in Creative Writing at the University of Gloucestershire. Her first novel, *Petite Mort* (2013), was nominated for the Desmond Elliott Prize, the Polari Prize, the Author's Club Best First Novel Prize and the Historical Writers' Association Debut Novel Prize, and was serialised on BBC Radio 4 as a ten-part Woman's Hour Drama. Her research interests include queer theory, happiness studies, historical fiction and twentieth-century lesbian and gay fiction. Her doctoral research examines the evolution of the 'unhappy queer ending' in the twentieth-century LGBT novel and aims to understand how an author might negotiate the long shadow of the unhappy ending when writing.

RICHARD KERRIDGE is a nature writer and literary critic. His book *Cold Blood*, about British reptiles and amphibians, their meanings and his fascination with them dating from childhood, was published in 2014. His nature writing has appeared in *Granta, Poetry Review* and *BBC Wildlife*. He leads the MA in Creative Writing at Bath Spa University, and has published widely on fiction and poetry, and on literature and environment.

KAREN V. KUKIL curates the Virginia Woolf and Sylvia Plath collections at Smith College in Northampton, Massachusetts. She also teaches in the Archives Concentration program and is the editor of the unabridged *Journals of Sylvia Plath* (2000) and co-editor of the two-volume *The Letters of Sylvia Plath* (2017 and 2018). Curated exhibitions include *'No*

Other Appetite': Sylvia Plath, Ted Hughes, and the Blood Jet of Poetry (2005) and *One Life: Sylvia Plath* (2017).

NOREEN MASUD is a Leverhulme Early Career Fellow in the Department of English Studies at the University of Durham. She holds a PhD from the University of Oxford, which is on the subject of aphorism and aphoristic aesthetics in the work of Stevie Smith. She organised the first one-day conference on the poet at Jesus College, Oxford, in March 2016. Recent publications include "'Ach ja': Stevie Smith's Escheresque Metamorphoses' in the *Cambridge Quarterly*. She is currently working on an article about flatness and surface reading in Smith's work and is co-editing a special issue of *Women: A Cultural Review*.

WILL MAY is Associate Professor of English at the University of Southampton. He is the author of *Stevie Smith and Authorship* and *Postwar Literature: 1950–1990* (both 2010) and editor of *The Collected Poems and Drawings of Stevie Smith* (2015). He is currently writing a study of poetry and whimsy.

MAEVE O'BRIEN completed her doctorate on the work of Sylvia Plath at Ulster University, where she is currently a Teaching Fellow. Her writings have appeared in *Plath Profiles, The Ted Hughes Society Journal* and *The Irish Times*. In 2017, she hosted Letters, Words and Fragments: An International Sylvia Plath Conference in Belfast, Northern Ireland. She is currently working on a monograph, *The Courage of Shutting Up: Strategies of Silence in the Work of Sylvia Plath*.

CORNELIA PEARSALL is Professor of English at Smith College. She is the author of *Tennyson's Rapture* (2008) and articles on Robert Browning, the Duke of Wellington, Virginia Woolf, W. H. Auden, Keith Douglas and Ted Hughes, amongst others. She is completing a book entitled *Imperial Disappearance: Tennyson and the Expansion of England*, on the interrelation of late Victorian poetry and imperial expansion. She is also working on two other books – one on Victorian mourning and memorialisation and the other on war poetry from Tennyson to Plath. Other projects study Browning and trauma; Queen Victoria and melancholia; and Miss Marple and sexuality.

ROBIN PEEL is a Visiting Research Fellow at Plymouth University, where until recently he was Associate Professor and Reader in English in the School of Humanities. Since 2000 his research has focused on the relationship between politics, culture and the work of three American writers, leading to three monographs: *Writing Back: Sylvia Plath, and Cold War Politics* (2002); *Apart From Modernism: Edith Wharton, Fiction and Politics* (2005); and *Emily Dickinson and the Hill of Science* (2010). Between 2009 and 2011 he led the two-year Arts and Humanities Council (UK)-funded research networking project, Separateness and Kinship: Transatlantic Exchanges Between Britain and New England 1600–1900. He is currently researching mid nineteenth-century transatlantic travel writing.

LAURA PERRY is a doctoral candidate in English at the University of Wisconsin-Madison and a Graduate Associate at the Nelson Institute's Center for Culture, History, and the Environment. She is an editor at *Edge Effects* magazine, a Mellon-Morgridge Graduate Fellow and a Public Humanities Exchange Fellow. Her research focuses on twentieth-century American literature, animal studies and the environmental humanities. Recent publications include 'Anthroposcenes: Towards an Environmental Graphic Novel' (2018) in *C21 Literature*. Her research on hygiene and cellophane in Sylvia Plath is partially supported by an Exploratory Research Grant from the Hagley Museum and Library.

NICOLA PRESLEY is Senior Lecturer in English Literature at Bath Spa University. She is currently completing her PhD on the intertextuality of popular culture in the work of Sylvia Plath and Anne Sexton. She has research interests in women's poetry, digital literature and post-war British and American fiction. Her article '"A Buried Land and a Blazing Source": Ted Hughes and William Golding' appeared in *The Ted Hughes Society Journal* (7.1, 2018). She is the Assistant Editor of *Irish Studies Review* and New Media Manager for William Golding Limited.

HOLLY RANGER is a postdoctoral Research Associate at the Institute of Classical Studies, University of London. She completed a PhD thesis (University of Birmingham) in 2016 on 'The Feminine Ovidian Tradition' in twentieth- and twenty-first-century women's writing. She has published on classical allusion in the work of Saviana Stănescu, Ali Smith and Sylvia Plath ('"I have tried to be blind in love": Psyche and the Quest for Feminine Poetic Autonomy in Sylvia Plath's House of Eros' [2019]). Her work has appeared in the *Classical Receptions Journal* and the *International Journal of the Classical Tradition*.

She is preparing a monograph on the influence of the classical tradition on the development of Plath's distinctive poetics.

ELENA REBOLLO-CORTÉS obtained her PhD from the University of Extremadura (Spain). Her dissertation is a historical, bibliographical and paratextual study of Plath's editions focusing on her canonisation process and the construction of Plath's myth and authorial identity. She holds a BA in Comparative Literature and Literary Theory as well as a BA in English, both from the University of Extremadura, where she currently holds a position as a Lecturer. She completed her education in Kingston University (UK) and Kalamazoo College (US) and she has presented her work at academic conferences in the United States, Britain, France and Spain.

FIONA SAMPSON has been published in more than thirty languages and received an MBE for services to literature. She's received a number of national and international honours, including the Newdigate Prize, a Cholmondeley, various awards from the Society of Authors and Poetry Book Society commendations, and international prizes in Bosnia, India, Macedonia and the United States. Twice shortlisted for both the T. S. Eliot Prize and Forward Prizes, in 2017 she published *Limestone Country* and *Lyric Cousins: Musical Form in Poetry*; and in 2018, *In Search of Mary Shelley: The Girl Who Wrote Frankenstein*. She is Professor of Poetry at the University of Roehampton.

ELEANOR SPENCER is Vice-Principal and Senior Tutor of St Chad's College at Durham University. She also teaches in the University's Department of English Studies and guest lectures in the School of Education. Her teaching and research interests are in twentieth-century and contemporary British and American poetry, and on literature in popular culture. She was awarded an AHRC Research Preparation Masters Award (2007–08) and an AHRC Doctoral Award (2008–11). She was a Frank Knox Memorial Fellow in the Department of English at Harvard University in 2011–12. Her recent publications include a chapter on the work of Kathleen Jamie (2014) and the *New Casebook on American Poetry since 1945* (2016). Forthcoming publications include essays in *The Blackwell Companion to British and Irish Poetry 1960–2015*.

PETER K. STEINBERG is the author of the biography *Sylvia Plath* (2004) and the 'Introduction' to *The Spoken Word: Sylvia Plath* (2010). He has published several articles on Plath that have appeared in *Fine Books &*

Collections and *Notes & Queries*, among others. He is a co-editor of the two-volume *The Letters of Sylvia Plath* (2017 and 2018) and a co-author of *These Ghostly Archives: The Unearthing of Sylvia Plath* (2017), a book of essays on Plath, research and the archive. He maintains the oldest continuously updated website dedicated to Sylvia Plath on the Internet: www.sylviaplath.info.

REBECCA C. TUITE is a fashion historian and doctoral candidate at the Bard Graduate Center in New York City, working towards her PhD in Decorative Arts, Design History and Material Culture. Her research interests include film and fashion, fashion photography and twentieth-century American fashion, as well as the history of women's higher education in the United States, with a particular focus on the clothing and campus culture at the Seven Sisters colleges. She is the author of *Seven Sisters Style: The All-American Preppy Look* (2014) and *The 1950s in Vogue: The Jessica Daves Years, 1952–1962* (forthcoming from Thames & Hudson).

LUCY TUNSTALL has taught at the universities of Exeter and Bristol and is the author of a collection of poetry, *The Republic of the Husband* (2014). Her work has appeared in *The Guardian, The Paris Review Daily, PN Review, English* and *New Poetries V*. She is the author of 'Aspects of Pastoral in Sylvia Plath's "Child"' (2009). She is currently working on a monograph, *The Limits of the Visual: Sylvia Plath and Modern Art*.

IAIN TWIDDY is a former Professor of English at Hokkaido University, Japan. He is the author of *Cancer Poetry* (2015), a study of cancer in contemporary poetry, including works by Paul Muldoon, Jo Shapcott and Christopher Reid. He is also the author of *Pastoral Elegy in Contemporary British and Irish Poetry* (2012), which includes chapters on Seamus Heaney, Ted Hughes and Michael Longley. His articles have appeared in a number of journals, including *Essays in Criticism, English* and *Irish Studies Review*.

ANDREW WALKER is Assistant Professor of English at Liberty University. He is the author of an essay on the early poetry of Robert Lowell in *Literature and Belief* and has an essay, 'The Uncertainty of Our Climate: Mary Kelly and the Rural Theatre', forthcoming in *Rural Modernity in Britain: A Critical Intervention*. He has research interests in poetry and poetics, theories of the lyric, modernism and modern and contemporary drama. In addition to a forthcoming essay on theatrical influence in Elizabeth Bishop's poetry, he is currently composing a book-length study of twentieth-century drama in verse, focusing on work by T. S. Eliot, W. B. Yeats, Gertrude Stein, Djuna Barnes, Robert Lowell and Derek Walcott.

GERARD WOODWARD is a novelist, poet and short story writer. He studied Fine Art at Falmouth School of Art, and Social Anthropology at the London School of Economics and Manchester University. His trilogy of novels concerning the Jones Family have won widespread critical acclaim, including shortlistings for the Man-Booker Prize and Whitbread First Novel Award. His five poetry collections have earned him a Somerset Maugham Award and two T. S. Eliot Prize shortlistings. His most recent publication is a novel, *The Paper Lovers*. He is a regular contributor to the *The Guardian*, *The Independent* and *The Times Literary Supplement* and is currently working on a new poetry collection.

Acknowledgements

I am deeply grateful to my editor at Cambridge University Press, Ray Ryan, for his passion and vision in commissioning this book. I am also grateful to Edgar Mendez at Cambridge for offering superb editorial support. Peter K. Steinberg kindly allowed me to put out a call for contributors on his SylviaPlathInfo blog, a vital resource for Plath scholars everywhere. That call was instrumental in shaping this volume. The large number of responses meant that the community of Plath scholars helped to mould this book. *Sylvia Plath in Context* has been a thrilling and happy project to work on, and I am very grateful to all of the contributors for making it so. I benefited from the wise counsel of Terry Gifford, who edited *Ted Hughes in Context*, and was generous in showing me the way and answering my countless questions. I would have made many mistakes without him. Charles Phillips is a superb copyeditor, with a sharp eye, elegant judgement and an exceptional depth of literary knowledge. I am deeply grateful to Bath Spa University for their support, in particular Professor Steve May, Professor John Strachan and Professor Andy Salmon. The university not only awarded me a period of research leave, but also paid for Paula Clarke Bain to produce the outstanding index. As ever, my inexpressible love and thanks to Richard, and to Imogen, Violet and Lily.

Chronology

1932

4 January — Otto Emil Plath and Aurelia Schober (Sylvia Plath's parents) are married.

27 October — Sylvia Plath is born in Boston, Massachusetts.

1934

Bumblebees and Their Ways, by Otto Plath, is published.

1935

27 April — Plath's younger brother, Warren Joseph Plath, is born.

1936

The Plath family move to Winthrop, Massachusetts.

1940

27 October — Sylvia Plath is eight years old.

5 November — Otto Plath dies of diabetes mellitus.

1942

Aurelia Plath moves with Sylvia and Warren to Wellesley, Massachusetts.

1950

Plath begins to publish stories, poems and articles in newspapers and magazines, which she will continue to do throughout her life.

Autumn	Plath begins her undergraduate degree at Smith College, having won a scholarship funded by the American novelist Olive Higgins Prouty.

1953

June	Plath is in New York, as guest editor for *Mademoiselle*.
24 August	Plath attempts suicide by taking an overdose of sleeping pills.

1953/1954

August–January	Plath undergoes treatment for psychiatric illness.

1954

30 January	Plath resumes her studies at Smith College.

1955

6 June	Plath graduates from Smith College *summa cum laude*.
September	Plath sails to England on the *Queen Elizabeth*.
October	Plath begins her studies at Newnham College, Cambridge University, on a Fulbright Scholarship.
December	Plath travels to Paris and the South of France.

1956

25/26 February	Plath attends *Saint Botolph's Review* party at Falcon Yard and meets Ted Hughes.
April	Plath travels to Venice and Rome.
16 June	Sylvia Plath and Ted Hughes marry at the Church of St George the Martyr in Queen Square, London.
August	Plath and Hughes honeymoon in Benidorm, Spain.
September	Plath and Hughes are with his family at The Beacon in Heptonstall.
1 October	Plath returns to Cambridge to resume studies, while Hughes works in London.
December	Plath and Hughes live together in Cambridge, at 55 Eltisley Avenue.

1957

June   Plath and Hughes leave Southampton for New York, sailing on the *Queen Elizabeth*.

September   Plath and Hughes move to Northampton, Massachusetts. Plath begins a teaching job at Smith College in the English faculty.

1958

June   Plath finishes her teaching job at Smith. She and Hughes move to Boston, having decided to dedicate themselves to writing.

1959

Summer   Plath and Hughes travel by car across the United States, including a visit to Yellowstone.

Autumn   Plath and Hughes spend two months at Yaddo, a retreat for artists, in Saratoga Springs, New York State.

December   Plath and Hughes return to England.

1960

January   Plath and Hughes move to London, renting a flat, 3 Chalcot Square, in Primrose Hill.

10 February   Plath signs a contract with Heinemann to publish *The Colossus and Other Poems*.

1 April   Sylvia Plath's first child, Frieda Rebecca Hughes, is born.

31 October   *The Colossus* is published by Heinemann in the UK.

1961

February   Plath suffers a miscarriage.

27 February   Plath receives one of *The New Yorker*'s 'coveted "first reading" contracts'.

Spring   Plath is 'working fiendishly' in the Merwins' study in the mornings, probably completing a full draft of *The Bell Jar* over this period.

Mid-June   Aurelia Plath arrives in England for a visit.

July   Plath and Hughes are guests of the Merwins at their house in France.

| 31 August | Plath and Hughes move into Court Green, a house in North Tawton, Devon. |
| 9 September | Plath wins a $2,000 Saxton Grant to work on her novel, which is in fact already finished. |

1962

17 January	Plath's second child, Nicholas Farrar Hughes, is born.
14 May	*The Colossus and Other Poems* is published in the United States by Knopf.
June	Aurelia Plath visits.
September	Plath and Hughes visit Ireland. Later that month, she and Hughes separate.
October	Plath writes 25 poems during this month, including 'Daddy', 'Ariel', 'Lady Lazarus' and her sequence of bee poems.
27 October	Sylvia Plath's last birthday. She turned thirty.
December	Plath moves to London with Frieda and Nicholas. She rents 23 Fitzroy Road, where Yeats once lived.

1963

14 January	*The Bell Jar* is published in the UK by Heinemann under the pseudonym Victoria Lucas.
11 February	Plath takes her own life.
18 February	Plath is buried in Yorkshire, in the village of Heptonstall.

1965

| 11 March | Faber and Faber publish *Ariel* in the UK. |

1966

| June | Harper & Row publish *Ariel* in the United States. |
| 1 September | *The Bell Jar* is published by Heinemann in the UK under Plath's own name. |

1971

| 14 April | *The Bell Jar* is published in the United States for the first time, by Harper & Row. |

1975

3 December   Harper & Row publish *Letters Home* in the United States.

1976

20 April   Faber and Faber publish *Letters Home* in the UK.

1977

17 October   Faber and Faber publish *Johnny Panic and the Bible of Dreams* in the UK.

1979

2 January   Harper & Row publish *Johnny Panic and the Bible of Dreams* in the United States.

1981

28 September   Publication of Sylvia Plath's *Collected Poems*.

1982

31 March   *The Journals of Sylvia Plath* published by the Dial Press (United States only).

12 April   *The Collected Poems* is awarded the Pulitzer Prize for Poetry.

1994

11 March   Aurelia Schober Plath dies.

1998

28 October   Ted Hughes dies.

2000

April   *The Journals of Sylvia Plath: 1950–1962* is published in the UK by Faber and Faber.

October   *The Unabridged Journals of Sylvia Plath* is published in the United States by Anchor Books.

2004

Ariel: The Restored Edition is published in the UK by Faber and Faber and the United States by HarperCollins.

2009

16 March   Nicholas Farrar Hughes, Plath's son, takes his own life.

2017

28 September   *Letters of Sylvia Plath Volume I: 1940–1956* is published in the UK by Faber and Faber.

17 October   *Letters of Sylvia Plath Volume I: 1940–1956* is published in the United States by HarperCollins.

2018

September   *Letters of Sylvia Plath Volume II: 1956–1963* is published in the UK by Faber and Faber.

November   *Letters of Sylvia Plath Volume II: 1956–1963* is published in the United States by HarperCollins.

Abbreviations and Textual Note

Where there is a difference in the editions used (for instance, in the US and UK editions of the *Collected Poems* as well as *Johnny Panic*, and in the multiple editions of *The Bell Jar*) the edition used is indicated in an endnote within the relevant chapter. All chapters use the short title form in end notes; full details for all references can be found in the Bibliography towards the end of this volume.

A Res.	Sylvia Plath, *Ariel: The Restored Edition* (London: Faber and Faber, 2007; New York: HarperCollins, 2004).
BL	Ted Hughes, *Birthday Letters* (New York: Farrar Strauss and Giroux, 1998; London: Faber and Faber, 1998).
BJ	Sylvia Plath, *The Bell Jar* (London: Heinemann, 1963 [under the pseudonym Victoria Lucas]; London: Faber and Faber, 1966; New York: Harper & Row, 1971).
CP	Sylvia Plath, *The Collected Poems*, ed. Ted Hughes (London: Faber and Faber, 1981) (New York: Harper & Row, 1981).
JP	Sylvia Plath, *Johnny Panic and the Bible of Dreams, and Other Prose Writings*, second edition (London: Faber and Faber, 1977) (New York: Harper & Row, 1979).
J	Sylvia Plath, *The Journals of Sylvia Plath: 1950–1962*, ed. Karen V. Kukil (London: Faber and Faber, 2000). *The Unabridged Journals of Sylvia Plath* (New York: Anchor, 2000).
LH	Sylvia Plath, *Letters Home: Correspondence 1950–1963*, ed. Aurelia Plath (New York: Harper & Row, 1975) (London: Faber and Faber, 1976).
LV1	Sylvia Plath, *The Letters of Sylvia Plath: Volume 1 (1940–1956)*, eds. Karen V. Kukil and Peter K. Steinberg (London: Faber and Faber, 2017).

LV2 Sylvia Plath, *The Letters of Sylvia Plath: Volume 2 (1957–1963)*, eds. Karen V. Kukil and Peter K. Steinberg (London: Faber and Faber, 2018).

LTH Ted Hughes, *The Letters of Ted Hughes* (London: Faber and Faber, 2007).

OED *Oxford English Dictionary.*

SPD Sylvia Plath, *Sylvia Plath: Drawings*, Introduced by Frieda Hughes (London: Faber and Faber, 2013).

TH:CP Ted Hughes, *Collected Poems* (London: Faber and Faber, 2003) (New York: Farrar, Straus and Giroux, 2003).

Key Archives

THA   Ted Hughes Archive, British Library, London.
EMORY   Ted Hughes Papers, Manuscript and Rare Book Library,
           Emory University, Atlanta, GA.
LILLY   Sylvia Plath Materials, Lilly Library, Indiana University,
           Bloomington, IN.
SMITH   Sylvia Plath Collection, Smith College, MA.

Introduction

Tracy Brain

In recent years, literary critics have engaged in a variety of new approaches to Sylvia Plath's work. Readers themselves are increasingly aware of the complex array of backgrounds and frameworks that shape Plath's writing. Bringing together an exciting combination of established and emerging thinkers from a range of disciplines, *Sylvia Plath in Context* is an important new landmark in this ongoing project. Across thirty-four chapters, this volume reveals Plath's complex responses to the writers she reads, her interventions in the literary techniques and forms she encounters, and the wide range of cultural, personal, artistic, political, historical and geographical influences that shaped her work.

Many of the chapters in this volume confront the specific challenges for reading Sylvia Plath today. Others evaluate her legacy to the writers who followed her. Reaching well beyond any simple equation in which biographical cause results in literary effect, all of them argue for a body of work that emerges from Plath's deep involvement in the world she inhabits. Situating Plath's writing within a wide frame of references that reach beyond any single notion of self, *Sylvia Plath in Context* will be a vital resource for students, teachers, scholars and general readers.

I. Literary Contexts

Jonathan Ellis situates Plath's work in relation to the American poetry scene of the 1950s and early 1960s. He analyses how a mid-century generation of poets like John Berryman, Elizabeth Bishop and Robert Lowell responded to modernism through the birth of confessionalism. Ellis draws on Plath's letters, journals, poems and stories to analyse her own role in and thinking about this aesthetic turn. He considers the impact of Plath's contemporaries, Adrienne Rich and Anne Sexton, as well as Edith Sitwell, Marianne Moore, May Swenson and Isabella

Gardner. Situating Plath's poetry in relation to the work of these poetic godfathers and godmothers, Ellis looks in particular at questions of gender and nationality.

Eleanor Spencer explores the topography of poetry in Britain during the 1950s and early 1960s, suggesting that what we find is a series of what Al Alvarez saw as reactions to and rejections of that which came before. Plath emerges from a period that saw the Movement's repudiation of the aesthetic and intellectual confusion of the New Romantics in favour of directness, communicability and an incisive New Critical sensibility. Just six years later, however, Alvarez's introduction to *The New Poetry* (1962) disavowed the 'gentility' of the Movement's 'academic-administrative verse', calling instead for a poetry that 'nakedly, and without evasion' registered the 'forces of disintegration' in the post-Second World War and Cold War era that threatened not only a familiar English way of life, but life itself.

Holly Ranger establishes a relatively neglected but crucial context for Plath's work, illuminating Plath's frequent classical allusions and her sophisticated intertextual dialogue with literary history. Among the many poems that Ranger helps us to see anew are the bee poems, shot through as they are with references to Virgil. All the while, Ranger reveals Plath's ambivalence towards her classical project, her impulse to reject this canon running up against her sense that it was impossible to ignore it.

Andrew Walker writes from the premise that one of Plath's most notable characteristics is her sense of the dramatic, her experimentation with multiple voices and personas. Walker establishes Plath's long-held interest in radio drama growing up in the United States, and the impact of contemporary radio dramas and the BBC's Third Programme on her work. Plath's radio play, *Three Women*, is influenced by Dylan Thomas's *Under Milk Wood* as well as Ted Hughes's *A Houseful of Women* and *The Wound*, which appear during key phases in Plath's poetic development. Walker accounts for a dramatic shift between Plath's earlier and later work, and demonstrates the importance of an overlooked yet highly vital poetic context.

In his expert analysis of Plath's correspondence with the editors to whom she submitted her poems at *The New Yorker*, Peter K. Steinberg provides a unique and critical new context for understanding Plath's compositional practices. Steinberg makes clear just how responsive those practices were to her professional aspirations for publishing her work, with *The New Yorker* being the pinnacle for those aspirations.

II. Literary Technique and Influence

Taking a 1962 fan letter that Plath wrote to the poet Stevie Smith three months before her suicide, Noreen Masud elucidates a key context out of which Plath's work emerged. Drawing on *The Bell Jar* and ranging through her poetry, Masud argues that Plath owes much to Smith's gendered perspective, dramatic monologues and ambivalent but darkly comic engagement with the stifling nature of suburbia.

Will May returns us to Plath's early reception, and finds there a vital but overlooked context for her work: the whimsical. Taking seriously Plath's fascination with the unthreatening fantasy worlds of children's stories and their attendant winsome philosophy, May rehabilitates a literary term that has often been used disparagingly by the Movement poets. Instead, he shows us how indebted Plath's dark comedy and verbal games are to whimsy. With close attention to her children's stories, May unveils Plath's cultural conversation with the domestic, the miniature and the absurd, though she herself was disingenuous about her interventions with whimsy. May debunks any notion that Plath's poetry and stories belong in separate spheres. Neither, he argues, does her children's writing.

In my own chapter, I discuss how Plath came into contact with the many common forms – literary and otherwise – in which we find the second person address. These include instructions such as user guides and recipes; questionnaires and interviews; advertising; letters; poems; and prose fiction. All of these second-person functions are utilised by Plath at various points in her work. I provide key examples of these uses and establish the context for the kinds of sources she drew upon. Plath's formulates a 'you' that is fluid and mobile, controlling the reader's distance from and closeness to the narrators of her poems and fiction.

Lucy Tunstall provides readers with a crucial understanding of Plath's conception of the lyric. Tunstall brings alive Plath's continuous, deliberate interventions in the lyric mode's possibilities and limits. She situates Plath's development of the lyric in the poet's childhood and college influences and traces it through to the *Ariel* poems and their seemingly incompatible registers. Tunstall shows us not just the unsurprising engagement with sound and voice, but with the visual, too, in Plath's unique conceptions of the lyric. Finally, Tunstall confronts the difficult questions raised by Plath's treatment of race in the context of her obsessive exploration of ideas of purity.

Iain Twiddy elucidates several strands of the pastoral that operate in Plath's poetry, 'including metaphysical or internal pastoral, the intimacy of pastoral with loss, mourning and elegy, and the influence of pastoral figures'. There is also Plath's engagement 'with classical pastoral in early poems'.

III. Cultural Contexts

Gerard Woodward explores Plath's complex relationship with the culture of food and cookery on both sides of the Atlantic and helps us to understand the ways in which food is treated in her poetry and fiction. Plath was a compulsive observer and cataloguer of what she ate and what she cooked. Yet the time in which she lived in was one of great contrasts and upheavals in the social and cultural attitudes towards food in Britain and the United States. In Plath's birth country food remained central to the American ideal of wholesomeness, represented most emphatically by Rombauer and Becker's *Joy of Cooking*, which Plath treasured. In Britain the national cuisine had been devastated by the Second World War and years of rationing. At the same time, in both countries, food was slowly acquiring new powers as a marker of status and aspiration, particularly for women.

The fashion historian Rebecca C. Tuite provides a detailed account of the pervasiveness of Plath's engagement with fashion throughout her literary and visual work, showing for the first time how powerful Plath's interest was from the outset, and remained throughout her writing life. Tuite reveals the contradiction in the Plath who was critical of the cultural and economic influence of fashion, but also able to draw on it artistically and aesthetically, as well as to take personal pleasure in it.

Lynda K. Bundtzen contextualises Plath's poetry with auteur cinema, the influx of principally European films into the American art house movie theaters in the 1950s and early 1960s. Drawing on Plath's known viewings of films by Luis Buñuel, Jean Cocteau, Federico Fellini, Ingmar Bergman and Alain Resnais, Bundtzen shows how Plath uses her writing to respond critically and emotionally to a cinema that is designed to showcase experimentation. Bundtzen focuses on the way in which the often surreal elements of Plath's imagery and the theatrical confrontations in her poems share the same experimental bravery of the directors whose work Plath so admired.

Nicola Presley establishes the increasing predominance of television in the American culture out of which Plath's work emerges. Drawing on advertisements for television in Plath's beloved *Ladies' Home Journal* as well as contemporary critical thinking on the subject, Presley accounts for Plath's deliberate engagement with television in her poetry and prose, making a case for Plath's horror of television's low artistic values and pernicious effects on those who watch it, yet also arguing for the undeniable visual impact of television on Plath's writing.

Jane Hedley accounts for Plath's descriptive and interpretive practice in the poems that take art as their subject. Plath's ekphrastic poems can be seen as interventions in a conversation with canonical predecessors from John Keats to W. H. Auden, and can be traced not just to her deliberate study of art history, but to the studies she made as a visual artist, before she made the decision in young adulthood to concentrate on writing.

IV. Sexual and Gender Contexts

Beatrice Hitchman situates *The Bell Jar* within an intriguing cultural moment for gay and lesbian fiction in the United States. She provides an original and fascinating account of the novel within the context of the boom in lesbian pulp fiction of the late 1950s and early 1960s, popular psychological writings, and the lesbian bar culture in New York's West Village during the period, all of which helped to place images of lesbians in a wider circulation. Hitchman reads Joan Gilling as a lesbian character, considering *The Bell Jar* in the context of lesbian fiction of the time, offering a new account of the novel within a cultural moment of acceptance/rejection of lesbian rights.

Contemporary readers tend to view *The Bell Jar* through a post-feminist lens. Kate Harding situates the novel within a cultural and historical moment that we too readily lose sight of. Harding reads the novel in the context of 1950s discourses in which the gendered roles that Esther resists are enforced by sexual violence. Drawing on mid-twentieth century rape laws, Harding reveals the disconnect between Esther's view of events and the contemporary reader's. Where the latter will see acquaintance rape and female victimisation, the former will see sexual availability and victim-blaming. In her brave and original response to *The Bell Jar*, Harding brings to light the pervasive rape culture that underpins Esther's story, and reveals the importance of this underpinning to our understanding of the novel.

Laura Perry argues that Plath's concerns with purity and cleanliness take the form of a poetics of hygiene. This poetics engages in conversation with a transatlantic discourse evident in post-war advertisements and government publications that trafficked in mid-century anxieties about biological containment, sexual purity and interracial contact. Perry shows how Plath links hygiene to gender, geopolitics and poetic form throughout her writings. She reframes Plath's search for transcendental purity by showing how this purity is embodied and historically located.

V. Political and Religious Contexts

Robin Peel explains the resonance of the execution of Julius and Ethel Rosenberg in *The Bell Jar*. As the event fades into history, its extraordinary impact on 1950s American psychology can easily be forgotten. The electrocution of the Rosenbergs for espionage is important to Plath's novel because of the resonance of their Jewishness, insider/outsider status and apparent vindication of Cold War paranoia. In addition, Peel reads the event from a retrospective and transatlantic perspective. The thirty-year-old adult woman writing in the persona of a senior student mirrors the simultaneous political engagement and distancing that has troubled so many readers.

Gail Crowther examines Plath's ambivalent response to religion by highlighting how the context of her religious upbringing lay at the root of her theological questionings. Crowther examines the impact of the Plath family's Unitarian faith on Plath's writing, her study of religion throughout her school and college education, and her adult position of reluctant atheism. Crowther shows how Plath's writing disrupts Judaeo-Christian ideas of patrilineage, instead putting Marian notions of love, care and redemption at the centre of her poems.

Richard Kerridge describes the literary, cultural and scientific context of Plath's interest in wild animals, landscape, climate and pollution. The letters and journals show that this interest was intense, but also that it was not scientific or systematic, even in a rudimentary way. Plath's strategy was to preserve the dramatic immediacy of unexpected encounters with wildlife, rather than frame those encounters with scientific information. Nevertheless, an emergent ecological consciousness and environmental concern are evident in her writing. Kerridge provides the historical and scientific background for this concern, by outlining the major conceptual shifts that were taking place in ecological science, the recent history of wild nature in literature and some of the changing popular attitudes in Britain and the United States.

Cornelia Pearsall reveals Plath's lifelong preoccupation with war, showing us how it permeates Plath's correspondence and filters into her poetry and prose, gaining in focus and momentum towards the end of her writing life. Pearsall establishes yet another crucial angle from which we can read Plath's deliberately outward-looking political and historical engagement, as opposed to any narrow view of merely personal and biographical concerns.

VI. Biographical Contexts

Sally Bayley traces Plath's emerging relationship to her journal persona and ideas about journal writing. Bayley focuses on the intense period of Plath's late teenage years and early adulthood, including the beginnings of her university education. She also reveals the importance of the diarists Plath read to Plath's own journal activities and larger poetic practices. Of special importance is Virginia Woolf, and Bayley helps us to see afresh Plath's oft-quoted exhilaration at Woolf's reference to cooking haddock and sausages, which says more about Plath herself than it does the subject of her comments. Bayley shows us how Plath's ideas about the 'melting', emerging self move from the journals and into poems such as 'Ariel' and 'Lady Lazarus'.

Amanda Golden addresses Plath's pedagogical strategies in order to shed new light on the ways that her identities as a student, teacher and poet overlap. Focusing on her teaching of Henry James, T. S. Eliot and James Joyce, Golden shows how Plath's later writing refashions the language she used as a teacher. Golden draws heavily on the teaching notes Plath made whilst working in the English Department at Smith College, combing through Plath's lists, lectures and the passages from critical texts that she highlighted.

Anita Helle provides transdisciplinary perspectives on electroshock therapy as a context for Plath's fiction. Counter to many critics and biographers, Helle does not 'diagnose' Plath. Rather, she historicises Plath's literary response to electroshock treatment from both sides of a highly mobile, linguistically multivalent and ideologically charged literary and medical spectrum. Plath's literary responses to electric shock treatment emerge in the context of post-Second World War social upheavals. They recall surrealist aims of shaping a counter-aesthetic 'convulsive beauty' in response to collective threat.

Peter K. Steinberg shows us how Plath used scrapbooks as an early means of honing her storytelling techniques and narrative skills, combining the linguistic and visual aptitudes that were present throughout her life and developing the art of self-performance and selection that are vital to any artist. Moreover, these relatively overlooked documents are a valuable source of key biographical data that amplify our understanding of the context out of which the work emerged.

Via the first volume of *The Letters of Sylvia Plath*, Karen V. Kukil traces the key themes and concerns that preoccupy the writer, providing an intellectual, cultural and personal biography. Thereby, Kukil establishes the key contexts out of which Plath's poetry and fiction emerge. After the well-documented deletions in *Letters Home*, and the dissatisfaction many readers felt at a selection that depicted Plath as ceaselessly happy, Kukil views the full and unabridged letters as akin to a full-length colour film after a black-and-white short.

VII.   Plath and Place

The poet and academic Sarah Corbett reveals Plath's profound response to Yorkshire's powerful and often threatening natural and human landscape, as well as to the writings of Emily Brontë and Ted Hughes. In a handful of poems, Plath can be heard sounding out a Hughesian strain of voice against the ghosts and rumoured angels of her own emergent poetic imagination. These West Yorkshire interludes show Plath making use of an ambivalent energy in the landscape to mirror her self/psyche, a technique that can be seen in many of the *Ariel* poems, and the beginnings of a working-out of the struggle between masculine and feminine voices that was to underpin much of her mature work.

Elaine Feinstein provides an expert and first-hand account of Plath's last months in London, which spans her search for a flat in November 1962 and her final move to the city in December that year. This is the period during which Plath wrote her final poems, and Feinstein's biography of Plath's time in London help us to understand better the context out of which these poems emerged.

Maeve O'Brien examines the geographical isolation Plath experienced when living in Devon, yet shows how these circumstances impacted her writing, contributing to the burst of creativity that came towards the end of her life and allowing Plath to mine her surroundings in direct ways. O'Brien shows us just how influenced by and receptive to her lived environment Plath was.

VIII.   The Creative Afterlife

Following Veronica Forrest-Thomson's lead, Gareth Farmer repositions Plath's work in experimental British, European and American lineages, testing the complexity of her 'poetic artifice' against Forrest-Thomson's theory and offering 'other' intellectual and literary contexts for her work.

Such contexts activate alternative questions for the poetry, such as the role and function of form in carrying epistemological and cognitive information, or the ways in which poetry offers a critique of lyric singularity, address and subjectivity. A more sustained concentration on Plath's poetic artifice offers new intellectual contexts, as well as alternative horizons for understanding the afterlife of her work.

Elena Rebollo-Cortés examines how the material features of Plath's final two books have played a key role in establishing a critical framework for the interpretation of her texts and in defining her posthumous identity as a writer. In the context of the publishing history and literary afterlife of Plath's works, Rebollo-Cortés shows us how the figure of Plath has been presented to readers through the visual and textual packaging of key editions of *Ariel* and *The Bell Jar*. These key works have had a wide readership and large presence in the literary market. Their editions have therefore played a major role in the creation and perpetuation of Plath's identification as a tragic figure. This concentration on books as historical and material objects presupposes that editions are (sometimes overlooked) vehicles of meaning, revealing, for example, that editions of *Ariel* disclose how Plath has been portrayed as a Faber poet, a woman poet or a myth, while editions of *The Bell Jar* have privileged biographical readings of the novel.

Fiona Sampson looks beyond any simplistic account of legacy in her nuanced tracing of Plath's continuing influence on British poetry. While Plath left no substantial or explicit articulation of her poetics, her early published work indicates some of her own literary debts. The free verse that eventually muscles its way out of that initial formality is closely related, in both rhythm and register, to exactly contemporary work by Ted Hughes. Almost universally read by contemporary British poets, she contributes a Plathian dimension to contemporary British poetics *as a whole*. This is less apparent in today's confessional free verse, which owes much to life-writing and oral forms, than in the continuation, alongside the Hardy/Larkin mainstream, of a more risk-taking, symbolic and higher-register tradition. Its protagonists include Sharon Olds, Louise Glück, Selima Hill and Denise Riley.

Heather Clark reveals the powerful impact of Plath biographers. Splicing the words pathology and biography with Plath's name, she coins the term P(l)athographers. Clark helps us to understand their cumulative practice of distortedly mythologising Plath and misdirecting readers' interpretations of her writing. For Clark, Plath's English Tripos exam at Cambridge offers us more understanding of Plath's poetics than her relationship with her dead father ever could.

Some of these lively and distinctive essays are written by traditional academics, others by creative practitioners. Every contributor to this volume brings to bear his or her own specialist perspectives and expert knowledge. What all of the chapters share are exciting and expert new ways of situating Plath's work and of understanding the different strands that formed it, as well as the ongoing story of its creative afterlife.

PART I

Literary Contexts

CHAPTER I

Plath and the American Poetry Scene

Jonathan Ellis

In her first journal, begun in July 1950 in the summer before she left home for Smith College, Sylvia Plath cites three Irish writers: Louis MacNeice, W. B. Yeats and James Joyce. 'Hold to the now, the here, through which all future plunges to the past' (*J* 7) she notes, quoting Joyce's *Ulysses*. In the pages of the journal itself, she rephrases Joyce in her own register: 'Nothing is real except the present, and already, I feel the weight of centuries smothering me. Some girl a hundred years ago lived as I do. And she is dead. I am the present, but I know I, too, will pass' (*J* 10). How did Plath understand 'the here' and 'the now' of the American poetry scene in the 1950s and early 1960s and which writers did she draw inspiration from and imitate? As a seventeen-, soon to be eighteen-year-old college student, Plath aspired not just to live in the present, but also to *be* the present. That double sense of 'passing' is always alive in her writing. Plath knows that, like the girl a hundred years ago, her body will pass away but not *this*, not her writing self. The repetition of 'I' three times in a sentence of just eleven words still astonishes with its audacious self-confidence. What does it say? It says: 'I know I' and that 'I, too, will pass.'

Mid-twentieth century American poetry was dominated by what we now call the modernists. When Plath was at Smith, Yeats had only been dead a decade. T. S. Eliot and Ezra Pound were very much alive and still publishing poetry, even if their best work had already been written. As an apprentice poet, Plath warned herself against 'blind worship of modern poets and not enough analysis and practice' (*J* 88). In her journals she kept to her word, favouring the modernist tradition not of Eliot and Pound but of female modernists like Amy Lowell and Elinor Wylie who have only recently entered the poetic canon. Plath was addicted to ranking poets, particularly in her journals. In a March 1957 entry, we find competitive comparisons of her poetry to various dead and living poets, all female. Edith Sitwell and Marianne Moore are identified as two 'ageing giantesses & poetic godmothers' (*J* 360). Of living poets she saw May Swenson, Isabella

Gardner and Adrienne Rich as her closest rivals. In a later journal entry, she writes of Elizabeth Bishop, 'Her fine originality, always surprising, never rigid, flowing, juicier than Marianne Moore, who is her godmother' (J 516).

This chapter focuses on Plath's poetry in relation to the work of these mainly American poetic godfathers and godmothers, looking in particular at questions of gender and nationality. Yet when we speak of an American poetry scene in the 1950s, it is important to remember that scene's international, transatlantic dimension, a fact Tracy Brain draws attention to in writing of Plath's 'perpetual displacement, a mid-atlanticism that is neither American nor English'.[1] In 1958 Plath was ambitious to become 'The Poetess of America' (J 360). Indeed, she 'arrogant[ly]' believed she had already written lines that qualified her for that title. Yet just a year later, she considered her 'tempo [to be] British' (J 521). Did Plath leave American poetry behind when she made the decision to move to England for good in 1959? Was she ever fully part of an American scene or just a sceptical observer? What actually is the American scene? Might it be more accurate to speak of it in the plural?

A short answer to this flurry of questions would be to state that Plath was always an Anglophile even as she remained an American citizen. Like W. H. Auden who was born and educated in England but spent most of his adult life elsewhere, or, travelling in the other direction, T. S. Eliot who was born and educated in the US but took on British citizenship, Plath's affinities and interests were of a hyphenated Anglo-American nature. She often divided poets, as we have seen, along gender lines, not national ones. It didn't matter to Plath where poets were born, but what they ended up writing about.

Steven Gould Axelrod believes that 'Plath's poetry evolved through four stages':[2]

> The first is the period of her juvenilia, culminating in the poetry she wrote at Smith College in 1950–55. . . . Plath's second stage, a period of growth and experiment, lasted from when she married Ted Hughes in 1956 to their permanent settlement in England in 1959. . . . The poetry of Plath's third stage, a dynamic period of passion and self-discovery, lasted from 1960 through the dissolution of her marriage in 1962. This period produced the texts that made her name and by which she is known today . . . Plath's final stage, a brief time of depression and withdrawal, occurred in the last weeks of her life in early 1963.[3]

Axelrod's periodisation roughly follows Ted Hughes's division of Plath's work into 'three phrases' in his introduction to the 1981 *Collected Poems*. It is worth revisiting it here.

'The first phase might be called her juvenilia', Hughes begins. 'A logical division occurs, conveniently, at the end of 1955, just after the end of her twenty-third year. The 220 or more poems written before this are of interest mainly to specialists' (*CP* 15).[4] From this pre-1956 period, Hughes selected what seemed to him the fifty best 'pieces' (note he does not call them 'poems') and printed them 'at the back of the book, as an appendix' (*CP* 16). Hughes extends the second phase of Plath's development a little further than Axelrod, suggesting that it falls 'between early 1956 and late 1960' (Axelrod ends this second phase a year earlier, in late 1959). According to Hughes, 'early 1956 presents itself as a watershed, because from later this year come the earliest poems of her collection, *The Colossus*. And from this time I worked closely with her and watched the poems being written, so I am reasonably sure everything is here' (*CP* 16). The logic of presenting 1956 as a 'watershed', at least partly because you were there to watch the poems 'being written', is convenient but not especially convincing. It is difficult to test its accuracy when less than a quarter of the poems have been made available to readers. I will come back to the status of the juvenilia in a moment. For Hughes, 'The third and final phase of her work, from the editorial point of view, dates from about September 1962. Around that time, she started the habit of dating the final typescript of each poem' (*CP* 17). The information Hughes gives us about Plath's habit of dating typescripts is helpful, but does this change in composition practice coincide with a change in form and subject matter as Axelrod's four-stage narrative contends? Putting aside the detail of dates and publication history, can Plath's career be divided into early/middle/late periods in this manner? Is it possible to speak of 'watershed' moments so neatly?

My own sense is that Plath's poetic development was less smooth and less summarisable than both of these accounts suggest. To go back to the juvenilia, and we have to go literally to the back of the *Collected Poems* to find them, I think Plath's early poems are worthy of study and not just by 'specialists'. The love poems, in particular, are stunningly sharp and witty examinations of courtship and rejection and of the discourse of the love poem itself. In 'Female Author', 'Cinderella', 'Bluebeard' and 'The Princess and the Goblins', Plath rejects the 'gilded fable' (*CP* 335) of traditional stories she had been taught as a child. The influence of the Victorian poet Christina Rossetti is clear. We know from Plath's letters to Aurelia Plath that she was reading Rossetti as early as December 1951 (*LV1* 406).

I suspect I am in the minority of Plath critics in finding time for this work.[5] For Tim Kendall, 'These poems are, with very few exceptions, unexceptional ... the juvenilia reflect a poet learning her art by imitating others: Auden, Stevens, Moore, Eliot, Dickinson and Dylan Thomas seem to have been among the more influential models. What appears most interesting now about Plath's early poems is her formal experimentation.'[6] While I disagree with Kendall about his estimation of the poems, I think he is right about Plath's models and her overall concern with fixed form at this point. Plath heard Auden read at Smith when she was a student and in an ecstatic letter to her brother dated 21 March 1953 she describes him as 'my conception of the perfect poet: tall, with a big leonine head and a sandy mane of hair, and lyrically gigantic stride ... I adore him with a big Hero Worship' (*LV1* 589).

A journal entry from the same period recalls being invited to meet him with other students in a teacher's living room:

> Auden tossing his big head back with a twist of wide ugly grinning lips, his sandy hair, his coarse tweedy brown jacket, his burlap-textured voice and the crackling brilliant utterances—the naughty mischievous boy genius, and the inconsistent white hairless skin of his legs, and the short puffy stubbed fingers—and the carpet slippers—beer he drank, and smoked Lucky Strikes in a black holder, gesticulating with a white new cigarette in his hands, holding matches, talking in a gravelly incisive tone about how Caliban is the natural bestial projection, Ariel the creative imaginative ... (*J* 180).

The journal entry brings Auden's physical presence vividly to life. Like the letter, it is another breathless and very funny example of a young poet's self-conscious and perhaps self-parodying 'Hero Worship' of one of her idols. Alongside the gushing prose, Plath's reference to Auden talking about Caliban and Ariel suggests an intertext for Plath's own poem, 'Ariel', and her decision to name her second collection after this poem. Auden, in other words, wasn't just a model she learnt and outgrew, but a poet whose public work and private words she remembered.

The same is true of the other poets Kendall mentions: Stevens, Moore, Eliot, Dickinson and Dylan Thomas. In the early letters and Smith-period journals, they are among the poets Plath mentions most frequently. And, as with Auden, we can listen to echoes of their writing in all of Plath's work, even if it is not immediately obvious. There have been many astute analyses of Plath's literary heritage. Jahan Ramazani has drawn attention to the elegiac tradition in the work of Stevens and Plath, among others. We can certainly hear one of Stevens's most famous lines, 'Let be be finale of seem', from 'The Emperor of Ice-Cream', in Plath's 'Pheasant': 'I trespass stupidly. Let be, let be' (*CP* 191). Vivian Pollak has written about Marianne Moore being an 'important friend to Plath, then to Hughes, then to Plath's dismay, not to the two of them together'.[7] One of Ted Hughes's poems from *Birthday Letters*, 'The Literary Life', also comments on this relationship. Although Plath was dismissive of the achievements of Eliot in a 1958 journal entry – 'let the <u>Wasteland</u> run how it may' (*J* 376) – her letters and poems are full of allusions to his work, including his plays. Jo Gill lists half a dozen poems that cite or rework lines from Eliot's poetry directly.[8]

Emily Dickinson's influence is less easy to trace but perhaps even more pervasive than that of Stevens, Moore or Eliot. Plath made a reference to Dickinson's influence on her poetry in a 30 April 1953 letter to her mother in which she included three poems: 'Tell me what you think of the poems ... any resemblance to Emily Dickinson is purely intentional' (*LH* 110). Angela Leighton links Dickinson and Plath's 'lifelong interest in effigies, dummies, casts, and heads'.[9] Their poems about 'dead women', she writes, 'are not forms of elegy, especially not forms of self-elegy, but elegies, rather, of perfect form'.[10] For Leighton, Dickinson and Plath are haunted by the aestheticist legacy of art for art's sake. They see poetic form 'not just as a matter of technique or pattern, though that is part of it, but also as a matter of resistance. It is the thing that cuts the poem off, from meaningful duties, civic or ethical, in order to be a thing in itself ... in the end it is what it is, and that is only a poem.'[11] Plath wrote frequently about the attractions (and limits) of poetic self-sufficiency. My own favourite poem of this type is 'Stillborn' in which the speaker grapples with the reality of the poem's not-quite-living life, so that the poems do little more than 'stupidly stare, and do not speak of her' (*CP* 142).

Plath's influences were not just American poets at this point. She didn't suddenly switch to reading British poets when she lived in Devon and London though perhaps they became more prominent in her mind (Stevie Smith is the best example of this happening). In a letter to Gordon Lameyer on 25 January 1954, for example, she casually namedrops the following five poets: 'we afterdinnercoffeed while listening to recordings of Eliot, eecummings, Nash, Marianne Moore ... and the lyric Welshman I've been mourning for these past months, Dylan Thomas' (*LV1* 670). Plath heard Thomas read from *Under Milk Wood* at Amherst College the year before and admitted to getting 'drunk just on the sound of the words' (*LV1* 671). At first glance, as the only non-American poet on Kendall's list of influences, Thomas might seem to stand out. Thomas was a key presence on American campuses and American reading lists in the early 1950s. For Plath, as for other American poets, he was one of the poetic voices they knew best, both in person and in print.

Stephen Burt's opening essay to *Close Calls With Nonsense*, a fantastic introduction to contemporary American poetry, includes a short history of American poetry in the mid-1950s, the period in which Plath was reading poetry and attempting to make her own name as a writer:

> By the mid-1950s most American poetry seemed predictable, passé; its elaborate stanzas reflected the safety of professors' lives. (Kenneth Koch epitomized and parodied their output in one line: 'This Connecticut landscape would have pleased Vermeer.') Rebels in San Francisco, in New York City, and in North Carolina translated poetry from French and Spanish, wrote tiny song-like poems or enormous ambitious ones rather than midsize, controlled, formal work, and published in obscure magazines they ran themselves (such as Cid Corman's *Origin*) rather than in well-established ones tied to academia. Some of these more adventurous poets, like Frank O'Hara and John Ashbery, hung out with abstract painters; others, like Allen Ginsberg and Gary Synder, hung out with, or were, the Beats. In 1959 Robert Lowell, once deemed an academic formalist, published *Life Studies*, whose poems (and prose) described in painful, self-inculpating detail Lowell's eventful life. Its broken, apparently rambling forms looked shockingly new (they were) and easy to imitate (they weren't though many so-called confessional poets tried).[12]

How does Plath fit in here? What did she make of Lowell's *Life Studies* or what came to be known as the War of the Anthologies between Donald Hall, Robert Pack and Louis Simpson's anthology of formal verse in *New Poets of England and America* (1957) and Donald Allen's anthology of so-called rebels in *The New American Poetry 1945–1960* (1960)? Was she a formalist or a rebel or something in between?

Among living poets, Robert Lowell was clearly an important mentor figure, as was Anne Sexton with whom Plath attended Lowell's poetry writing workshop in Boston in 1959 (Plath and Sexton famously bonded over martinis after class at the Boston Ritz-Carlton). Plath spoke several times about the significance of *Life Studies* for her own writing. 'I've been very excited by what I feel is the new breakthrough that came with, say, Robert Lowell's *Life Studies*',[13] she explained to Peter Orr in 1962. Significantly, she went on to discuss the work of her friend Anne Sexton: 'I think particularly of the poetess Anne Sexton, who writes about her experiences as a mother; as a mother who's had a nervous breakdown, as an extremely emotional and feeling young woman.'[14] The 'breakthrough' myth still has traction among Plath critics. Like Susan Rosenbaum, I am not convinced of 'an explosive transformation' in Plath's style.[15] If there were, I certainly don't think it would be traceable simply to reading Lowell or Sexton. As Rosenbaum observes: 'The narration of Plath's "break-through" ignores her continuing sense that to sell her work successfully, she had to style it, to negotiate generic conventions and audience expectations.'[16] There is a change in poetic style, then, but not a sudden one, and not a change that ignored the demands or tastes of poetry readers, much as it pushed at what was formerly considered acceptable subject material for women writers.

As Deryn Rees-Jones points out in a wide-ranging essay on Plath and the gendered self, Plath's relationship to women poets was 'largely rivalrous or dismissive'.[17] While, as we have seen, Plath frequently prefers women poets to men or at least spends more time talking about them, she repeatedly falls back on a narrow and very traditional association of prose as feminine and poetry as masculine. She isn't always as subversive as we want her to be. In 'A Comparison', published in 1962, Plath explicitly genders the novelist as a woman:

> I imagine him—better say her, for it is the woman I look to for a parallel—I imagine her, then, pruning a rosebush with a large pair of shears, adjusting her spectacles, shuffling about among the teacups, humming, arranging ashtrays or babies, absorbing a slant of light, a fresh edge to the weather and piercing, with a kind of modest, beautiful X-ray vision, the psychic interiors of her neighbors—her neighbors on trains, in the dentist's waiting room, in the corner teashop (*JP* 56).

Poems, by contrast, are objects that aren't necessarily tied to a particular person. She compares them to 'round glass Victorian paperweights' (*JP* 56). As Rees-Jones states, 'this description of the poem sounds very much in line with imagist aesthetics'.[18] Plath even cites Pound's 'In a Station of the Metro' in the essay. Plath is not often seen as an Imagist, or even a Post-Imagist. We have known for years about her interest in the visual arts, however, and her own proficiency as a collagist, illustrator and painter. Kathleen Connors and Sally Bayley's book, *Eye Rhymes: Sylvia Plath's Art of the Visual* (2007), and Frieda Hughes's edition of *Sylvia Plath: Drawings* (2013) both show Plath's debt to an international art scene that Plath was able to experience first-hand in both America and England. She wrote two poems inspired by Giorgio de Chirico, two by Henri Rousseau and four by Paul Klee. In a 1958 interview, she spoke of having 'a visual imagination. . .. my inspiration is paintings and not music' (*SPD* viii). Any appreciation of her artistic development must engage with this visual world as well, a world that encompasses advertising, cinema, painting and sculpture.

As an American poet living in England, a relatively rare occurrence in the 1960s (young artists like David Hockney went the other way, relocating from London to Los Angeles), Plath was often commissioned to speak and write about American culture. 'America! America!' (1963) and 'Ocean 1212-W' (1962), non-fiction pieces about her American childhood, were both written in England. One of her most important commissions was to edit *American Poetry Now*, a pamphlet anthology of American poetry published by the Welsh journal *Critical Quarterly*. Plath worked on the anthology in the first half of 1961. Her final selection included twenty-six poems by seventeen poets. Plath didn't believe anthology editors should include their own work. She also considered but later omitted three out of four members of what Thomas Travisano's book, *Midcentury Quartet* (1999), identifies as a loose group of some of the most influential American poets of the 1950s. Travisano's four poets are Bishop, Lowell, Randall Jarrell and John Berryman.

On the verso of the first page of the first draft of Plath's own poem, 'Mirror', she made three columns of possible poets, some with poems next to their name. Bishop and Lowell are the first names in the first column. Perhaps Plath was acknowledging their centrality to mid-century American poetry before dismissing their inclusion as too obvious and not sufficiently 'now'? For Bishop, Plath had three poems in mind, 'Wading at Wellfleet' and 'Large Bad Picture' from her first collection, *North & South* (1946), and 'The Prodigal' from her second collection, *A Cold Spring* (1955). Lowell was represented by 'Skunk Hour' and 'Inauguration Day: January 1953', both from *Life Studies* (1959). John Berryman had no poems next to his name. Randall Jarrell wasn't even mentioned. Delmore Schwartz, Karl Shapiro and May Swenson were also named in the first column, only for Plath to cut them from her final selection. A second column on the page added Theodore Roethke, Richard Eberhart and Stanley Kunitz. A third column listed names only, including Gregory Corso and James Merrill. None of these poets were eventually selected.

Who did Plath choose? Here are the seventeen poets she anthologised in the order in which they appear: Daniel Hoffman, Howard Nemerov, George Starbuck, William Stafford, Denise Levertov, Louis Simpson, Barbara Guest, Richard Wilbur, E. Lucas Myers, Adrienne Rich, Anthony Hecht, Hyam Plutzik, W. S. Merwin, Edgar Bowers, Robert Creeley, Anne Sexton and W. D. Snodgrass. Peter K. Steinberg discusses these choices in a fascinating chapter on Plath's work as an editor and reviewer. He speculates, rightly in my opinion, that 'the poems in *American Poetry Now* were chosen subconsciously to illustrate Plath's current poetry', in particular her shift from 'formal rhyming in favor of free verse'.[19] Steinberg also draws out several compelling comparisons between individual Plath poems and work included in the anthology, demonstrating a far wider circle of influences than has sometimes been acknowledged. Often it feels as if critical analysis of influence in Plath's poetry begins and ends with Ted Hughes, with occasional reference to Boston-based poets that Plath knew like Lowell and Sexton. By looking at Plath's journal entries and letters, not to mention her other creative projects, including her editing and reviewing, we discover a more complex and contradictory intellectual history.

Plath's anthology, like any selection, is a snapshot of one person's perspective on American poetry; it is not a history of American poetry per se, whatever that might be. Although it gives us a taste of American poetry at the beginning of the 1960s, in particular what was already becoming known as the Confessional School after M. L. Rosenthal's influential 1959 review of *Life Studies*, I can't help being struck by Plath's omissions, some accidental, others deliberate. The New York School poets are represented not by John Ashbery or Frank O'Hara but by Barbara Guest, another example of Plath's tendency to champion female members of poetic movements over their louder, often more celebrated male peers. There are no Beat poets, just one Black Mountain poet (Creeley) and not a single Objectivist. African American poetry is completely ignored. If she had been able to include British poets, it is difficult to see how she could have omitted two of her favourite women poets, Edith Sitwell and Stevie Smith, and of course her husband, Ted Hughes.

Plath read widely and voraciously but had blind spots and prejudices like all of us. Her American scene was by and large a Smith College student's idea of mid-century American poetry, augmented and challenged by her own bold and idiosyncratic reading of modernist and contemporary writing, particularly by women poets she considered rivals. In a journal entry written on 1 May 1958, on one of her last days as a Smith College instructor, she admitted to feeling impatient at having to read and presumably teach Marianne Moore and Wallace Stevens. 'I am already in another world—or between two worlds, one dead, the other dying to be born' (*J* 376). As she prepared to become a full-time writer, the poets she admired were already 'dead to her' but she needed them to help her own poems come to life, even if they were not quite ready 'to be born'. Becoming the present – what Joyce described as 'the now, the here, through which all future plunges to the past' – was a much more difficult process than her journal self could have predicted.

Notes

1. Brain, *The Other Sylvia Plath*, 46.
2. Axelrod, 'The Poetry of Sylvia Plath', 75.
3. Axelrod, 'The Poetry of Sylvia Plath', 75, 76, 80, 87.
4. References throughout are to the UK edition of *The Collected Poems* (1981) published by Faber and Faber.
5. See also Brain, *The Other Sylvia Plath*, 36–8, and Gill, *The Cambridge Introduction to Sylvia Plath*, 30–3.
6. Kendall, *Sylvia Plath*, 1–2.
7. Pollak, 'Moore, Plath, Hughes', 95.
8. Gill, *The Colossus* and *Crossing the Water*, 92.
9. Leighton, *On Form*, 254.
10. Leighton, *On Form*, 254.
11. Leighton, *On Form*, 257.
12. Burt, *Close Calls with Nonsense*, 6–7.
13. Quoted in Cox and Jones, 'After the Tranquillized Fifties', 107.
14. Quoted in Cox and Jones, 'After the Tranquillized Fifties', 107.
15. Rosenbaum, *Professing Sincerity*, 144.
16. Rosenbaum, *Professing Sincerity*, 144.
17. Rees-Jones, *Consorting with Angels*, 121.
18. Rees-Jones, *Consorting with Angels*, 125.
19. Steinberg, 'What's been happening in a lot of American poetry', 137.

CHAPTER 2

The Dominant Trends in British Poetry of the 1950s and Early 1960s

Eleanor Spencer

For contemporary readers, Sylvia Plath is an epoch-making figure; however, when Plath died in February 1963, she was still relatively unknown outside of London literary circles, the majority of her writing unpublished. In a tribute in *The Observer* shortly after her death, the poetry editor Al Alvarez wrote that her last poems 'represent[ed] a totally new breakthrough in modern verse' and that 'the loss to literature [was] inestimable'.[1] This undoubtedly struck many as hyperbole, given that Plath had only a slim collection, *The Colossus and Other Poems* (1960), to her name but set the tone for the posthumous apotheosis of Plath that would gain momentum with the publication of her excoriating final poems in *Ariel* (1965). Perhaps because Plath came to real prominence only after 1965, or because these poems struck British readers at least as so neoteric, critics and readers alike have tended to extricate her from her literary context, or to focus myopically on the creative relationship between Plath and Hughes, rather than to look more broadly at her influences and stimuli during the 1950s and early 1960s.

If Alvarez was partly responsible for igniting popular interest in Plath's life and work with her inclusion in the revised edition of *The New Poetry* (1966) and his later study of suicide *The Savage God* (1972), he also significantly, though not necessarily helpfully, shaped the way in which we understand the trends and developments in British poetry during the decades after the Second World War. In his seminal anthology for Penguin, Alvarez suggests that 'Since about 1930 the machinery of modern English poetry seems to have been controlled by a series of negative feedbacks'.[2]

Alvarez claims that English poetry in the 1930s had responded to the experimental verse of the modernists including T. S. Eliot and Ezra Pound with a reactionary pendulum swing back towards traditional forms that was not entirely disguised by the 'highly up-to-date' idiom adopted by the

likes of W. H. Auden and Louis MacNeice.[3] However, when the formal
precision and intelligent 'occasional' verse of the 1930s had become the new
status quo in English poetry, there was a counter swing away from political
realism towards high emotion:

> The reaction to Auden took the form of anti-intellectualism. He was
> thought to be too clever and not sufficiently emotional for the extreme
> circumstances of the forties. The war brought with it a taste for high, if
> obscure, rhetoric. The log-rolling thirties were followed by the drum-rolling
> forties.[4]

The work of the so-called Neo-Romantics (also called the New
Apocalyptics, after the 1939 anthology *The New Apocalypse*), including
Dylan Thomas, Vernon Watkins and George Barker, was characterised
by renewed interest in surrealism, mythopoeia and expressionism. Alvarez
decries this second 'negative feedback' as 'a blockage against intelligence',
dismissing these poets as slavish followers of Thomas for whom 'all that
mattered was that the verse should sound impressive'.[5]

Plath's journals and letters evidence that she was well versed in the
poetry of both Auden and Thomas, and in an interview with Peter Orr
in 1962 she said, 'When I was at College I was stunned and astounded by
the moderns, by Dylan Thomas, by Yeats, by Auden even: at one point
I was absolutely wild for Auden and everything I wrote was desperately
Audenesque.'[6] This yen for Auden was to become a near obsession with
Thomas; having 'imitated and idolized [him] as the perfect example of the
modern poet, excessive in language and life' whilst in high school, she was
disconsolate after missing the opportunity to meet him during her stint at
Mademoiselle magazine in New York in 1953.[7] She reportedly loitered
outside the White Horse Tavern and the Chelsea Hotel for two days in
the hope of seeing him, but to no avail (this was one of several cruel
disappointments that preceded her first suicide attempt later that year).
Amongst Plath's early work we find a significant number of 'exercises' in
the style of Auden and Thomas.[8]

Plath arrived in England to take up her Fulbright Scholarship at the
University of Cambridge in 1955, one year after the phrase 'the new
movement' had first been used in an anonymous article published in *The
Spectator* (now known to have been written by J. D. Scott, the paper's
literary editor), heralding the emergence of a new group of poets committed to writing in, about, and for 'modern Britain'.[9] This 'new movement' shortly came to be known as the Movement. This decorous rebuff to
the 'wild, loose emotion' of the Neo-Romantics is what Alvarez calls 'the

third stage' of these negative feedbacks. Though this article named only two poets – Donald Davie and Thom Gunn – when D. J. Enright's *Poets of the 1950s* (1955) and Robert Conquest's *New Lines* (1956) anthologies were published the grouping was expanded to admit Enright and Conquest themselves, alongside Kingsley Amis, John Holloway, Elizabeth Jennings, Philip Larkin and John Wain.

These poets were ostensibly the antithesis of the 'blindly inspired' bard Thomas; of the nine poets included in *New Lines*, six were university teachers, two were librarians and one was a civil servant. Alvarez suggests that these poets, with their 'academic administrative verse', took it upon themselves 'to show that the poet is not a strange creature inspired; on the contrary, he is just like the man next door – in fact, he probably is the man next door'.[10]

More so than any previous 'feedback', the poets of the Movement were explicit their condemnation of the perceived misdemeanours of their immediate poetic predecessors, castigating the Neo-Romantics for their bombast and emotional incontinence. In the introduction to *New Lines*, Conquest writes of 'the corruption [of] the general attitude to poetry in the last decade', stemming in part from 'the debilitating theory that poetry must be metaphorical'.[11] The poets of the 1940s, he claimed, 'were encouraged to produce diffuse and sentimental verbiage, or hollow technical pirouettes'. It is through these rejections and eschewals that the Movement was defined. Conquest admitted: 'It will be seen at once that these poets do not have as much in common as they would if they were a group of doctrine-saddled writers forming a definite school complete with programme and rules. What they do have in common, perhaps, is at its lowest little more than a negative determination to avoid bad principles.'[12]

Despite *The Spectator's* insistence on the 'newness' of the Movement, Conquest is at pains in his introduction to make clear that what these poets are advocating 'is not new, but merely the restoration of a sound and fruitful attitude to poetry, of the principle that poetry is written by and for the whole man, intellect, emotions, senses and all'.[13] The Movement poets rejected what they saw as the modernists' lack of regard for their readership – wilful obscurantism and formal experiment for its own sake – and sought instead to produce poetry that could both communicate *and* be understood by the reader. This new emphasis on the increased accessibility of poetry was part of a wider cultural strategy in the UK that saw the establishment of the Arts Council of Great Britain several years earlier in 1946, and the creation of the Poetry Book Society in 1954, both with the *raison d'être* of creating an arts-literate public.[14]

The Movement poets' rejection of modernist experimentalism was not only an aesthetic decision but also a moral imperative. To Davie's mind, it was the immoderations of modernism that created the febrile conditions for fascism. In his critical volume *Purity of Diction in English Verse* (1952) he writes that 'the development from imagism in poetry to fascism in politics is clear and unbroken . . . to dislocate syntax in poetry is to threaten the rule of law in the civilized community'.[15] Neil Corcoran suggests, 'Syntax, measure and a logic of statement were, in the Movement poem, almost an act of post-war reconstruction: to build the decorous shape of the poem was to provide a defence against barbarism.'[16]

It was, however, precisely this decorousness at which Alvarez takes aim in *The New Poetry*. Though Davie and the other Movement poets saw their principled recourse to traditional form and rationality as a necessary corrective post-1945, Alvarez viewed it as a diffident psychic retreat from the threat of 'mass evil' and 'mass extermination' represented by the Holocaust and the Cold War:

> . . . the concept of gentility still reigns supreme. And gentility is a belief that life is always more or less orderly, people always more or less polite, their emotions and habits more or less decent and more or less controllable; that God, in short, is more or less good.[17]

What was called for in this post-war age, Alvarez suggested, was a 'new seriousness', characterised 'simply as the poet's ability and willingness to face the full range of his experience with his full intelligence; not to take the easy exits of either the conventional response or choking incoherence'.[18]

Alvarez offers up the speaker of Larkin's 'Church Going' (1955) as an embodiment of this mannerly conventionalism, yet fails to recognise that this figure is also struggling with 'serious' existential questions of belief, consolation and meaning. Larkin's speaker 'often' finds himself unconsciously drawn to places of Christian worship, yet is clearly embarrassed by this inarticulable 'compulsion'.[19] The ability to admit doubt or uncertainty – what we might even call a radical incertitude – is characteristic not only of Larkin's poetry but the work of the other Movement poets, too. Whilst their imagery may have been crystalline in its clarity, there can be no such philosophical confidence; where Alvarez demands bold absolutism, the Movement poets instead offer brave but balanced contemplation.

If the Movement poets represent all that Alvarez deems outmoded in British poetry, then it is the American poets, foremost amongst them Robert Lowell and John Berryman, that he posits as the future. Tracing their line from Eliot's 'radical revaluation of literary tradition', he credits them with producing 'poetry of immense skill and intelligence which coped openly with the quick of their experience, experience sometimes on the edge of disintegration and breakdown'.[20] He suggests that the British heir apparent to this poetry of unflinching psychic verisimilitude is Hughes, and offers a comparative reading of Larkin's 'At Grass' and Hughes's 'A Dream of Horses' for illustration. This crudely dichotomous positioning of Larkin and Hughes as the 'old' and the 'new' of British poetry was to become engrained, not only in the minds of the academy but also for the poets themselves. Ryan Hibbett suggests that 'Larkin makes use of Hughes as a kind of straw man' even in the late 1970s.[21] Hughes, though only eight years younger than Larkin, conceives of himself as part of a different generation altogether: 'Now I came a bit later. I hadn't had enough. I was all for opening negotiations with whatever happened to be out there.'[22]

What this false Larkin-Hughes dichotomy obscures is not only the shared background of these poets (both were lower-middle-class, scholarship-winning, Oxbridge-educated poets from the country's regions) but also the extent to which both were 'opening negotiations' with the horrors of the mid-twentieth century. One need look only at Larkin's 'Myxomatosis', 'Deceptions' or 'Next, Please' (all 1955) to see that this 'genteel' poet was, in his own way, just as *au fait* with trauma as the purportedly more robust Hughes. Perhaps the most significant difference between these poets is in their siting of the grotesque and the horrific. Hughes's world is one of nature turned nightmare in which the mythopoeic and the archetypal are made flesh in shocking visceral imagery, as in 'Complaint' (1957): 'Jack Horner's hedge-scratched pig-splitting arm, / Grubbing his get among your lilies'.[23] Larkin's world, on the other hand, is real rather than surreal and the horror is simultaneously existential and kitchen-sink, in the debility of his human subjects, lonely, disillusioned and unfulfilled.

Alvarez's clarion call to break out 'Beyond the Gentility Principle' found a willing respondent in Plath. Shortly after its publication, she said, 'I think it [contemporary English poetry] is in a bit of a strait-jacket ... [Alvarez's] arguments about the dangers of gentility in England are very pertinent, very true.' Like Alvarez, she sees the likes of Lowell and Anne Sexton (with whom she attended Lowell's creative writing seminars in Boston in 1958) as the American liberators of the emotionally repressed English: 'Perhaps this is an American thing: I've been very excited by what I feel is the new breakthrough that came with, say, Robert Lowell's *Life Studies*, this intense

breakthrough into very serious, very personal, emotional experience which
I feel has been partly taboo.'[24]

In 1962, only six years after the publication of *New Lines*, Davie himself
acknowledged that 'the new movement' had now become old news. He
lamented that 'a poetic programme less than ten years old, which called for
a return to rational order and control, has been overturned from within its
own ranks, by writers like Gunn and Alvarez who dwell instead upon the
pain and violence of physic disturbance'.[25] Both Davie and Larkin decried
those poets whom they saw as unscrupulously making poetic capital out of
their personal traumas, Davie noting that 'poets nowadays know that it
helps their reputations and sales if they can manage a spell in the psychiatric ward'.[26]

Plath, too, was alert to this growing appetite for the literature of
mental breakdown and intended to capitalise on it with the 'pot-boiler'
(*LH* 472) that became *The Bell Jar*. In 1959, she wrote in her journal,
'Must get out *Snake Pit*. There is an increasing market for mental-
hospital stuff. I am a fool if I don't relive, recreate it' (*J* 495). In
1961 Elizabeth Jennings published *Song for a Birth or a Death*, which
reconnoitres the darker side of the human psyche. In the volume's title
poem, Jennings's characteristic rhythmical precision is still in evidence
but the diction and imagery is much changed from her earlier work:
'The fox's bark, the owl's shrewd pounce, / The crying creatures – all
were there'.[27] Her later collections *Recoveries* (1964) and *The Mind Has
Mountains* (1966) would explore with a new frankness her period in
a psychiatric institution following a nervous breakdown in the early
1960s.

Though by the early 1960s, the Movement aesthetic was no longer *au
courant*, it was not without lasting influence. In 1989, the Welsh poet
Dannie Abse suggested that 'the pitch, tone, strategy, and bias of the
Movement poets has predominated, with modifications, to the
present day'.[28] Abse was an unswerving opponent of the Movement
ethos, co-editing with Howard Sergeant the 1957 anti-Movement anthology *Mavericks*, which refused on principle to include the work of any poet
who had been included in Conquest's *New Lines*, instead including Abse
himself, Vernon Scannell, Jon Silkin and David Wright. John Lucas
suggests that, despite this apparent drawing of battle lines, 'it wasn't easy
to decide quite what, quality of production apart, separated the two
anthologies. Not a few of those who contributed to *Mavericks* especially
John Smith, Michael Hamburger and W. Price Turner, would have looked
at home in *New Lines*.'[29]

More obviously radical than *Mavericks* was the quarterly magazine, *Stand*, edited by Silkin. Founded in 1952, the magazine was so titled to '"Stand" against injustice and oppression, and "Stand" for the role that the arts, poetry and fiction in particular, could and should play in that fight'.[30] The poetry often did so by forcing readers to engage with difficulty, in direct opposition to the Movement shibboleths of clarity and rationality. Silkin's own poetry was unapologetically 'difficult' with its contortions of syntax and principled confrontation of pain and cruelty.

If the poetry of 1950s had, as Alvarez suggested, been characterised by an insularity borne of post-war enervation, the early 1960s saw a new interest in, and availability of, European and world poetry in translation. Lowell published *Imitations* in 1962, Penguin Modern European Poets series began in 1963 with Alvarez as advisory editor, and the magazine *Modern Poetry in Translation* was founded by Ted Hughes and Daniel Weissbort in 1965, with poems by the Czech Miroslav Holub, the Serbian Vasko Popa, the Polish Zbigniew Herbert and the Israeli Yehuda Amichai in the first issue. What this poetry in translation offered was a shot in the arm for British poets: 'This poetry is more universal than ours', Hughes and Weissbort claimed, and should 'stimulate poetry-making in this country'.[31]

These new voices were explicit in their often radical left-leanings. Poetry as performance had gained attention in the late 1950s when poet Christopher Logue and jazz drummer Tony Kinsey collaborated on the 1959 vinyl record *Red Bird, Jazz and Poetry*, and poetry-and-jazz meetings in the 1960s attracted a young and politically literate audience who swiftly became disillusioned with the Labour government's support of US military involvement in Vietnam. A febrile poetry of the 'Underground' (also termed the 'British Poetry Revival') developed, associated with 'rock music, festivals, "happenings" and anti-war protest'.[32] It was this poetry, explicitly political (or polemical) and formally experimental, rather than that of Abse's *Mavericks*, that represented the true repudiation of Movement restraint.

If Alvarez occupied a central role as a poetic king- (or queen-) maker during this period, a lesser-known though arguably equally significant figure was Philip Hobsbaum. It was not as a poet, though, but as a lodestone for bringing together other poets and writers, that he is most significant. Heavily influenced by F. R. Leavis and the tenets of the New Criticism whilst studying at Cambridge, he formed a weekly verse-speaking group in late 1952. Early members included Rodney Banister, David Jones and Peter Redgrove. Early on, members began to submit their own poems for discussion; these were typed and distributed on what became known as the 'Group sheets'. If the premise of the Group sounds familiar or even imitative to a contemporary reader, it is because the Group was an important precursor to the creative writing workshop 'industry' that has become so widespread on both sides of the Atlantic in the decades since the 1960s. Hughes was, perhaps surprisingly, never a member of this Cambridge Group during his student days as he belonged to another loose grouping of writers associated with St Botolph's Rectory (it was at the launch party for the *St Botolph's Review* that Plath and Hughes were to first meet in February 1956).

In 1955 Hobsbaum relocated to London, and a new incarnation of the Group was born with members including Edward Lucie-Smith, George Macbeth, Alan Brownjohn, Peter Porter, David Wevill (the husband of Hughes' later partner, Assia Wevill) and, though his attendance was sporadic, Hughes himself. Plath put herself forward for membership of this London Group in the late 1950s, but was knocked back by Hobsbaum, who later recalled:

> She sent me four meticulously typed poems, but I didn't like her early work at all – real college girl stuff – and I didn't respond appropriately. I was wrong of course. I think I was very cerebral in those days, and they were callow poems . . . two have never been republished and one was republished in very revised form. All very silly and sentimental . . . but I never thought of her as I think now.[33]

Hobsbaum's rejection of Plath had evidently been forgotten by the time he co-wrote the Foreword to the volume *A Group Anthology* in 1963, as he and Lucie-Smith stress what they evidently regard as the radical inclusivity of the Group: 'anyone who asked if he could come was welcome to do so. No one has ever been expelled or excluded.'[34] Heather Clark notes that 'Hobsbaum's use of the male pronoun here hints at the social barriers which would discourage women writers from joining Hobsbaum's London and Belfast Groups.'[35] When Hobsbaum moved to Sheffield in 1959, the Group continued under the chairmanship of Lucie-Smith, meeting at his house in Chelsea. At around this time the membership diversified to include Edwin Brock, Zulfikar Ghose, Shirley Toulson and Fleur Adcock.

The aesthetic identity of the Group was even more difficult to discern than that of the Movement. Hobsbaum explained that 'There was no recognizable "Group" poet; we were not a "school" of poetry. Certain writers in the Group had traits in common, of course, but similar traits could be found in writers who never came near our meetings ... What the Group did have as a basis for its activity was a belief that poetry could be discussed and that the writer was likely to be the better for having his or her work set before an interested audience.'[36] However, when in 1963 Lucie-Smith and Hobsbaum edited *A Group Anthology*, they clearly felt it was incumbent on them to articulate something of the values and ambitions of the collective. In the foreword, they identify 'frank autobiographical poems ... a poetry of direct experience' as their aim.[37] This would seem to clearly align the Group with the Confessional poets and makes Hobsbaum's earlier rebuff of Plath all the more ironic.

How amidst these diverse groupings and trends of the 1950s and early 1960s can we most usefully read Plath's work? Though by the time she wrote her *Ariel* poems the wistfully painted Massachusetts seascape of her childhood had largely been overwritten by the ill-omened English countryside, Plath admitted that she found little to inspire her in contemporary British poetry: 'I must say that the poets who excite me most are the Americans. There are very few contemporary English poets that I admire.'[38] Much of what has been written about Plath's work has, intentionally or incidentally, perpetuated the impression that her macabre imagination and arresting diction were without precedent or peer in British poetry. It is less romantic but more illuminating to recognise that her work, whilst surely the most successfully realised of its ilk, is not unique in its urgent ransacking of the 'myth kitty'. We see a similar receptivity to the 'weird mishmash' of 'astrology, black magic, Jungian psychology, Celtic myth and pagan superstition' in the work of Group member Redgrove.[39]

Redgrove was also born in 1933 and was a contemporary of Plath at Cambridge, and, like her, fused a naturalist's eye for the details of the world around him with the occultist's ear for incantatory diction and rhythm. Plath and Redgrove appeared back to back in the September 1959 issue of *Poetry*. Indeed, as M. L. Rosenthal (who coined the term 'Confessional poet' in his 1959 review of Lowell's *Life Studies*) pointed out in 1967, a reader could be forgiven for mistaking much of Redgrove's verse in the later 1950s and early 1960s for that of Plath.[40]

Unflinching and urgent in their confrontation of psychic distress, the poems of *The Colossus* and *Ariel* are the 'extremist poetry' or 'depth poetry' called for by Alvarez. However, like their author, who is hallowed as both poster-girl for mid-century female liberation and as a mythological type, they are simultaneously an integral part of the poetic history of the early 1960s *and* peculiarly resistant to contextualisation.

Notes

1. Alvarez, 'A Poet's Epitaph', 23.
2. Alvarez, 'The New Poetry', 21.
3. Alvarez, 'The New Poetry', 22.
4. Alvarez, 'The New Poetry', 23.
5. Alvarez, 'The New Poetry', 23.
6. Orr, *The Poet Speaks*, 170.
7. Butscher, *Sylvia Plath*, 34.
8. Butscher, *Sylvia Plath*, 92.
9. Scott, 'In the Movement', 399–400.
10. Alvarez, 'The New Poetry', 23.
11. Conquest, *New Lines*, xii.
12. Conquest, *New Lines*, xv.
13. Conquest, *New Lines*, xiv.
14. Corcoran, *English Poetry since 1940*, 82.
15. Davie, *Purity of Diction in English Verse*, 107.
16. Corcoran, *English Poetry since 1940*, 83.
17. Alvarez, 'The New Poetry', 25.
18. Alvarez, 'The New Poetry', 28.
19. Larkin, *The Complete Poems*, 35–6.
20. Alvarez, 'The New Poetry', 28.
21. Hibbett, 'The Hughes/Larkin Phenomenon', 111.
22. Faas, 'Ted Hughes and Crow', 201.
23. Hughes, 'Complaint' (1957), *TH:CP*, 32.
24. Orr, *The Poet Speaks*, 168.
25. Morrison, *The Movement*, 278 (quoting Davie, 'Reason Reversed', 640).
26. Morrison, *The Movement*, 278 (quoting Davie, 'John Clare', 964).
27. Jennings, *The Collected Poems*, 87.
28. Abse, *The Hutchinson Book of Post-War British Poets*, xiii.
29. Lucas, 'Value and Validity in Contemporary Poetry', 250.
30. Byrne, 'Poetry and Class', 119.
31. Hughes and Weissbort, 'Editors' Note', 1.
32. Corcoran, *English Poetry since 1940*, 135.
33. Quoted in Clark, *The Ulster Renaissance*, 49.
34. Hobsbaum and Lucie-Smith, *A Group Anthology*, vi.
35. Clark, *The Ulster Renaissance*, 49.
36. Hobsbaum, 'The Group: An Experiment in Criticism', 88.
37. Hobsbaum and Lucie-Smith, *A Group Anthology*, 'Foreword', v–ix.
38. Orr, *The Poet Speaks*, 168.
39. Alvarez, 'Ted, Sylvia and Me'.
40. Rosenthal, *The New Poets*, 215.

CHAPTER 3

Plath and the Classics

Holly Ranger

Sylvia Plath's approach to the use of Graeco-Roman myth in contemporary poetry may be suggested by her review of C. A. Trypanis's *The Stones of Troy*. She finds Trypanis's engagement with the classical past too self-consciously done and she comments, 'There is always the danger [in classically-inspired texts] that the poet will not transform the material, will not, in some way, make it freshly his own or ours':

> The weakest poems ... are those where the gap between 'contemporaneity and antiquity' is uncomfortably straddled: where the mythic material remains inorganic and untransformed in the context of the modern poem; where the parallel between old and new is pointed at, rather than realised in the poems' shape and texture.[1]

If, she continues, the poet chooses metaphor to infuse classicism into a poem, then it must be 'intrinsic to the poem, working back and forth on itself, not expressed prosaically at the close, like the moral in a fable'. In Plath's own classically infused poems, her engagement with her literary models is subtle and organically embedded; and when classical tales are referenced explicitly, she uses them knowingly as stage-props, observing herself in the process of reception with a detached critical eye: 'I borrow the stilts of an old tragedy' (*CP* 116).

One consequence of the dominant biographical mode of reading Plath is that her intertextual engagement with an extensive range of Graeco-Roman classical texts has been neglected. Her turn to Homer's Penelope, for example, as a model for herself as a resisting woman translator of the canonised classical past, sitting at home with dictionaries and working covertly at her literary task, a 'Penelope weaving webs of Webster, turning spindles of Tourneur' (*J* 233); and her playful inversion of such models in letters to lovers, casting the sailor Gordon Lameyer as Penelope to her 'female ulysses' (*LV1* 953; 894; 1046), or figuring herself as Ceres to Richard Sassoon's absent Proserpine and a 'feminine pygmalion' to J. Mallory

Wober's Galatea (*LVi* 1018). The anxiety Plath expresses elsewhere regarding her male peers' assumed or actual classical education, and her comparative 'ignorance' in this field (*LVi* 978; 1085; 1122), is belied by her calculated yet playful erudition – embedding letters to classicising recipients with subversively gendered allusions. Her recurring self-characterisation as Pygmalion from Ovid's *Metamorphoses* is employed to alternately mould her male lover and critique her complicity in the self-creation of the 1950s man-made woman (*J* 191; 510; *CP* 221, 69, 158). The shared female gaze of 'In Plaster' – between *Pygmalione* and her 'new absolutely white' creation – also reveals how Plath's approach to myth frequently removes the male antagonist to open up the ancient text and create a space – if ambivalent – for female dialogue.[2]

Although ancient tragic heroines are commonly invoked in Plath scholarship – she is variously described as an Electra, Medea, Clytaemnestra, Phaedra or Dido – they are used to mythologise the poet herself, and the construction of Plath-as-myth has overshadowed her literary artistry.[3] Such fatalistic and biographical readings of Plath as a doomed heroine trapped in a Freudian cycle of perpetual mourning for her father overlook her arguably more redemptive reading of Sophocles' *Oedipus* ('we have free will & must be responsible', *J* 335; cf. 329, 333–5; cf. *LH* 195, 209, 229). They also overlook her interest in the archetypal figure of feminine rebellion, Antigone (*J* 216, 222, 333, 340, 554). Antigone suggests a productive route for exploring Plath's use of the classics to create an alternative and highly ironised 'feminine' Oedipus complex to represent her relationship with 'Jocasta' and her literary mother(s). For while Plath was first introduced to Latin by her father, a trained classicist, she developed her personal classicism in dialogue with other women.[4] Plath was influenced by female acquaintances who were classical scholars including her college Latin teacher Eleanor Shipley Duckett (*LH* 252), Smith colleague Pat Hecht and her Cambridge philosophy supervisor Dorothea Krook, as well as by the feminist anti-bourgeois take on the classics developed by writers such as Stevie Smith, Anne Sexton and Christine Brooke-Rose (*LH* 369). As Virginia Woolf looked to Jane Harrison, Plath may have looked to these women as models to validate both her life as a writer and her gendered approach to the classics, self-consciously positioning herself within a tradition of women readers and rewriters of the classics.

Plath's classical allusions often sit in an intertextual chain of earlier women's receptions: her use of a Psyche-narrative in her Yorkshire Moor poems, for example, reworks the tale's earlier appearance in the novels of the Brontë sisters. Plath probably first read Apuleius' recombination of Platonic myth and folk-tale in *Cupid and Psyche* in his *Metamorphoses* in her 1940s school Latin class (*LVi* 87, 106–7, 137) – US contemporaries of Plath, Rachel DuPlessis and Alicia Ostriker, both recall reading Apuleius at school and both have written their own Psyche sequences – but her bathetic presentation of the House of Eros in 'Two Views of Withens', and its use to foreground a difference between masculine and feminine poetic vision, is clearly filtered through its dilapidated appearance in *Jane Eyre*. Similarly, the bridal imagery of 'The Bee Meeting' (*CP* 211) plays with Sappho fr. 13 ('Neither honey nor bee for me') via the sexual undertones of the plundering bees in H. D.'s Sappho poem, 'Fragment 113'; and both Plath and Anne Sexton make wry use of Ovid's tale of Daphne to explore female sexuality and cast a disdainful eye upon cultural imperatives to chastity in their respective poems 'Virgin in a Tree' and 'Where I live in this honorable house of the laurel tree'.

It is Woolf, however, who informs Plath's antagonistic relationship with the traditional guardians of classical literature. Cramming for a history lecture in her first year at Smith College, Plath feels 'faceless' before the 'centuries to comprehend before I sleep', and colours her journal entry with a distinctly Woolfian scepticism about the benefit of rote classical learning: 'millions of lives to comprehend before breakfast tomorrow ... To stop with the German tribes and rest awhile: But no! On, on, on. Through ages of empires, of decline and fall' (*J* 26–7). In Woolf's coming-of-age story, *The Voyage Out*, Edward Gibbon's six-volume *The Decline and Fall of the Roman Empire* (1776–89) is a key comedic prop in the text, as the socially awkward Cambridge scholar Hirst attempts to 'educate' the young Rachel Vinrace. Hirst exclaims his shock upon learning that Rachel has reached the age of twenty-four without reading Gibbon – he believes that appreciating the work is 'the test' to establish a woman's intellectual 'capacity' (Rachel's guardian, Helen Ambrose, argues that it is not Gibbon the naive Rachel needs, but 'the facts of life').[5] Woolf's use of Gibbon here is thematically reprised in *Jacob's Room* and *Between the Acts*, where an elite classical education is shown to hold no preparatory value for sexual encounters, romantic or aggressive: upon seeing Florinda's naked body, Jacob 'knew that cloisters and classics are no use whatever'.[6] The contrast between sex and the classical tradition in Plath's college journals implicitly echoes Jacob's thoughts, yet both she and Woolf suggest that it is not so much the classical past itself that is useless, but rather the ideologically loaded way that the classics have been taught and their reduction to the 'lives of great men', set texts and rote-learning. As Plath observes of the rows of 'girls, girls everywhere' reading Gibbon together in the library, 'Huxley would have laughed. What a conditioning center this is!' (*J* 26; 328).

As a student, Plath laughs at the banal indoctrination of the classics; but as a teacher at Smith College a few years later, her disappointment in those entrusted with the classical past is clear. At a faculty meeting, Plath's eyes and concentration flit about the room, mixing the contemporary with the classical:

> No eyes met mine . . . A roomful of smoke and orange-seated black-painted chairs. Sat beside a vaguely familiar woman in the very front, no one between me and the president. Foisted forward. Stared intently at gilt leaved trees, orange-gilt columns, a bronze frieze of stags, stags and an archer, bow-bent. Intolerable, unintelligible bickering about plusses & minuses, gradu-ate grades. On the backcloth a greek with white-silver feet fluted to a maid, coyly kicking one white leg out of her Greek robe. Pink & orange & gilded maidens . . . Haven't you heard? Mr Hill has twins (*J* 318).

Plath's disillusionment is heightened by the contrast between the culturally esteemed classical art and the 'unintelligible bickering' of the staff around her; she conveys a sense of loss and belatedness in recognising that, as a woman in the 1950s who has finally gained access to the classical learning that men have controlled for centuries, she is too late – the classical greats have been reduced to 'pluses and minuses, graduate grades' (or, perhaps, it is a recognition that the classics have always been so). If we read the neo-classical frieze at Smith as depicting Diana and Actaeon, then Ovid's story of trespassing and vision highlights Plath's sense of exclusion from acade-mia – an outsider looking in – alongside a sense that in witnessing the behind-the-scenes bureaucracy of teaching, she has seen something she regrets being privy to – something she may be disproportionately punished for glimpsing.[7] The scene gains a Woolfian colour when the journal entry is compared to the account provided in a letter to her brother. Plath writes how disillusioning it is to find that those whom she admired as a student now 'gossip, especially the men . . . with those on tenure getting pot-bellies' (*LH* 341). The portly classical scholar is a recognisably Woolfian type. In her essay on Gibbon, Woolf describes the scholar as 'ridiculous' in body, 'prodigiously fat, [and] enormously top-heavy'; while the sight of classical philologist Erasmus Cowan in *Jacob's Room* moves the authorial voice to wonder, 'what if the poet strode in? "*This* my image?" he might ask, pointing to the chubby man, whose brain is, after all, Virgil's representative among us, though the body gluttonise, and as for arms, bees, or even the plough ... But ... [n]owhere else would Virgil hear the like'.[8]

Plath's journal sketches of her classical colleagues at Smith are essays in Woolfian pastiche. Recounting a dinner party at which a male peer expresses his hostility towards the women classicists of Smith College ('Paul spoke of ... Pat Hecht's "Knowing more about Greek plays", or pretending to, than he', *J* 326), Plath clearly dislikes Paul Roche's attempt to disparage Hecht's learning. Both Roche (English) and Hecht (Art History) were possible candidates for a Classics professorship, and Roche seems threatened by Hecht's classical credentials. Well versed in the classics herself, Plath resents his affected scruples concerning the new wave of women scholars entering the 1950s (male) academy. The interplay between the personal and the scholarly – between gender and the classics – informs Plath's presentation of herself as an academic battling endemic sexism at work alongside endless domestic chores. Teaching Sophocles to undergraduates in between late nights and grocery shopping (*J* 334–5), and attempting to prepare class notes while running a house and cooking for dinner guests ('to hell with Sophocles', *J* 329–30), Plath wryly contrasts the high art and 'mysteries' of *Oedipus* with her own domestic tragedies. Observing the mouldering apples in her fruit bowl that 'mock' her, Plath imagines that the great demand the gods make of her is simply (in the face of Oedipus' trials) to get out of bed (*J* 334). Plath struggles, clearly exhausted, yet berates herself for her 'sloth ... & weakness', observing the clash between her own life and the lives of the male academics around her who effortlessly succeed (*J* 507). She describes Roche, too, in ironically classical terms that increasingly hold negative connotations in her writing when associated with male writers. Plath notes with a hint of fascinated disgust his face, 'adonis-boy looks lost', and his 'professionally dewy blue-eyed look and his commercially gilded and curled blond hair on his erect, dainty-boned aristocratic head looking as if it had been struck on a greek coin that since has blurred & thinned from too much public barter and fingering' (*J* 326, 354). Later, Plath discovers that Paul is a 'palpable sham':

> what machinations lead him to set about doing Greek translations ... ? to impress [his wife's] parents, to stall (until they come across handsomely by leaving a fortune) under the aura of a specialist scholar's life work? One can't help wanting to know. He is 'successful' in getting money, getting an audience ... [but] what does he do? The translations are a front: he uses a lexicon. Stanley claims to have seen the lexicon & Louis MacNeice's translation on his desk, open, and his own page a kind of elaborate synthesis.

So he is a fraud. One suspects, one knows, this—and yet one wonders: how, so beautifully, does he keep it up? (*J* 383–4).

Plath sees through the neoclassical pretences of these male frauds, mocking their classically decorated houses and classical posing as 'saccharine' – artificially sweet (*J* 503).

Like Woolf, Plath reserves her greatest scepticism for the guardians of the classical past, interrogating the fetishised value assigned to signifiers of a classical education and the ways in which the classical past is transmitted. This distinctive attitude is also found in Plath's poetry, but is, I think, always present alongside a self-reflexive critique of her own modernist anxieties – a reproach to break away from modernist classicising impulses. In 'Private Ground', for example, the speaker mocks the unsuitability of 'those Greek beauties you brought | Off Europe's relic heap | To sweeten your neck of the New York woods' (*CP* 130), while the speaker of 'The Colossus' is 'none the wiser' for her thirty years of labour reconstructing the fragmented colossus of the past (*CP* 129); in 'Insomniac', ineffective sleeping tablets are described as 'worn-out and silly, like classical gods . . . [they] do him no good' (*CP* 163).

Yet the pull of both ancient and modernist poetic traditions remained forceful. Plath repeatedly reveals in her poems an intimate knowledge of ancient languages and texts through close verbal echoes and allusions. 'Ouija' wittily recalls 'every foul declension' (*CP* 77) of her school Latin lessons, while her fear of miscomprehension is conveyed by the 'unintelligible syllables' of her new bee hive 'like a Roman mob . . . I lay my ear to furious Latin' (*CP* 212). Her personal library contained a broad range of ancient Graeco-Roman texts including Sappho, Plato, Aristotle, Thucydides, Quintilian, Marcus Aurelius and Augustine, and many of these are bilingual Harvard Loeb Classical Library editions, suggesting that Plath worked from translated texts containing the Latin or Greek on the facing page. Works of classical reception such as Racine's *Phèdre*, Anouilh's *Antigone* and Marguerite Yourcenar's *Memoirs of Hadrian* (*J* 233, 383–4, 399; *LH* 149, 256, 307), alongside representations of mythological characters in visual art (the films of Jean Cocteau and the paintings of Paul Klee, Henri Rousseau, José Clemente Orozco and Giorgio de Chirico), also acted as key stimuli for Plath's classicism. Undoubtedly, her 'Roman time' in the spring of 1956 (*J* 336; *LVi* 1160) shades poetic references to tourist sites including the Roman Forum (*CP* 129), and 'Aqueducts, the Baths of Caracalla' (*CP* 170).

In an extended example of Plath's classical engagement, her cycle of bee poems (*CP* 211–19) innovatively translate and rewrite Virgil's guide to beekeeping in *Georgics* 4. According to one biographical tradition, Virgil, like Plath, had a beekeeper father; but the links between their works extend beyond the personal. Alongside repeated references to the Latin language, Rome, Romans and Caesar (cf. *Geo.* 4.506), each of the five poems that form Plath's sequence corresponds directly to a section of Virgil's poem, and holistically rework his use of the bee society as an allegorical figure for civil, domestic strife. More explicitly, 'The Swarm' borrows the extended war metaphor at *Geo.* 4.67–87, but updates Virgil's references to Caesar to describe the swarm as the bee-emperor Napoleon and his troops battling at Waterloo. An understanding of how Virgil's fourth *Georgic* informs the bee cycle can therefore illuminate, in part, the integral role of 'The Swarm' – a critically neglected poem that Plath herself left in parentheses.

Her use of 'African hands' in 'The Arrival of the Bee Box' to describe the speaker's first sight of the bees reminds the classical reader of Virgil's own African bees, the Carthaginians, compared to bees building a new city for the queen bee, Dido, when the hero Aeneas first catches sight of the new city at *Aeneid* 1.430–6. Like the speaker of Plath's poem, Aeneas stands marvelling at the great 'din' (*strepitum*, 1.422) emitted by the workers, uncertain whether he meets friends or enemies. 'Stings' also follows the Latin closely in its account of the old queen, 'Her wings torn shawls, her long body | Rubbed of its plush', and the 'Honey-drudgers' who 'thought death was worth it' (*saepe etiam duris errando in cotibus alas | attriuere, ultroque animam sub fasce dedere: | tantus amor florum et generandi gloria mellis*, 'Often they even wear down their wings as they bumble against the hard rocks, and freely give their lives under the load: so great is their love of flowers and the glory in making honey', *Geo.* 4.203–5).

Plath also uses Virgil's text to foreground the woman who is the necessary yet unspoken condition of the poetic pastoral paradise, subverting the *Georgics* to challenge the male poetic tradition that uncritically praises the pastoral life. 'Stings' in particular implies that the man's idyll has come at the expense of the woman's cultural starvation and hard work: 'for years I have eaten dust | And dried plates with my dense hair'. A poetic sequel to her Woolfian journal entries, the poems darkly allegorise the ambivalent 'value' of a classical education in a period when women were expected to abandon their university studies for marriage.

The bee poems present an ambivalent response that both endorses and refutes her classical model. Plath problematises Virgil's imperial paean whilst drawing heavily upon it, flaunting her classical training at the same time as questioning the cultural authority that the classics hold (literalised in her text through the dominating and dangerous presences of Caesars and Napoleons) by expressing a self-reflexive anxiety regarding the power her speaker does not necessarily want to hold – and regarding a poetic tradition from which the poet has not quite yet broken free. Reading Plath reading Virgil resists biographical accounts of the apian poems that explain her thematic interest solely in relation to her father, at the expense of her intricate allusion – an obfuscation enacted, for example, by Hughes's poem 'The Bee God', in which the bees' Latin is rewritten as German 'gutturals' (*BL* 150).

The bee cycle forms part of Plath's larger engagement with Virgil. Virgil's own bee poem is notable for its description of Octavian – future father of the country, *pater patriae*, Augustus – as 'thundering in battle' (*fulminat ... bello, Geo.* 4.561). This is the first instance of the Latin verb *fulminare* ('to thunder') used of a mortal (it is previously only used of the father god Jupiter) – a linguistic conceit neatly reflected in the 'thundering' father of 'Among the Bumblebees' (*JP* 259, 261). 'Elm' (*CP* 192), meanwhile, 'inhabited by a cry. | Nightly it flaps out' reworks the *ulmus opaca*, the shady elm filled with false dreams encountered in the Underworld of *Aeneid* 6.282–4. Plath's engagement with Virgil is clear and deep; but it is Ovid's *Metamorphoses* which most often lends characters and themes to her work.

Her poems display a sustained thematic interest in metamorphosis, meditating on the transmutations of insects and the changing moon, and using metamorphic imagery in a specifically gendered way to describe pregnancy and the ill or menstruating body (in, for example, 'Metaphors' and 'Cut', *CP* 116, 235). Mental ill-health is also repeatedly figured in the poems as a kind of metamorphosis, most frequently represented by images of women overwhelmed by plant-life. This echoes the many traumatised women of Ovid's epic poem who are transformed into flowers, shrubs and trees. We see the unsettling blur between human and vegetable as a woman melts into the flower-patterned carpets in 'Miss Drake Proceeds to Supper', and in the suffocating flowers of 'Poem for a Birthday', 'Leaving Early', 'Tulips' and 'I Am Vertical' (*CP* 41, 131, 145, 160, 162). Metamorphic imagery dissolves the boundaries between self and other, and poems highlight the fragility and permeability of such boundaries by juxtaposing the Ovidian with modern images of surgery and tattooing (as in 'The Surgeon at 2 a.m.', *CP* 170). There are also allusions to or reworkings of many specific stories found together in Ovid's *Metamorphoses*, perhaps most strikingly to Philomela – sister of Procne, raped by Tereus, mutilated of her tongue, metamorphosed into a bird and inspiration for Shakespeare's Lavinia – in 'The Courage of Shutting-Up' (*CP* 209), and 'The Snowman on the Moor'.

Alongside the imagery of birds, purple mouths, tongues and bruises (*purpureas ... notas*, *Met*. 6.577), the poems share with Ovid a thematic interest in the interrelation between sexual violence and speech and silence (the word 'mouth' and its cognates appears sixty-seven times across Plath's poems, the Latin equivalent *os* 250 times across *Metamorphoses*). The story of Procne and Philomela (metamorphosed respectively into a swallow and nightingale) shades many other poems linked by their close association of sisters, birds, tongues and bloody mouths ('The Shrike', *CP* 42, 'Three Women', 180, 'The Rabbit Catcher', 193, 'Poppies in July', 203, and 'The Detective', 208). In 'Blackberrying' (*CP* 168), the 'blue-red juices' of the blackberries (cf. the bloodstains on the metamorphosed sisters' breasts, *Met*. 6.577; *caedis ... notae*, 669–70) stain the speaker's hands in 'a blood sister-hood', while overhead 'cacophonous flocks' wheel: 'Theirs is the only voice, protesting, protesting' – a mournful cry that recalls the Sophoclean tradition in which the birds Procne and Philomela lament for eternity.

A recognition of Plath's sophisticated and explicitly gendered classicism impacts beyond her own work. Both Plath and Sexton, for example, were working on their Daphne poems when they met in Robert Lowell's poetry class in Boston in 1958. While the link between Lowell, Plath and Sexton is usually figured in terms of their poetic dramatisation of autobiographical material, an understanding of Plath's classicism impels a reassessment of the 'confessional' school of poetry in terms of the role played by classical mythology. Similarly, any exploration of the poetic interaction between Plath and Hughes must integrate her classical scholarship. Allusions to Plath in his *Tales from Ovid and Oresteia* may be read not as allusions to Plath-the-woman, but rather as allusions to her own classical work.

Simultaneously rejecting yet drawing upon the classical tradition, Plath wrote at a time before she had the political framework to negotiate her ambivalence to the literary canon that informed her work. But her transformations of classical literature represent a poetic attempt towards such a negotiation, using old texts to explore new ways of representing herself as a lover, a mother and a poet. Plath approached her classical models, her poetry and her life with characteristic irony and humour, creating a place for herself in life and the classical tradition as a woman and as a writer.

Notes

1. Plath, 'Review'; 'contemporaneity and antiquity' quotes T. S. Eliot's 1923 *The Dial* review of James Joyce, 'Ulysses, Order, and Myth'.
2. On ambivalent, female, classically infused spaces, compare Plath's heavily ironic title 'Lesbos' to describe not a Sapphic idyll, but 'viciousness in the kitchen' (*CP* 227).
3. Lowell, 'Foreword'; Newman, 'Candor', 45; cf. 'Pythia, Cassandra, the Whore of Babylon', Newman, 'Candor', 55; Nausicaa, Calypso, Dido, Circe, Artemis, Aphrodite (Lameyer, quoted in Wilson, *Mad Girl's Love Song*, Simon and Schuster, 10); a 'vestal . . . initiate[. . .]' (Howard, 'I have no face', 82); 'Isis' (Sagar, *Laughter*; Rollyson, *Isis*); Tiresias (Axelrod, *The Wound*, 175).
4. *LH* 37; Butscher, *Method*, 10; Kirk, *Biography*, 31; Wilson, *Mad Girl's Love Song*, 87.
5. Woolf, *Voyage Out*, 172, 183.
6. Woolf, *Jacob's Room*, 69.
7. Compare 'The Snowman on the Moor' (*CP* 58), in which the speaker finds herself in the role of Actaeon, fleeing a lover's quarrel as the man 'send[s] police and hounds to bring her in'; Hughes inverts these subject positions in *Tales from Ovid*, casting Plath as Diana and himself as Actaeon (Hughes, *Tales from Ovid*, 105).
8. Woolf, 'The Gibbon'; Woolf, *Jacob's Room*, 33.

CHAPTER 4

Plath and the Radio Drama

Andrew Walker

In an early journal entry, Sylvia Plath reflects on the medium of radio. In a philosophically speculative discussion, she imagines the ways we respond to and create our sense of reality. For Plath, the radio dramatist – like the poet – imagines an audience: 'The sound is potential, even if no one is there to hear it. Just as radio programs are all around us, clogging the air, needing only a certain sensitive mechanism to make them a reality, a fact' (*J* 121). Plath was concerned not just with broadcasting but with receptivity, further noting the ways that we 'all live in own dream-worlds and make and re-make our own personal realities with tender and loving care' (*J* 121). These characteristic concerns for Plath – of audiences both imagined and real, audiences receptive and solipsistic – find a unique place in poetic output, particularly in performance and dialogue, monologue and drama. For Plath, the radio drama carries potential that is both good and ill. Although a young and precocious Plath would acknowledge the ways that the pervasiveness of radio keeps 'us in contact with the world', she nevertheless wondered if it brought all too much 'over the airwaves to hypnotize those who are too lazy to think for themselves' (*LVi* 159–60). For Plath, the radio drama might present an opportunity for connection and receptivity, yet it might also weaken the strengths of the lyric form, its individuality and sensitivity to interior perception.

That Plath was generally interested in the radio and its possibilities for reaching mass audiences has been well acknowledged by critics who have largely focused on her most well-known readings and radio interviews, beginning with her 1957 approaches to the British Broadcasting Corporation's D. S. Carne-Ross for the series *The Poet's Voice*. Although it is not until 1960 that Plath's work is accepted by Ross, who takes her poem 'Candles', she reads her own work three times for American radio during 1958 and 1959, and would eventually contribute more than a dozen radio broadcasts between November 1960 and January 1963. In these broadcasts, Plath reads her poems, discusses her work with Hughes and takes now widely repeated critical stances, both on the nature of her own work and that of others. Yet her most significant contribution to the medium is her only adult radio drama, Three Women. This work remains somewhat obscure in its generic and contextual origins, since it belongs to that dramatic subspecies the poetic radio play, relatively common at the time but under-examined nowadays.

Of the distinguishing characteristics of Plath's poetry, few are more notable than her sense of the dramatic, her sense of alternate voices and personas. Known primarily as a lyric poet writing in a lyric age, Plath here makes a foray into the dramatic that arises nonetheless out of a larger mid-century interest among poets in plays for radio and the stage and an historical milieu steeped in radio performance both pulp and experimental. As her journals and letters show, Plath's sense of dramatic language and genre were decisively formed by dramatic forms of poetry and radio dramas. Three Women, however unique in Plath's own corpus, looks far less out of place considering a context that includes other poetic dramas of the period – for instance, Dylan Thomas's Under Milk Wood and Ted Hughes's The Wound, amongst others. Throughout Plath's development as a poet, from her early journal entries to her final drafting, radio plays and verse dramas appear during key moments and prove distinct in their influence on the poetic art she practises. In accounting for some of the context surrounding the genre during her poetic development, we are better able to account for the decisive shift that occurs in Plath's poetry between October 1961 and the spring of 1962, helping us to see Three Women as a unique articulation of Plath's dramatic poetics in a moment of transition.

Early Radio Drama and *The Shadow*

In a letter to her friend Margot Drekmeier in August 1946, Plath's early fondness for radio dramas appears in a recounting of a seemingly unbroken evening of radio listening. Beginning by describing shows like *A Date with Judy* (a comedy series for a largely teenage audience) and *The Grand Marquee* (a romantic comedy series), Plath's letter typifies the radio drama's inter-spersed nature, describing the ways the half-hour programs are interrupted with popular, romantic tunes. Yet, on this evening, Plath's recounting includes a statement of unusual praise, to say that she had 'heard just about the best program I've ever heard … It was titled "Disputed Passage"' (*LVI* 82). A radio adaptation of the Lloyd C. Douglas novel, *Disputed Passage* was, in Plath's words, a 'moving story of two doctors, one old—one young—only a delightful speck of romance to give it more human flavor. I guess its [sic] hard to live without if you want to be a success. (Or so they say)' (*LVi* 82).

The basic features that Plath alludes to – her focus on doctors and the drama of the maternity ward – appear not only in her own radio drama but in another of the dramas significant to Plath's early interests. In a notable exchange with her mother in February 1952, Plath would write to encourage her mother to 'Work on Dr Christian' (*LVi* 411), a radio serial modelled on the eponymous obstetrician in the 1936 film *The Country Doctor*. As Aurelia Plath has noted, her daughter was encouraging her to work on her submission to a yearly writing contest held by the radio program. Though Sylvia Plath's encouragement is largely that of the supportive daughter, her confidence was nonetheless grounded in her mother's facility with the language of motherhood that would mark Plath's own radio drama, urging that Aurelia must write every year 'until you win. You have the background and technical terms. Go to it!' (*LVi* 412).

In the same 1946 letter to Drekmeier, Plath ends with a postscript, a modified tagline that identifies one of the radio dramas most influential on Plath's work: *The Shadow*. The tagline – 'Crime doesn't pay!' – is rendered in Plath's wry style with her addition of a parenthetical 'well enough' (*LVi* 83). This sign-off was the marker of an enormously popular radio program that reached an audience of 'more than 15 million listeners', resulting in its 'becoming the highest rated dramatic program on the air'.[1] Plath's reference to the show's tagline demonstrates an early interest in a program – one of the longer running and more influential radio dramas of its era – that would reappear as an influence on both her own radio drama and her fiction. Plath would most substantively rely on the hard-boiled radio drama in her 1959 short story of the same name. At the time of her drafting, she would describe her thematic reliance on a 'Feeling of badness in world unconquerable by good: war, death, disease: horror radio programs' (*J* 453), precisely that of the world heard on *The Shadow*.

The short story's central theme makes use of key metaphors from Plath's poetry, with the radio drama's pulp morality serving as a dramatic guide-rail. In her initial development of the story, Plath gestures towards her central theme demonstrating an 'awareness of a complicated guilt system whereby Germans in a Jewish and Catholic community are made to feel, in a scapegoat fashion, the pain, psychically, the Jews are made to feel in Germany by Germans without religion' (*J* 453). In Plath's story, in which a young girl bites a playmate on the leg, only to be ostracised by the community of adults who blame her actions on her non-churchgoing,

German parents, the childhood sense of justice and the world's reaction are largely tied to dramatic forms. Leroy, the young boy bitten by Sadie Shafer, is described reading science fiction magazines and having constructed a radio that 'tuned in on regular programs like "The Shadow"' (*JP* 144). It is ultimately through this receiver that the Shadow, who knows 'what Evil lurks in the hearts of men', helps the children to find the 'accumulating evidence of the warped, brutish emotions current in the world beyond Washington Street and the precincts of the Hunnewell School', and telling them 'how mean people can be' (*JP* 147).

In Plath's story, the Shadow becomes an ethical instructor and experiential guide. For Plath, writing self-consciously in the aftermath of the Holocaust, the radio drama theme functions as a moderating voice against those who would claim a moral high ground. In the world of the story, as the narrator points out, the world coming through the radio was one where the children 'had no cause to wonder: *Will* the good people win? Only: *How?*' (*JP* 148). The world Plath addresses in her writing is not so optimistic. The story's ending instead foreshadows the kind of direct psychological presentation she would make in her later work: 'The shadow in my mind lengthened with the night blotting out our half of the world, and beyond it; the whole globe seemed sunk in darkness' (*JP* 151).

Dramatic Verse and *Under Milk Wood*

Plath's interest in dramatic verse and its radio production appear in more literary examples, as well, including not just radio broadcasts but their reproduction and the communal potential of the poetic voice. Among her many visits to see films and plays, she describes in one memorable instance an evening spent at 'our Unitarian Young people's meeting where we heard and discussed the records of T. S. Eliot's "Cocktail Party"' (*LVI* 395). In a later letter in January 1954 to Gordon Lameyer – to whom she would also write something of a radio farce mimicking the police procedural *Dragnet* (*LVI* 775–76) – she describes Eliot's play *The Confidential Clerk* as 'Excellent ... entertainment. Though not as clearly defined as was the "Cocktail Party"' (*LVI* 669). In the same letter, Plath goes on to describe her fascination with listening, noting with fondness time spent in the post-meal coffee period of a dinner party listening to Eliot, E. E. Cummings, Marianne Moore and Dylan Thomas. However much Plath would take courage from the performances of these poets, it was ultimately to the last one that she would return in her own radio drama and as a key contributor to her sense of the poet's speaking potential. The untimely death in

November 1953 of Thomas, the 'lyric Welshman', would put Plath 'in mourning' for several months (*LVi* 670). Plath's affection for Thomas is evident in the fact that his verse drama, *Under Milk Wood*, was one of the key precursors to *Three Women*. She even duplicates his subtitle, *A Play for Voices*.

From the beginning Thomas conceived *Under Milk Wood*, which premiered on the BBC in 1954, as a radio piece. Yet, like *Three Women*, *Under Milk Wood* has been performed on stage, read aloud and enjoyed in print, troubling its status as a distinctively radio drama. The play is widely considered a masterpiece and for this reason has been the object of a great deal of critical and scholarly discussion. As Amanda Wrigley notes, the audience reactions to the 1957 television production, based on the audience questionnaire, were much less positive (scoring a mere 48) than the radio performance received (which scored in the 80s).[2] One of the chief reasons for this discrepancy is the play's achievement in poetic speech and direct psychological treatment of character. In fact, many assessments of the play's primary achievement and subsequent praise would describe its success as being 'closely related to Thomas' linguistic dexterity, poetic sensibility and imaginative flights of fancy'.[3] The play's language and poetic imagination was, in fact, what drew Plath's attention. Though Thomas had first performed the work in a solo reading in Cambridge, Massachusetts, in May 1953, as well as in New York, Plath's first exposure had been his reading of the drama at Amherst (*LVi* 671). Although she would eventually receive the 'tear sheets' of *Under Milk Wood* from Cyrilly Abels at *Mademoiselle*, where the drama had been first published in the February 1954 edition, Plath's commentary is almost wholly concerned with the play's use of sound: 'I could get drunk just on the sounds of the words' (*LVi* 671). After her extensive quotation of the opening of the work, Plath offers more of an apologia than a proper apology: 'I didn't mean to dive off the deep end in quoting, but the introduction was just too rhythmic and musically vowelish to cut short. And I can just hear his voice reading, the lovely curlyheaded, boozing hefty poetman' (*LVi* 672).

In Thomas's drama, the focus on sound is so pervasive that the characters seem to contribute little in the way of a central plot. Instead, the radio drama's characters appear as curiosities for psychological examination more than causal agents. Douglas Cleverdon, the drama's first producer, noted that it 'had no plot', but contended that it had 'all the other ingredients for a stage success'.[4] For Cleverdon, radio drama itself lacks any distinct rules governing 'what can or cannot be done', for though 'it may be in dramatic form, it has no need of a dramatic plot'.[5] Rather than focus on dramatic plot, the voices of the characters instead land on a quality much like the one that marked *The Shadow* and its invisible protagonist. First read by Richard Burton, the First Voice in Thomas's radio drama maintains a dreamlike quality that would reappear in Plath's own play for voices. Thomas's drama is one in which 'Only you can hear and see, behind the eyes of the sleepers, the movements and countries and mazes and colours and dismays and rainbows and tunes and wishes and flight and fall and despairs and big seas of their dreams. From where you are, you can hear their dreams.'[6] Such dreamlike qualities would reappear throughout Plath's text, relying on the ways that the radio drama featured as a medium less suited to plotting than to speech, sensory detail and psychological realism.

Ted Hughes and *The Wound*

The historical moment in which Plath would write *Three Women* was that Hughes had found recent success leading up to the couple's move to Devon. Hughes had composed a number of dramatic pieces throughout 1960, contributing translations of *The Odyssey* to the Third Programme and his *The House of Aries* had been recently performed by the Poets' Theatre Company in Cambridge, Massachusetts. His second play, *The House of Taurus*, was in drafting stage, and he was additionally at work on an opera libretto based on the *Tibetan Book of the Dead*.[7]

When Hughes recounted the development of his central radio drama of the period, *The Wound*, he would juxtapose his long-weltering libretto with the flash of insight that wrought his radio drama. In an interview preceding a later performance of the play, Hughes describes the play as coming to him in a dream, what he would himself call a 'freak production'. According to Hughes, the dream was the play itself, the entirety of its action. The morning after, writing in a feverish manner – 'it was very early' – Hughes tried to 'catch' the text. Although Hughes imagines his attempt to be half-finished (he believed himself to have 'lost the text') he finished with a distinctly 'poetic text', a 'sort of poetic-prose text'. Given that Hughes was 'interested in writing a radio-drama at the time', he resists the visual nature of his dreamed action, replacing it with what he would eventually note as a 'commentary rather than monologues . . . a narrative description of what's going on'.[8]

Plath initially considered such a dreamlike production ill-suited to their current position and needs. Recounting one of Hughes's recent dreams in her journal, Plath goes on to note that he is beginning to 'type his play. Ill advised, said yesterday wished it were realistic. Of course, I want a broadway hit in the cheap surface mind, an easy street' (*J* 522). Yet, as later drafts of their work demonstrate, both Plath and Hughes would rely on notes from his play *The Calm* for later poems, with both Hughes and Plath taking up some of the images and lines from the unrealised play, demonstrating their poetic and not-merely-financial potential. Plath would even use some sheets from the typescript for some of her most memorable poems later in the year.[9] Thus, to see the drama as a play predominantly for financial gain neglects the immediate poetic possibilities of Plath's aspirations.

Three Women

For Plath, the situation in which she found herself drafting *Three Women* was hardly advantageous to the experimental work she would develop. Having left London in 1961, Plath and Hughes's move to Devon and their new home, Court Green, resulted in a creative quiet that lasted much of the winter for Plath. Partially as a result of the birth of their second child in January 1962, Plath would write very little from October 1962 until the beginning of a creative outburst that year marked by her drafting of *Three Women*. Hughes's note in *The Collected Poems* clarifies the inciting motivation, noting that the drama was 'written for radio at the invitation of Douglas Cleverdon' (*CP* 292), who had produced Hughes's recent dramas. Responsible for producing work on the BBC's Third Programme, Cleverdon would ultimately shepherd *Three Women* to its debut on 19 August 1962.

According to then BBC Director-General Sir William Haley, who was responsible for its launch in 1946, the purpose of the Third Programme was to 'seek every evening to do something that is culturally satisfying and significant', something 'directed to an audience that is not of one class but that is perceptive and intelligent'.[10] Hosting avant-garde radio dramas like Samuel Beckett's *Embers* and *All that Fall*, the Third Programme was not averse to experimental work. Its listeners would expect intellectual seriousness and be familiar with the avant-garde performance style common to this kind of programming. Like many of the experimental radio dramas featured on the Third Programme, *Three Women* was vibrantly attuned to the dreamlike and spectral qualities Plath had begun to explore in 'The Shadow'.

Plath's explicitly stated influences for the thematic subject of *Three Women* were diverse in their origin, coming not just from the doctor-centred radio dramas of her childhood but also from the cinema. Plath first acknowledges the influences on *Three Women* in a letter of 7 June 1962, where she describes the work as a 'long poem (about 378 lines) for three voices', noting that it is about 'three women in a maternity ward. Inspired by a Bergman film' (*LH* 456). She is referring to the Swedish director's 1958 film *Brink of Life*. Plath would directly take up the plot of Bergman's film, depicting the lives of three women in a maternity ward each contemplating keeping or giving up her baby. In a brief working outline – one of the few drafts of the work extant – Plath originally titles the piece 'Waiting Women/Three Voices', and records the chief characteristics of each voice: 'the first does not want a baby, the second loses a baby, and the third wants the baby she has'.[11] Plath's journals may give an earlier suggestion as well, from one of Plath's original ideas for her lost novel. In this entry, Plath writes of her having an idea for a novel 'still titled <u>Falcon Yard</u>: story of three women, or mainly one: C—, with her illegitimate baby and mental hospital, just as Marty, her closest tagalong friend was discovering she couldn't have a baby', with Plath describing the work as 'Much easier to work up because not personal' (*J* 483).

Three Women is anticipated by other, earlier dramatic attempts, including Plath's 1957 or 1958 'verse dialogue' piece, 'Dialogue over a Ouija Board' (*CP* 276). In addition, Plath had a long-held practice of speaking her poems aloud. Unlike the production of Hughes's *The Wound*, however, *Three Women* functions less as a drama than a set of layered monologues, with each of the voices weaving a form of lyric production. Relying on such a performative methodology, Sandra Gilbert sees borrowings from Virginia Woolf's *The Waves*, especially in Plath's use of narrative patterns.[12] *In the case of Three Women*, this presentation of voices heightens the work as an experimental drama, though it also presented something of a problem for the initial broadcast. Two of the actors chosen to portray the three women had to be replaced at short notice, resulting in voice styles that were said to be difficult to distinguish on listening. Thus, in performance, many would hear Plath's lone direct attempt at a dramatic form in a way that seemed to rely upon an essentially lyric presentation of monologue, directly presenting the kind of intense subjectivity that would mark her later work. First Voice proclaims, 'I talk to myself, myself only, set apart' while Second Voice tells us, 'I find myself again. I am no shadow / Though there is a shadow starting from my feet' (*CP* 187).

Although *Three Women* was first published by Turret Books in 1968, the limited edition of 180 copies did little to advance the work's critical recognition or widen its public reception. Not until it was reprinted in 1971, in *Winter Trees*, was the work more closely considered. Some critical estimates have since placed it among the most socially important of Plath's work, noting that it 'meditates on ways that female subjects may resist the effects of centralized authority and bureaucratic will', and calling it 'Plath's longest poem and her most sustained effort to approximate the voice of the other'.[13]

Three Women presents Plath's voice at its most simple but also most dramatic, revealing her shift towards a more direct treatment of psychological processes. In her decision not to give the characters conventional first names but instead designate them as voices, as well as her avoidance of direct dialogue and causal plotting, Plath's experimental turn towards the dramatic is influenced by a host of early police procedurals like *The Shadow*. It also engages with more recent models by Thomas and Hughes, assisting in her move towards a poetic perspective that is visual in its imagination, and sonic in its outworking. Written within a year of her death, *Three Women* stands as a decisive transition in Plath's poetics, demonstrating a poetry that is at once clear, lyrical and eminently dramatic.

Notes

1. Mortenson, 'What the Shadows Know', 102.
2. Wrigley, 'Dylan Thomas' *Under Milk Wood*, 83.
3. Wrigley, 'Dylan Thomas' *Under Milk Wood*, 79.
4. Cleverdon, 'The History of a Radio Classic', 6.
5. Drakakis, 'Introduction', 10.
6. Thomas, *Under Milk Wood*, 3.
7. Stevenson, *Bitter Fame*, 201–2.
8. Skea, 'Ted Hughes: *The Wound*'.
9. Middlebrook, 'The Poetry of Sylvia Plath and Ted Hughes', 164–6.
10. Paulu, *British Broadcasting*, 152–3.
11. Crowther and Steinberg, *These Ghostly Archives*, 73.
12. Gilbert, 'In Yeats' House', 216.
13. Axelrod, 'The Poetry of Sylvia Plath', 86.

CHAPTER 5

'Sincerely Yours': Plath and The New Yorker

Peter K. Steinberg

The letters from Sylvia Plath to the editors at *The New Yorker* exhibit a different epistolary dimension from those to her family. They enrich our understanding of how Plath created and revised poetry, as well as how she marketed her work. We see her building up the credentials towards earning her 'coveted "first reading" contract' (*LV2* 583), and see Plath through the eyes, as it were, of her peers. *The New Yorker* letters provide insight into her poetic vision via her authorial comments on poems such as 'The Rival' and 'Elm', rounding out our exterior view of Plath's creative process. In these letters we witness Plath's close and respectful working relationship with *The New Yorker*'s editors.

Plath was often amenable to *The New Yorker*'s criticism and always responded with professionalism to their editorial advice, even when she disagreed with their reading of her poetry. By exploring the business correspondence between Plath and *The New Yorker*, primarily held in *The New Yorker* records at the New York Public Library, we see Plath interacting with her editor-peers, demonstrating instances where she stood firm with regards to her work and offering her own authorial comments on her poetry. These explanations offer an untapped source of Plath's own attitude towards her poetry and what she was trying to do. Plath communicated with several different editors at the magazine, including Robert Hemenway, Rachel Mackenzie, William Maxwell and, most frequently, Howard Moss.[1] Additionally, the conversations sometimes record otherwise undocumented changes to the poems.

Most readers only know of Plath's family-oriented letters published in *Letters Home*. In that volume, there is largely just the one voice projected. To Harriet Rosenstein, reviewing the book for *Ms.*, *Letters Home* is 'embarrassing to read, painful to contemplate. Its pages constitute a sustained plea for maternal recognition by a girl who could not quite sustain or recognize herself.'[2] It is important to highlight Plath's non-familial letters for the ways in which she presents herself to the recipient, be it a boyfriend, her husband, a friend or, as is the focus of this essay, her professional contacts.

Plath was an astute marketer of her own work from an early age. She often sent out a batch of poems immediately after she brought a sufficient number to completion. In her late teens and early twenties, Plath first sought acceptance in *Seventeen* and *Mademoiselle*. By February 1953, Plath was sending her recent villanelles such as 'To Eva Descending the Stair', 'Doomsday' and 'Mad Girl's Love Song' to *The New Yorker*. In a letter to her mother, Plath was categorically encouraged by 'the most tantalizingly sad' rejection from the magazine in early March of two villanelles (*LV1* 577). It was her practice to send them first to *The New Yorker*, and then to other periodicals such as *The Atlantic* and *Harper's*. She read academic journals, too, and routinely turned to these if she met with refusal from the magazines. In the absence of a submissions list, such as exists for Plath's September 1959 to 1963 works, the correspondence with *The New Yorker* may provide a way to roughly assign creation dates for many of her undated works written from 1958 to August 1959.

By 1958, two years into her marriage to Ted Hughes, Plath had placed her poetry in many major literary magazines and academic journals – except for *The New Yorker*. In June of that year, she finally broke through when Howard Moss accepted 'Mussel Hunter at Rock Harbor' and 'Nocturne'. Plath wrote letters immediately expressing her thrill to her mother, brother and Olive Higgins Prouty. In her journal she consecrated the day as 'starred' and recorded a cinematic scene-by-scene recap of her opening the 'shockingly, hopefully thin' envelope (*J* 397).

The New Yorker's acceptances came with a caveat. Moss wrote that there were 'some problems, as always', saying that the main obstacle was the length of 'Mussel Hunter at Rock Harbor'.[3] As a result the poem might not be printed until the summer of 1959, unless there was a forthcoming book in which case they would attempt to schedule it more quickly.

The letter from Moss offers fascinating insight into the behind-the-scenes editorial discussions that went into accepting, or possibly rejecting, poems. In speaking for himself and some unnamed editors, Moss felt the last two lines of 'Mussel Hunter at Rock Harbor' read ambiguously and sought clarification. There was some confusion over the number of and kinds of crabs about which Plath wrote. Plath answered Moss two days later declaring how pleased she was with the acceptances. To quell their misreading, Plath explained that the last lines of 'Mussel-Hunter at Rock Harbor', 'this relic saved / Face, to face the bald-faced sun' (*CP* 97), should be read idiomatically as 'to save face' (26 June 1958). Regarding the crab conundrum, Plath wrote that the crabs in 'mottled mail / Of browns and greens' (*CP* 96) are specifically fiddler-crabs; and that the dead crabs are more generic, representing all 'Crabdom' (*LV2* 254).[4] Plath pleaded for the poem to appear more quickly than the summer of 1959 stating that she planned to have a book to a publisher by autumn. Her phrasing allows her to be creative with the truth, for it gives the impression that she had a publisher in line when in fact she did not.

As for 'Nocturne', Moss suggested a title change, saying: 'We have no really valid reason for this; we simply don't like titles like "Nocturne," "Aubade," etc., very much'.[5] Plath's accepted the title change and she countered Moss's suggestion of 'A Walk in the Night' with the more concise 'Night Walk', which is how the poem appeared when printed in the 11 October 1958 issue.[6]

On 2 July 1958, Plath returned page proofs for the poems with a letter. The proof was the stage at which Plath was able to see their editorial punctuation and spelling decisions. For 'Mussel Hunter at Rock Harbor', Plath was satisfied with the additions of commas and the omission of hyphens. However, she did enforce her own preference in several instances. *The New Yorker* seems to have made Plath's 'Backtracking' from the first line of the second stanza a hyphenated word: 'Back-tracking'. However, she explains that her intention was for the word to be the gerund of the verb 'backtrack' (*LV2* 257).[7] It was changed. Plath also included a comma in the last line of the poem in order to eliminate an undesirable ambiguity, causing the reader to pause after the word 'Face'. These corrections show that Plath, despite fulfilling a literary ambition, was not prepared to simply accept *The New Yorker*'s suggestions at the expense of her vision for the poetry.

Upon publication of 'Mussel Hunter at Rock Harbor' six weeks later on 9 August 1958, Plath pronounced in her journal: 'I am awestruck, excited, smiling inside creamy as a cat ... in a rapt contemplation of my poem ... the title in that queer wobbly, half-archaic type I've dreamed ... about for eight years' (*J* 413).

Eight months later, after refusing six poems,[8] *The New Yorker* rejected four additional poems ('The Other Two', 'The Thin People', 'Landowners' and 'The Bull of Bendylaw') yet accepted two: 'Watercolor of Grantchester Meadows' and 'Man in Black'. Moss suggested slight changes to the poems. In her reply, Plath agreed to the addition of the geographic subtitle of '(Cambridge, England)' to 'Watercolor of Grantchester Meadows'. Plath was clued-in to *The New Yorker*'s bias for *place*, as she commented in an earlier letter to her husband Ted Hughes that 'the secret is to go where noone's ever been' (*LVI* 1270).⁹ But she expressed reservation at another of Moss's ideas, which was to modify the last line of the first stanza, 'Flits nimble-winged in thickets, and of good color' (*CP* 112). Moss sought to have the line end 'and is of good color'. Plath's worry was that this would both change her meaning and hold up the line's 'movement' (*LV2* 314).¹⁰ What is unclear, generally, is how extensive this kind of editorial counselling was to those writers whom *The New Yorker* published. In Plath's other business letters there is scant attention given either to improving the submissions or to altering an author's intention. In any event, Plath won this round: the 'is' was not there when the poem was published on 28 May 1960.

Plath's pre-1960 poems are difficult to trace because she did not appear either to save early drafts or to date completed poems as fastidiously as those written after she moved back to England. Though Ted Hughes placed 'A Winter's Tale' in 1958 in Plath's *Collected Poems*, Plath does not appear to have seriously marketed it until mid-1959. On 9 June, Moss wrote that with the exception of a single line he liked 'A Winter's Tale', and encouraged Plath to resubmit the poem later in the year.¹¹ Moss typed the line he disliked: 'Hair blonde as Marilyn's', which does not appear on any archival typescript of the poem. Plath sent the revised poem from Yaddo in September 1959. In her covering letter, Plath recapitulated Moss's suggestion about modifying 'the line (stanza 3, line 3)' and included two recent poems 'Magnolia Shoals' and 'Yaddo: The Grand Manor' (LV2 360).¹² Rachel Mackenzie rejected the two new poems, but accepted 'A Winter's Tale' on 6 October. Thus the edited-out line removes what is probably Plath's only explicit poetic reference to Marilyn Monroe; and may have played into the dream that Plath recorded in her journal two weeks later in which Monroe gives her an 'expert manicure' (*J* 514).

In early November 1959, towards the end of her stay at Yaddo, Plath submitted five recently composed poems: 'The Sleepers', 'Polly's Tree', 'The Net Menders', 'Memoirs of a Spinach Picker' and 'Dark Wood, Dark Water'. This is a somewhat rare instance where, according to her submissions list, Plath tried the poems elsewhere – *Harper's*, *Harper's Bazaar* and *The Atlantic Monthly* – before submitting to *The New Yorker*. *The New Yorker* accepted 'The Net Menders' and, as with 'Watercolor of Grantchester Meadows', the magazine sought a geographical subtitle to place the poem for its readers. Plath acquiesced, and in the first of two letters sent on 28 November 1959, suggested 'THE SPANISH NET MENDERS, THE NET MENDERS OF BENIDORM, or THE NET

MENDERS (Benidorm, Spain)' (*LV2* 370).[13] On 8 December 1959, *The New Yorker* sent Plath a cheque for 'The Net Menders', adding the subtitle 'Benidorm, Spain' on the payment slip. The following day, Mackenzie wrote to Plath with queries on behalf of both the fact-checking and proof departments. The fact-checkers sought information about Tomas Ortunio (the man for whom the street was named in Benidorm where Plath and Hughes lived in the summer of 1956). The proof department wanted Plath to consider the additions of commas and hyphens.

Writing from Heptonstall, England, on 18 December 1959, Plath was not able to supply much information about Tomas Ortunio other than that he may have been a 'local hero'. She accepted the punctuation revisions the magazine proposed (though curiously not all of these changes were kept when published in her *Collected Poems*). Plath refuted other editorial 'fussiness' such as capitalising the 'm' in 'madonna' (stanza 4, line 1) and pluralising 'bride's lace' (stanza 3, line 4).[14]

The last batch of poems Plath sent while a resident of the United States, on 28 November 1959, was rejected by Mackenzie in a letter dated 18 December 1959. The poems Plath submitted were 'A Winter Ship', 'Two Views', 'Flute Notes from a Reedy Pond', 'The Burnt-Out Spa' and 'Mushrooms'. It is unclear if this was 'Two Views of Withens' or 'Two Views of a Cadaver', though the former seems more likely. Smith College holds a typescript of 'Two Views of Withens' with a 3 Chalcot Square, London, return address. After Plath received Mackenzie's December letter, she submitted 'Two Views of Withens' to *The Atlantic Monthly* on 25 January 1960.[15]

With 'You're', Plath marketed 'Sleep in the Mojave Desert', 'On Deck' and 'Two Campers in Cloud Country' (more poems of place) to the magazine on 9 July 1960. The long silence since December 1959 was due to setting up home at 3 Chalcot Square, London, and giving birth to her first child, Frieda Hughes. When editor Robert Hemenway wrote accepting 'Two Campers in Cloud Country' and 'On Deck' later in the month, he suggested changes to Plath's imagery in both poems.

Hemenway comments that in the version of 'On Deck' Plath sent, '"Shuffleboard" suggests daytime games, when all the rest is midnight ... Wouldn't another wording without the misleading connotation strengthen the poem?'[16] Plath agreed and changed 'shuffleboard' to 'bingo' in stanza two, line five. Plath stated that that her focus was the shift from 'players of ship's games to players with emotions' (*LV2* 500).[17] Plath also explained that her usage of the word 'players' in 'On Deck' referred to those who either 'habitually' play or those freshly returned from an activity, including people who had left the playing room to get fresh air (*LV2* 500).[18]

Regarding 'Two Campers in Cloud Country', which Plath herself subtitled '(Rock Lake, Canada)', Hemenway suggested changes to the sixth and seventh stanzas that he though would help to clarify the poem, accommodatingly quoting her typescript submission (Plath mss). About stanza six, Hemenway wrote, 'we're not sure, but don't lichens grow practically everywhere, even on such rocks?' He also queried the line: 'In a month we'll forget what plates and forks are for', asking: 'isn't that statement a little too strong? The campers would, after all, bring plates and forks of some sort along.'[19] In her long reply, Plath agreed with these concerns and changed 'lichens' to 'herbage' to encompass 'all vegetation' and 'forget' to 'wonder' because after a period of camping 'plates and forks' would appear 'fancy and superfluous' (*CP* 145; *LV2* 500).[20] These are not significant changes to the two poems, but they do show collaboration on bringing the poems to a final state, and additionally show Plath to be receptive to constructive criticism.[21] Later in the year, Plath sent 'Love Letter', 'Leaving Early', 'Candles', 'Home Thoughts from London', 'Magi' and 'Words for a Nursery'. Although the magazine rejected the batch on 1 November, Moss wrote that he personally liked 'Love Letter' and 'Leaving Early'.

In late February 1961, Plath went to London's St Pancras Hospital for an appendectomy, staying there for a week. While there, Ted Hughes brought her a first-reading contract with *The New Yorker*. The contract buoyed Plath's readiness for the procedure and she wrote to her mother on 1 March with the details: a check for $100 for signing the annually renewable contract, one-quarter more payment per accepted poem, a cost-of-living increase and a higher rate for '<u>exceptional</u>' work (*LV2* 583).[22] The backstory to the issuance of the contract is interesting.

On February 19, in New York, W. S. Merwin wrote to Howard Moss asking if his opinion of the work of Plath or Hughes would be high enough to offer one a first reading contract. Merwin added that they were in 'financial straits' and that the poets were two of his 'best friends', which was the reason for his voluntary involvement. Moss replied on 23 February, agreeing that Plath should have a first reading contract and sent it to her the following day.[23] Simultaneously, on 21 February 1961, Plath sent 'Morning Song', 'Parliament Hill Fields', 'Whitsun', 'Night Thoughts' ['Small Hours'] and 'A Life'. Plath thought about sending 'Face Lift' but crossed the poem out of her tracking list. There is a peculiar irony that in the midst of W. S. Merwin championing Plath's poetry to *The New Yorker* she considered sending her poem 'Face Lift', a verse on the surface about a procedure Dido Merwin underwent. All were rejected on 7 March.

In a letter to the Merwins, Plath wrote 'O Bill you don't know how it sustained me & you are an angel to have nudged the Mossy stone into action. As I blacked out I thought of it with great joy & it was signed soon after, under the influence of morphia, but genuinely' (*LV2* 588).[24] Though all were rejected, her first poems to *The New Yorker* post-contract were 'I am Vertical', 'Private Ground', 'Stillborn', 'In Plaster', 'The Hanging Man', 'Heavy Woman' and 'Zoo Keeper's Wife'. Plath then sent 'Insomniac', 'Widow' and 'Tulips', the last of which the magazine accepted on 14 June. While it was written the same day as 'In Plaster', Plath withheld 'Tulips' initially, probably because the poem was written on commission for the Poetry at the Mermaid festival in London that summer. Plath did not explain this genesis of 'Tulips' but asked, on 17 June, if the poem could be printed in the poetry festival programme. Moss acceded.

Later in 1961, Plath's submission of 'The Rival' led to a fascinating discussion. Moss admired its 'hostility', elegant vocabulary and tone; however, the editors could not reconcile the title to the poem.[25] Originally a poem in three sections, Plath offered to omit the second part and was open to a title change, explaining that 'The Rival' is a 'contrast between two women': the speaker (a plain housewife and mother) and another (a dominating 'superhuman' figure) (*LV2* 645).[26] In spite of Plath's elucidation, *The New Yorker* remained baffled by the poem, rejecting it outright stating that without Plath's 'accompanying letter' the poem did not make sense.[27]

Plath sent two additional groups of poems to *The New Yorker* in 1961. Moss accepted 'Blackberrying' but rejected 'The Surgeon at 2 a.m.', 'Wuthering Heights' and 'Finisterre' on 27 October. Moss sought clarification in two lines of the final stanza of 'Blackberrying', which originally read: 'To the hills' northern face, their faces are orange rock. / They look out on nothing . . .' (Plath mss). Plath's revision to 'To the hills' northern face, and the face is orange rock / That looks out on nothing . . .' refines the imagery of the scenery (*CP* 169). On 12 December, *The New Yorker* took 'The Moon and the Yew Tree' and 'Mirror', while rejecting 'Last Words' and 'The Babysitters'. Candidly, Moss asked Plath to change the poem 'Mirror Talk' to 'Mirror' because of a prejudice against the word 'Talk' in a title.[28] In Plath's equally frank answer, she felt herself to be 'a rather numb hand at titles' (*LV2* 706).[29] A researcher working with Plath's manuscripts cannot help but notice the frequency with which Plath revised titles. This is true not just for her poetry, but also in her prose. For example, consider Plath's story 'This Earth Our Hospital', which she modified to 'The Daughters of Blossom Street' at the *London Magazine*'s prompting. Plath's longer prose was subject to working titles as well: *Diary of a Suicide* became *The Bell Jar*, and her later, unfinished novel had several titles: *The Interminable Loaf, Doubletake* and *Double Exposure*. Plath's journals also record numerous title changes for her 'early' poetry collections compiled between 1957 and 1959.

In his letter accepting Plath's 'Among the Narcissi', Moss wrote about 'the most extravagant praise of TULIPS', which was published in the 7 April 1962 issue.[30] Plath expressed her delight about its reception on 21 May, when she also submitted 'Three Women', 'Elm', 'Event' and 'The Rabbit Catcher'.[31] As with 'The Rival', the correspondence concerning 'Elm' reveals provocative background information. On 27 June, Moss wrote to Plath that they were 'drawn to' 'Elm' and found it 'impressive' but 'obscure', in large part because of the relation between the poem's subject and its dedicatee, Plath's poet-friend Ruth Fainlight. Plath held off replying until 31 August as Moss had advised they were closing for the summer. She resubmitted 'Elm' *sans* dedication, explaining that there was no relationship between Fainlight and the poem. The speaker of the poem is the elm and as such, could be entirely put in quotes. The tree is speaking to a woman who 'contemplates her' (*LV2* 815).[32] They share 'moods', particularly that of 'anguish' (*LV2* 815).[33] Plath admitted the poem was 'wild & desperate' but hoped, too, more clear in light of her explanation (*LV2* 815).[34] When Moss accepted 'Elm' he suggested a title change to either 'The Elm Speaks' or 'Speaking Elm' explaining that the magazine assumes its 'readers will have the same trouble' they did, which was an acknowledged 'injustice'.[35] Plath wrote to Moss on 10 October saying this acceptance was her happiest yet.

Since signing her first reading contract, Plath's submission rate had been fairly steady despite intervals of comparative quietude due to familial and domestic obligations. During the spring and summer of 1962, when her marriage to Hughes unravelled, there was sparse new work to send. However, throughout the autumn Plath harassed *The New Yorker* with her new poems, sending five batches in October, three in November and one in December.[36] In all, Plath sent a total of forty-two new poems.

In her first October offering, Plath dispatched 'A Birthday Present', 'The Detective', 'The Courage of Quietness' ['The Courage of Shutting-

Up'], 'For a Fatherless Son' and 'Bees', her shorthand title for her five bee poems. Undated on her submissions list, her second batch included just two poems, 'The Applicant' and 'Daddy'.[37]

It is not known what the effect this rapidity of submission had on the editors of *The New Yorker*. We do know, though, that this blitzkrieg was met coolly. Though Moss found 'Wintering' to be 'particularly fine', he accepted nothing.[38] 'Amnesiac', submitted on 22 October, the day after it was written, contained two parts. Moss saw no clear relation between the two parts, and preferred the second over the first. Plath resubmitted it in November with the declaration that it was 'quite independent' from its first part which was 'simply about the town forgotten' (*LV2* 903).[39] Moss accepted the poem on 30 November 1962.

Plath's final two submissions to *The New Yorker* came on 30 January and 4 February 1963. The former was comprised of 'Totem', 'The Bald Madonnas' ['The Munich Mannequins'], 'Child', 'Gigolo' and 'Paralytic'; and the latter of 'Kindness', 'Mystic', 'Words', 'Edge', 'Balloons' and 'Contusion'. It is worth noting that the last poem on her submissions list, 'Contusion', which was written on 4 February 1963, was added to the list in Plath's hand. The rest were typed. This suggests both that Plath decided to include 'Contusion' almost as an afterthought and that Plath did not actually send the submission the day she dated it on her list as she wrote 'Edge' and 'Balloons' the day after 'Contusion', on 5 February. There are several other instances on her submissions lists where the dates do not accurately align with other evidence. 'Mystic' is the only poem that was accepted, and that was done posthumously. At the suggestion of the Merwins, Moss wrote to Hughes expressing his 'shock' at the news of Plath's death and that her poems were 'extremely admired'. On her submissions lists, Plath exclusively underlined acceptances in a red pencil. 'Mystic' is underlined in black ink.[40]

Notes

1. The letters from *The New Yorker* editors to Plath are held either by Smith College (originals) or the New York Public Library (NYPL, carbon copies). Plath dealt with Maxwell for her short fiction submissions in 1959. Plath also submitted ten drawings to *The New Yorker* from Yaddo on 14 September 1959, though the editor to whom these were directed is unknown.
2. Rosenstein, 'To the Most Wonderful Mummy', 45.
3. Howard Moss to Sylvia Plath, 24 June 1958.
4. Sylvia Plath to Howard Moss, 26 June 1958.

5. Howard Moss to Sylvia Plath, 24 June 1958.
6. The title of the poem was eventually changed to 'Hardcastle Crags' by the time it appeared in Plath's first poetry volume, *The Colossus and Other Poems* (Heinemann, 1960).
7. This is peculiar, as in Plath's typescripts of the poem the word is hyphenated. See copies held by the Lilly Library and the poem as enclosed in a letter to her brother, 11 June 1958.
8. Howard Moss to Sylvia Plath, 8 October 1958. Moss rejected: 'Night Shift', 'Above the Oxbow', 'The Times are Tidy', 'Runaway' ['Whiteness I Remember'], 'Sculptor' and 'Green Rock, Winthrop Bay'.
9. In the letter to Hughes, Plath was discussing specifically their 'Our Far-Flung Correspondent' feature; but Plath's poems of place certainly fell within the theme of unusual locations. A search of *The New Yorker* archive on 31 October 2016, which admits its optical character recognition can be inaccurate, yields just six results for 'Grantchester' (none of which were for Plath's poem) and one for 'Benidorm, Spain' (which was Plath's poem 'The Net Menders'). Please note that *The Collected Poems* prints 'The Net-Menders' with a hyphen, but *The New Yorker* omits the hyphen.
10. Sylvia Plath to Howard Moss, 23 April 1959.
11. Howard Moss to Sylvia Plath, 9 June 1959. In this letter, Moss rejected: 'In Midas' Country', 'Goatsucker', 'The Eye-Mote' and 'Alicante Lullaby'.
12. Sylvia Plath to Rachel Mackenzie, 20 September 1959.
13. Sylvia Plath to Rachel Mackenzie, 28 November 1959.
14. Rachel Mackenzie to Sylvia Plath, 9 December 1959.
15. A point in favour of it being 'Two Views of Withens' is *The New Yorker*'s aforementioned preference for geographical poems. 'Two Views of a Cadaver' appeared in *The Times Literary Supplement* on 6 November 1959 and in *The Nation* on 30 January 1960. Neither poem was tracked on Plath's submissions list.
16. Robert Hemenway to Sylvia Plath, 29 July 1960.
17. Sylvia Plath to Robert Hemenway, 7 August 1960.
18. Sylvia Plath to Robert Hemenway, 7 August 1960.
19. Robert Hemenway to Sylvia Plath, 29 July 1960.
20. Sylvia Plath to Robert Hemenway, 7 August 1960.
21. This letter closed with an inquiry regarding the copyright of 'Watercolor of Grantchester Meadows' for which Plath had received a request to have included in an anthology.
22. Sylvia Plath to Aurelia Schober Plath, 1 March 1961. Plath's contract was renewed for 1962 and 1963.
23. Letters held by New York Public Library.
24. Sylvia Plath to Dido and W. S. Merwin, 7 March 1961.
25. Howard Moss to Sylvia Plath, 29 August 1961.
26. Sylvia Plath to Howard Moss, 11 September 1961.
27. Howard Moss to Sylvia Plath, 26 September 1961. In Plath's *Collected Poems*, the second and third sections are printed in the 'Notes' (p. 291).

28. See Howard Moss to Sylvia Plath, 12 December 1961. In this letter Moss refers to a Rodgers and Hammerstein song called 'Happy Talk'.
29. Sylvia Plath to Howard Moss, 18 December 1961.
30. Howard Moss to Sylvia Plath, 18 April 1962. Moss rejected 'An Appearance', 'Crossing the Water' and 'Little Fugue'.
31. Plath's submissions list records the date of submission as 8 June.
32. Sylvia Plath to Howard Moss, 31 August 1962.
33. Sylvia Plath to Howard Moss, 31 August 1962.
34. Sylvia Plath to Howard Moss, 31 August 1962.
35. Howard Moss to Sylvia Plath, 26 September 1962.
36. Submissions dates were on 10, 12, 22, 26 and 30 October; 5, 15 and 17 November; and 3 December 1962.
37. These were added by hand beneath the previous submission.
38. Howard Moss to Sylvia Plath, 23 October 1962. Letter held by New York Public Library.
39. Sylvia Plath to Howard Moss, 15 November 1962.
40. Howard Moss to Ted Hughes, 21 February 1963.

Literary Technique and Influence

PART II

Literary Technique and Influence

CHAPTER 6

Plath in the Context of Stevie Smith

Noreen Masud

In November 1962, soon after her thirtieth birthday, Sylvia Plath wrote a letter to a sixty-year-old novelist and poet:

> Dear Stevie Smith,
>
> I have been having a lovely time this week listening to some recordings of you reading your poems for the British Council, and Peter Orr has been kind enough to give me your address. I better say straight out that I am an addict of your poetry, a desperate Smith-addict [...]
>
> I am hoping, by a work of magic, to get myself and the babies to a flat in London by the New Year and would be very grateful in advance to hear if you might be able to come to tea or coffee when I manage my move – to cheer me on a bit. I've wanted to meet you for a long time.
>
> Sincerely,
> Sylvia Plath[1]

Born Florence Margaret in the northern British city of Hull, 'Stevie' Smith trained as a secretary, and wrote poems in spare moments. Her first collection of poems was rejected, and Smith was famously told to 'go away and write a novel'.[2] So Smith produced *Novel on Yellow Paper* (1936), typed on yellow foolscap from her office.

Novel on Yellow Paper made Smith's name. By the time Smith received Plath's letter, she had published three novels and several collections of poetry (illustrated with her own drawings). More hauntingly, she had retired from her secretarial job after a public but half-hearted suicide attempt in the office. Now she spent her days in her suburban London home, with her formidable aunt, who called her 'Peggy' and was lovingly indifferent to her poetic efforts. After breaking off an engagement in the 1930s, Stevie had never married.

In the early 1960s, while Plath struggled with two children in a cold Devon house, Smith was building her reputation as a popular performance poet. In these eccentric displays, she sang and chanted her poems in a quavery voice, dressed like a child in Peter Pan collars and leather shoes:

> At school I always walk with Elwyn
> Walk with Elwyn all the day
> Oh my darling darling Elwyn
> We shall never go away . . .[3]

Smith's characteristic sing-song nursery-rhyme rhythm lends itself, like Plath's 'Daddy', to being read aloud. In fact, Plath wrote to Smith after hearing her perform on a record. Nevertheless, her interest in the older poet predates the letter. In February 1962, Plath enthused about Smith's poems: they 'seem born all-of-a-piece, not put together by hand'.[4]

Linda Anderson has discussed how Smith and Plath's poetry both use voice and performance to escape their fixed position in the confining 'place of the feminine',[5] while Deryn Rees-Jones suggests that Smith's use of dramatic monologue and nonsense verse influenced Plath's writing.[6] This chapter builds on this initial work to investigate Plath's engagement with suburban roleplay in the context of Stevie Smith, exploring the forms of 'knowing' that the poets promise and withhold.

Suburbs and the 'Heavenly'

Both Stevie Smith and Sylvia Plath had suburban childhoods, scraped together in the aftermath of familial tragedies. After Smith's father vanished when she was three, the family moved to the London suburb of Palmers Green. Thirty-seven years later, in the United States, a not-yet-ten-year-old Sylvia Plath also lost her father, and Aurelia moved the family to Wellesley, a suburb west of Boston.

Clashing with these narratives of trauma is the suburb as classic 'everyday' or average experience. Neither Plath nor Smith fits comfortably here; both their autobiographical first novels – Smith's *Novel on Yellow Paper*, Plath's *The Bell Jar* – grapple with the burden of how to inhabit suburban banality. Smith's *Novel on Yellow Paper* sets her protagonist Pompey in the lightly fictionalised suburb of 'Bottle Green'. Living, like Smith, in near-solitude with her aunt, Pompey observes Bottle Green from a tongue-in-cheek anthropological perspective:

> I have wandered about having a *nostalgie* for this suburb but no means of getting into the inside-of it . . . And Freddy has been my guide, my Virgil, in these regions . . .

> They are very kind and solid the people are, and they are very nice for
> a visit, say you come in from a walk and you are invited to tea. And there is
> a kind lady that is his mother. And there are scones for tea. And they draw
> up to the fire and there is talk about how awfully common the other people
> in Bottle Green are being all the time.[7]

Pompey as outsider descends into the infernal depths of the suburb, with
her fiancé Freddy to translate. Of course, the trivial details – scones, walks,
gossip – are meant to seem, as Smith later specifies, 'too warm and too
close'.[8] The people are 'kind and solid': the social graces that make them
'very nice for a visit' also make them impenetrable. Ultimately, Pompey
breaks off her engagement when she realises that she cannot fit herself to
Freddy's model of suburban femininity.

But reading this passage simply as satire misses its tonal ambivalence.
Ged Pope recognises that Smith associates the bourgeois suburbs with
'ways of belonging . . . family, community, homeliness and happiness'.[9]
And 'kind and solid' praises suburbanites sincerely even as it establishes
their limitations. In Plath's hands, however, suburban associations become
overwhelmingly negative. Arriving home from New York, Esther in *The
Bell Jar* feels alienated by the suburb's excessive, indiscriminate benevo-
lence: '. . . the motherly breath of the suburbs enfolded me. It smelt of lawn
sprinklers and station wagons and tennis rackets and dogs and babies.
A summer calm laid its soothing hand over everything, like death' (*BJ*
109).[10]

Plath tips the suburb into horror by defining it as thoroughly, suffocat-
ingly known. The brutally paratactic list excludes any possibility of chance:
rackets and dogs and babies and nothing else. Suburban life lays down
a claustrophobic pattern that Esther cannot survive.

For Plath, suburban aesthetics extend even to her Devon home, portrayed alternately as haven and prison. 'What is so heavenly here is the utter
peace', she writes to her mother in 1961. 'Very nice tradespeople, a retired
couple from London at the end of our drive . . .' (*LH* 428). Devon is not-
London but oriented towards it; an annexe of the city, still defined in its
terms. And in 'Eavesdropper', Plath ascribes the same suburban impulses –
malevolent-maternal – to its residents and neighbours. Plath's speaker
imagines her 'nosy' neighbour spying through the window at night, but
all smiles and generosity by day. In what seems at first to be a delighted
exclamation at a kind offer, the poem begins, 'Your brother will trim my
hedges!' (*CP* 260). Only as the poem proceeds does it transform into a gasp
of horror. The neighbour is threatening to invade, we realise; her excessive
attention colonises the speaker's very body, like a spreading 'mole'.

Suburban knowledge derives from surveillance, and is experienced as violation. Only the proper city offers escape: New York in *The Bell Jar*, and the hallowed 'flat in London' in her letter to Smith. Sylvia Plath's personae experience these places as revitalising because they rule out the possibility of being known completely.

Smith and the 'Heavenly': Knowing and Not Knowing

Unlike Plath, Smith survived the suburbs, and stayed there all her life. The neighbours were unaware that she was a prominent poet, because she played the role of her auntie's dutiful 'Peggy' so well. For Smith, Pope argues, the ex-centric position of the suburb means that it cannot – contra Plath – be known or experienced directly.[11] Suburbs remain fascinating for Smith because they offer an opportunity for roleplay that lets her protagonists become alien unto themselves. In her essay 'Syler's Green', Smith's memories of the suburbs consist of early make-believe games and transforming hatboxes into jungle scenes with paint.[12] Even 'Peggy' is a performance, a playacting of normalcy whose relationship to reality can never be wholly known. This section explores such knowing, unknowing roleplay of suburban aesthetics, experienced lightly for Smith and heavily for Plath.

Smith's Pompey felt safe to enjoy the suburbs in limited, careful ways. She could 'visit' the suburbs and then remove herself. This glancing, gradual knowledge offers pleasure to Smith's characters, though it makes Plath shudder. Plath presents Esther Greenwood as psychologically at risk from a suburban aesthetic that repels her, but which she cannot effectively resist. The poet herself dutifully inhabits this hated role, particularly in letters to her mother:

> ... [the midwife] sat on one side of the bed and Ted on the other, gossiping pleasantly together ... while I breathed in my mask whenever I had a strong contraction and joined in the conversation [... after the birth] I immediately sat up and felt wonderful – no tears, nothing.
>
> It is heavenly to be in my own home – I'm in the guest room, which is ideal (*LH* 443).

Plath is anxious to emphasise how socially competent she was during Nicholas's birth. She plays the good girl-next-door: keeping up her side in the conversation, managing her own pain, sitting straight up afterwards. Then she comes back to her 'heavenly' home, establishing herself within the meticulous, fussy hospitality of the 'guest room'.

'Heavenly' – that earnest, well-schooled girl's word – recurs in Plath's letters, part of the performance of suburban acceptability. Ireland is 'heaven', but so is her ambivalent Devon idyll: 'What is so heavenly here is the utter peace . . .' (*LH* 428). Plath connects the word with roleplaying, performing the homemaker, the designer of idyllic interior spaces: 'I adore my own study, and after I get my great plank table, paint the woodwork white, get a rug and maybe an upholstered armchair, it will be heavenly . . .' (*LH* 429).

'It will be heavenly.' Stevie Smith parrots this social cliché in 'The Frog Prince' (1966). An enchanted frog, mostly contented, describes his life in language which, as Romana Huk notes, 'resounds of solitude in suburbia rendered stagnant by complacency':[13]

> I am happy, I like the life,
> Can swim for many a mile . . .[14]

This is the voice of the placid retiree, who enjoys the mundanity of doing lengths in the local pool. But the frog does look forwards sometimes, he admits, to the kiss that will lift the numbing spell:

> . . . It will be *heavenly*
> To be set free . . .[15]

Smith's italics tend to suggest inappropriate or excessive emphasis. In 'Mutchmore and Not-So' they underline an exaggeratedly gossipy tone: 'Gerald has such a *peculiar* sense of humour.'[16] Both Smith and Plath often associate emphasis with gossip, and thus with the untrustworthy: emphasis casts content (both contentment and poetic content) into doubt. In Plath's 'Eavesdropper', an insistent exclamation mark demands that we stress the first line: 'Your brother will trim my hedges!' Yet the strength of that emphasis elides its ambiguity: does the stress suggest warmth, horror or outrage?

Similarly, italics in Plath's 'The Tour' cue us into the chatty voice of the suburban gossip, perhaps the 'kind lady' we met in Smith's *Novel on Yellow Paper*. 'Not a patch on *your* place, I guess' (*CP* 237), 'It'll be *lemon* tea for me', 'Well I *hope* you've enjoyed it, auntie!' (*CP* 238). Plath reveals the grisliness underlying bright social chatter: images of savage furnaces and carnivorous pools alternate with talk of biscuits and tea. Though Smith's 'The Frog Prince' is less explicitly troubled than Plath's 'Eavesdropper' or 'The Tour', her italics encourage us to read her 'heavenly' as pastiche. Smith reminds us that these social niceties are spoken by a frog masquerading as an affected suburban gossip. He is, of course, also a prince masquerading as a frog. Layers of roleplay are operating. We are not sure who to credit for these lines: frog, prince or Smith herself.

But pastiche levels out with the final verse. The poem ends with an invocation to the girl who will, ambiguously, 'disenchant' him. Will heaven, that socially prescribed heaven of refined human life, be an experience of disenchantment, rather than happiness? Or is Smith suggesting a moral dimension to this experience, where it is sobering, but saintly, to see things as they are and be who one is? She foregrounds no interpretative line. Despite its emphatic italics, the divinely oracular promise of 'heavenly' is undercut. We are prevented from 'knowing' the poem reliably.

'A Desperate Smith-Addict': 'Lady Lazarus' and Excess

Smith has been hampered by readings insensitive to her wryness. Jack Barbera describes how her illustrations, for instance, were considered excessively personal at a time when good poetry was meant to be impersonal.[17] The similarity with Plath is clear: as a 'confessional' poet, who praised Robert Lowell's 'breakthrough into very serious, very personal, emotional experience',[18] Plath's biographical legend has been conflated frequently with her writing.

Like Smith, Plath's best work renders excess with gravity; undercuts the confessional with the humorous. Accordingly, her letter to Smith lays audibly jokey claim to the role of the penitent sinner, confessing before a priest. 'I am an addict of your poetry', she admits, 'a desperate Smith-addict'. But describing herself as a 'desperate ... addict' further allows Plath to couch her reading and artistic life in terms of excess. Smith is to understand her as ardent, passionate; not quite in control of her reading and writing appetite; prone to overstatement.

Plath has in fact, as Karen Jackson Ford notes, been discussed in the gendered language of 'excess' for writing too much, revealing too much and developing her poetics 'too far'.[19] Stevie Smith received similar criticism; a publisher's reader, 'E.B.', despaired over the poems she submitted, deeming them 'too many'.[20] Her style often creates the impression of exceeding its own form, with unexpectedly long lines bursting past their limits. In a stanza from her most famous poem, 'Not Waving But Drowning', for instance, the third line overextends, before stopping short in an anticlimactic, pokerfaced 'They said'.[21] Smith signals that excess is a display. The overproducing poet is a role that she can assume and put off at will. In a letter to John Hayward in 1942, she half-laments, half-boasts how, in a moment of inspiration, she produced 'six more poems and . . . 24 new drawings', and the 'room . . . looks like a paper-chase'.[22] So Plath's self-description as a 'desperate Smith-addict' signals to her predecessor that she can live up to the Stevie Smith legend. Smith may overproduce, may signal her brilliance through her rhetorical and performative excess, but Plath the 'addict' is on the same plane: she can consume everything Smith produces and still beg for more.

For Ford, Plath developed her own 'excessive' style late. While earlier in her career she tried to fit herself to the demands of magazine editors, her later work developed excess as a strategy to resist the limitations of standards of decorum.[23] Like Smith's deadpan, barely inflected humour, however, Plath positions her later poems in conversation with that decorum. They marshal excess with a knowing playfulness or gravity. Her explicitly 'theatrical' poem 'Lady Lazarus' stages a 'strip tease' (*CP* 245) of lurid imagery:

> I have done it again.
> [. . .]
> My right foot
>
> A paperweight.
> My face a featureless, fine
> Jew linen.   (*CP* 244)

Plath transfigures each part of her speaker's body into grisly historical artefacts: the linen and lampshade speaking testaments to Nazi atrocities. And yet the diction is methodical. Plath uses deliberate, discursive language to 'manage' (even the feat of rebirth is described in bureaucratic terms) the flow of horrors. Lady Lazarus as 'walking miracle' is tempered by her 'sort of': she can be casual even about her most extreme claims. And Plath's characteristic sharp full stops bring the poem grinding repeatedly to a deadpan halt:

> I do it so it feels like hell.
> I do it so it feels real.
> I guess you could say I've a call.   (*CP* 245)

They weigh it down, like Nazi 'paperweights' barely holding down the swelling piles of euphemistic bureaucracy. As in Smith's 'Not Waving But Drowning', these acts of formal discipline frame and emphasise the excess that they restrain. Both Smith and Plath perform the dry affectlessness that lies on the other side of overproductive mania: excess that could, with just a little twist, really be nothing at all.

'Wild as a Cat'

When Plath calls herself 'a desperate Smith-addict', then, the excess is both jokey and serious. Linda W. Wagner-Martin describes how, in early November 1962, Plath veered between buoyancy and desperation as she sought authoritative reassurance. After viewing a London flat, Plath opened Yeats's collected plays at random, and interpreted the lines she saw as a sign that she was 'in touch with good spirits'.[24]

In turning to Yeats, Plath was seeking spiritual and literary blessing: a gesture of approval from an ancestral authorial voice. We sense the same impulse in her letter to Smith. When she confesses 'I better say straight out that I am an addict of your poetry, a desperate Smith-addict', Plath performs her own self-abnegation before Smith as literary/maternal authority. Smith is meant to laugh, but also to recognise a call for 'enfolding' support. Plath channels the language of the prodigal daughter: confessing all, hoping for forgiveness and help.

What help does Plath want from Smith? We can hear an implicit request in this letter for Smith to participate in a 'work of magic'. Plath's phrasing in the *London Magazine* casts Smith as a witch: 'The poets I delight in are possessed by their poems as by the rhythms of their own breathing. Their finest poems seem born all-of-a-piece, not put together by hand ... [for instance] a very great deal of Stevie Smith ("Art is wild as a cat and quite separate from civilisation").'[25]

Here Plath imagines Smith as a medium. Her poems do not seem 'put together by hand'; Smith appears to channel them intact from some source that is at once 'wild' – primal, beyond herself – and profoundly bodily, caught up in 'the rhythms of [her] own breathing'. Plath craves this model of reliable, controlled truth, delivered with oracular finality in opposition to the slow, insidious 'grow[th]' ('The Eavesdropper') of gossip-knowledge. The same hunger drew Plath to the Ouija board: it similarly combines the bodily and unbodily, moved at once by its users' hands and by an independent spirit. Yet in 'Dialogue over a Ouija Board', Plath associates Ouija experience not with oracular authority but with doubt, tedium and argument:

> SIBYL: F- I-N-E, he says. You feel him pull
> Under your finger? I mean, you don't push
> Even a little?
> LEROY: You know I don't, and still ...
> SIBYL: And still I'm sceptic. I know. I'm being foolish. (CP 277)

The voice lacks a convincing wholeness, needing to be spelled out. In another poem on the subject, 'Ouija', the spirit 'dribbles' out his messages slowly and messily, 'maundering' between letters (*CP* 77). He is not 'succinct' (*CP* 78): his messages do not come 'all-of-a-piece', as Plath described Smith's best poetry. The line she quotes from Smith's poem 'The New Age' – 'Art is wild as a cat and quite separate from civilisation' – has the 'perfected' self-sufficiency (to use a key word from Plath's 'Edge') of something finished.

Yet, despite its aura of absolute knowledge, this completeness has a deadening quality. When Smith finally wrote back to Plath, the same effect of finished finality is audible – but this literary ancestress offers no oracular reassurance:

> I was glad to hear from you & glad you enjoyed the Harvard record . . .
> . . . I do hope your novel goes well & I do hope the move in the New Year goes well too – if only as you suggest, so that we can meet some time.
> I feel awfully lazy most of the time [. . .] as for poetry, I am a real humbug, just write it (?) sometimes but practically never read a word . . .[26]

Smith's niceties are exaggeratedly bland. Her repetitions – 'glad', 'I do hope' – flag up their own banality, and harden the good wishes into opacity: a social front that is hard to penetrate. Much about this letter reads as Smith detaching herself from Plath, from the urgency with which the younger poet attempted to cast Smith as confessor, cheerleader, life-saver. Stevie Smith's language refuses to get involved: it dips into suburban courtesies, then withdraws itself.

Notes

1. Plath, quoted in Smith, *Me Again*, 6.
2. Sternlicht, 'Introduction', 66.
3. Smith, *Collected Poems*, 413.
4. Plath, 'Context', 46.
5. Anderson, 'Gender, Feminism, Poetry', 184.
6. Rees-Jones, *Consorting with Angels*, 121.
7. Smith, *Novel on Yellow Paper*, 181.
8. Smith, *Novel on Yellow Paper*, 182.
9. Pope, *Reading London's Suburbs*, 107.
10. All citations from *The Bell Jar* are from Faber's 1966 edition.
11. Pope, *Reading London's Suburbs*, 108.
12. Smith, 'Syler's Green' in *Me Again*, 87–9.
13. Huk, 'Eccentric Concentrism', 253.

14. Smith, *Collected Poems*, 472.
15. Smith, *Collected Poems*, 47–8.
16. Smith, *Collected Poems*, 508.
17. Barbera, 'The Relevance of Stevie Smith's Drawings', 236.
18. Plath, *The Poet Speaks*, 167.
19. Ford, *Gender and the Poetics of Excess*, 10.
20. Barbera and McBrien, *Stevie*, 71.
21. Smith, *Collected Poems*, 347.
22. Stevie Smith to John Hayward, 2 January 1942: King's College, Cambridge. Quoted in Spalding, *Stevie Smith*, 161.
23. Ford, *Poetics of Excess*, 11–13.
24. Wagner-Martin, *Sylvia Plath*, 229.
25. Plath, 'Context', 46.
26. Barbera and McBrien, *Stevie*, 242–3.

CHAPTER 7

Plath's Whimsy

Will May

Tracy Brain's landmark study *The Other Sylvia Plath* begins with a call to arms: to rethink Plath we must return to the impressions of her first readers. The cover blurbs gathered for *The Colossus and Other Poems* (1960) provide an intriguing starting point, identifying a 'skill with language that is curiously masculine in its knotted, vigorous quality, combined with an alert, gay, sometimes whimsical sensibility that is wholly feminine'.[1] The troubling binary of male skill and female sensibility echoes the recurring 'double bind' Jane Dowson and Alice Entwistle have identified in their account of twentieth-century women's poetry: Plath inhabits the female 'wholly', but the male 'curiously'.[2] Yet the sharper surprise from one of her first critical readers is yoking Plath not to the feminine, but the whimsical. This chapter will suggest it is a mode central to Plath's poetry but expediently peripheral to its reception.

What made Plath write? In her journal, she attributes it to 'a tendency toward introversion begun when I was small, brought up as I was in the fairy-tale world of Mary Poppins and Winnie-the-Pooh' (*J* 34). Her account roots itself in a children's fantasy land largely without threat: these are stories of winsome philosophy, homespun Edwardian kitsch and fantastical exits and entrances. Balloons may pop, bees might sting, but the disappearing nanny always returns. Yet this entrancing cosmos of talking bears, bottomless carpet-bags and magic umbrellas is rarely glimpsed amidst the shelves of Plath criticism, perhaps for good reason. Whimsy is a term often used pejoratively. Geoff Dyer states the objection plainly: 'whimsy is for low stakes'.[3] The grudging ordinariness of Movement poetry had a particular disdain for it: Donald Davie glosses it as 'tiresome writing' that is 'allied to circumlocution'.[4]

Its association with a feminine sensibility is not accidental. Mary Wollstonecraft noted that educated women in the eighteenth century were assumed to be 'teeming with capricious fancies';[5] whimsy was the note of caution holding them in check. Since its first recorded use, the word has been used to measure or contain the intellectual role of women in society. Even Margaret Cavendish's utopian play, *The Female Academy* (1662), characterises female wit as whimsical and excessive. This vexed cultural history goes some way towards explaining why we downplay the comedy and verbal games of Plath's work. Tellingly, Plath's contemporary Stevie Smith asked an American publisher to remove the word 'whimsical' from the blurb of a selected edition in 1963: 'it is rather handing a gun to critics'.[6] It is safe to attach the adjective to Plath's drawings, but not her words. By 1996, Faber could confidently publish *The It-Doesn't-Matter-Suit and Other Stories*, but the relatively recent appearance of her children's stories suggests their existence might matter a great deal.

The 1960s blurb-writer was not alone in detailing the competing polarities of Plath's poems. Marjorie Perloff has acknowledged Plath's 'peculiar ability to fuse the domestic and the hallucinatory'.[7] Marsha Bryant, reading Plath's poems alongside the *Ladies' Home Journal*, constructs a 'topography of the domestic surreal',[8] their images of electric currents, levitating objects and indoor chaos juggling women's magazines alongside Henri Lefebvre and Giorgio de Chirico. Yet readers and scholars are reluctant to follow the breadcrumbs when they lead to the kitchen or playroom. Bryant wonders aloud why Plath's 'cultural conversation'[9] with the domestic, the miniature and the absurd has gone largely unremarked.

At times, the trail is deliberately hidden by the author. In a letter of 1957 to the playwright Michael Frayn, Plath apologises for two recent short stories, identifying their 'elaborate style and whimsy' as 'a kind of safeguard against the impact of the actually ghastly naked situation – which in both cases is a complete annihilation of the creative identity'. Her confession of weakness is, characteristically, accompanied by a determination to do better: 'perhaps I'll be able to write that straight out, bang crash, someday, without getting fancy and hedging'.[10] Her confession offers up whimsy and play as 'hedging', failing to tell the truth, a creative cop-out. For a burgeoning writer it works as a get-out clause, an obstacle to writing it 'straight out'.

Plath scholars have observed this ruthless 'hedging' by charting the leap from her prose to poetry. Jo Brans shows how the 'devices' of Plath's letters are 'mercilessly banished' from poems – including 'parenthetical asides' and 'cute closings'.[11] Some readers might mourn the loss. Sometimes the poetic voice itself does the mourning – 'What I want back is what I was' (*CP* 109), says the speaker of 'The Eye-mote', starkly. The 'elaborate' quality that appalled Plath in her short stories comes under a tighter rein in the poems: the genre, perhaps, offers fewer temptations to elaborate.

Recent critical responses to the first volume of letters suggest Plath's queasiness at the cute whimsy of her writing was well-founded. In those teenage lines Rachel Cooke finds the tone so 'bright' as to be 'monotonous'.[12]

Yet Plath's poetry and prose do not live in separate spheres, and the it-doesn't-matter suits of her children's stories have something to say to Esther Greenwood's clothes wrapped in a ball under the bed. Tellingly, the poem 'Mad Girl's Love Song', published in *Smith Review* in Spring 1953 and *Mademoiselle* in August 1953, finds a more obviously literary home in the May 1957 issue of *Granta* at Michael Frayn's request.[13] It is later included in Lois Ames's biographical note accompanying the US publication of *The Bell Jar* in 1971, suggesting whimsical prose and vigorous poetry might share common ground. The poem pivots on the refrain: 'I think I made you up inside my head' (*BJ*, x). Its self-mocking appearance alongside *The Bell Jar* conjures various readings: has Esther Greenwood constructed her own author for us? Either we have made up a Plath who finds no room for the whimsy her first readers found such a distinctive part of her aesthetic, or Plath's later works turn away from 'hedging' so completely that the earlier, discarded armour seemingly never belonged to them.

Allaying Whimsy

In January 1955, Plath spent three absorbing days in New York. Hughes would call the year that followed a writing 'watershed' (*CP* 16). On a trip to the Museum of Modern Art, she is compelled by the silent French film *The Passion of Joan of Arc* (1928), which was screened with piano accompaniment. At first, the contrast between the high drama of the image and the casual, playful soundtrack bothered her: on reflection, she realises 'it absorbed some of the tremendous tensions aroused, and made the emotion more supportable'. Reeling from its penitential punch, she walked laps of Central Park, where eventually she 'was treated to a ride in a horse cab, fed a lump of sugar to horse, and felt better'. The 'agonisingly' depicted martyrdom needs the relief of tinkling ivories to make it palatable to a general audience, and the comfort of childhood indulgence to resettle Plath, its more specific one. In an enthused letter to Gordon Lameyer, she remains haunted by the 'close-up shot of a baby sucking its mother's nipple, turning casually to the final agony of the saint, and then calmly resuming sucking': a mild diversion offsets the terror. Plath's only means of recovery can be 'wine and cognac and aperatifs, oysters, steaks, lamb chops, eclairs and pastries, and all those other delights our sinful flesh is heir to' (*LV1* 870). The transformed spectator offers petty sins unworthy of a saint's sacrifice all the better to forget it. To mangle the words of Plath's much-cherished Mary Poppins, the sugar helps the martyrdom go down.

Poems from this period often work in the same way, helping absorb emotional and technical powers that, untempered, might themselves prove too absorbing. They speculate on whether any reader would willingly enter a Plath poem unmediated by whimsy – 'Who'd walk in this bleak place?' (*CP* 22) – then deck the poems with verbal strategies to entice them: 'fabulous lutes and peacocks' (*CP* 21), a 'watermelon sun' (*CP* 26), 'arab-esques and trills' (*CP* 75), often served with generous helpings of 'cookies and Ovaltine' (*CP* 75). Fierceness is balanced by 'quibble' (*CP* 28), and the black-feathered birds are all 'bell-tongued' (*CP* 69). The 'persistent bric-à-brac' (*CP* 65) of these early poems joins things together, offering one answer to the final knotty question asked in 'Conversation Among the Ruins': 'What ceremony of words can patch the havoc?' (*CP* 21). Sometimes, ceremony alone cannot do the patching. Often, there is only a playful soundtrack to join one frame to the next.

This offers a chronological story about Plath with much traction. Her true authorial voice arrives only once the bric-à-brac is tidied away. Ted Hughes's introduction to the 1981 *Collected Poems* offers the supporting curation. To arrive at *Ariel* is to abandon the 'enclosed cosmic circus' (*CP* 16) of earlier poems. Finally, Plath leaves the old 'sugar-faceted' voice (*CP* 13) behind. The dizzying ensemble of a poem like 'Alicante Lullaby' seems to bear this out. The poem's world is discrete, habitual, and its stakes are low. We hear 'Rumbas and sambas no ear-flaps can muffle', but we will not be pressed to listen to anything that will make us pause or give us undue concern. If we can hear a hint of Edward Lear, it is without his cruelty. Wallace Stevens sounds out, but without the surreal. These edgy omissions can make the poem seem diverting verbal play, rich and sonorous as it is ('spumily', 'kumquat-colored trolleys'). The poem's closing apostrophe – 'O Cacophony' – calls for quiet from the thing it praises, reminding us that this a honeymoon poem, written during her week in Benidorm in 1956. Its particular capriccio is love-addled: it seems closer to Richard Strauss's final opera *Capriccio* (1942), a courtship conversation piece, than, say, the terror and unblinking satire of Goya's *Los Caprichos* (1799). Here, perhaps, Plath bids a fond farewell to the whimsy of what Hughes called her 'juvenilia', though his silencing is more deliberate than her speaker's.

Yet the poem's candied phonic confections (*prestissimos*/pillow/*pia-nissimo*) hide the soft surprise of the final line, where the speaker asks to be 'Lullayed by susurrous lyres and viols'. A poem that makes no inventive demands leaves it until its final verb to puzzle us, Plath's neologism 'lullayed' an apparently sleepy elision of 'to allay' and 'to lullaby'. The conflation is telling: the whimsy that puts us at ease also reveals the anxiety it does not quite keep at bay. The verb cannot quite allay the speaker or the reader. It is a wakeful whimsy that calls on Cacophony to give them a rest. Is Plath's whimsy then something to be allayed?

Toying with Success

The playful poetic mode is silenced more frequently and more completely in her later works, but the absence is often pragmatic. Hughes's introduction to *Ariel* nuances his story of girlish whimsy forsaken by comparing Plath's writing and revising practice to an artisan: 'if she couldn't get a table out of the material, she was happy to get a chair, or even a toy' (*CP* 13). The metaphor displaces the narrative of the poet awaiting breakthrough with that of the dextrous woodworker, and might give us pause. The offcuts that become her toys might be expedient in their creation, but no less well-made than her tables and chairs. While we have long ago learned how to dine out on Plath's work or settle down again amongst the familiar furniture of her story, we have less understanding of how to play with her *toys*.

One such toy might be 'Ella Mason and Her Eleven Cats', written in 1956, rejected by *The New Yorker* in the same year, and not included in *The Colossus and Other Poems* (1960). The poem spies out the 'red-faced' (*CP* 53) and 'blowsy' (*CP* 54) Ella Mason in her 'ramshackle' house with its attendant felines, a 'spinster' who is 'run to fat' (*CP* 53). The final stanza reluctantly rethinks her from childhood figure of fun to 'green-eyed and solitary'. Yet the switch from preposterous to merely lonely is little recompense: the poem enjoys its snickering and her 'mammoth and blowsy' (*CP* 54) frame more than the moment it must consider her views on marriage. The poem's reluctance to accommodate its own subject is matched by the critical response to the work itself. Plath returns from Cambridge to find 'a sweetly pencilled New Yorker rejection of Ella Mason, etc., begging me, too, to try again' (*LV1* 1256). The imploring saccharine of the rejection letter mimics the poem's own cruel sketch. The poem finds 'no good reason' (*CP* 53) for Ella Mason's cat-hoarding, and literary editors can find no good reason for the poem. Subsequent critics, who pass it by embarrassed, have tended to follow suit.

Yet the letter Plath writes to Hughes recounting its rejection is evidence for considering it at more length. It is a decisive and compelling missive, hovering between conscious restraint and ecstasy. The letter promises him something 'wonderful and incredible' (*LV* 1255) but waits for the second paragraph. News of the poem's fate must come first, followed by Plath's account of the doggerel littering recent issues of *The New Yorker*: 'colossal amount of fables by [James] Thurber about Grizzly Bears and Gadgets, Oysters and Philosophers [. . .] poems by John Malcolm Brinnin (one huge long funny type fake poem; probably picked a word from a published poem here, there, and pasted them together$()$, Adrienne Ceceile Rich, getting richer but duller; Ogden Nash, the lucre-monger' (*LVI* 1256). These disappointments are first scrutinised against the poems of Plath's they have rejected and Hughes's 'excellent adult fables', yet to receive any response at all from that 'glittering rag' (*LV* 1254), then pitched against the 'latest serious poems' (*LVI* 1256) published in *The New Yorker*, suggesting how keenly Plath trained herself to make the division between the two modes.

The selection of poems in *The New Yorker* replacing Plath's preferred contributors – herself and Ted – is not incidental. Ogden Nash's 'Ms. Found Under a Serviette in a Lovely Home' is a brittle riposte to Nancy Mitford's characterisation in *Noblesse Oblige* (1956) of Americans as pre-occupied by money: the poem's epigraph quotes its popular formulation that Americans relate life itself to the dollar. Nash's poem dusts it down to nonsense: 'we loosened our collars / And resumed our conversation about dollars'.[14] Yet for Plath, navigating the value of her own poetry, the 'lucre' Nash's own poem earns prompts a snarling dismissal. Anything the editor of *The New Yorker* is prepared to pay for can be worth no more, perhaps, than whimsy. Their rejection of 'Ella Mason and Her Eleven Cats' prompts a mutual rejection by Plath of its poetic mode.

This final parting is strengthened by Henry Rago accepting six of her poems for *Poetry* on the same day:

> (I can just hear Leftover Cravenson's pitying lisp: 'I don't think you'll sell much of such poetry . . . I wish I could help you, poor wayward girl') [. . .] it is the consecration of my new writing, which properly, began with you and 'Pursuit' and ramped on through spring and summer (*LVI* 1257).

The word 'wayward', repeated here in the quick delight of comeuppance, calls up the Dickinson tradition of female literary experiment untested by tradition, but also pits the question of form against commercial and literary value – she is 'poor' not because she is pitiable, but because her work has spiritual powers that outflank its commercial potential: it is 'consecration', not affirmation. The acceptance of six poems for *Poetry* speeds up Plath's rejection of her whimsical poems, and her conscious attempt to banish the whimsical from her work. In 1957, Plath complains, 'I write my good poems too fast – they are on objects, not <u>themes</u>, thus concrete, limited' (*J* 403). The objects, and the cabinet of curiosities they construct, must be left to one side.

Yet toys, as Plath's own work makes clear, have the power of distraction, which elevates the toymaker to an artist with prodigious gifts. They make no bid for immortality, but immerse us thoroughly in the meantime. 'Perseus, The Triumph of Wit Over Suffering' (1958) finds the whimsical mode not abandoned altogether, but embodied. The poem balances its vision of a world 'Fisted to a foetus head' with 'feathers to tickle', a 'fun-house mirror' and a 'cosmic / Laugh'. Too much grief would petrify us all, and 'turns gods, like kings, to rocks' (*CP* 83). Recalling her vision of Joan of Arc, a suffering martyr consoled by the incongruous, Plath's vision of playful martyrdom is, tellingly, directed to Perseus as an artwork, invoking *Perseus with the Head of Medusa* (1804–6). He avoids being turned to stone so the nineteenth- century Italian sculptor Antonio Canova can cast him in white marble. The poem imagines him gobbling up all former pietàs in the Met, confident that the person with the biggest belly can swallow up all our suffering and still have the last laugh.

The poem's language of suffering is dismissive, guffawing at the 'unstitching, plaguey wounds' (*CP* 83) of the consummate martyr. Yet the voice of the poem is accusatory towards its subject, too: Perseus uniquely can be the heroic gorgon-slayer, devouring 'what centuries alone digest' (*CP* 82). Meanwhile, Antigone, Phèdre and the Duchess of Malfi are outflanked, the Medusa reduced to a 'sullen doll' (*CP* 83). History and myth accord women the power to kill, but not to be playful. Whimsy is a not a question of genre, but identity: only those who naturally assume can afford the risk of being unassuming about it.

Subsequent poems widen their dynamic range by making the whimsy uncanny – the 'cuddly mother' and 'turnipy chambers' of 'Dark House' (*CP* 133), or tethering the 'cloud-stuff' in 'Polly's Tree' to 'bleeding hearts' (*CP* 129). The neutral and blank ramp up their power, too, from the 'stomach of indifference' (*CP* 136) in 'The Stones' to the 'Perfectly voiceless' and 'bland-mannered' chorus of the 'edible' in 'Mushrooms'. If Plath-as-artisan made fine tables and chairs, she had learned what to do with the leftover wood by 1959, where the fungus grows with low-stakes whimsy ('asking / Little or nothing') but has an unnerving number of shapes ('shelves' and 'Tables'). The nudging and shoving of Plath's poetry is mode-shifting as well as shape-shifting: even now, it may have airs, moods and merits we are yet to 'Acquire' (*CP* 139).

So what might be the purpose of training our ears and eyes to be more alert to Plath's whimsy rather than to tidy it away into so much juvenile bric-a-brac? Plath was alert to its limitations, its tendency to act as a get-out clause: it can be the easy response of a writer or their reader unable to face suffering head-on. As a critical term, it can also inflict particular damage on the standing of a female artist. Plath critics might have more reason to avoid 'Ella Mason and her Eleven Cats' than Eliot critics do to studiously ignore *Old Possum's Book of Practical Cats*. Yet whimsy's total excision from both the works we value and the responses we permit to those works is a loss. If it is a mode that can overload art with bathos or perpetually lower the stakes, it can release us from the everyday as often as it reminds us of it. While Plath assiduously sought to downplay the whimsical in her own writing, she found no better term to describe to her lover Richard Sassoon the moment when human love transforms us, momentarily, from erring mortals into heavenly creatures. Searching for a word to explain that seemingly arbitrary divine choreography, 'the kind of radiance that suddenly comes over you when I look at you dressing or shaving or reading and you are suddenly more than the daily self we must live with and love, that fleeting celestial self which shines out' – Plath acknowledged 'the whimsical timing of angels' (*J* 54). Now may be time to develop a keener taste for aspects of her work she sought to leave behind.

Notes

1. Plath, The Colossus (Heinemann, 1960), cover blurb.
2. Dowson and Entwistle, *A History of Twentieth-Century British Women's Poetry*, 1.
3. Dyer, *But Beautiful*, 43.
4. Davie, *Purity of Diction in English Verse*, 57.
5. Wollstonecraft, *A Vindication of the Rights of Women*, 103.
6. Stevie Smith to James Laughlin, 25 November 1963. Department of Special Collections and University Archives, McFarlin Library, University of Tulsa. Previously cited in May, *Stevie Smith and Authorship*, 14.
7. Perloff, 'Icon of the Fifties', 283.
8. Bryant, 'Ariel's Kitchen', 228.
9. Bryant, 'Ariel's Kitchen', 211.
10. Quoted in Frayn, 'An Uncollected Poem by Sylvia Plath'.

11. Brans, 'The Girl Who Wanted to be God', 213.
12. Cooke, '*The Letters of Sylvia Plath*'.
13. See Frayn's account in 'An Uncollected Poem by Sylvia Plath'.
14. Ogden Nash, 'Ms. Found Under a Serviette in a Lovely Home', *The New Yorker*, 22 September 1956, 24.

CHAPTER 8

Sylvia Plath and You

Tracy Brain

The American writer and actor Lena Dunham asked her millions of Twitter followers what *The Bell Jar* meant to them. 'My favorite response', Dunham tells us, 'was a simple "it made me feel less alone." Because that's how it made me feel, too.'[1] One of the fundamental ways that Plath makes readers 'feel less alone' is having her fictional characters and poetic persona speak to them directly. The second person direct address that she deploys repeatedly in her writing is a key mechanism for achieving this.

Plath famously said, 'I think that as far as language goes I'm an American, I'm afraid, my accent is American. My way of talk is an American way of talk. I'm an old-fashioned American.'[2] Integral to that 'way of talk' is Plath's fluent use of the second person narrative viewpoint, and the intimacy and immediacy it can convey. This is in keeping with Joshua Parker's observation that 'the "you"-designated protagonist in a text often seems to develop out of an author's desire to give an effect of spoken word'.[3]

What is crucial about second person narrative is that it establishes a relationship between the speaking 'I' and the 'you' who is being addressed. At the same time, it cements a bond between these 'I' and 'you' persona and the reader, who is made to occupy both of these positions at once. That is to say, the reader is simultaneously located as the person speaking and the person spoken to. Hence, there is a fluidity and mobility inherent in the second person. To put this negatively, 'second person narration is semantically unstable'.[4] To put it positively, 'Narrative "you" generates a complex series of perspectives whose multiple angles deserve to be explored.'[5] We will see that there can be an intensity, too, in second person narration. In Plath's case, this is often amplified through additional rhetorical and/or poetic devices, such as repetition, rhyme and even sudden shifts in point of view. The latter force the reader to experience different positions in relation to the story, subject matter and characters.

84

Plath came into contact with the many common forms – literary and otherwise – in which we find the second person address. These include instructions such as user guides[6] and recipes; questionnaires and interviews; advertising;[7] letters; poems; and prose fiction. All of these second person functions are utilised by Plath at various points in her work. My purpose in this chapter is to provide key examples of these uses and establish the context for the kinds of sources she drew upon.

Letters

We might begin by asking why the second person was second nature to Sylvia Plath. The answer partly lies in her lifelong practice of prolific letter writing. The epistolary form is fundamentally a second person form. Aurelia Plath tells us, 'It may seem extraordinary that someone who died when she was only thirty years old left behind 696 letters written to her family between the beginning of her college years in 1950 and her death early in February 1963' (*LH* 3). Yet the letters to Plath's family were only a fraction of her epistolary practice. Mrs Plath does not mention the letters and postcards Plath wrote throughout her childhood,[8] nor those she addressed to numerous other correspondents during her life.

Those who are lucky enough to study the original letters in the archives will be struck by their sheer quantity, by the blue airmail paper Plath favoured while living in Europe and by Plath's tendency to use every millimetre of paper. She sometimes surrounds the recipient's address on the envelope with her continued message. In the early months of 1960, Plath even types letters to her mother, brother and Sappho the cat on the reverse side of a kitchen wallpaper sample that she wants to share with them.[9] Liz Stanley reminds us that a letter's 'power for the recipient' is that 'it bears many traces of its writer, such as their handwriting, touch on the paper, and licking of stamps'.[10] Plath's presence is everywhere in her letters, as anyone who has ever handled the rose-covered bedroom wallpaper sample she touched with her own fingers will know.

But you do not need to handle Plath's actual letters to experience her presence. You've only to read the letters to identify with the 'you' she addresses; indeed, to step into the shoes of this you, as it were, and feel as if you are part of a continued and intimate conversation with Sylvia Plath. As Plath herself puts it, discussing her correspondence with Gordon Lamayer, 'the letters were really close to talking' (*LV1* 660). And as a reviewer of *The Letters of Sylvia Plath* recently said of Plath and her audience, 'she has never stopped speaking to us'.[11]

In her letters, says Nigel Nicolson, 'Virginia Woolf varied her approach from one person to another'.[12] Joanne Trautmann Banks believes we can play a 'parlour game' with Woolf's letters: 'Give the players a letter to one of Virginia's major correspondents. Cover up the name of the addressee and see if the image of the implied reader is so particular that the correspondent can be correctly guessed.'[13] In a good letter, Trautmann Banks's reasoning goes, the person to whom it is addressed should be implicit in every word. That 'you' should be fully formed and individuated, revealed by the circumstances of the letter and the nature of the way the writer talks to them. Elaine Showalter writes of Plath, 'Her letters to friends, relatives, teachers, editors and boyfriends are performances; she is always choosing which face to present, which voice to adopt.'[14] Erica Wagner makes a similar point. 'One of the fascinations of reading these letters', she writes, 'is seeing Plath present varied accounts of the same events to different correspondents: mother, brother, whichever young man (or young men) was the object of her attention at the time.'[15]

Trautmann Banks's parlour game could be played with Plath's letters, too. 'When and if you have a chance, could you send over my *Joy of Cooking*? It's the one book I really miss!'[16] Can you guess to whom Plath is writing here, given her ease at making the request, and also the fact that the addressee is in possession of her book?

Plath is, of course, writing to her mother, Aurelia Plath.

Recipes

Of the hundreds of letters I could have selected for the parlour game, I chose one with a reference to *Joy of Cooking* because it was a book that Plath actively studied. Moreover, it is a book that is grounded in the second person point of view. Plath writes in her *Journals*, 'Yesterday I read through the vegetable section of my blessed Rombauer . . . to cull all the sauteed [sic] dishes' (*J* 250–251). If we look at one of the sautéed dishes Plath was likely to have read, we encounter the typical rhetoric and instruction of the recipe book: 'Quickly deglaze the delicious brown residue in the sauté pan —unless you have been cooking with a strongly flavored fish—with stock or wine. Reduce this sauce and pour it over the sautéed food. If you heat sautéed food in sauce you steam it too much.'[17] This is the second person direct address with which Plath was so familiar, where 'you' is either explicitly named (in sentences one and three) or implicitly present (the command given in sentence two).

It is noteworthy how authoritarian, and even scolding, the recipe is. It seems less aspirational, less cheerleading and encouraging, than more recent cookery books.[18] Rombauer counts on the reader's willingness to obey the writer and trust in her expertise, and assumes at least a modicum of culinary ability in the addressee, who is expected to know how to 'deglaze' and 'Reduce'. While I rather enjoy loving what Plath loves, I find *Joy of Cooking* bossy and irritating, largely because I feel whenever I read it as if I am being rebuked for my domestic ineptitude. However much Plath adored *Joy of Cooking*, it is precisely this sense of being told off that she comes to exploit in *The Bell Jar* and in poems such as 'The Applicant'.

In her 1962 calendar, Plath interweaves her daily professional activities with the foods she was cooking and baking. On 19 August, for example, there is a seamlessness between her reference to the radio broadcast of 'Three Women' and her plan to cook roast lamb, cauliflower and apple cake.[19] It is natural that domestic and literary activities, the daily stuff of Plath's life, and their respective narrative strategies, should penetrate each other. The authoritative, instructional tone of a recipe operates in Plath's 18 November 1960 poem, 'A Life'. The poem begins with an implicitly second person command and the air of confident expertise and experiential knowledge that are the currency of recipe writing: 'Touch it: it won't shrink like an eyeball'. The second stanza begins with the direct second person address, and another directive, followed by a cool explanation of what will result if you take the prescribed action: 'Flick the glass with your fingernail: / It will ping like a Chinese chime in the slightest air stir' (*CP* 149, 150). You can imagine a comparable construction in a recipe. *Beat the egg with a whisk: It will thicken like cream in a freezer.* Similarly, in her 1962 short prose piece, 'A Comparison', she likens the 'smallish, unofficial garden-variety short poem' to a 'round glass Victorian paper weight' or 'clear globe', and goes on: 'You turn it upside down, then back. It snows. Everything is changed in a minute' (*JP* 56).

Advertising

Plath's internship at *Mademoiselle* in June 1953 has been well documented by biographers and critics. Elizabeth Winder provides a thorough description of the numerous products advertised in the August 1953 issue that Plath helped to edit.[20] These mostly fall into the categories of beauty products and fashion. I want to draw attention to the advertisement that appears on the same page as Plath's 1953 poem, 'Mad Girl's Love Song'.

The page reveals the insistent coexistence of advertising with literary writing, and the second person 'you' weaves its way through both.

The advertisement is for a coat, and the reader is told that it is a 'Perfect example of the Ardmoor talent for making you look terrific'.[21] Beside the second person advertisement, the second person refrain in Plath's villanelle is '(I think I made you up inside my head)'.[22] Of course, Plath could not have known that her poem would eventually appear beside the advertisement. But it is easy to see the two adjacent pieces and come away with the impression that the grammar of the entire page insisted on a consistent use of the second person. What we can safely say is that the second person was in the air, and it always has been. Angelina Mirabella reminds us that the 'Second person has various iterations, all of which hinge on two questions: who is "you" and who is addressing "you"?'[23] In 'Mad Girl's Love Song', the speaking I (or 'person addressing "you"') is a young woman, and you is her fantasy lover, who she dreams 'bewitched me into bed'.[24] In the advertisement, the 'you' is a young woman who would have much in common with the poem's speaker, her head full of a young man she wants to impress.

The world of 'you' penetrates everywhere in Plath's work, from her less well-known poems to her most famous. 'You're', written in January or February 1960, puts the second person in its very title, which must be spoken as part of the poem for it to make sense. By this I mean that the poem should not begin, 'Clownlike, happiest on your hands', but rather, 'You're Clownlike, happiest on your hands' (CP 141). If we return to Mirabella's question, the 'You' in 'You're' is an unborn child, and the speaking I is his or her pregnant mother.

And the 'you' gains in sophistication, knowingness and irony, as Plath and her work mature. An instance of the latter occurs in 'Lady Lazarus', where the second person is invoked to mimic advertising strategies that will grab the attention of the 'peanut-crunching crowd'. The product the speaker is trying to sell, here, is her very self. 'Gentlemen, ladies / These are my hands / My knees' (CP 245), she tells them, seeming to perform a magic trick. Plath recognises, and plays with, the fact that '"you" (as well as "I" itself) can be a dangerous pronoun which advertising and journalism may corrupt'.[25]

That October …

On 16 October 1962, Plath had this to say: 'I am a writer. I hate teaching. I am a genius of a writer, I have it in me. I am up at 5 writing the best poems of my life, they will make my name'.[26] If you accept the argument that a good letter will be so personal you can deduce a great deal about the identity of 'you' from the way it is written, have a guess at the person Plath addresses here.

To do this, you might pause to admire Plath's unashamed and confident declaration of her talent. Which raises another question. What kind of person would she make such a declaration to? You might also consider a number of likely characteristics for this person: somebody Plath knows intimately and trusts; somebody for whom she needn't put on a pretence of false modesty; somebody she knows will not regard her as conceited or arrogant; somebody who will want to agree with and celebrate such a stance. In this instance – and you probably did guess before you came to my prompts – the 'you' Plath is addressing is, again, her mother.

Tim Kendall reminds us that 'Many of Plath's poems written between "Daddy" and "Lady Lazarus" address a specific individual.'[27] Moreover, a dozen of the twenty-five October poems are written in the second person,[28] most of them in a sustained address to you, whilst a few occasionally deploy it. There isn't space to look closely at them all here, and I have examined Plath's use of the 'simultaneously first- and second-person narrative point of view' elsewhere,[29] but it is worth pausing to consider two. 'Daddy' may well be regarded as one of Plath's most famous – and notorious – poems. Of the many and various points made about it, what isn't often discussed is the fact that Plath puts the second person in the first word, and it is a word that insistently determines the obsessive, powerful 'oo' rhyme scheme that winds its way through the entire poem.

'You do not do, you do not do' (*CP* 222) the daughter-speaker tells her father. Jay Arnold Levine defines the verse epistle as 'that kind of poem, presented as a letter, which discusses serious matters of individual, social, or political conduct in an intimate or middle style'.[30] Plath's second person poems are not traditional epistles – the title is not 'To Daddy' – and the poems are not presented as explicit letters. In other words, Plath's second person poems are not generically epistolary, but they have epistolary qualities, and owe much to her apprenticeship as a letter writer. They certainly work through an 'intimate . . . style'. But unlike Levine's conception of the verse epistle, Plath's interventions in the form often speak of 'individual, social' and 'political conduct' all at once, rather than choosing any single one.

'The Applicant' is another noteworthy second person poem from October 1962. It engages in a 'performative satire'[31] in order to parody the interview form, or even a consumer questionnaire. The poem begins,

'First, are you our sort of a person?' (*CP* 221). Here, the speaking 'I/we' is a kind of agent or marriage broker. The 'you' they are addressing is the single client who is seeking a partner (or, more likely, who is forced to seek one). It is worth observing that any critical impulse to identify Plath herself as the speaking 'I' is thwarted by the poem's deployment of the second person.

Fiction and the Flexible 'You'

Plath's apprenticeship with the second person was also served through her reading of fiction. Jane Eyre's declaration, 'Reader, I married him',[32] is probably one of the most famous second person addresses to a reader in the English novel. It is a novel that Plath certainly knew. Her Eighth Grade 'Certificate for Reading' *Jane Eyre* was awarded on 7 June 1946[33] and she refers on multiple occasions in her diaries to reading it as well as to loving the film so much she watched it twice.[34] It is worth mentioning, also, that her copy of Charlotte Brontë's *Villette* is heavily underlined and annotated.[35]

Another key fictional context for Plath's development of the second person was J. D. Salinger's *The Catcher in the Rye*. She refers in a 1956 letter to 'my copy' (*LV1* 1187) of the novel. The following year, she writes: 'I could write a terrific novel. The tone is the problem. I'd like it to be serious, tragic, yet gay & rich & creative. I need a master, several masters. . . . I have that fresh, brazen, colloquial voice. Or J. D. Salinger. But that needs an "I" speaker, which is so limiting' (*J* 276–77). Plath finds a way to use Salinger, learning from Holden Caulfield's talky, confiding, colloquial voice, but without being limited. One of her strategies for achieving this in *The Bell Jar* is an intermittent, flexible second person that she had experimented with in her 1958 story, 'Johnny Panic and the Bible of Dreams'. That is to say, Plath allows Esther to slip into the second person at key moments for a variety of effects and ends, but does not sustain it through the novel.

The Catcher in the Rye famously begins: 'If you really want to hear about it, the first thing you'll probably want to know is where I was born, and what my lousy childhood was like, and how my parents were occupied and all before they had me, and all that David Copperfield kind of crap, but I don't feel like going into it, if you want to know the truth.'[36] *The Bell Jar's* opening deploys the second person at the end of the novel's first paragraph. Esther tells us, 'It had nothing to do with me, but I couldn't help wondering what it would be like, being burned alive all along your nerves. I thought it must be the worst thing in the world' (*BJ* 1).[37] *The Catcher in the Rye's* initial 'you' is a version of 'one' that positions the reader as a kind of interrogating enemy who will not prevail against the narrator, and is kept at a distance from him.

The Bell Jar's first 'you' works differently. It establishes the reader's close relationship with the speaking 'I', and their shared positioning. Both are implicated in the act of imagining. Both are also the subject of the act that is being imagined. By not saying 'my' (as in 'burned alive all along my nerves'), Plath also allows Esther – and the reader with whom she merges – to establish some degree of rhetorical detachment from the horror of what happened to the Rosenbergs, all the while highlighting any supposed safety in the position as illusory. What in many contexts would be exaggeration – 'the worst thing in the world' – is actually a fair assessment.

There are instances in *The Bell Jar* when Plath uses 'you' as a stand-in for 'one', though always achieving the direct talkiness that is so important to her. We see this, for instance, when 'Buddy stopped for a breath, the way you do in the middle of climbing something very steep' (*BJ* 88). More typically, though, simple cases of you being substituted for one, when examined, reveal that they are anything but simple.

Esther tells us in *The Bell Jar*, 'The trouble about jumping was that if you didn't pick the right number of storeys, you might still be alive when you hit bottom. I thought seven storeys must be a safe distance' (*BJ* 131). The key thing here is that the change in narrative address at this instant highlights the intense and personal nature of Esther's disclosure. It is when she imagines the impact of jumping but surviving, severely injured, that Esther deflects the impact from herself with the change of pronoun, abandoning 'I' for 'you', which Plath uses three times in that first sentence, before returning to 'I' in the next one.

Joshua Parker tells us, 'Many [authors] admit that second person is a disguised first person, a way of putting distance between themselves and an embarrassing or traumatic past experience'.[38] But I would qualify Parker's account. My own experience leads me to see this strategy as a way of demonstrating a *character's* psychological truth and emotional detachment from the terrible events he or she recounts, rather than the *author's* need to construct alterity between their writing and lived experiences. As Jarmila Mildorf reminds us, 'one cannot "know" the real-life author and his or her intentions'.[39]

The Bell Jar is not Plath's only work of fiction in which she deploys the intermittent second person. Whilst there are numerous instances of the sustained second person in the poems, we also find them in Plath's short fiction, as in her children's story, *The Bed Book* (where you is the reader) and her short story 'A Day in June'. There is not scope in this chapter to look further than this taster of key instances of her use of the second person, and the generic contexts out of which this use was formed. Early in *The Bell Jar*, Esther says of Doreen, 'Everything she said was like a secret voice speaking straight out of my own bones' (*BJ* 7). The same could be said of Plath's numerous speakers, who talk to and from us at once, as if out of our bones, through one of the twentieth century's most accomplished and powerful uses of the second person narrative viewpoint.

Notes

1. Dunham, 'Sylvia Plath: Reflections on her Legacy'.
2. Orr, *The Poet Speaks*, 168.
3. Parker, 'In Their Own Words', 169.
4. Marcus, 'A Contextual View of Narrative Fiction', 48.
5. Morrissette, 'Narrative "You" in Contemporary Literature', 2.
6. Plath refers to the 'travel books' (*LH* 414) or ('travelbooks' [LV2]) she has been reading (17 March 1961) and reviews Miroslav Sasek's children's picture book *This is Venice* (Plath, 'General Jodpur's Conversion', 698) on 10 November 1961. Here is a taste of the latter: 'Near one end of the bridge, you will find "the Erberia" market and the little church of San Giacomo' (Sasek, *This is Venice*, 41).
7. It seems odd that an essay with the title 'Who Talks Advertising? Literary Theory and Narrative "Point of View"' does not have a single reference to the second person. See Stern, 9–22.
8. Now available in *LVi* 2–157, which reprints all extant letters from the 1940s. The Lilly Library holds a box of Plath's family correspondence that dates back to when Plath was six years old. *LILLY*. PLATH MSS. II, Box 1, Correspondence, 1938–Apr. 1951.
9. See Brain, *The Other Sylvia Plath*, 60. This letter can be found in *LILLY*. PLATH MSS. II, Correspondence, 1960, Jan.–Apr., Box 6.
10. Stanley, 'The Death of the Letter?', 244.
11. Sehgal, 'Sylvia Plath's Letters'.
12. Nicolson, 'Introduction' to *The Letters of Virginia Woolf*, xxiii.
13. Trautmann Banks, 'Introduction' to *Congenial Spirits*, x.
14. Showalter, 'Sunny Sylvia'.
15. Wagner, 'The Many Selves of Sylvia Plath'.
16. *LVi* 1178. The reference is here given in an endnote to reduce the risk of spoiling the parlour game.
17. Rombauer, *Joy of Cooking*, 127.
18. See for instance Mitchell, 'The Rhetoric of Celebrity Cookbooks'.
19. Sylvia Plath, Personal Papers, Calendar 1962. *SMITH*.
20. Winder, *Pain, Parties, Work*, 210–13.

21. *Mademoiselle*, August 1953, 358.
22. *Mademoiselle*, August 1953, 358.
23. Mirabella, 'The Other Point of View', 64.
24. *Mademoiselle*, August 1953, 358.
25. Morrissette, 'Narrative "You" in Contemporary Literature', 3.
26. *LV2* 861. The reference is here given in a footnote, again to reduce the risk of spoiling the parlour game.
27. Kendall, *Sylvia Plath*, 161.
28. 'The Swarm', 'A Secret', 'The Applicant', 'Daddy', 'Medusa', 'Lesbos', 'Stopped Dead', 'Fever 103°', 'By Candlelight', 'The Tour', 'Nick and the Candlestick' and 'Lady Lazarus'.
29. Brain, 'Story, Body and Voice', 70.
30. Levine, 'The Status of the Verse Epistle before Pope', 661.
31. Brain, 'Medicine in Sylvia Plath's October Poems', 23.
32. Brontë, *Jane Eyre*, 370.
33. *LILLY*. PLATH MSS. II. Box 9 – Memorabilia; Folder 12 – School Awards and Promotions.
34. *LILLY*. PLATH MSS. II. Box – Diaries and calendars, 1944–57; Folder 1 (entries for Wednesday 5 April 1944, Saturday 8 April 1944, Sunday 16 April 1944, Friday 26 January 1945).
35. *LILLY*. iucat.iu.edu/catalog/144090. See 'Sylvia Plath's *Villette*' in Brain, *The Other Sylvia Plath*, 161–74.
36. Salinger, *The Catcher in the Rye*, 5.
37. All citations from *The Bell Jar* refer to the fiftieth anniversary edition published by Faber and Faber in 2013.
38. Parker, 'In Their Own Words', 170.
39. Mildorf, 'Studying Writings in the Second Person', 74.

CHAPTER 9

Plath and the Lyric

Lucy Tunstall

Like the unborn child in Plath's 'You're' ('A clean slate, with your own face on') (*CP* 141) the term 'lyric' is both immanent and impossible to pin down. It is sometimes defined as a brief poem, usually in the voice of a single speaker, expressing a personal emotion or thought, or capturing a moment in time. As a genre, however, it is amorphous and mobile with a tendency to subsume any number of poetic subgenres[1]; as a mode, it is frustratingly quasi-spiritual: '"Lyric" escapes from prose meaning almost as the soul, or the spirit, escape from the body in pneuma, the Greek word that meant both "spirit" and "breath".'[2] In *The Government of the Tongue*, Seamus Heaney's definition of what a lyric poem *is* relies on images of transcendence, lightness and elevation:

> The achievement of a poem, after all, is an experience of *release*. In that *liberated moment*, when the lyric discovers its *buoyant completion* and the timeless formal pleasure comes to fullness and exhaustion, *something occurs* which is equidistant from self-justification and self-obliteration.[3] [my emphases]

The mysterious potency that seems to inhere in lyric ('something occurs') was a lifelong fascination for Plath; her work can be read as a continuing dialogue with the workings, possibilities and hostilities of the lyric mode. In her short memoir (or lyric essay), 'Ocean 1212–W', Plath recalls her mother reading aloud from Matthew Arnold's 'The Forsaken Merman': 'I saw gooseflesh on my skin. I did not know what made it. I was not cold. Had a ghost passed over? No, it was the poetry. A spark flew off Arnold and shook me, like a chill' (*JP* 118).[4]

Plath pursued that chilling 'spark' of poetry at Smith College where she was steeped in the modernism of T. S. Eliot and W. B. Yeats, and trained in the New Criticism of John Crowe Ransom and Cleanth Brooks. She developed a close working relationship with the Eliot scholar Elizabeth Drew (*LVI* 436, 445, 679, 684, 695) and through Drew, met W. H. Auden, who told Plath he found her writing 'too glib' (*LV1* 682). Like those very early childhood influences – the poetry of Emily Dickinson (Aurelia Plath's 'bible'), for example (*LH* 5), as well as Arnold's watery ballad – the writers she encountered at Smith continued to shape Plath's mature work. 'Mystic', written in 1963 right at the end of her career, draws on Eliot's themes of martyrdom and his New England coastal landscapes. The peacocks 'blessing / Old ground' (*CP* 272) in 'Balloons' (one of Plath's final poems) evoke the peacock-stalked terraces of Yeats's 'Ancestral Houses'.[5] Plath's college set texts are heavily annotated, not just with class notes, but also her own idiosyncratic interventions. Cleanth Brooks's discussion of lyric structure in *The Well Wrought Urn* is decorated with 'lovely' and 'Bravo!'[6] Among her verse anthologies and collections it seems every instance and variant of 'glittering' is underlined: Jonathan Swift's 'Vice in all its glittering dress' in 'Stella's Birthday',[7] Christopher Marlowe's 'The flattering sky glitter'd in often flames' from *The First Book of Lucan*,[8] and W. B. Yeats's 'Their ancient, glittering eyes, are gay' from 'Lapis Lazuli' and 'The glittering eyes in a death's head' from 'Demon and Beast' as well as the 'abounding glittering jet' of 'Ancestral Houses'.[9] 'Glitter' is a word that continued to occupy Plath, reasserting itself much later, to appear again and again in the poems of 1963. In 'The Munich Mannequins' 'black phones' are 'Glittering / Glittering and digesting' (*CP* 263); 'Totem' has a 'glitter of cleavers' (*CP* 264); the 'Gigolo' 'Glitter[s] like Fontainebleau // Gratified' (*CP* 268); and in 'Mystic', some sort of interrogation involves torturous 'hooks' or unanswerable 'Questions' that are 'Glittering and drunk as flies' (*CP* 268).

What Plath seemed to want from these writers and critics was to learn something about that uncanny, glittering 'spark' that 'flew off Arnold and shook me, like a chill'. She was interested all her life in the mechanics of lyric poetry and many of the *Ariel* poems, particularly those incendiary poems of October 1962, dramatise their own bizarre, over-reaching compulsions and peculiar processes. 'Fever 103°' makes vividly apparent some unexamined assumptions about lyricism and transcendence. The poem begins with a question in the form of a catechism: 'Pure? What does it mean?' (*CP* 231). Rather than a prescribed answer given by rote, Plath's speaker embarks on a spectacular display of physical suffering, disease and immolation all serving to purge the woman/artefact/patient/burlesque performer/saint of her inessential identities as she ascends, theatrically, to paradise. The concluding conceit is an incandescent grand finale in which the parenthesised undressing is a last purification before the uprush of the speaker's acetylene-fuelled lift-off.

These themes of purification and ascension draw on an array of hagiographic, iconographic and literary sources. Both Yeats and Eliot deal with themes of martyrdom and purgation. Eliot's *Murder in the Cathedral* is much annotated in Plath's copy of *The Complete Poems and Plays*. The 'miracle' 'golden' bird of 'Byzantium' and the 'hammered gold' bird of 'Sailing to Byzantium'[10] inform the speaker's migrainous head of 'gold beaten skin' (*CP* 232) in 'Fever 103°'. In Plath's poem the exquisite golden *object* that exists outside time and nature is also a delicate patient *subject* with a hammering headache. Discussing Plath's 'debased art objects' Angela Leighton explains that 'the subject of these poems cannot withstand the assumption from the "antique" that a woman belongs on a vase, or perhaps in a poem'.[11] The *Ariel* lyrics are not ekphrastic in any straightforward manner, but they do create artifacts ('gold beaten skin') and sometimes give the impression of dramatising visual artworks. 'Purdah', with its stillness and its decorative odalisque, might be understood as a temporal text trying to escape from a spatial one, or a poem that cannot quite free itself from the orientalist and Fauvist paintings that shape it. 'Fever 103°' is a kind of animation of Renaissance depictions of the Assumption of the Virgin. These works, by Titian, Rubens, Botticini and many other artists, follow a strict schema in which gathered male figures witness a levitating Mary rising through the clouds attended by cherubs, towards God who waits to crown her Queen of Heaven.[12] In something of a Plathian twist, many versions show Mary casting away her girdle to be caught by (doubting) Thomas as proof of her ascension and her chastity.[13]

One of the lyrical interventions made by 'Fever 103°' is the mixing of incompatible registers, or the drawing-out of inherent peculiarities and contradictions: the kitsch of Catholic iconography, or the reimagining of the Girdle of Thomas as 'old whore petticoats'. Heaney's 'release', 'pleasure' and 'self-obliteration'[14] carry implicit sexual undertones. By contrast, 'Fever 103°' debauches the language of passionate piety. There is a long lyrical tradition which, in the work of John Donne, for example, casts God and penitent as lovers. This uneasy propriety cannot withstand the unwholesome suggestiveness of Plath's imagery, which is both lascivious – 'a lecher's kiss' (*CP* 231), and 'auto-erotic':[15] 'All by myself I am a huge camelia / Glowing and coming and going, flush on flush' (*CP* 231). Plath's speaker makes a spectacle of herself because that is the price of lyric elevation, it is what the 'achievement'[16] of the poem demands and exacts. 'There is a charge', says Lady Lazarus, 'For a word or a touch' (*CP* 246). Lyric has a tendency to (at best) commodify the thing it wants to celebrate; the incandescent Virgin, like Lady Lazarus, pays for her transcendence with more than a pound of her own flesh.

A 'charge' is also the firing of a weapon, and a 'spark'– the storing and releasing of electrical energy. If 'Fever 103°' is to reach its apotheosis (release its 'charge') there is nothing for it but for the speaker herself to be transfigured, and the possibility of this is signalled exactly halfway through the poem where, like a faulty electrical light, she begins to become illuminated: 'flickering, off, on, off, on'. The first half of the poem makes abortive attempts to rise, but the sulphuric smokes 'catch and anchor' (*CP* 231). When the transcendent image arrives – the stock-in-trade of romantic and post-romantic lyric poetry – the reader is warned to expect it: 'I think I am going up' (*CP 232*). What is delivered is exhilarating, but also preposterous, melodramatic and close to comic. This staginess works in tension with the elevated consciousness and rarefied emotion that are the more expected payouts of the lyric poem, the place where 'timeless formal pleasure comes to fullness and exhaustion, and something occurs'.[17]

Heaney's 'The Indefatigable Hoof-taps' is an important document in Plath studies not least for the high regard it demonstrates for her 'constellated lyrics'.[18] Few critics of Heaney's standing and profile have paid such careful attention to her work. His final assessment, however, has been both influential and obfuscating. With a note of exasperation in his emphasis, Heaney allows that 'There is nothing *poetically* flawed about Plath's work'. It falls down in the end, according to Heaney, where 'self-forgetfulness' gives way to 'the intense personal need of the poet':[19]

> what counts is the quality, intensity and breadth of the poet's concerns between the moments of writing, the *gravity* and *purity* of the mind's appetites and applications between moments of inspiration. This is what determines the *ultimate human value* of the act of poetry.[20] [my emphases]

'Purity', 'gravity' and 'ultimate human value' are suggestive, but vague, compared with the forensic interrogation of the meanings and implications of those qualities in 'Fever 103°'. For Heaney, it is self-evident that 'we' all know what we mean by 'purity' and agree that it is a required condition for the 'achievement' of lyric poetry.[21]

In 'Fever 103°', 'purity' is an altogether more troubling concept. How might purity be achieved in a poem, it asks, and what might it cost a woman speaker or a woman poet? If a mystic must fast, pray and denounce all worldly bonds to achieve enlightenment, or an alchemist burn away all dross in a fiery crucible, what terrible process might lyrical elevation demand? What exactly do we mean by purity? Is it artistic, spiritual or carnal, and how are these aspects connected? How is purity in art bound up with material costliness and the rarefied object? What combinations of register are permissible in a lyric poem, and how are notions of perfection in poetry connected with repression, oppression, neuroticism or tyranny? And not least: what exactly are we looking at when we find transcendence in a poem? If the poem is the answer to the question, 'What is purity?', it is difficult, having read the poem, to give a clear answer, but we are in a position better to understand the urgency and complexity of the question.

Lyric is often associated with sound and voice (whether in contemporary song, classical verse to be sung to the accompaniment of the lyre, or the confessional 'I' of untrammelled self-expression). However, lyric is also inextricably bound up with vision and looking, the object as well as the subject: Keats's urn; Yeats's Byzantine bird; Plath's golden, lantern-like head. Recent years have seen a growing interest in Plath's artwork and the visuality of her practice.[22] As a freshman at Smith (1950–51) she majored in fine art as well as English (*J* 619 n). Abstract expressionism had made New York, for the first time, the centre of the international avant-garde and all its galleries were within easy reach. She visited museums and churches in London, France and Italy, sometimes 'drawing line facsimiles' or 'taking color notes' (*J* 317). She went on to audit classes on modern art (*J* 691 n), produced art writing[23] and ekphrases[24] and often cited painting as a 'source of inspiration' for her poetry (*LH* 336, *SPD* viii). This expertise in fine art – theoretical, historical and experiential – is instrumental to the new articulation of lyric in *Ariel*. It is not just that Plath brings in to her poetry iconic images from the visual arts, or that she borrows compositional practices (although these things are extremely significant);[25] Plath's *Ariel* poems take flight at the moment that naturalistic perspective is dismantled and she finds a way to mobilise in her poetry a painter's understanding of 'the ineluctable presence of the surface'.[26]

The dismantling of depth perspective and its apparatus – vanishing point, fixed eyeline, convergence – has been said to define modern painting. It represents an evolution in representation that cuts through all twentieth-century movements, such as cubism, Fauvism and surrealism, which have been linked with Plath's poetics or with particular poems; and through the work of all Plath's favourite post-impressionist painters: 'Henri Rousseau, Gauguin, Paul Klee, and De Chirico' (*LH* 336):

> The limitations that constitute the medium of painting – flat surface, the shape of the support, the properties of the pigment – were treated by the

Old Masters as negative factors that could be acknowledged only implicitly or indirectly. Under Modernism the same limitations came to be regarded as positive factors, and were acknowledged openly.[27]

Giorgio de Chirico holds a special place in Plath's assembly of artists with his surrealistic parody of mathematical perspective and impossible vistas and architectures.

Like one of Giorgio de Chirico's faceless mannequins, the speaker of 'Tulips' (an early *Ariel* poem) tries to gauge her coordinates in three-dimensional space by observing sunlight and shadows, but sees that she is 'flat' and has 'no face' (*CP* 161). The painterly and expressionistic use of colour in the *Ariel* lyrics has sometimes been read as a brave rejection of New Critical formality for the unbounded self-expression represented by visual art: 'the alluring savagery of "no well-bred lilies" and unexplored poetic vistas'.[28] Plath's mature style represents, in fact, an expansion of modernist visuality (the verbal *icon*, the *well-wrought urn*) [my emphasis], as Fan Jinghua explains: 'New Criticism's fastidious analysis of formal aspects of poetry prepares her for the coming maturity in poetic pictorialism.'[29] Plath's poetry demonstrates that the logical conclusion of New Critical formalism (energised by twentieth-century evolutions in visual art) destabilises all kinds of lyrical conventions so that accepted notions of tone, point of view, objectivity, confessionalism, for example, begin to shift and buckle.

'Tulips' is a 'transitional'[30] and conflicted poem in which painterly flatness is at odds with naturalistic detail and narrative episode. The success of the poem in conveying realistically the experience of passing time in a hospital ward – the nurses' rounds, the slow movement of daylight across the ward, the detailed scene-setting – hinders its competing drive towards uncompromising visuality. Speaking to Peter Orr in 1962, Plath explained that domestic details sit uneasily in her poetry: 'I feel that in a novel, for example, you can get in toothbrushes and all the paraphernalia that one finds in daily life.'[31] There is not quite a toothbrush in 'Tulips', but there is a catalogue of domestic miscellany as well as the wish to jettison this 'baggage' (*CP* 160). The poem performs a kind of decluttering: 'I watched my teaset, my bureau of linen, my books / Sink out of sight' (*CP* 161).

Once the tulips' devouring redness has entered the poem, all established rules of representation are in jeopardy. There is no attempt at a naturalistic depiction of the flowers. Their vivid colour is presented without modulation or nuance; they embody the inherent properties of pure red pigment: advancing 'vigour' and 'determined . . . powerful intensity'.[32] The wild and

'dangerous' red of the tulips also relates to the Fauve ('wild beast') painters
of the early twentieth century whose work is characterised by vivid,
unmixed colours. Plath's expressionistic, painterly use of red brings into
the poem the post-impressionists' refusal to paint the illusion of foreground and background, or subject (woman speaker) and decorative but
subordinated setting (the tulips and the interior space of the hospital). The
air of the ward 'snags and eddies' around the flowers (*CP* 161), condensing
into a kind of liquid, like paint, or like the 'weight of the space on that
circular form'[33] in Paul Cezanne's seminal paintings of apples and oranges.
When painting is no longer structured around vanishing point, foreground
and background, modelling, or the mimetic reproduction of an observed
scene from a fixed viewpoint, painted forms can 'seem to float' (*CP* 161) or
to share a shifting picture space, or to recede from or advance towards the
viewer in unexpected ways:

> Their redness talks to my wound, it corresponds.
> They are subtle: they seem to float, though they weigh me down,
> Upsetting me with their sudden tongues and their color,
> A dozen red sinkers round my neck. (*CP* 161)

Remarkably, 'Tulips' seems to understand that a new kind of painterly
lyric, one that is both more more stylised and more exposed, will bring with
it 'upsetting . . . sudden tongues' and a drawing-out of woundedness
('Their redness talks to my wound'). It is as if the speaker has an apprehen-
sion of the confessional label, and the accusations of solipsism, the fetishis-
ing of psychic pain, verbal excess and self-indulgence, which have indeed
featured in the reception of Plath's later work.

If 'Tulips' represents the lyric in flux, 'The Moon and the Yew Tree',
written six months later, is unequivocally pictorial: 'This is the light of the
mind, cold and planetary. / The trees of the mind are black. The light is
blue' (*CP* 172). Here Plath achieves, for the first time, the emphatic
delivery, visual patterning and expressionistic use of colour so characteristic
of *Ariel*. Set by Hughes the exercise of describing the view from the
bedroom window of their Devon house, Plath takes down the scene
much as a visual artist takes 'color notes' and 'facsimiles' (*J* 317).
A painter studying the natural world in this practical way might look for
horizontal and vertical lines and forms, repeated motifs of colour or shape,
areas of coolness and warmth, light values, soft and hard edges and so on;
'The trees of the mind are black. The light is blue' sounds very like the sort
of observations that might be found in an artist's notebook. The composition is highly patterned: a vertical triangle points up to a circular moon;

forms mirror, repeat and transpose, and are geometric and gestural rather than sculptural or naturalistic; the palette is radically restricted.

In modern painting, the eye is guided by the articulating elements of the design. In 'The Moon and the Yew Tree', the strong, black, vertical of the yew 'lifts' (*CP* 173) the eye of the reader from the grasses underfoot to the moon above just as post-impressionist painters create an illusion of space that 'can be traveled through, literally or figuratively, only with the eye'.[34] The barefoot waif is lost and cannot locate her destination, or the route from 'here' to 'there', because there simply is no 'there'. Pockets of apparent depth appear, such as the line of headstones which, for a moment, appears to mark a boundary between house and churchyard. It seems unlikely to keep out the 'spiritous mists', however (*CP* 172); the most determined function of the structure is as a strong horizontal balancing the verticals of tree and (in a different key) the spire of the church.

In this flat, painterly, pictorial world, the subject is in a treacherous and attenuated position. The reader struggles to attach subjectivity or point of view to this unreliable 'floating' figure. The hospitalised speaker in 'Tulips' had (the remnants of) 'history', 'name', 'family' and domestic possessions, but *Ariel's* more characteristic female figures are both anonymous and heroic, flatter and more startling. The waif of 'The Moon and the Yew Tree', the decorative odalisque in 'Purdah', the fiery virgin of 'Fever 103°', the precipitous rider in 'Ariel' and the death-defying 'Lady Lazarus' all possess only the most iconic or unexpected of identifying possessions (which are never quite separate from the body of the woman) – a galloping horse, a gold tooth, red hair, bare feet, a lioness, a head of beaten metal. The undermining of naturalistic perspective raises questions of how and whether subjectivity might exist in a textual artifact (a lyric poem). The speaker of 'The Moon and the Yew Tree' stands, at first, with her bare feet in the weeping, 'Prickling' grasses (*CP* 172), suggesting a direct, visceral connection with personal emotion and with the natural world. This moment of immediate communication is shadowed, however, by the longed-for, but absent, maternal gaze of the Madonna Eleusa that rests with great 'tenderness' (*CP* 173) on the infant in her arms. Those sensuous grasses and imagined maternal embrace are counterpoised with the ascetic retreat of the hovering saints inside the church, the inscrutable silent yew and, compositionally superior to all, the extreme remove of the traumatised and traumatising moon. By the final stanza, the floating waif has lost touch entirely with the earth and finds everywhere about her only self-absorbed, absent or retreating figures.

A lack of appropriate distance, that is, of perspective, is exactly the problem with Plath's mature poetry for some readers. Joyce Carol Oates disapproves of what she reads as egotism in Plath's presentation of the natural world: 'Plath's landscapes become pictorial without any intermediate stage, so that we discover ourselves "in una selva oscura where associations multiply endlessly, but where each tree looks like every other one . . ."' That is the danger risked by those minimal artists of our time whose subject is solely the agony of the locked-in ego: their agonies, like Plath's landscapes, begin to look alike.'[35] What Oates is missing is the painterly aesthetic at work in this new kind of lyric, that is seeking precisely something 'pictorial without any intermediate stage' and is delighted to discover itself in a dark forest 'where associations multiply endlessly'. Painters know that naturalistic representation and mimesis require elaborate sleight of hand. In literary criticism there has sometimes been a tendency to look for an impossible ideal in lyric rendering of the natural world, a connection between words on a page and 'out there' unmediated by the ego of the poet. Any lyric poem, whatever its degree of authorial detachment, objectivity of tone or rhetorical restraint, is a representational pose. Even found text has been curated, and a poem driven by a conceptual motor has to be set running. To speak (however indirectly) in or through a lyric poem is a power position, though the power is sometimes unappreciated by those for whom lyric discourse has always been available and comfortable: 'The avant-garde's "delusion of whiteness" is the specious belief that renouncing subject and voice is anti-authoritarian, when in fact such wholesale pronouncements are clueless that the disenfranchised need such bourgeois niceties like voice to alter conditions forged in history.'[36]

What does it mean to look at and define another person, to say, in a lyric poem, 'you are' (or 'You're' as Plath puts it) (CP 141)? 'The Arrival of the Bee Box' is a poem much concerned with looking and power, and with art and representation: 'I put my eye to the grid' (CP 213). A grid is a textual and graphic device for the purpose of tabulation or classification. As the single most prevalent motif in twentieth-century painting, the grid is 'emblematic of the modernist ambition' becoming, from pre-war cubism onwards, 'ever more stringent and manifest'.[37] A grid is also an aperture and 'The Arrival of the Bee Box' contains an absence the speaker cannot properly perceive or name. She looks very closely into this negative space, positioning her body as close as physically possible, but still cannot see what it contains, discerning only an uncharacteristically vague *feeling* of African hands' [my emphasis] (CP 213).[38] Something about this missing piece is too terrible to face and provokes a desire for extreme decorative passivity. In a fantasy of classical (Ovidian) transfiguration she becomes part cherry tree, part stereotypical Antebellum Southern belle, with blonde ringlets and frothy petticoats – all very silent, and very white. In 'Wintering', as well as 'The Arrival of the Bee Box', the speaker is 'appall-[ed]' (*CP* 218, 213) (made pale, blanched) by unknowable blackness as if the encounter (or missed encounter) not only dismays and horrifies, but also sharpens and reinscribes a sense of her own whiteness.

Plath's work is alert to the potential for damage (by intrusion, calcification, domination or commodification) in all lyric poetry, including her own: 'Not this troublous / Wringing of hands' entreats the mournful narrator of 'Child' (*CP* 265). Nonetheless, the poems can sometimes be blind to their own specific instances of harm. There are moments of effacement or dehumanising, casual aggressions: the image of darkness in 'Ariel', 'Nigger-eye / Berries' (*CP* 239), relies on the terminology of racial slur; 'African hands' ('The Arrival of the Bee Box', *CP* 213) has the effect of dissecting black bodies into parts, and Africa becomes a shorthand for nameless horror. These are the self-unseeing parts of Plath's lyric that the most generous assessment of her perception of whiteness – its deathly passivity and mindless power – cannot absorb.[39] Heaney argues that the poet needs 'to get beyond ego' (whatever that might mean) 'in order to become the voice of more than autobiography'.[40] Plath's *Ariel* poems shows it is not ego that scuppers lyric, but the forgetting of ego, those moments where the ego is unaware of its own limited subjectivity and the partiality of its own perceptions.

Notes

1. 'In Western poetics, almost all poetry is now characterized as lyric' (Jackson, 'Lyric', 826).
2. Burt, 'What Is This Thing', 428.
3. Heaney, *The Government of the Tongue*, xxii.
4. All references from *Johnny Panic and the Bible of Dreams* refer to the 1979 Faber and Faber edition.
5. SMITH, Yeats, *Collected Poems*, 225.
6. SMITH, Brooks, *The Well Wrought Urn*, 201, 204.
7. SMITH, *The Oxford Book of Eighteenth Century Verse*, 70.
8. SMITH, *The Oxford Book of Sixteenth Century Verse*, 459.
9. SMITH, Yeats, *Collected Poems*, 339, 209, 225.
10. SMITH, Yeats, *Collected Poems*, 281, 218.
11. Leighton, *On Form*, 49.

12. See, for example 'The Assumption of the Virgin', reproduced in Phillips, *Titian*, 55.
13. See, for example, Rylands, 'Palma Vecchio's "Assumption of the Virgin"', 244–50.
14. Heaney, *The Government of the Tongue*, xxii.
15. Kendall, *Sylvia Plath*, 164.
16. Heaney, *The Government of the Tongue*, xxii.
17. Heaney, *The Government of the Tongue*, xxii.
18. Heaney, 'The Indefatigable Hoof-taps', 151. All citations from this essay are from *The Government of the Tongue*.
19. Heaney, 'The Indefatigable Hoof-taps', 168.
20. Heaney, 'The Indefatigable Hoof-taps', 170.
21. Heaney, *The Government of the Tongue*, xxii.
22. Connors and Bayley, *Eye Rhymes*; Bayley and Brain, *Representing Sylvia Plath*.
23. Connors, 'Living Color', 96.
24. See, for example, 'The Ghost's Leavetaking' (*CP* 90) and 'Battle-Scene' (after Paul Klee) (*CP* 84), and 'Yadwigha, on a Red Couch, Among Lilies' (after Henri Rousseau) (*CP* 85).
25. See, for example, Jinghua, 'Sylvia Plath's Visual Poetics'; and de Nervaux-Gavoty, 'Coming to Terms with Colour'.
26. Greenberg, 'Modernist Painting', 86.
27. Greenberg, 'Modernist Painting', 86–7.
28. de Nervaux-Gavoty, 'Coming to Terms with Colour', 119.
29. Jinghua, 'Sylvia Plath's Visual Poetics', 211–12.
30. Kendall, *Sylvia Plath*, 199.
31. Orr, *The Poet Speaks*, 171.
32. Kandinsky, *Concerning the Spiritual in Art*, 40.
33. Picasso quoted in Gilot, *Life with Picasso*, 219.
34. Greenberg, 'Modernist Painting', 86.
35. Oates, 'The Death Throes of Romanticism', 518.
36. Park Hong, 'Whiteness and the Avant Garde'.
37. Krauss, 'Grids', 5.
38. 'It is difficult for the white eye to see itself seeing white' (Miller, 'Sylvia Plath and White Ignorance', 138).
39. For a discussion of Plath's depictions of whiteness see Curry, 'White: It Is a Complexion of the Mind'.
40. Heaney, 'The Indefatigable Hoof-taps', 148.

CHAPTER 10

Plath and the Pastoral

Iain Twiddy

At first sight, pastoral might seem an unproductive context for the work of Sylvia Plath, especially given her succinct guiding comments for a radio reading of 'Sheep in Fog': 'It is December. It is foggy. In the fog there are sheep' (*CP* 295). The poem that follows, however, makes clear how infused with pastoral principles much of Plath's work is. Riding her horse slowly, the speaker describes hills withdrawing, stars or people behind lit windows that she disappoints, and fields that 'melt' her heart as they threaten to allow passage to 'a heaven / Starless and fatherless, a dark water' (*CP* 262). In its quixotically clipped lines, the poem is focused less on the external world than on the ways in which that world is inimically filtered through the speaker's foggy perception. If pastoral is a sanitised representation, in which harmonious human ideals are imposed upon nature, then the perspective here is equally extreme, in the use of landscape to foreground a psyche unguarded against invasion or internal collapse, and unguided against loss.

Although 'Sheep in Fog' takes place in the countryside, pastoral is not constitutionally rural. It is a loose but encompassing term for the process whereby things, people, times and places (whether internal or external) become intensely, contrastively valorised. In this, as William Empson identified, pastoral offers a means of 'putting the complex into the simple'.[1] This description suggests fluidity more than dichotomy: the complex can inhere within the simple, and the simple can negotiate – by concentration, reduction or diffraction – something more complex. But what appears simple or simplifying – such as the childhood conception of a divine pastor – can turn out to be more complex in the revelations of lived experience. Pastoral is a mediation, rather than a permanently lived state, a perspective that enables a traversing of terrain, a simple guiding idea that may make sense of complexity beyond.

'Sheep in Fog' reveals several pastoral strands that appear in Plath's poetry, including metaphysical or internal pastoral, the influence of pastoral figures and pastoral's intimacy with loss, mourning and elegy. Plath did engage with classical pastoral in early poems, such as pastoral elegy motifs in 'Tale of a Tub' and 'Winter Landscape, with Rooks', and in her eclogue, 'Bucolics', but the effect was as hollow as the voice of 'Conversation Among the Ruins', with its constricted diction and synthetic images, where a figure tracks through the portico of the speaker's grand house, unsettling the cornucopia of fruit, lutes and peacocks, 'rending the net / Of all decorum which holds the whirlwind back' (*CP* 21). The interest in Plath's engagement with pastoral lies not in strained classical and neoclassical exercises, but in her poetry's devastating liberation from personal constructions of pastoral.

The first of these versions concerns childhood. In the late memoir 'Ocean 1212-W', writing in England, Plath describes her *locus amoenus*, a literal, littoral space:

> My childhood landscape was not land but the end of the land— the cold, salt, running hills of the Atlantic. I sometimes think my vision of the sea is the clearest thing I own. I pick it up, exile that I am, like the purple 'lucky stones' I used to collect with a white ring all the way round, or the shell of a blue mussel with its rainbowy angel's fingernail interior; and in one wash of memory the colors deepen and gleam, the early world draws breath (*JP* 117).

This location was changed by an event tersely recorded at the essay's end: 'My father died, we moved inland. Whereon those nine first years of my life sealed themselves off like a ship in a bottle—beautiful, inaccessible, obsolete, a fine, white flying myth' (*JP* 124). Following the loss of a pastoral figure, the pleasurable formative environment becomes hypercathected,[2] its vivid encryption assisted by a lack of reality-testing, given the geographical removal, and given that Plath did not attend her father's funeral, nor visit his grave until age twenty-six. Plath's poetry shows how this metaphysical space shells well into adult life, before a forcible breaking open.

Being indelibly cut off, the formative environment is one of plenitude, but also potential, since the suddenness of the loss and the brevity of the prelapsarian time indicate that it could have or should have continued. In 'Ocean 1212-W', recalling how her mother stopped her attempt to crawl straight into an oncoming wave, Plath writes how she 'often wonder[s] what would have happened', had she 'managed to pierce that looking-glass' (*JP* 117). In their failures to return, to smash through that glassy green wave, the 1958 poems 'Full Fathom Five' and 'Lorelei' articulate the grievous desire for the force that held that location together. The former, written in the descent form of *terza rima*, ends with the muted cry 'Father, this thick air is murderous. / I would breathe water' (*CP* 93), while the slant-rhyme *terza rima* of the latter, with its roots in Plath's Germanic heritage, goes deeper, ending with an appeal to the sirens:

> Deep in your flux of silver
> Those great goddesses of peace.
> Stone, stone, ferry me down there. (*CP* 95)

Flanked by two dissonant rhymes, the suspended 'peace' attempts to sink stonily, searching for its binding rhyme.

These companion poems show how pastoral is not always protective in its effects.[3] The place of 'breath' may be a refuge, but it also embeds two breathless anxieties: one, melancholia that the pastoral was so idyllic that nothing can ever compensate for its loss; and two, paranoia that should happiness actually be found elsewhere, since paradise was lost once, it may be lost again. Thus, the compensatory state may be more closely guarded, in actions so forceful that they catalyse its degeneration.

Pastoral thinking perpetuates joy, but it also conserves the hurt of loss, to the self-damaging depth 'Lady Lazarus' will describe, remembering how she 'rocked shut // As a seashell', and people 'had to call and call / And pick the worms off me like sticky pearls' (*CP* 245). This surfacing is beyond the capability of speakers of poems that would have made up, as Plath wrote in October 1959, a 'soggy book' (*J* 518). 'Full Fathom Five' and 'Lorelei' suggest Plath's creative block after landing back in Massachusetts in June 1957, attempting to graft back on to her original landscape, and gain financial security in an academic career, teaching miserably at Smith for a year. In renewing therapy sessions with Dr Ruth Beuscher in 1958, Plath took the first steps towards a radical shake-up of this pastoral, deferent mindscape. In approaching the father's grave for the first time, 'Electra on Azalea Path' is groundbreakingly candid in its opening admission of abject hurt: 'The day you died I went into the dirt' (*CP* 116). The poem comes to map the dimensions the pastoral has assumed by assessing the physical conditions of the grave, where the dead are crammed in 'foot to foot, head to head' and 'no flower / Breaks the soil' (*CP* 117). There is no idyllic regeneration here, no comforting thought of immortality, only the perennial nature of guilt when attempting to distance the dead: 'O pardon the one who knocks for pardon at / Your gate, father – your hound-bitch, daughter, friend.'

If the speaker of 'The Beekeeper's Daughter', with her 'heart' (*CP* 118) under her father's foot, is similarly unable to squirm free, at least 'The

Colossus' recognises the attempted recovery and reconstruction of the fragments of a figure 'pithy and historical as the Roman Forum' (*CP* 129) to be futile. The classical description conveys how psychological weight gathers with time, rather than dissipates through distance, even though the ending announces separation: 'No longer do I listen for the scrape of a keel / On the blank stones of the landing' (*CP* 130). Whether this refers to Electra waiting for Orestes, or Penelope for Odysseus, it is clear that freedom from the dead involves diminishing the status of the colossus and its domain, in poems of dissent rather than descent.

Plath not only opens the borders of the pastoral space, but also vanda-lises it in poems like 'Daddy' and 'Medusa', developing the process she began in 'Green Rock, Winthrop Bay'. The result is that revisiting a location leads the speaker to a blunt assessment of a 'tawdry harbor', 'the rock's dwarfed lump' and the 'drabbled scrum' of a place now 'churlish' (*CP* 105), rather than childishly delighting. These poems can be considered pastoral elegies, of which three types are informative. Firstly, idyllic pastoral elegy, which imagines the dead in an ideal place, whether earthly or divine, can be a deferent form of denial that perpetuates the dead. Secondly, realistic or natural pastoral elegy is holistic, in combining the sublime and the mundane. Since nature is vastly indifferent to human concerns, and humans are intrinsically part of nature, there is no need to place the dead in a separate paradise. Just as nature recycles, the psyche can inherit, regenerate and perhaps derive consolation in this ongoing process. Thirdly, anti-pastoral elegy subverts artificial, idyllic ideas about death and nature, thus exposing – devastatingly – the fact that humans are too feeble to snatch comfort from the teeth and claws of nature. This perspective may be as unnatural as that of idyllic pastoral elegy, in the implication that humans are unique in requiring (unobtainable) consolation. In Plath's poetry, since a particular realm has been so deeply valorised, the anti-pastoral process is necessary, in the form of vandalism, to reach the more moderate assessments of relationships, grief and selfhood intrinsic to natural pastoral elegy.[4] Although the motion is inverse, the goal of the process is that of Milton's assuaging in 'Lycidas', where an artificially beneficent vision of nature is used to 'interpose a little ease'[5] between the intensity of grief and the return to a more mundanely grievous world.

This need for intervention is made explicit in Plath's externalisations of how the guarded, pastoral perspective has left the self paradoxically open, unremittingly paranoid that invasion can reoccur. We see this in the 1961 poems 'Tulips', where the flowers open threateningly 'like the mouth of some great African cat' (*CP* 162), 'Wuthering Heights', where 'The horizons ring me like faggots' (*CP* 167), 'Blackberrying', where, while bushes grotesquely, profusely press on every year against death, a wind 'slap[s] its phantom laundry in my face' (*CP* 169), and 'Finisterre', where the mists 'stuff my mouth with cotton', and 'When they free me, I am beaded with tears' (*CP* 169). In 'The Rabbit Catcher', the following year, the 'constriction' of present experience by bonds 'too deep to uproot' (*CP* 194) is figured in the snare,[6] in a 'place of force', with 'The wind gagging my mouth with my own blown hair, / Tearing off my voice' (*CP* 193).[7] Propelled by formal relaxation – not in terms of stanzas, but in line length and fixed requirements of metre and end rhyme – the anti-pastoralising *Ariel* poems tear up this restrictive terrain.

'Daddy' and 'Medusa' exemplify the process. In the former, the pastoral state has been outgrown like a black shoe, and the pastoral figure symbolically killed by being defaced as frightful, marmoreally pompous, and aberrantly proportioned. Pristine originary environments are matter-of-factly polluted – 'The snows of the Tyrol, the clear beer of Vienna / Are not very pure or true' (*CP* 223), and, recalling the speech-ripping wind and choking snares in 'The Rabbit Catcher', pastoral rejection is figured in speech. Attempting to learn German, the daughter's tongue:

> stuck in a barb wire snare.
> Ich, ich, ich, ich,
> I could hardly speak.

The icky proximity of 'stuck', 'ich' and 'speak', on a tongue sticky with this 'gobbledygoo' articulates how the pastoral has become loathsome in its own deliciousness, taking grotesque figures like the huge grey toe, which indicates the father's diabetes and resultant gangrene. This flavour is concentrated in the mixture of facetiously twee nursery-rhymey language – 'I do, I do' (*CP* 224) – and high camp – 'A man in black with a Meinkampf look' – that Plath ramps up into the fairy-tale revenge, where 'There's a stake in your fat black heart', and the villagers continually stamp on the father's grave.[8] This is intentional, petulant, look-at-your-naughty-daughter excess: the father is both vampire and Nazi, his heart fat as well as black; not only does she hate him but all the villagers do, too. The speaker assumes the autocratic behaviour of which she accuses the father, but if his representation is unrealistic or unfair, it is to suggest the daughter's unreasonable suffering. The humiliation bears the self-aware absurdity of the adult speaker still being stamped by grief for a man possibly not a tyrant in his living, but in the crime of his dying, given the child's understanding that parents somehow have power over life and death.

'Medusa', completed four days later, cuts the speaker's connection – conceived as an umbilical transatlantic cable – to a mother who is disconcertingly 'always there, / Tremulous breath at the end of my line' (*CP* 225). The speaker rejects this 'Blubbery Mary', the 'Bottle in which I live', declaring 'There is nothing between us' (*CP* 226). The bottled pastoral presented at the end of 'Ocean 1212-W' is here smashed, although the ending is as equivocal as the triumphant (self-)destruction of 'Daddy'; here there is both no connection, and an intimate nothingness mutually harming the two.

In rejecting in extreme terms these two extremely pastoral forces, fantasy – or at least exaggeration – theoretically cancels out earlier unrealistic conceptions. But because those connective tissues constituted part of the self, the practical danger is that the liberated self, as the endings of both poems suggest, progresses rawly into a wilderness. Initially, in October and November 1962, Plath's poetry moved into greater self-possession, not least in its command of traditional pastoral elements. Although Ted Hughes writes in *Birthday Letters* that 'When you wanted bees I never dreamed / It meant your Daddy had come up out of the well' (*TH:CP* 1140), the bee sequence performs a species of exorcism. The bee connection goes beyond family, back to Virgil's link between poetry and beekeeping, and to classical figures of the pastoral and Orphic poet.

The size of this poetic inheritance is measured in the speaker's hesitation in 'The Arrival of the Bee Box', where she asks, given that she seems to have 'ordered a box of maniacs', 'How can I let them out?' (*CP* 213). Following incomprehension of the 'furious Latin' – the surging force of words that will come in poems after the 'temporary' 'box' of this one – comes anxiety over responsibility in 'Stings'. Yet, having rejected a repetitive, suppliant role like other rural women, the speaker declares that she has 'a self to recover, a queen', asking forcefully 'Is she dead, is she sleeping?'[9] and where she could have been, 'With her lion-red body, her wings of glass' (*CP* 215). The leonine figure here is the old queen usually ejected when the new one hatches (*J* 658). The poem may be rooted in the domestic circumstances of a husband's adultery, but it gains ascendant force from classical gravitas: the old queen rises into perhaps vengeance, perhaps transcendence, but certainly into 'terrible' self-possession above 'the engine that killed her— / The mausoleum, the wax house' of domestic containment. In moving free of this restricted living, the speaker is more Medea (able to conjure herself into flight), than abject Eurydice (in need of rescue from the underworld or from the attempted rape by Aristaeus that led to her death).[10]

In her ordering of the bee poems for *Ariel* – 'The Bee Meeting', 'The Arrival of the Bee Box', 'Stings', 'The Swarm', 'Wintering' – Plath moves from the inheritance of power, through learning how to conjure, to a masterful, prophetic declaration of prosperity the following spring. Despite professing to her mother on 12 October 1962 to 'hate this cow life' (*LH* 466), distant from the cerebral pleasures of London, Plath's move to self-possession is exemplified in 'Letter in November', where the speaker is 'stupidly happy' and possibly 'enormous' (*CP* 253) in her command of a fruitful poetic domain, no longer the suppliant of the hieratic figure in 'The Beekeeper's Daughter', or the onlooker of Orpheus in 'Ode for Ted' and 'Faun'. This progression is inextricable from the pastoral role of motherhood. Ted Hughes attested that with the birth of Plath's first child, suddenly she could 'compose at top speed, and with her full weight. Her second child brought things a giant step forward' (Hughes, *Winter Pollen* 162). Self-possession comes through self-replication, through the elevation of status from daughter to nurturing pastoral figure, which brings the sublime feeling of 'Morning Song', where the floral-nightgowned, breastfeeding speaker listens to her baby daughter trying her 'handful of notes; / The clear vowels rise like balloons' (*CP* 157). This release from the grievous history of her own childhood continues in Plath's poems about her son. 'Nick and the Candlestick' is a response to the perceived harm in 'For a Fatherless Son'. In the latter, a pastoral longing will develop organically, once the child becomes conscious of an 'absence' that grows next to him like 'A death tree, color gone, an Australian gum tree' (*CP* 205).[11]

In 'Nick and the Candlestick', a taming, neatly rhyming, children's-story-titled poem, Plath brings her son the world, telling him about – amongst other things – mines, stalactites, bats, plums, icicles, newts and piranhas, establishing their home as a refuge: 'love, / I have hung our cave with roses' (*CP* 241). This is pastoral in the tradition of 'The Passionate Shepherd to His Love', with the 'beds of roses / and a thousand fragrant posies'[12] the speaker will provide, but the relationship is mutually sustaining; the son is:

> the one
> Solid the spaces lean on, envious.
> You are the baby in the barn.   (*CP* 242)

For all the tenderness of the half-rhymes of 'love', 'have' and 'cave' above, the mother needs the stabilising presence of her son as much as he needs her, a feeling that is carried by the restive sonic plantings of 'one', 'lean', 'on', 'envious' and the concluding 'barn'.

Although pastoral can tame or simplify, that does not mean that pastoral roles are not complex or difficult to maintain. Through the lens of maternal pastoral we see the surrender of the *Ariel* momentum, in three late poems in particular. A possible origin for the imagery of 'Child' may be Regent's Park, given its proximity to Fitzroy Road: the poem's scenario could be a mother walking her son in his pram through the park, looking into his eyes and articulating the 'zoo of the new' (*CP* 265) she wants him to see, with all the captivating words for it. The son's 'clear eye'[13] is imagined as a pool, which should reflect classical columns, figures of a world as solid and long-lasting as his mother's presence. In this reflection, there is a beautiful symmetry in the infant's exploratory hand actions and the speaker's grievous hand-wringing, while the distressing, disorientating lack of a star at the poem's end recalls the 'starless' heaven of 'Sheep in Fog'. In 'Balloons', imagining 'A funny pink world he might eat on the other side', the son bites a balloon and is left with 'A red / Shred in his little fist' (*CP* 272). The shred reprises the children figured as red roses in 'Kindness', and intimates their depiction as curled-up white snakes in 'Edge', where the maternal pastoral most lucidly fails. A female figure has killed her children. The guiding force is the dead, monochrome moon, whose gravity is shown in the final half-rhyming couplet – 'She is used to this sort of thing. / Her blacks crackle and drag' (*CP* 273): by weight of accumulation, the anchoring, stressed 'a' sounds tug like a grapnel at the 'in' of 'thing', voiding the possibility of difference and forcing collapse. This power drains the colourful fertility of 'Morning Song', and lays waste the domestic refuge of 'Nick and the Candlestick'.

Against the gravity of mental illness, the poetically fertile, independent maternal role was ultimately not resilient enough to shepherd Plath through the savage winter of 1962–3 in London. In a pastoral reading of Plath's poetry, the extreme anti-pastoralising actions might well have effected self-possessed freedom from the restricting pastoral perspective, yet left the self so exhausted by the work of upheaval that inimical circumstances – sub-zero temperatures, flu, the wrong kind of antidepressant, frozen water pipes – prevented the spirit of *Ariel* from reaching the blossom in spring.

The demolition poetics of poems like 'Edge' may seem incongruous with the generically reassuring repetitions of pastoral, or the regenerative drive of pastoral elegy. But Plath's poetry is extraordinarily productive in its groundbreaking articulation of the experience of childhood, mother-hood and grief, and in its exploration of the subconscious and the bound-aries of the self. Its pastoralism is vast in terms of poetic influence, not least upon the work of Ted Hughes. In *Birthday Letters* and *Howls & Whispers*, Hughes repeats Plath's anti-pastoralising, border-opening, vandalising Orphic actions by making public a private story of grief, an action that left him – although sadly too late – thrillingly 'unguarded'.[14] Finally, given Plath's death at thirty, in the spring of her writing life, it may be tantalising, as Anne Sexton wrote to Hughes in 1967, to think of 'the more' (Sexton 307) she could have written. Yet even in the relatively small crop of poems Plath left, it is abundantly clear that amidst the fierce flames of personal distress, the golden lotus had been lastingly planted.

Notes

1. Empson, *Some Versions*, 25.
2. Freud posits 'hypercathexis' in 'Mourning and Melancholia' (1917): in grief, 'Each single one of the memories and expectations in which the libido is bound to the [lost] object is brought up and hyper-cathected, and detachment of the libido is accomplished in respect of it', by means of reality-testing (Freud, *Complete Psychological Works*, vol. XIV, 245).
3. In *The Bell Jar*, Esther is torn between following streetwise Doreen and 'Pollyanna Cowgirl' Betsy, as part of the larger conflict that culminates in the basement overdose: 'The silence drew off, baring the pebbles and shells and all the tatty wreckage of my life. Then, at the rim of vision, it gathered itself, and in one sweeping tide, rushed me to sleep' (*BJ* 169). (All citations from *The Bell Jar* refer to the 1971 Harper & Row edition.)
4. This anti-pastoralising exemplifies the 'fury' Freud identifies as sometimes necessary for relinquishing a hyper-cathected lost object (Freud, *Complete Psychological Works*, vol. XIV, 257).
5. Milton, *Complete English Poems*, 54.
6. The relationship-as-snare conception may relate to Plath's image of 'two over-lapping circles', in her journal entry for 15 May 1952 (*J* 105).
7. This is a leitmotif for Plath: as well as in 'Finisterre', variations appear in 'Parliament Hill Fields' ('The wind stops my breath like a bandage' (*CP* 152)), and 'Elm' ('A wind of such violence / Will tolerate no bystanding: I must shriek' (*CP* 192)).
8. 'Daddy' echoes Esther's description of her 'German-speaking father' who 'came from some manic-depressive hamlet in the black heart of Prussia' (*BJ* 33).
9. D. H. Lawrence's liberating influence on Plath is clear when recalling his description of rabbits in 'The Wild Common': 'Are they asleep?—are they living?' (Lawrence, *Selected Poems*, 27).

10. In Book IV of the *Georgics*, in fidelity to Eurydice's memory, Aristaeus' bees desert him (*Georgics* IV, ll. 453–9, ll. 531–4 (Virgil 124, 126–7)). In 'Stings', the bees attack the disloyal male.
11. This figure stems from one in 'Little Fugue', where 'Death opened, like a black tree, blackly' (*CP* 188).
12. Marlowe, *Complete Poems*, 207.
13. This may be both metaphorical and literal, given Plath's worry about one of Nicholas's eyes, which Hughes mentions in a letter to Aurelia Plath on 13 May 1963 (*LTH* 219–20).
14. Hughes twice uses this word, writing to Keith Sagar (*THL* 720 and Sagar, *The Letters of Ted Hughes and Keith Sagar*, 267).

PART III

Cultural Contexts

CHAPTER 11

Plath and Food

Gerard Woodward

Sylvia Plath's *Collected Poems* contains 224 poems that Plath wrote between 1956 and 1963. Around a third of these contain a direct reference to food. If we also include poems that contain more oblique references, for instance to its absence ('Frog Autumn', *CP 99*) or to the processes of digestion and swallowing ('Perseus', *CP 82*) or to things that may or may not be food ('Pheasant', *CP 191*) then the figure is a little higher. While a third may sound like a large proportion, in fact only a small number of poems have food as their main subject. Food in Plath's poetry is a constant but offstage presence, most often serving to provide a powerful but fleeting simile, something to strengthen the main theme of the poem or to trigger some other line of thought or incident. It might make as brief an appearance as the 'bitten clean' corn cobs and the juice of the 'hot nectarine' that appear towards the end of 'Ouija' (*CP 77*), or in the sudden evocation of burnt turkey and the 'vinegary fume' that give a grim reality to the corpses on view in 'Two Views of a Cadaver Room' (*CP 114*) – an early example of Plath's lack of squeamishness when it comes to thinking about food. Plath can associate food with abundance and new life, as in the string of similes for a newborn that make up 'You're' (*CP 141*) – 'O high-riser, my little loaf', or with betrayal and suspicion (the 'earwig biscuits – creepy-creepy' of 'The Tour' [*CP 237*]), or with death, as in 'Mary's Song', where in a welter of religious imagery the oven in which the Sunday lamb 'cracks in its fat' (*CP 257*) evokes the ovens of the death camps.

Food is an equally insistent presence in Plath's prose fiction. The emotional energy of the early story 'The Day Mr Prescott Died' is contained, at the end, in the obese body of Mrs Mayfair, who'd 'gorged herself on three desserts' at Mr Prescott's wake, now carried 'huffing and puffing' down the steps on her way to the funeral parlour (*JP 47*).[1] In *The Bell Jar* Esther Greenwood declares that she loves food 'more than just about anything else' (*BJ 25*).[2] An early scene in that novel sums up the complex emotions Plath associated with food, when a feast of avocadoes and caviar at the *Ladies' Day* banquet results in a violent bout of food poisoning and abject vomiting, after which Esther is soon eating again – '"Bring it in [the soup]," I said, "I'm starving"' (*BJ* 51). From feeding to vomiting to feeding again within a few pages – another example of Plath's non-squeamishness, but also of the ravenousness, the greediness, of her attitude to food, which was a theme in her journal keeping and letter writing, and a key strand in her thinking about herself.

What is startling, then, is not so much the number of works, both of poetry and prose, that mention food, but the range of ways in which food imagery is used to convey, tighten or suggest differing meanings and emotional states. In some ways this should not be surprising, as Plath is a poet of things and of the senses, and food is an essential part of her sensory world. At the same time, food occupies a special place for Plath among sensory phenomena. Food for Plath was, in some ways, an extension of the bodily self and a conveyor of identity, something through which she negotiated her place in the world. But what world was it in which Plath found her food? What did this great poet of eating and cooking actually eat?

Outside of her poetry and fiction the main sources of information about Plath and her relationship with food are her letters and journals. In addition, there are assorted documents that provide further information – for instance, a calendar for the year 1962 resides in the Lilly Library archive, detailing her menus and shopping lists for that turbulent year. And then there are the accounts of people who knew her, contained in the many biographies and memoirs that have appeared since her death.

From these sources it is possible to assemble a picture of Sylvia Plath's life as a journey through several overlapping yet distinct culinary phases, from the corn chowders of her Massachusetts childhood to the cold, grey stews of the Newnham College refectory, to the love food of steaks and veal cutlets that typified her relationship with Ted Hughes, to the pies and pottages of his Yorkshire homeland through to the endless apple pies and honey of her Devon life, to her final months of frugal diets, of forgetting to eat, right down to the last meal she ever made, that scant breakfast of bread and milk she left for her children on the morning of her suicide.

Food, in the days before she was known as a poet, was often one of the criteria through which people formed opinions about Plath. One of the earliest mentions of Plath in the letters of Ted Hughes is a reassurance to his parents not to worry that she will be a 'drag' on him. 'She is a very fine cook', he announces, only mentioning a few lines later that she is also 'very, very bright' (*LTH* 45). Some months later, married and living in Cambridge where Hughes is working in a secondary school, he writes to Plath's mother in a tone that is perhaps also trying to be reassuring, 'Our home is fine. And each day, when I get home Sylvia has a speciality ready out of her cook-book' (*LTH* 90). In contrast, Dido Merwin's eviscerating memoir of Plath, 'Vessel of Wrath', included in Anne Stevenson's biography *Bitter Fame*, takes rather a different view of Plath and food, seeing her as a consumer rather than a provider, a guest who was a taker of more than her fair share, helping herself in the morning to food that had been put aside for lunch. Merwin is one of the first to be troubled by Plath's appetites, and to misunderstand her greediness, her ravenousness.

The cook-book mentioned in the letter above was *Joy of Cooking*, Irma S. Rombauer's vast compendium of recipes, an American bible of household cookery first published in 1936 and in continuous print since then.[3] This is the book that Plath begged her mother to send her, shortly after she met Hughes, and which acted for her like a beacon lighting the darkness of British cookery, providing an arsenal of dishes with which to feed her new husband. This book, in which can be found the recipes for many of the meals that Plath mentions in her letters and journals – from tomato soup cake to lemon meringue pie – was an immensely popular volume and embodied the wholesomeness of pre-war home cooking. Both American and British cuisines were in a poor state after the Second World War, though rationing had ended in the United States as early as 1946; it lingered on in Britain until 1954, just a year before Plath first crossed the Atlantic. American cookery was also suffering from the onslaught of new mass-food-production techniques and the rise of convenience food. The early 1950s was the age of the TV dinner, of artificial food colouring and Jello-O with everything. Books like Poppy Cannon's *The Can Opener Cookbook*, published in 1951, replaced *Joy of Cooking* on the bestseller lists.

As far as we can tell, Plath was mostly protected from this wave of pre-packaged food, though she was aware of its dominance in the wider world. As she writes to a pen friend in 1948, 'While a good deal of the cooking here is tasteless, I am very fortunate to have an Austrian grandmother who cooks good European dishes for us' (*LV1* 137). Indeed, when Plath is being nostalgic about the food of her childhood, it is often to her grandparents' cooking that she refers. In 1956, writing to her ailing grammy and grampy, she reassures them how much their cooking meant to her: 'grammy's marvellous cooking, and sour cream sauces, and fish chowder, and those feathery, light pastry crescents filled with hot apricot jam – our wonderful lobster dinner under the pines . . .' (*LH* 209).

Plath's unusually intense interest in food is apparent from a young age. Plath's mother recalls that her daughter learnt the alphabet by reading the labels on food packets (*LH* 16). Sylvia's earliest letters home, written from summer camp in the 1940s, contain matter-of-fact lists of what she's eaten, often proudly itemising their excesses. 'How're these menus: <u>Lunch</u> – two bowls of vegetable soup, loads of peanut butter, four pieces of coffee cake, chocolate cake and marsh mellow sauce, three cups of milk. <u>Supper</u> – Haddock, nineteen carrots, lettuce and tomatoes, cucumber, punch, two potatoes, four slices of water melon! Boy!' (*LV1* 24).[4] Otherwise food is most often mentioned in a context of luxury or celebration. In her letters home she describes reading her short story 'Sunday at the Mintons' when it appeared in *Mademoiselle*, alone on the beach with a bag of peaches and cherries, feeling 'the happiest I ever have in my life' (*LH* 91). News of this story's success came to her when she was in a rather tense relationship with food – in her summer waitressing job she had been relegated to serving in the side rooms and was denied the more prestigious role of serving in the main dining hall. 'The more I see the main hall girls expertly getting special dishes, fixing shaved ice and fruit etc, the more I get an inferiority complex . . .' (*LH* 88).

Plath valued the traditional and the homely in cooking. Although she could be impressed, even awe-inspired, by luxurious *haute cuisine* such as was provided by the *Mademoiselle* buffet she fictionalised in *The Bell Jar* or by the breakfast delivered in great copper tureens at the mansion of a wealthy acquaintance that is one of her most vivid early descriptions of food in the *Letters Home* (*LH* 75), it was the simpler home cooking – the pies, steaks, chowders and stews – that she seems most to have appreciated. This is evidence not only of a dislike of pretension – Esther's physical rejection of the *Ladies' Day* Buffet in *The Bell Jar* can be seen to mirror Plath's distaste for what she saw as the corrupt and shallow world of high fashion – home cooking represented basic nourishment, the fuelling of the body, the maintenance of health and therefore life. Her fondness for blood-saturated protein in the form of steaks and beef stews, a fondness that found its full expression in her relationship with Ted Hughes, represents perhaps the most potent form of this particular meaning of food for Plath.

This wariness of the fussy and the pretentious in cooking might help throw light on the tensions between Plath and Dido Merwin that gave rise to the latter's extraordinary memoir. Merwin's account of their difficult relationship is full of disdainful remarks about Plath's attitude to food, complaining of her greediness when a guest at her French farmhouse, helping herself to things from the fridge, 'downing the Fons *foie gras* as though it were "Aunt Dot's meat loaf".[5] Earlier in London, it was Merwin who supported Plath by sending round home-cooked dishes after she had given birth to her first child. Plath, always complimentary in her letters to her mother about Merwin's cooking, records these provisions – 'trout in aspic with eyes turned to pearls and lemon slices arrayed about them, blanquette de veau' (*LH* 376). Even at these times Merwin can't help cooking to impress, and seems to have provided just the sort of showy food that was coming into vogue in Britain at the time with the emergence of TV cooks like Fanny Cradock.

It is interesting to contrast Merwin's trout in aspic with a different type of fish dish, which Plath describes in her journals, in which she seems to be trying out a possible scene for her Cambridge novel:

> The girl picked up the cracked metal tin of salt and snowed it into the bag. Then, taking the cut-glass bottle of vinegar, she showered the fish, lifted the edge of it, and doused the potatoes. . . .
> . . . She burnt her fingers, pulling off part of the fried skin, with the fish sticking succulent to her fingers. She licked them as they strolled slowly down Russell Street.
> 'I'd rather eat fish and chips on a rainy night than anything,' she said . . .
> (*J* 278).

Plath wasn't always so enthusiastic about British food, and indeed the quality of food available was a source of frustration for her throughout the whole of her time in England. While she tried to be positive, especially in the letters to her mother, and while she does find delights in certain aspects of British food culture – for instance she loves the traditional cream tea – for the most part Cambridge offers a dour and enervating eating experience.

Plath was quite unprepared for the drabness of English cooking. She sails for England in late September 1955, but by the beginning of October, in a letter typically effusive about Cambridge, she is already thinking about home food: 'I would welcome any cookies ... to remind me of home' (*LH* 184). In her letters, always anxious to reassure her mother, she talks positively about the mist and the rain, and even the cold: 'Our rooms are cool enough to keep butter and milk in!' (*LH* 187). By November she writes about her routine: 'I eat my soggy, sludgy mass of daily starch foods.' In the same paragraph she describes redeeming this experience by filling her room with fruit: 'I now have my big earthenware plate heaped with a pyramid of fruit: apples, oranges, pineapples, bananas, grapes ...' (*LH* 196). In a 1956 letter, she writes, 'Cambridge restaurants are probably the worst in the world' (*LH* 256). Her feelings about British food are probably best summed up in a letter to her mother in which she parodies the kinds of recipes found in British women's magazines: 'Lard and stale bread pie garnished with pig's feet' or 'left over pot roast in aspic' (*LH* 438).[6]

Although she found a food soulmate in Ted Hughes there is, in the torrent of fervent letters she wrote to her mother about him, a suggestion that she was not wholly appreciative of the food world he came from. During Sylvia's first visit to Yorkshire in September 1956, she writes that she continues to cook for herself and Hughes while his mother, in her 'tiny kitchen . . . makes us starchy little potages and meat pies. (I'll be so happy to have an American kitchen . . .)' Later in the same letter she mentions how she was unable to make a stew out of a rabbit Hughes had shot because it was a doe with young 'and I didn't have the heart to make a stew out of it' (*LH* 269). Although enthusiastically carnivorous, Plath cannot see the living animal as food in the way that Hughes can – a complex divergence that is explored in, among others, their respective poems entitled 'The Rabbit Catcher'.

In another letter from the same Yorkshire visit Plath expresses frustration with not having a kitchen of her own: 'How weary I am of living off Other People's kitchens and houses . . .' (*LH* 272). She frequently looks forward to taking Hughes to the United States and introducing him to real American food, and her family's home cooking, 'corn and fish chowders, apple pie, apricot jam half-moons, etc . . .' (*LH* 272). The underlying suggestion here is that the sharing of Hughes's mother's tiny kitchen might have been a cause of tension, and also that she was discomfited by the food culture of Hughes's home environment – of shot, pregnant rabbits and 'starchy little pottages'. If there was something unsatisfactory about Hughes in those early days of their relationship, Plath seems to have seen it first in terms of food.

Otherwise, the relationship with Hughes sparked the most exuberant and intense food phase of her life. Frequently her letters mention how she and Hughes ate and read at the same time. She 'cooks steaks, trout on my gas ring and we eat well. We drink sherry in the garden and we read poems' (*LH* 235). In another letter written later in the same month, perhaps the most effusive of the early Hughes letters to her mother, full of biblical references and written in a tone almost of divine ecstasy, she describes Hughes as 'the first man who really has a love of food'. She then goes on to describe a meal of trout and shrimps after which 'Ted just lay groaning by the hearth . . . with utter delight, like a huge Goliath' (*LH* 244). This letter seems to bring those three fundamental values of Plath's – food, health and love – together into a single experience.

With Plath's intense nostalgia for the food she grew up with and her eagerness to share it with Hughes, it is surprising to note that some of her most negative food commentaries occurred while she and Hughes were in the States in 1958–9. 'Brains for supper last night. Ugh, I gag to think of it. I made them with a pungent wine sauce and they were ghastly. Even Ted couldn't eat all of them. Soft, flabby obscene meat: food for mental invalids. Gah.' In the same entry she notes how a drop of blood from a raw chicken in the icebox fell onto 'my pristine white cheesecake. Dreamed of catching a very tiny white rabbit last night: a menstruating dream?' (*J* 486). Earlier in her journals, she writes of a faculty dinner at which she 'spooned up watery red soup ... Then the uncuttable tough florid-pink tongue, the watery orange turnip ... slippery-dressinged lettuce' (*J* 315). During another Boston social event she refers to 'thick slabs of roast beef, watery string beans, roast potatoes and some ghastly ice cream' (*J* 353).

Plath and Hughes's residence at the artists' colony at Yaddo was a high point in their food journey across the United States – 'We have elegant dinners here: sweetbreads, sausages, bacon, mushrooms; ham and mealy orange sweet potatoes; chicken and garden beans' (*J* 502). She enthuses about the Yaddo food in her letters to her mother – 'Greetings! As usual our main news is that we are well fed' (*LH* 355). In the journals, however, when food is mentioned, as in the above reference to the 'elegant dinners', it is in a curiously detached way, as part of an entry otherwise filled with anguish and self-doubt. The food is listed, rather than described. The entry doesn't relish food, but merely acknowledges its presence, among the many other delights of the Yaddo manor.

The move to Devon in 1961 brought a new food phase to Plath's life, and one that promised to immerse her ever deeper into English cooking and food traditions. The letters from here give, at times, a sense of her being overwhelmed, or even overburdened, by the produce that the land attached to Court Green yielded. She writes to her mother asking for suggestions as to what to do with all the rhubarb, and she eats apple pies for breakfast (something she had done as a teenager in the United States) to use up the huge stock of fruit they had harvested. Indeed, her food life in Devon is dominated by the apple. Court Green had a large orchard, and her first letter to her mother from her new home mentions making apple sauce from a harvest of windfalls (*LH* 428). Apple pies seem to crop up everywhere in her life at this time, even during Christmas lunch (*LH* 441). In a curious way this prevalence of apple pies suggests an Americanisation (apple pie being an emblematic staple of traditional American home cooking) of the Devon cuisine.

Given that she always strives to be positive in her letters to her mother, it is almost shocking to hear Plath express negative thoughts about cooking, but by 1962, with her marriage beginning to fail, she writes that she is tired of her own cooking and has no energy to try the exotic recipes in the *Ladies' Home Journal* (*LH* 455). By June she is expressing her fatigue with the constant string of guests, mostly Ted's family. She doesn't say as much, but the suggestion is that it is the constant cooking that is a burden, and also the sense that there is another clash of cooking cultures, of American versus Yorkshire cooking (*LH* 455). At this time some of her most positive mentions of food are away from Court Green – in Ireland, for instance, in September 1962 (after the first separation from Ted) where she talks enthusiastically of eating oysters and brown bread (*LH* 461).

If the *Letters Home* were our only source of information, we would have to conclude that Plath's interest in food drops dramatically following the collapse of her marriage. After the summer of 1962, when Plath was living as a single mother at Court Green, she mentions food rarely, and then usually in the context of the struggle to eat, and of her increasing thinness. In a letter of September she mentions how she eats at the same time as she feeds Frieda, as a way of reminding herself to eat at all (*LH* 464). By October she writes to both Aurelia and Warren of her emaciation, 'the flesh has dropped from my bones' (*LH* 465), her 'bones sticking out all over' (*LH* 468). It may have been an exaggeration. The calendar for 1962 that is preserved in the Lilly Library archive shows that she continues to write memos to herself to bake banana bread, lemon meringue pie, to order joints of beef, legs of lamb, eggs and potatoes all through October and November. In the accounts of her final weeks, when she was generously and warmly supported by her friends Gerry and Jillian Becker, she is observed to have eaten heartily. The day before she died she had Sunday lunch with them 'with Sylvia's usual exclamations over its excellence'. She returned home 'after tea and cake',[7] and killed herself that night.

Plath's enthusiasm for food never faltered, or if it did, it was only momentary. This enthusiasm is sometimes read as a form of self-centredness, of greedy self-interest and relentless self-indulgence, as it is by Dido Merwin, who suggests also that it seems to point to an absence of some social norm. When Esther Greenwood eats her soup enthusiastically so soon after vomiting up the *Ladies' Day* Banquet, or when Plath herself can write to her mother about eating a tuna salad 'with gusto' shortly after vomiting up a meatloaf at the start of her labour with Frieda (*LH* 374) we can wonder about her grip on social norms. Elizabeth Winder would see it as an act of social courage and an admirable lack of gender conformity: 'Having a hearty appetite was considered unfeminine, maybe even more so than it is today. Today, you have actresses and models who say: "I eat hamburgers and fries every day and I just happen to look like this." In the '50s, even if you looked great, having a big appetite was considered a male quality.'[8] Or we could say that this simply shows how deeply ingrained was Plath's appetite for living, and for experience. In her reading of 'Esther's bulimic consumer impulses',[9] Renée Dowbnia would see this as an 'example of the binge/purge cycle of consumer capitalism, which is most keenly revealed in her ambivalence towards consumption throughout' *The Bell Jar*.[10] If, in her final year, it seemed that outwardly Plath might sometimes want to give, in her letters to her family, an impression of helplessness, what the 1962 calendar shows is that she maintained a strong desire to keep to her routines, to hold things together, to survive and go on living and eating.

Notes

1. All references to *Johnny Panic and the Bible of Dreams* are from the edition published by Faber and Faber in 1979.
2. All references to *The Bell Jar* are from the edition published by Faber and Faber in 1966.
3. *The Joy of Cooking* had been published privately by its author in 1931. The year 1936 saw it first commercial publication by the Bobbs-Merrill Company. The 1931 and 1936 editions had the word *The* in the title, but later publications were generally called simply *Joy of Cooking*.
4. The practice of keeping her mother informed, through letters, of her eating habits continued throughout Plath's life.
5. Stevenson, *Bitter Fame* (Penguin 1989 edition), 340.
6. This letter is written more than a year after the one that mentions Dido Merwin's trout in aspic.
7. Stevenson, *Bitter Fame*, 295.
8. Winder, 'On Sylvia Plath's Food and Body Issues'.
9. Dowbnia, 'Consuming Appetites', 572.
10. Dowbnia, 'Consuming Appetites', 569.

CHAPTER 12

Plath and Fashion

Rebecca C. Tuite

From the full skirts and nipped waists of Dior's 'New Look', to the Shetland sweaters and Bermuda shorts of US college girls, and even the tanned bodies and flirty bikinis of mid-century pin-up stars, Sylvia Plath's fashion life places her at the nexus of many iconic moments in fashion history.[1] Interested in fashion from an early age, Plath even considered becoming a designer (*LH* 30).[2] Her expansive collection of childhood handmade paper dolls and costumes demonstrates an early affinity for clothing construction and a firm grasp on everything from current trends to showgirl glamour, historic costume to Hollywood style.[3] Plath exhibited an instinctual understanding that fashion did not exist in a vacuum, but rather functioned across boundaries of history, culture, art and design, and her own relationship with fashion demonstrates its influence across the full breadth of her creative endeavours.

Fashion looms large in Plath's journals, where she candidly shared everything from her shoe-shopping struggles ('I bought mine too tight as usual & got frightful heel blisters . . .') to 'buyer's remorse' ('And I feel dry and a bit sick whenever I say "I'll take it" . . .') (*J* 419; 183). However, she also had a profound relationship with fashion that went far beyond the superficial. From the fashion sensibilities detailed in her journals and correspondence, to fashion's influence on her poetry, prose, artwork and even her own forays into the professional realm of fashion as an editor and a journalist, Plath occupies a fascinating place within and without the fashion industry at the mid-century.

Fashion, Identity and Womanhood: Sylvia Plath's 'Split-Screen' Fashion Life

During her first year at Smith, Plath created the collage 'Woman Behind Screen', featuring an image of a brunette model emerging from behind a frosted screen.[4] She is wearing a fashionable, white, lace-trimmed, off-the-shoulder peasant blouse (not unlike the one that Esther Greenwood of *The Bell Jar* wears on her return from Manhattan) (*BJ* 112).[5] Half of her painted face, coiffured dark hair, bare shoulder, lace puff-sleeve and one manicured hand is visible, while half of her is in silhouette, open palm pressed upon the partition; a spectral shadow. The photograph shares striking similarities with other contemporary fashion visuals in which the image of a woman is 'split', many of which Plath would probably have been familiar with. For example, the March 1948 cover of *Seventeen* similarly featured a model stepping out halfway from behind a frosted screen, *Mademoiselle*'s March 1947 cover showed a model's face cut into two halves and rearranged, and Erwin Blumenfeld's famous January 1950 *Vogue* cover presented a model's face quite literally reduced to half of her heavily made-up features.[6] Plath's 'Woman Behind Screen' represents the culture of conflicting messages for women at the mid-century; a culture that manifested itself not only in Plath's poetry, where, as Sally Bayley has noted, Plath developed 'a split model of womanhood' and a 'divided female self' that defined several of her poems, but in a 'split-screen' approach to fashioning identity.[7]

Plath came of age at a time when the fashion pendulum had swung back to ultra-femininity. During the Second World War, shortages and restrictions rendered fashions more utilitarian, with boxy silhouettes and shorter skirts.[8] However, in 1947, Dior's 'New Look' collection heralded a return to luxury and womanliness: wasp-waisted suits, calf-length skirts and dresses with prominent bust lines all created an accentuated 'hourglass' silhouette, the influence of which was felt across the fashion industry and into the US juniors markets to which Plath would have been attuned.[9]

However, fashion's new femininity dovetailed with a growing emphasis on traditional sex roles – ideas that were perpetuated in women's magazines.[10] The American designer Anne Fogarty even published *Wife Dressing: The Fine Art of Being a Well-Dressed Wife* (1959), which decreed: 'The first principle of wife-dressing is Complete Femininity.'[11] As fashion historian Valerie Steele has observed, these developments:

> ... helped position fashion as a pillar of 'the feminine mystique.' ... expressing as it did, a veritable cult of femininity. From stiletto heels and waspie girdles to white gloves and aprons, women's fashion promoted restrictive images of femininity: wife-and-mother and/or *femme fatale*.[12]

This was also the era of Revlon's 'Fire and Ice' campaign, which promoted 'a *new* American Beauty ... she's tease and temptress, siren and gamin, dynamic and demure'.[13] In 1954, Plath was seemingly perfectly aware of such dual categories of womanhood, using Revlon-style advertising copy to muse on whether to 'release the lady? or the tiger?' (*LV1* 662).[14] Plath also understood how fashion shaped each side of the binary: 'the eggs-and-bacon-and-coffee girl in a housecoat who can also exist on olives, Roquefort and daiquiris while clad in black velvet' (*LV1* 661–2).[15] Certainly, Plath had a 'lifelong interest in feminine fashion as a form of theatre', and used fashion, like writing, to explore the 'many possibilities of selfhood'.[16] However, her split-screen fashion life also speaks to ideas of transformation and the struggle to become 'whole'.

'I still can't believe I'm a SMITH GIRL!' Plath excitedly wrote home shortly after arriving at college in 1950 (*LH* 46). While she had attended Smith College for its academic excellence, it also had a reputation for style superiority that was not lost on her: Plath was a *Smith* girl, not just a college girl.[17] Fashion at Smith was a particularly clear example of 'split-screen' style identity: as *Flair*'s college issue noted the year Plath started school, Smith students lived 'a double life, wardrobe-wise'.[18] During the week students wore casual Bermuda shorts, crew-neck sweaters, blue jeans, button-downs and penny loafers (*LV1* 178; 199; 667; 832).[19] At the weekend, students transformed by assuming the trappings of ladylike fashion for dates and parties: dresses, skirts, heels, kid-leather gloves and matching accessories.[20] Plath paid close attention. Fellow students recall Plath looking every bit the '"Ivy League College Girl"', while she herself adored the rituals of the weekend and would later explore the power of clothing in all-female school environments in 'Initiation' (*LV1* 183; 211; 395; 667; *JP* 198–307).[21]

One dress particularly conveys Plath's embrace of the social transformation: her silvery strapless prom dress of 1953. Plath bought the dress 'splurgingly' and excitedly wrote to her mother with all the details and a sketch (*J* 177; *LV1* 572–5). She planned her hair (a fashionable pageboy that she had trimmed perfectly) and her jewellery, with which, she hoped, 'I should look like a silver princess—or feel like one anyway' (*LV1* 576). With the right 'silver high heels', Plath believed the outfit was an emotional and physical departure from 'the white naïve flatfooted Puritanism' of two years earlier and admitted her desire to dress for a man's attention: 'I want to be silverly beautiful for him: a sylvan goddess' (*J* 177). She would later wear the dress at a *Mademoiselle* rooftop party and the photograph of her, silvery, smiling and sipping cocktails, appeared in the magazine and her own scrapbook.[22]

However, Plath felt increasingly conflicted about the 'split-screen' style of Smith life, and following her return to college in 1954 after her first suicide attempt, she decided to embrace a singular Smith self. Plath famously had blonde/brunette personalities, but when she reverted to brunette, she explained that the divide was sartorial as well as cosmetic: Her 'serious, industrious, unextracurricular' brunette self wore the week-day uniform of 'Bermudas, knee socks and loafers instead of racy red heels, parachute skirts and an aura of chanel' (*LVI* 807).[23] Even her 'most exquisite formal' was viewed differently with time: when the moment was recast for *The Bell Jar*, the dress on Esther Greenwood is just 'a skimpy, imitation silver-lamé bodice stuck onto a big, fat, cloud of white tulle [. . .]' reflecting Esther's own imitation of outward conformity to prescribed ideals of fashionable womanhood (*LVI* 572; *BJ* 2).[24]

When beginning the phase of her life as a wife and mother, she pitted these domestic roles against her professional self. In a letter to her best friend, Marcia Brown, in 1955, Plath distilled the split-screen: 'The new job, Marty, sounds at last really worthy of you: what a tremendous double-perspective you must have on Cambridge life: pink Brooks Bros. shirts versus tattered diapers!' (*LVI* 1056). That Plath could adeptly reduce the identities of wife/mother/professional in this way is telling of her engage-ment with contemporary fashion (the Brooks Brothers' women's pink shirt had been an iconic womenswear development), but also of how she continued to associate specific garments with professional experiences and achievements as a woman.[25] Plath would dress carefully for her teach-ing job, believing that the 'right' wardrobe could directly impact her performance: '. . . I am sure I teach better in certain dresses whose colors & textures war not against my body & my thought' (*J* 335). She also took care to dress appropriately for major professional milestones, including when she signed her first book contract and wrote home of being 'resplen-dent in black wool suit, black cashmere coat, fawn kidskin gloves from Paris . . . and matching calfskin bag (from Italy)' (*LH* 365–6).

When Plath and Hughes separated, Plath again used fashion as a way to reinvent her split-screen self: casting aside her wifely skirts, polka dots and headbands (and the clothes she had worn since Smith), she began with a new camel suit and a few other pieces, hoping 'her new London life could "begin over from the skin out."'[26] Once in London, the transformation continued with 'a Florence-Italy blue and white velvet overblouse, a deep brown velvet Italian shirt, black fake-fur toreador pants, a straight black velvet skirt and metallic blue-and-black French top' (*LH* 491). The clothes were particularly fashionable (especially Toreador pants, which were tight, cropped pants inspired by those worn by Spanish bullfighters that had been popular through the 1950s and 1960s) and exhibited sleeker silhouettes than Plath tended to wear.[27] This was a confident, empowering, texturally full wardrobe for a new start.

'More Taste Than Money'

Throughout her life, Plath was the embodiment of what *Vogue* magazine called 'More Taste Than Money', meaning that she shopped carefully and made a dollar stretch fashionably far.[28] Nonetheless, Plath sometimes ignored actual dollars and cents, and calculated how many outfits she could buy per published poem, once proudly listing, 'For three villanelles I have a blue-and-white pin-striped cotton cord suit dress, a black silk date dress and a grey raincoat with a frivolous pink lining' (*J* 183).[29] She dreamed of fine fashion, admitting that, 'if I were wealthy, my idea of extravagance would be to have a closet full of colored shoes . . .', but would 'kick myself where I deserve to be kicked for such horrible and mercenary afflictions of wishful thinking' (*J* 558; *LVI* 367).

Plath's fashion frustrations intensified at Smith, where she was a scholarship student surrounded by wealthy girls, referring to herself as a 'Smith Cinderella'.[30] Plath noted the difference when her suitcase was stolen in NYC:

> . . . because when one is supporting oneself, one does not replenish wardrobe, one wears dungarees for a year. so I will wear dungarees for a year. and pretend I have become an ascetic. You know: just cawn't beah cashmeah sweatehs, so vulgah. materialism, these tweed dresses! Back to natcah! (*LVI* 850).

However, Plath was resourceful: she borrowed and made clothes, and shopped the sales (*LVI* 285; 294–5; 309; 323; 854; 858; *J* 460). Even her silvery gown was bought in a sale, quite unlike those students buying pricey prom designs from the Northampton designer Violet Angotti (*LVI* 572).[31] Plath made frugal choices look fashionable, once feeling 'most chic in mackintosh, ironically, because of its swaggery cut', and when a boyfriend remarked on her 'practical gabardine coat', she remained steadfast: 'I enjoyed it – and would never feel quite at home in fur' (*J* 558; *LVI* 285).

However, Plath took pride in dressing well on a budget. When attending a formal party as a freshman, she wrote to her mother: 'I am sure you would have been supremely happy if you had seen me. I know I looked beautiful. Even daughters of millionaires complimented my dress' (*LH* 76). Being a 'Smith Cinderella' was an acknowledgement of achievement and she often tried to remind herself of the way she had risen: 'Five years ago, if I could have seen myself now: at Smith (instead of Wellesley) with seven acceptances from <u>Seventeen</u> & one from <u>Mlle</u>, with a few lovely clothes, and one intelligent, handsome boy – I would have said: that is all I could ever ask!' (*J* 151).

Living Wearing: Plath's Wardrobe of Colour, Fabric and Feeling

If Plath connected with writing because, as Kathleen Connors has observed, she felt it 'could be experienced with the full force of the senses', then perhaps her love of fashion stemmed from the fact that it similarly offered her a whole gamut of sensory pleasure.[32] There was colour, which Plath was profoundly affected by, but also the touch of different fabric; as she once admitted, she 'dressed, conscious of color and the loveliness of being thin and feeling slink, swank and luxurious in good fits and rich materials' (*J* 379).[33] There was the sound of garments in motion, with Plath often noting auricular details: 'Girls in beautiful gowns clustered by the stair. Everywhere there were swishes of taffeta, satin, silk' (*LH* 75). Plath was also intoxicated by the scent of worn fabrics and the bodies they dressed, often remembering the almost chemical reactions between her favourite perfumes and her clothes, such as the time she was 'fresh and apple-scented in the lovely shimmering tie-silk dress with the lavendar design on the silvery-beige background' (*J* 329; *LVi* 807; *J* 109).[34] In addition, there were the tactile delights of embellishment, accessories and fastenings, with a young Plath preferring 'the clean quick flash of zippers' as opposed to those 'round, fingered little objects on shirts and sweaters' (*J* 52). Above all, there was the intimate, *lived* experience of clothes in all their euphoric glory, bitter disappointment, fitful rage, any number of other emotional states one might experience. Plath's own favourite colours and fabrics repeat across her wardrobe and her writings; fashion choices that are rooted in contemporary trends, but that become imbued with emotional, physical and symbolic significance both for her and written characters.

Although Plath revelled in paler colours, like aqua, yellow and white (which highlighted her best accessory: her tan), her favourite colour was red, a circumstance that Ted Hughes wrote of in his *Birthday Letters* poem, 'Red' (*J* 9; 74; 90; 108; 114; 161; 561; *BL* 197).[35] Red was Plath's official class colour at Smith, and she always kept her wardrobe filled with crimson, feeling most 'chic' in red skirts, sweaters, scarves and polka dots (*J* 561; 51; *LVi* 534). Plath also had well-loved red ballet shoes, (*J* 364) which were fashionable since the designer Claire McCardell had paired Capezios with her sportswear in 1941.[36] However, Plath favoured red Pappagallos, perhaps the most coveted preppy flats for American college girls, and even warned her mother to send her an authentic pair while studying in Cambridge: 'You can tell them by the striped red & white inside. Don't take a reasonable facsimile! Only the gen-you-ine article!' (LVI 1004).[37] Plath was even wearing a 'lovely red headband', however infamous it was to become in biographical debate, when she met Ted Hughes (J 212). Wearing red awakened her senses, once famously observing in her journal: 'For the first time put on my red silk stockings with red shoes – they feel amazing, or, rather, the color feels amazing – almost incandescent fire silk-sheathing my legs: I can't stop looking . . .' (J 379).[38] Plath's obsession with matching red accessories was also on trend: In 1957 Vogue had confirmed that, 'Red with red is the idea' (LVI 395; 518).[39] The following year, Plath caught a glimpse of herself in a shop window, 'lost, red-heeled, red-gloved . . .' and around the same time she wrote, 'Stone Boy With Dolphin', in which Dody wears ribboned red shoes, a red belt and red fingernails (J 325; JP 182; 197; 199). In 'Mothers', a rather autobiographical short story from 1962, the American character, Esther, strongly parallels Plath in many ways, not least in the fact that she wears a matching red cashmere coat and turban (JP 10). But the depth of Plath's affection for red accessories is best indicated by her sorrow at losing them: '. . . and that was the last party at Saint John's where I lost the red glove, as tonight I lost the red bandeau which I loved with all the redness of my heart' (J 213).

Plath's preferred colour combination was red, black and white; a love that likely came from both her 'color-driven sensibilities' and the popularity of the 'tricolour' trend.[40] In one of her earliest letters home from Smith, Plath mentions Flair magazine, which in its August 1950 issue included a feature entitled 'Red-Black-White', in which outfits appeared on pages spliced in half, giving the reader the opportunity to combine different tops and bottoms by flipping the flaps back and forth (LH 46).[41] Plath took pleasure in the 'stark' contrast of the colours, and the immediate confidence even an 'old black jersey and red skirt' could give her (J 176; 51).[42] On honeymoon, she wore a 'black linen skirt, white jersey, red belt and polka-dotted scarf to be bright and wifely for Alicante' (J 253). Plath also lamented the fact that when she was stood up for a date, '[. . .] every time I am dressed in black, white and red: violent, fierce colors' (J 233).[43] These colours and their associated passions, seemingly leapt from her wardrobe and into her typewriter, with scholars noting that her 'poetic palette' became increasingly 'loaded with black, white, red and blue', particularly in her later poems.[44]

Ever texturally driven, Plath took pleasure in the 'snug' fit of jersey as it clung to her every curve and when *Vogue* wrote about being 'Young and in love with velvet' they might as well have been describing Plath, who would write of feeling 'sexy' in her black velvet dress, and revelling in the 'caress' of her velvet skirt (*J* 329; 146; 28).[45] However, Plath also adored tweed, unsurprising given its capacity for colour and texture combinations. Photographs of her in nubby tweed dresses and suits abound, and she associated tweed with celebration, achievement and sophistication, once dreaming that she and her future husband would have a life filled with work, friends, art, literature, culture '. . . and I will be able to buy all the poetry books and tweed suits I want!'[46] Plath had visceral reactions to these fabrics and they appear across her poetry and prose, imbued with sensual and symbolic power; even nature wore tweed to herald the return of Spring in her poem 'Apparel for April': 'Hills sport tweed / for april's back' (*LV1* 883).

One particularly special garment fuelled poetic expression and emotional connection: Plath's pink knitted wedding dress. 'And I am married to a poet', Plath wrote in her journal, describing, 'Ted in his old black corduroy jacket & me in mother's gift of a pink knit dress. Pink rose & black tie' (*J* 270). The colour and texture combination, the emotional gift and the fact that the dress was particularly fashionable at the time create the perfect Plath wedding style story.[47] That pink knitted dress came to represent so much of their union: life, love and marriage woven into the yarns. Plath would remember the dress's first outing whenever she wore it again and Hughes never forgot the moment he saw her, 'In your pink wool knitted dress / Before anything had smudged anything / You stood at the altar. Bloomsday' (*LH* 311; *BL* 34).

Plath's Fashion Career Explored

When Plath submitted her entry to the 1955 *Vogue* Prix de Paris competition, she listed her fashion skills and interests, emphasising: 'This is not mere nebulous dreaming. This is practical experience.'[48] Indeed, by this point, Plath had already won a place on the prestigious *Mademoiselle* Guest Editorship program, spending the summer of 1953 'hatted + heeled', working at the magazine (the experiences of which would provide material for *The Bell Jar*).[49] Plath attended fashion shows and parties, met major designers, including Pauline Trigère, wrote features on everything from poetry to plaid fashion and was photographed by celebrated fashion photographer Hermann Landshoff.[50] Plath would go on to win

Honourable Mention in *Vogue*'s Prix de Paris, write fashion journalism and model for *Varsity* while in Cambridge and earn the acclaim of major editors, including Cyrilly Abels and Jessica Daves.[51]

Plath was always conscious of the way visuals could elevate her writing about clothes, with fashion sketches appearing in her notebooks, letters and journals, and this inclination fed her professional fashion work.[52] As Elizabeth Winder has observed:

> Sylvia was the perfect candidate for fashion journalism. Like Alexander Liberman, Diana Vreeland, and the rest of the midcentury Condé Nast heavyweights, Sylvia was intrigued and inspired by the spark between fashion and the visual arts.[53]

Although her time at *Mademoiselle* was dominated by writing, Plath paid close attention to the visual side of the magazine, parlaying this into her *Vogue* submission, where she specifically mentioned 'analyzing layouts and inventing feature and fashion displays that will attract the *Vogue* reader'.[54] Plath demonstrated a knack for commercially appealing yet artistic fashion layouts. For an unsubmitted *Vogue* piece, Plath suggested a layout of children's fashions with a nursery rhymes theme, using pull quotes from the original texts blended with evocative photographs and typical fashion copy to tug at the strings of childhood nostalgia.[55]

Plath's process of *writing* fashion shows careful study and development; Plath was sensitive to descriptions of clothing in literature when developing her own deeply evocative style.[56] She studied magazines carefully to shape her voice, and, by the time she reached *Mademoiselle*, could easily slip into breezy fashion copy: 'Foremost in the fashion constellations we spot Mlle's own tartan, the astronomic versatility of sweaters and men, men, men – we've even taken the shirts off their backs!' (*LH* 35).[57] Her journal entries and correspondence often served as practice, such as in a letter to her mother from 1951, where she blends an elegant college weekend with fashion description that could be lifted from *Mademoiselle*: 'Picture me then, in my navy-blue bolero suit and versatile brown coat, snuggled in the back seat of an open car, whizzing for two sun-colored hours through the hilly Connecticut valley!' (*LV1* 376).

Plath also understood fashion as an entry into an entire way of living; an entire way of being and fashion magazines increasingly promoted fashions as 'lifestyles'. As international travel became ever more available to middle-class Americans, vacation wardrobes emerged as a lucrative business, and the collegiate market similarly embraced an image of American college students enjoying a lifestyle of elite education and social merriment on ivy-covered campuses to sell clothes.[58] Plath was aware of these kinds of features and their effect. Her submission to the *Vogue* competition was particularly savvy: a piece entitled, 'Wardrobe for Six Weeks in Europe', which was exactly the kind of article the magazine liked to print at the time.[59]

Plath could balance elevated fashion copy with real *lived* experience, and much of her fashion writing is relatable, entertaining and eminently practical. When Plath described a capsule wardrobe for travel, it was realistic and stamped with her personal style, even down to the colours she chose (her favourites: grey, black, white, aqua, red).[60] When she talked about college fashion in her submissions to *Mademoiselle*, she translated her own experience as a budget-shopper, highlighting the pieces that had given her the most versatility (*LVi* 314).[61]

For all this, however, Plath was still caught in the mixed messages of mid-century fashion. When she had her first interview for *Mademoiselle*, Plath immediately panicked:

> I can't think of a thing to wear. All my clothes are brown, navy or velvet. No matching accessories. Hell, how I've piddled off money, penny by penny for unmatching items. How can I expect to criticize the country's leading fashion mag when I can't even dress correctly myself? (*J* 533).

Yet she could so easily craft the exact kind of breezy, instructional fashion copy that would set up such notions, because Plath existed on both sides of the fashion industry: a savvy and industry-aware fashion editor who could inhabit the language, craft the images, market the trends and promote the products; and a young woman simultaneously caught up in, yet directly challenging, the contradictory resulting expectations.[62]

Thus, to understand Plath and fashion is to understand an intensely personal relationship. Fashion elevated her emotional experiences, her creative expression and her understanding of selfhood. However, it is also a unique glimpse into mid-century fashion trends, photography and journalism, through Plath's own singular vision and interpretation.

Notes

1. I would like to thank the Bard Graduate Center for their generous support of this chapter.
2. *LH* citations refer to the HarperPerennial 1992 edition.
3. Connors, 'Living Color', 71, Pl. 15; Bayley, 'Costume of Femininity', 191; Winder, *Pain, Parties, Work*, 19–20.
4. *LL*, Art Scrapbook #4, c. 1950–1.

5. All *BJ* citations refer to the HarperPerennial Modern Classics, 2005 edition. Peasant styles became particularly fashionable in the 1940s and 1950s. See 'Peasant Clothes', 88–9.

6. *Seventeen* (March 1948), photographer: Francesco Scavullo; *Mademoiselle* (March 1947), photographer: Gene Fenn; *Vogue* (1 January 1950), photographer: Erwin Blumenfeld. See also *Seventeen* (June 1949); *Vogue* (1 January 1952), photographer: Erwin Blumenfeld.

7. Bayley, 'Costume of Femininity', 184. See also 189, where Bayley develops a 'split-level' metaphor of 'double self'.

8. Steele, *Fifty Years of Fashion*, 8.

9. Most notably, designer Anne Fogarty. Milbank, *New York Fashion*, 188; 'Fogarty Was Ahead of Dior', 76.

10. Bayley, 'Costume of Femininity', 185; Bryant, 'Ariel's Kitchen', 211–35; Bryant, 'Plath, Domesticity and the Art of Advertising', 17–34; Leonard, 'The Woman Is Perfected', 60–82; Smith, 'The Feeding of Young Women', 1–22.

11. Fogarty, *Wife Dressing*, 6.

12. Steele, *Fifty Years of Fashion*, 29. Pelt also identifies this promoted image of femininity in her study of fashion in *BJ*. See, Pelt, 'Esther's Sartorial Selves', 17–18.

13. Quoted in Winder, *Pain, Parties, Work*, 153.

14. See also *J* 111.

15. Also quoted in Bayley, 'Costume of Femininity', 200–1.

16. Bayley, 'Costume of Femininity', 191; Connors, 'Living Color', 2.

17. Tuite, *Seven Sisters Style*, chapters 1–4.

18. 'Four BWOC', 49. 'BWOC' stands for 'Big Woman on Campus' (*LVi* 176 n).

19. See also Tuite, *Seven Sisters Style*, 40–59.

20. Tuite, *Seven Sisters Style*, 60–85.

21. Jane Baltzell Kopp, quoted in Rollyson, *American Isis*, 96. All *JP* citations refer to Harper Perennial Modern Classics, 2008 edition.

22. Mathers, 'Memo from the Guest Editor', *Mademoiselle* (August 1953), 54; LL, PMII, Smith Scrapbook, Oversize no. 8.

23. Quoted in Bayley, 'Costume of Femininity', 199.

24. See also Crowther, 'The body does not . . .', 118.

25. Tuite, *Seven Sisters Style*, 86–7, 89, 92–5.

26. Wagner-Martin, *Sylvia Plath*, 226; for 'cycles of self-improvement', see Connors, 115.

27. 'Spanish Styles', *LIFE* (21 August 1950): 57–61.

28. 'More Taste Than Money', 76–89.

29. See also *J* 478.

30. Quoted in Ames, 'Biographical Note', in *BJ* 5. LL, PMII, Smith Scrapbook, Oversize no. 8.

31. Lazaro, 'Beautiful Clothes Violet Angotti', 39–56.

32. Connors, 'Living Color', 73.

33. See also *LV1* 367; for color, see Connors, 'Living Color', 19 and throughout; de Nervaux-Gavoty, 'Coming to Terms with Colour', 110–28.
34. See also Winder, *Pain, Parties, Work*, 95.
35. See also Winder, *Pain, Parties, Work*, 19.
36. Yohannan, *Claire McCardell*, 63.
37. For Pappagallo: Tuite, *Seven Sisters Style*, 18 and 56.
38. See also Connors, 'Living Color', 114.
39. 'The New Charm of Red – Disarming', 133.
40. Connors, 'Living Color', 20; 'Summer Fashion on a Tricolour Basis', 115.
41. 'Red-Black-White', 37–43.
42. See also *LV1* 230, 534, 607.
43. See also *J* 176.
44. Gubar, 'Afterword', 231; Connors, 'Visual Art', 84–6.
45. 'In Velvet . . .', 126–7. See also *LV1* 717, 1156, 1303.
46. Quoted in Wagner-Martin, *Sylvia Plath*, 119.
47. 'Heyday – and Evening – Of the Knitted Dress', 128.
48. Quoted in Connors, 'Living Color', 72.
49. Quoted in Ames, 'Biographical Note', in *BJ*, 5.
50. See Winder, *Pain, Parties, Work*, for an account of this summer.
51. 'Who Won Vogue's 1955 Prix de Paris', 142; 'Sylvia Plath Tours the Stores', 6–7; Telegram from Jessica Daves to SP (15 May 1955), regarding Vogue's 20th Prix de Paris, LL, Box Oversize 8, Folder 41.
52. See Plates 14, 20 and 21 in *LV1*. Letters where such illustrations are indicated include *LV1*, 80, 310, 435.
53. Winder, *Pain, Parties, Work*, 93.
54. Quoted in Connors, 'Living Color', 72.
55. Quoted in Connors, 'Living Color', 72; Original in LL, PMII, Box 9, Folder 2.
56. Connors, 'Living Color', 73; See also LL, PMII, Box 12, Folder 1, where Plath mentions the significance and descriptions of dress in the novel, *Sister Carrie*, in her notebook.
57. 'Mlle's Last Word', 235.
58. Forthcoming Tuite, *The 1950s in Vogue: The Jessica Daves Years*, Thames & Hudson (2019); Tuite, *Seven Sisters Style*, 86–107.
59. 'Wardrobe for Six Weeks in Europe' (essay, 1954). LL, PMII, Box 9, Folder 2; 'Capsule Trip, Capsule Wardrobe', 154–5; '44lb. Travel Wardrobe', 58–61, 106–10.
60. 'Wardrobe for Six Weeks in Europe' (essay, 1954). LL, PMII, Box 9, Folder 2.
61. Analysis of the College *Mademoiselle* Issue. LL, PMII, Box 12, Folder 7.
62. Leonard, 'The Woman Is Perfected', 60–82. See also Bayley, 'Costume of Femininity', 199–203; and Smith, 'The Feeding of Young Women', 3–4.

CHAPTER 13

Experimental Bravery: Plath's Poetry and Auteur Cinema

Lynda K. Bundtzen

During Sylvia Plath's 1959 stay at Yaddo,[1] she went to see Ingmar Bergman's *The Magician*, noting in her journal:

> Not as gripping and terrifying as the Seventh Seal, but fine, magnificently entertaining. Photography, haunting scenes and characters faces strong – – – recognized the cast of the other film. Why can't America, even England, produce something like the good Swedish and Italian and Japanese films? (*J* 522).

Plath was not alone in questioning American movie-making for valuing Hollywood's studio production, star system and box office receipts more than artistic merit or experimentally daring film directors like Bergman, Federico Fellini or Akira Kurosawa. Plath remembers Bergman's actors from *The Seventh Seal*, intuiting this director's reliance on an ensemble of skilled players rather than a casting director's choice and is moved by his allegiance to black-and-white cinematography and natural light. Both undergird Bergman's 'haunting scenes', as does his signature move with the camera: probing close-ups of actors' expressive faces. *The Magician* is by an *auteur*, intent on fulfilling his personal vision of humanity and not dependent on a hired screenwriter.

What did Plath imbibe from the influx of foreign films by directors wielding the *caméra-stylo* during the 1950s?[2] Initially we glimpse their inspiration in her swooning voice when writing about Richard Sassoon after seeing Jean Cocteau's surrealist masterpieces *La Belle et La Bête and Orphée*. Sassoon speaks to her 'through every word of French, through every single word I look up bleeding in the dictionary'. She hears 'the wounded, miraculous furry voice of the dear *bête* whispering so slow through the palace of floating curtains. And the Angel Heurtebise and Death [from *Orphée*] melt through mirrors like water.' Entranced with Sassoon's 'image', she alternately constructs masks for him or begs Sassoon to 'break' his image and 'wrench it' from her (*J* 216–17). Cocteau's mirrors in *Orphée* are a melting gateway between our world and netherworld ruins where the dead wander aimlessly. Echoes of the mirror's power to transport us into another realm and in Cocteau's words to 'bring us closer to death'[3] are echoed in Plath's pleading: 'You [Richard] know I am not strong enough to live merely in that abstract Platonic realm out of time and flesh on the other side of all those mirrors' (*J* 216–17).

For poetic experiments equal to Cocteau's surrealistic imagery, however, we must look to Plath's *Ariel*. Sandra Gilbert, 'barely a published poet' when *Ariel* appeared, and 'secretly competitive' with Plath, remembers a shift in her perception reading 'Berck-Plage' for the first time. Earlier, she had 'been disappointed by Plath's poems' – 'their apparent docility, their "good girl" decorum'. Familiar only with the 'careful texts of *The Colossus*', she 'stumbled on "Berck-Plage"' and was 'baffled, envious', and astonished by its power.[4] The 'docile' 'good girl' poet disappeared and was now both dangerous and transgressive.

'Berck-Plage' was prompted by the death of Plath's Devon neighbour Percy Key, and her obsessive fascination with his 'end, even of so marginal a man, a horror' (*J* 672). Plath's setting, however, is a French seaside town distant from Devon. Plath and Hughes visited Berck-Plage the year before on holiday, and 'what might have been a carefree vacation spot was from the start blighted by the ubiquitous medicalization of the place',[5] dominated by its hospital and the 'mutilated war veterans and accident victims —who took their exercise along the sands'.[6]

'Berck-Plage' reads like a nightmare pilgrimage. The speaker oddly observes herself with 'two legs, and I move smilingly', as if to defend herself from being 'scalded by these bald surfaces' (*CP* 196). There is nothing here to smile about, and later she confides, 'I am not a smile' (*CP* 198), despite her demeanour. What she envisions are surrealistic fragments in a 'pervasively diseased geography':[7] a sun-seared landscape peopled by a priest in a 'black cassock', 'pale girls' scooping 'electrifyingly-colored sherbets', and 'mackerel gatherers' handling fish 'like the parts of the body' (*CP* 196). Percy Key enters later, but already he is 'vanishing' with 'no help' for his 'weeping wife'. Gone are his 'eye-stones, yellow and valuable, / And the tongue, sapphire of ash' (*CP* 198). Such images recall the metaphysical poets, violently yoking together soft eyes with hard gems, the moist tongue with dust. For Gilbert, Plath may well be '*the* poet of modern death',[8] denuded as this elegy is, in Plath's words, of 'hope, it is given up' (*CP* 201) – a final diffident shrug.

If Plath wins fame for 'her often death-drenched work',[9] she thereby resembles directors she admired. Bergman was obsessed with death, personified in *The Seventh Seal* as a chalk-faced, black-caped chess player and trickster. Death sometimes arrives as a prank played upon the unsuspecting – like the figure with the 'beak' in Plath's 'Death & Co.' that 'Claps sidewise' at the speaker who worries, 'I am not his yet' (*CP* 254). Bergman's plague-ridden landscape, with its pilgrim-flagellants in haircloth, stretches of sand and sea, and priests casting incense, might inspire 'the great abeyance' of the sea and the 'sandy damper' that 'stretches for miles' in 'Berck-Plage' (*CP* 196). In Cocteau's *Orphée*, as in Plath's 'Death & Co.', Death arrives with an entourage. Cocteau's Death is a Princess in love with Orpheus, the archetypal poet who, in turn, loves and pursues her. She appears later as a white goddess: her black robes and hood turn white, her hair, lips, eyebrows and eyelashes are white, and like Plath's Death, whose 'eyes are lidded / And balled' (*CP* 254), Cocteau's Princess has flat white disks on black hollow sockets.

Cocteau insists, 'Death in my film is not Death represented symbolically by an elegant young woman but the Death of Orpheus.'[10] Hence, when she chooses the younger poet Cégeste for death, she also 'abolishes herself to make the poet [Orpheus] immortal'. For Plath's 'Lady Lazarus', 'Dying / Is an art' (*CP* 245) performed repeatedly to achieve perfection and resurrection as a rarefied phoenix figure. In this she mimics Cocteau's conception of the poet's immortality: 'The successive deaths through which a poet must pass before he becomes ... changed into himself at last by eternity.'[11] Next to this immortal artist-figure in Plath's poems are mere mortals confronting death's finality: in 'Totem', there are 'only suitcases / Out of which the same self unfolds like a suit' (*CP* 264) and 'the one / Death with its many sticks' (*CP* 265); or it might be anybody when the speaker menacingly intones, 'Somebody's done for' (*CP* 255) in 'Death & Co.'. That Plath could sustain both figurations – the poet enacting death's successive incarnations, and the 'flies' in 'Totem' that 'buzz like blue children' while caught 'In nets of the infinite' (*CP* 265) – illustrates the 'austere ferocity' Gilbert admired in Plath's *Ariel*.[12]

Some speakers in *Ariel* are caricatures, like the broadly conceived neurotic clients in *Rêves à Vendre* (*Dreams that Money Can Buy*), an *avant-garde* film directed by Dada theorist Hans Richter. The fast-talking salesman in 'The Applicant' with his infomercial guarantees – 'I have the ticket for that' – and sham-wow promises – 'It is waterproof, shatterproof, proof / Against fire and bombs through the roof' (*CP* 221) – resembles the 'droll ... and disturbing' incidents and tone (*J* 560) delighting Plath when she saw *Rêves à Vendre*.[13] The film's major character is an ordinary Joe, but he discovers his own stream-of-consciousness in the mirror of his rented room. Joe sets up business selling dreams to various client-applicants. The first, titled *Desire*,[14] parallels the marital negotiation in 'The Applicant', with a couple arriving mismatched in their dreams. Bored with her bank clerk husband, Mrs. A asks for a dream that will widen his horizons and heighten his ambitions, but the husband's desire is erotic, not materialistic, and the dream Joe sells him resembles phone sex. The thrice repeated refrain of a woman's voice dreamily beckoning him to join her under a 'warm white gown' may have inspired Plath's salesperson, who hammers the applicant to 'marry it, marry it, marry it' (*CP* 222).

Mirrors are everywhere in Plath's poetry, too, and associated with anguished self-probing and feminine anxiety over appearances. The speaker in 'The Courage of Shutting-Up' has her tongue 'cut out' – no longer 'loaded' with accusations of 'Bastardies, usages, desertions and doubleness' – but as long as she has eyes, 'Mirrors can kill and talk.' They reflect 'torture' and 'the face of a dead man' who deserted the speaker (*CP* 210). In 'Face Lift', the initial speaker disappears quickly, listening to a 'you' bringing 'good news' (*CP* 155) about her face lift: 'Now she's done for, the dewlapped lady/ I watched settle, line by line, in my mirror' (*CP* 156). 'Mirror' itself claims in one poem, 'I am not cruel, only truthful' (*CP* 173), even though the woman examining her reflection has 'drowned a young girl' and watches an 'old woman' rising in her place (*CP* 174). The 'Second Voice' in *Three Women* miscarries, yet 'The mirror gives back a woman without deformity', blurring the truth of how she sees her body. Like the mirrors in *auteur* cinema, Plath's mirrors open consciousness into a troubled psychic realm.

In the Hollywood *film noir*, mirrors suggest the *femme fatale*'s duplicity. She is doomed by overweening ambitions for money, for power, for a more exciting life. Yet she is disabled by her gender from pursuing her desires without a male conspirator. Seduced by her beauty and ambitions mirroring his own desire, he may kill and steal, leading to their shared fatality. As Laura Mulvey observes, the 'male gaze projects its fantasy onto the female figure, which is styled' to reflect men's desire;[15] or, as the cartoon *femme fatale* Jessica Rabbit explains her voluptuous body in *Who Framed Roger Rabbit*, 'I'm not bad. I'm just drawn that way.' Similarly, Phyllis Diedrickson in Billy Wilder's *Double Indemnity* offers no explanation for why she is 'rotten to the core'. It stands as the clichéd premise of her character.

In *auteur* cinema, the *femme fatale* has more dimensions. Like Cocteau's Princess/Orpheus's Death, she is a muse. Truffaut's Catherine in *Jules et Jim* is, perhaps, the most vivid representation of the *femme fatale* as regal mistress of her own fate as well as the fate of Jules and Jim, who see her as an embodiment of the eternal feminine. The men surrender control of their future when they vow to pursue Catherine. Mulvey argues woman as image 'work[s] against the development of a story-line, to freeze the flow of action in moments of erotic contemplation'.[16] Unless, of course, she refuses to assume the passive role of '*to-be-looked-at-ness*'[17] and actively contrives the narrative as Catherine does. Jules and Jim forgive Catherine for being capricious, wilful and manipulative. She cheats at life, following her heart's whims. Ultimately, though a more complex figure than the *film noir femme fatale*, Catherine inevitably lures Jim to his death and her suicide.[18]

Plath also experiments with the *femme fatale* as more complex, with motives beyond greed or sexual manipulation of a male dupe. Lady Lazarus, no longer the puppet of Herr God, Herr Lucifer, ends with the promise to 'eat men like air' (*CP* 247). Self-revelation of a being in full possession of her powers is also the climax of 'Stings'. As the queen bee takes flight 'With her lion-red body' (*CP* 215), she leaves her male 'scape-goat', unmasked by stinging bees, 'Molding onto his lips like lies', putting a triumphant end to deception. The speaker in 'Purdah' may be Plath's greatest *femme fatale*, an 'enigmatical' creature garbed in the all-enveloping clothing of purdah and confined in the harem's 'rustling appurtenances' (*CP* 242–3). A mistress of deception, she 'gleam[s] like a mirror' and her 'visibilities hide'. Like her *film noir* sisters, she reflects what the male gaze desires – his own ego and image magnified, believing he is 'Lord of the mirrors!' (*CP* 242). He is not doomed by a woman's duplicity, but by his prideful delusion that she is his possession. Plath harks back to the original for all these fatal women in Clytemnestra, luring Agamemnon, blinded by *hubris,* into 'The shriek in the bath / The cloak of holes' (*CP* 244).

Since *Ariel*'s 1965 publication, Plath has aroused critical anxiety for appropriating historical tragedy to enhance her own personal struggles.[19] For European directors prominent in the 1950s, intertwining private confession with history was a technique for bearing witness to the Second World War's horrors. Alain Resnais's *Hiroshima Mon Amour* is both an intimate conversation between a man and woman, lovers and adulterers, and a meditation on atomic devastation. 'She' is a French actress in Hiroshima to make a film about peace; 'he' is a Japanese architect. The architect's parents were Hiroshima victims, and he challenges his lover's claim to have seen the images Resnais incorporates to confront the viewer as well: photos and newsreel footage of bodies burned beyond recognition, a city flattened to rubble and deformed children.

While Plath may lack the political intent of Resnais, the director encouraged Plath to venture opportunistically into recent history for imagery to heighten her reader's emotional response. The opening of *Hiroshima Mon Amour* clearly had an impact on Plath in 'Fever 103°'. Resnais depicts the bodies of a woman and man making love, but the image is tightly cropped and suffocating. Suddenly they are covered with atomic dust, intertwining lovemaking and death. When the grainy image of the ash-covered lovers dissolves into a photographically clear image, the ash becomes beads of perspiration. Likewise, the 'radiation' in Plath's poem greases 'the bodies of adulterers / Like Hiroshima ash and eating in' (*CP* 231). Resnais's film challenges the audience with a narrative relying on flashbacks, elliptical dissolves and voiceover narration that feels circular, repetitive and unresolved. Similarly, Plath's poem progresses as a fevered dream, with images rapidly dissolving into one another – tongues into the 'aguey tendon' of Cerberus, smoke from a 'snuffed candle' into Isadora Duncan's scarves, an orchid into a 'devilish leopard' (*CP* 231). The images cohere obscenely into a sexual fever of a woman 'flickering off, on', and in conversation with a 'darling' who watches as she transcends her fevered body, 'coming and going, flush on flush' (*CP* 232) – at the end, 'a pure acetylene / Virgin', rising to 'Paradise' as Mary does in her Assumption.

Plath borrows imagery and, possibly, intimate conversation between lovers from *Hiroshima Mon Amour*, but she boldly reinvents Bergman's *Brink of Life* for the BBC broadcast of *Three Women*. As in Bergman's film, the setting of Plath's poem is a maternity ward with three women characters. In Bergman's film, these are Cecilia, a secretary who miscarries, Stina, a wife ecstatic with her pregnancy, and Hjördis, a single young woman undecided about keeping her baby. While Bergman relies on close-ups – what Béla Balázs calls the 'silent soliloquy' of cinema[20] – to express their inner feelings, Plath provides dramatic monologues for her women. Her First Voice parallels the life-affirming joy of Stina. She is a 'great event' (*CP* 176), 'a seed about to break' and utterly 'calm' (*CP* 179) yielding herself up to the miracle of birth. She is a stereotype of the maternal instinct, not only when 'Dusk hoods [her] in blue, like a Mary' (*CP* 180), but in her wonder at the birth of a son. She asks, 'What did my heart do, with its love?' (*CP* 181) before his birth and wills him 'To love me as I love him' (*CP* 186). Bergman denies Stina such maternal triumph. Instead, her baby is stillborn and final close-ups show a woman emotionally crushed and deadened. Perhaps Plath, composing her poem in March 1962, celebrates the birth of her son Nicholas earlier, on 17 January. She records feeling 'immensely proud' of her labour, and like her First Voice, she invokes Mary and the birth of Christ: 'It felt like Christmas Eve, full of rightness & promise' (*J* 647).

Plath's Third Voice and Bergman's Hjördis share a sulky sense of injury, of life being unfair. Plath's student isn't 'ready' and has 'no reverence' for the 'face' that goes on 'shaping itself with love' in her womb (*CP* 178). Bergman's Hjördis is a puzzled observer in the maternity ward. While she gradually comes to experience her surroundings as benign, Plath's student regards the birthing room as a torture 'chamber with its instruments. / It is a place of shrieks. It is not happy' (*CP* 180). She wishes she had aborted the baby, while Hjördis finally chooses motherhood. Plath's student leaves her baby daughter behind, along with the 'clothes of a fat woman I do not know' (*CP* 184), believing this abandonment restores her former self, and the birth 'was a dream, and did not mean a thing' (*CP* 185). Plath finally burdens her student with a sense of loss. Despite her affirmation, 'It is so beautiful to have no attachments!' she is haunted with the question, 'What is it I miss?' (*CP* 186).

Plath's secretary is closest to Bergman's Cecilia in the aftermath of a miscarriage. Cecilia believes her husband never wanted a child – an *idée fixe* that convinces her he is responsible for the miscarriage and wishes to end the marriage. Plath's secretary perversely blames men, and projects her body's inadequacy on to men's 'jealousy of anything that is not flat' and a Father God and Son deciding, 'Let us flatten and launder the grossness from these souls' (*CP* 179). Both Bergman and Plath explore psychological projection in their depiction of women who feel their bodies failed them. Plath's student and secretary regard men with hostility because they are immune to the consequences of sex and blameworthy for women's ambivalent feelings about their bodies. 'All' her student sees in sex is 'dangers: doves and words, / Stars and showers of gold—conceptions, conceptions!' (*CP* 178). Plath alludes to Danae and Leda, as if the student were ravished by Zeus, a victim of male lust on 'A hot blue day [that] had budded into something' (*CP* 178). For the secretary, her body betrays her: 'I lose life after life' (*CP* 181), and subject to the menstrual cycle, 'Month after month, with its voices of failure', she can only 'create corpses' (*CP* 182). Bergman wanted 'to kill the myths about "the despair and happiness of motherhood"'.[21] Such a way of thinking helps to explain Plath's liberty to experiment with the same culturally constructed ideas about motherhood. Both artists at times support these myths and at others offer more nuanced representations of motherhood and women's psychology.

Bergman's *Through a Glass Darkly* may be the last film Plath saw.[22] His heroine is Karin, a schizophrenic recently released from a mental hospital and recuperating on a Baltic island with her husband Martin, her father David and her adolescent brother Minus. Bergman focuses on the fraught relationships between Karin and the men, but especially on her cold and distant father. David is a novelist and one of Bergman's predatory artists, who sees his daughter and her mental deterioration as potential material for a novel. Karin discovers his diary where he plans 'To make use of her'.[23] When Karin and her brother are left alone for a day on the island, they have sex in the hold of a rotting shipwreck. For both Karin and Minus, incest is shattering. Minus tells his father, 'reality burst in pieces for me',[24] and Karin relapses into hearing voices and having hallucinations.

I suspect that Plath felt a kinship with Bergman as he began exploring his own stormy relationship with his father and his anxieties over the silence of God, themes like Plath's fears of 'a heaven / Starless and fatherless' (*CP* 262). Then, too, Plath was no stranger to mental illness, and Karin's delusion of a God who will reveal himself to her resembles the daughter's longing in 'The Colossus'. When Karin is about to be sent back to a mental hospital, she hallucinates the arrival of a spider-god who assaults her: 'All the time I saw his eyes. They were cold and calm.'[25] While Karin enacts this rape, her father coldly observes her hysteria. One cannot help but draw an analogy between Karin's spider-god and the distant father and greedy artist who confesses to Minus his own 'emptiness', his 'dirty hopelessness',[26] as if this confession of existential despair will help his son's desperation. The final line of *Through a Glass Darkly* is Minus's whispered revelation, 'Daddy spoke to me!'[27] The line probably resonated with Plath, whose daughter in 'The Colossus' labours 'To dredge the silt' (*CP* 129) from the throat of her father-god, a silent ancient ruin; or the daughter in 'Daddy', who 'never could talk to you' (*CP* 223). Then there are Karin's hallucinations, which recall Ted Hughes's poetic address to Plath in 'The God', '"God is speaking through me," you told me', and his frightened response, 'That is horribly unlucky!' (*BL* 191)

Finally, there is an uncanny resemblance between Plath's speaker in 'Mystic', one of her last poems,[28] and Bergman's description of Karin: 'A God descends into a human being and settles in her.' As he becomes 'more known to her', she 'learns to love him', but finally 'he leaves her empty and burned out, without any possibility of continuing to live in this world'.[29] Plath's speaker in 'Mystic' begins, 'Once one has seen God, what is the remedy?' (*CP* 268), an unanswerable question followed with a sense of being 'used utterly' – a 'complete emptiness' like Karin's. Yet both Bergman and Plath finally seize – perhaps unconvincingly – on love's remedy.[30] Later, Bergman mocks his 'desperate attempt to present a simple philosophy: God is love and love is God',[31] while Plath's Mystic finds 'bright pieces / Of Christ in the faces of rodents' and hopefully asks,

'Is there no great love, only tenderness?' Even after being seized up, possessed by God, Plath's speaker assures, 'The heart has not stopped' (*CP* 269).

Notes

1. Yaddo is an artist's retreat in upstate New York providing room and board for artists to pursue their work.
2. This metaphor was coined by Alexandre Astruc to 'mean that the cinema will gradually break free from the tyranny of what is visual, from the image for its own sake, from the immediate and concrete demands of the narrative, to become a means of writing just as flexible and subtle as written language'. Astruc, 'The Birth of New Avant-Garde', 32.
3. Cocteau, 'Poésie de Cinéma', 158.
4. Gilbert, 'On the Beach', 126.
5. Gilbert, 'On the Beach', 124.
6. Ted Hughes, note to 'Berck-Plage', *CP* 293.
7. Gilbert, 'On the Beach', 124.
8. Gilbert, 'On the Beach', 123.
9. Gilbert, 'On the Beach', 121, author's italics.
10. Cocteau, 'Poésie de Cinéma', 155.
11. Cocteau, 'Poésie de Cinéma', 158.
12. Gilbert, 'On the Beach', 133.
13. Plath saw this film on Easter break from Cambridge in 1956.
14. This sequence was created by Max Ernst.
15. Mulvey, 'Visual Pleasure', 19.
16. Mulvey, 'Visual Pleasure', 19.
17. Mulvey, 'Visual Pleasure', 19, author's italics.
18. In *Chapters in a Mythology*, Judith Kroll notes that Plath refers to *Jules et Jim* in the notes for the novel she was writing about Ted Hughes's affair with Assia Wevill, a beautiful rival Plath may well have perceived as a *femme fatale* resembling Catherine (229, note 52).
19. Irving Howe takes issue with the admirers of 'Daddy': 'There is something monstrous, utterly disproportionate, when tangled emotions about one's father are deliberately compared with the historical fate of the European Jews; something sad, if the comparison is made spontaneously.' Howe, 'The Plath Celebration', 232–3.
20. Balázs, *Theory of the Film*, 58.
21. *Ingmar Bergman Archives*, 224.
22. In a letter to her mother dated 21 December 1962, she mentions seeing a 'marvelous new Ingmar Bergman movie' (*LH* 491) that corresponds to its screening in London.
23. Bergman, *A Film Trilogy*, 35.
24. Bergman, *A Film Trilogy*, 59.

25. Bergman, *A Film Trilogy*, 58–9.
26. Bergman, *A Film Trilogy*, 61.
27. Bergman, *A Film Trilogy*, 61.
28. It is dated 1 February 1963 in *CP* 269.
29. *Ingmar Bergman Archives*, 279.
30. In my experience, audiences for *Through a Glass Darkly* are dumbfounded by Minus's upbeat declaration at the end, as if a father's love could erase the guilt of incest.
31. *Ingmar Bergman Archives*, 279.

CHAPTER 14

Plath and Television

Nicola Presley

Sylvia Plath declared in a letter to Myron Lotz in 1953, 'I never watch television' (*LV1* 639),[1] and her sentiments are echoed in a journal entry in 1952 in which she writes 'of the gross crudities of soporific television, of loud brash convertibles and vulgar display' (*J* 112). In the early 1950s, she imagines television programming to be at the low end of culture, an opinion that was held by many social commentators at the time. Lynn Spigel writes, 'Even when critics praised television as a source of domestic unity and benevolent socialisation, they also worried about its harmful effects, particularly its dissemination of debased knowledge and its related encouragement of passive minds and bodies.'[2] However, throughout the decade, Plath recognised that television could be a possible destination for her writing. She wrote to her mother in 1953: 'TV is a rising thing ... I wonder what it would be like to write for it' (*LV1* 638) and by 1957 she pushed this idea further, writing in her journal: 'TV: try that' (*J* 296).

Plath's engagement with the medium of television has received little attention from critics, and while she certainly had an ambivalent attitude to the technology, there can be little doubt that the medium itself, as well as the reaction to it in publications like *Ladies' Home Journal*, had an effect on her writing. Critics have, however, noted the influence of particular films on Plath's work: Tracy Brain discusses the influence of the 1959 film *Hiroshima Mon Amour* on Plath's 'Fever 103°';[3] Robin Peel cites Ingmar Bergman's film *Brink of Life* as a source of inspiration for Plath's poem 'Three Women', which was written for radio and broadcast by the BBC in 1962;[4] Deryn Rees-Jones makes a convincing case that Plath was inspired by Alfred Hitchcock's 1959 film *North by Northwest* when she wrote 'The Colossus'.[5] Although film and television are treated differently by Plath, there are of course some similarities between the two media, particularly their emphasis on the importance of the visual, a trope that frequently appears in Plath's work.

For Plath, television was part of low culture with little artistic credibility. However, Jacqueline Rose rightly argues that 'Plath took pleasure in the multifarious forms of the culture, both high and low'[6] and she certainly recognised the power and influence of television on society and how the impact of television had increased the public's voyeuristic appetite. Writing about the impending execution of the Rosenbergs, Plath wonders if it would receive more attention from the masses if it were shown on television:

> There is no yelling, no horror, no great rebellion. That is the appalling thing. The execution will take place tonight; it is too bad it cannot be televised . . . so much more realistic and beneficial than the run-of-the-mill crime program (*J* 541–2).

Reading and hearing the news no longer stirred people's emotions. This is not necessarily negative; as William Y. Elliott questioned in 1956, 'will television's impact on the future of our race be felt in terms . . . of an increased stimulus to morally responsible understanding?'[7] Later, in *The Bell Jar*, Esther Greenwood tells us: 'I liked looking on at other people in crucial situations. If there was a road accident or a street fight or a baby pickled in a lab jar for me to look at, I'd stop and look so hard I never forgot it' (*BJ* 12).[8] She asserts that the act of looking commits the image to the mind, permanently imprinting it on the memory. Similarly, in 'Little Fugue', the speaker 'couldn't stop looking' (*CP* 187) and as Sally Bayley writes, 'for the speaker, looking is a compulsive act'.[9]

Tracy Brain draws attention to 'The Thin People' as a poem that dissects media representations of war and disaster: 'the outline / Of the world comes clear and fills with color' (*CP* 65). Brain argues that the poem 'remarks upon the way that this terrible material stays with those who see it, and may also refer to the increasing popularity of Technicolor film'.[10] It is also possible to apply this to the growing ubiquity of television sets, creating a continuous stream of images into the household and eventually 'into our bad dreams' (*CP* 64). The fact that the thin people 'persist in the sunlit room: the wallpaper / Frieze of cabbage-roses and cornflowers pales / Under their thin-lipped smiles' (*CP* 65) suggests an invasion into the private sphere of the home; an allusion to the presence of the television set, and its eventual omnipresence.

As George Lipsitz demonstrates, 'the number of televisions in use in the USA increased from 14000 in 1947 to one million in 1949 to four million in 1950'.[11] By 1959, Martin Halliwell states, 'nearly ninety percent of homes had a TV set [. . .] as a cultural artefact it was virtually impossible to avoid'.[12] John Keats's *The Crack in the Picture Window*, published in 1956, is a blistering and humorous polemic against the development of the suburbs and the false nirvana that it promised for young couples and families. One of Keats's criticisms of the suburbs were the huge windows that provided an illusion of space and openness:

> Through their picture window, a vast empty eye with bits of paper stuck in its corners, they could see their view – a house like theirs across a muddy street, its vacant picture eye staring into theirs.[13]

As Keats shows, the picture window exposed the suburban family and reduced them to what Spigel calls 'the goldfish bowl effect' causing a 'sense of claustrophobia' and bringing 'an enormous amount of pressure to conform to the group'.[14] Thus we begin to see that families – and particularly housewives who were charged with running the home – felt the pressure of the omnipresent neighbour-spy. In addition to this invasion of privacy, a new threat to spatial privacy was, in Keats's words, 'perched on a table was a tiny box with a picture window'.[15]

Complicating the threat to privacy from the suburbs and television was the fear and paranoia created by the Cold War. To counter the predominant anxiety about the threat of Russia and its nuclear programme the US government introduced a number of initiatives related to the privacy of the individual and the nation's duty to free the United States from the threat of communism, which can be summarised as policies of 'containment'. Deborah Nelson's exemplary book on the issue of privacy in the Cold War United States discusses the way in which 'television and suburbia were both stirring new and very public debates over privacy'.[16]

As an example of this, Plath's poem 'Lesbos' is, on the surface, about a nosy, annoying woman who seems to be a gossiping neighbour. But the threat to privacy evidenced in the poem suggests something more sinister:

> Viciousness in the kitchen!
> The potatoes hiss.
> It is all Hollywood, windowless,
> The fluorescent light wincing on and off like a
> terrible migraine (*CP* 227).

These opening lines create a feeling of claustrophobia in the kitchen with no natural light or place to look through to the outside world. The repeated 's' sounds of 'viciousness', 'potatoes hiss' and 'windowless' evoke a whispering sound that adds to this claustrophobia and suggests a betrayal, perhaps by the speaker's neighbour who enters in the second stanza. This sibilance is also reminiscent of the sound of a television broadcasting static white noise. This electrical noise is created due to poor signal reception, disrupting the programming. This same sound in the poem alerts the speaker that her own home is also disrupted by an unwelcome presence. The flickering light suggests a kind of torture as if the speaker is waiting to be questioned and is compelled to answer, and, in addition, implies the electrical flickering of a television screen.

'Lady Lazarus' with its 'peanut-crunching crowd' is perhaps Plath's most famous poem on spectacle and spectators. The line 'What a million fila-ments' alludes to the electrical elements that produce a picture on a television or cinema screen, broadcasting the speaker's 'big strip tease' (*CP* 245). This electric motif continues throughout the poem: 'And there is a charge, a very large charge / For a word or a touch' (*CP* 246). In 'The Detective', the speaker asks, 'Was she at the window, listening?' (*CP* 208). 'Eavesdropper' features a nosy neighbour whose eyes are 'flicking over my property, / Levering letter flaps' (*CP* 261). In 'Insomniac', the male char-acter lives 'without privacy' (*CP* 163). Marsha Bryant reminds us that in 'A Birthday Present', 'the speaker senses a spectral presence'[17] while cooking: 'I feel it looking' (*CP* 206). In 'The Courage of Shutting-Up', the speaker demonstrates a fear of surveillance: 'But how about the eyes, the eyes, the eyes? / Mirrors can kill and talk, they are terrible rooms / In which a torture goes on one can only watch' (*CP* 210). Here, Plath emphasises the passivity of the audience and the inability to alter events that are viewed, and links back to the presence of the television set in 'The Thin People'.

Plath uses a television set in her 1956 story 'The Wishing Box' and in doing so reflects contemporary concerns about television's 'utopian promise of increased social life and the dystopian outcome of domestic seclusion'.[18] The protagonist, Agnes, is a frustrated and bored house-wife who feels isolated and uninspired in her current situation. Clues are provided that she is an educated woman; for example, she has probably read, and at least owns, a copy of Sigmund Freud's *The Interpretation of Dreams*. However, she does not seem to be able to exercise her intelligence as a housewife. It seems likely that Plath is responding to contemporary cultural attitudes about women; the pre-valent idea here is that women go to college to make themselves marriageable, rather than to pursue a career.

When Plath graduated from Smith College in 1955, Adlai Stevenson gave what has become an oft-quoted speech in which he advised the female graduates to use their intelligence to be good wives and mothers and not to feel frustrated that they now write 'laundry lists' rather than poetry:

The assignment for you, as wives and mothers, has great advantages. In the first place, it is homework – you can do it in the living room with a baby on your lap, or in the kitchen with a can opener in your hands. If you're really clever, maybe you'll even practice your saving arts on the unsuspecting man while he's watching television.[19]

Agnes's husband Harold describes his extremely vivid dreams to Agnes, who is at first fascinated but becomes increasingly bitter and envious of his imagination. Agnes's jealousy of Harold's dreams is an allegory for her envy for his life outside the home. Not only can Agnes not share his dreams, she is also excluded from his professional life: Agnes begins attending movie theatres in a bid to 'exorcise the dead silence in her head' and eventually persuades Harold, 'by dint of much cajolery' (*JP* 54),[20] to buy a television set so she can escape from her numbness without leaving the house.

'The Wishing Box' was written in October 1956. In the previous year, NBC television ran a series of advertisements aimed squarely at housewives. In one, published in *Ladies' Home Journal* in February 1955, the tagline reads 'Your friends from breakfast to bedtime' with pictures of television hosts Dave Garroway, Arlene Francis and Steve Allen.[21] The text encourages the viewers – who must be housewives if they are available to watch television all day – to wake up with, eat lunch with and spend the evening with NBC. Deliberately playing on the fact that housewives were often isolated during the day, the ad refers to the presenters as 'friends – exciting friends' coming 'into your home'. A similar ad had appeared for NBC radio the previous month, entitled 'Afternoon Social' in which the housewife is pictured darning socks, while hosting a tea party with the wireless as the only guest. The text begins rhetorically with 'A cup of coffee and a chat with friends. What could be more satisfying?' The difference between the two adverts is that the housewife is clearly expected to continue her housework while the radio plays but 'with these folks around the house, your chores get done almost without your knowing it'.[22] The mobility of the radio is also highlighted as a benefit as the text encourages the housewife to take the radio with her in whichever room she is working in. The television set is immobile (at least until the introduction of portable TVs) but the TV ad seeks to reduce this fear of passivity by promising that the lunchtime show *Home* 'helps around the house', featuring experts on 'things vital to America's women – fashions, work-savers, beauty hints, shopping news'.[23] However, the TV ad cannot escape from the fact that watching television is an activity that holds the attention of the viewer in a passive state and is a distraction; as Todd Gitlin puts it, television is an 'entertainer, painkiller [and] companion to the lonely'.[24]

The loneliness and isolation suffered by some housewives was the subject of a fascinating article in *Ladies' Home Journal* (February 1955), featuring a forum of housewives, journalists and three experts on family matters. Entitled 'The Plight of the Young Mother' the article discusses issues such as 'is our society asking too much of the young mother' and 'is it possible for her to give her children the best care when she must work as long as 100 hours a week – much more than is expected of people in business and industry – with no relief?'[25] Dr Popenoe, one of the family experts, summarises the main problem for housewives:

> The common complaint of homemakers is not that the work is too hard but that is too confining, too lonesome. As these mothers have pointed out, they want to be with adults, hear adult rather than merely child talk, have more contact with other human beings.[26]

The responses from the housewives suggests that they were overworked, often isolated and in some cases, had lost their individual identities.

In 'The Wishing Box', Agnes's jealousy is marked by her own infrequent nightmarish dreams that she cannot even remember clearly in the morning. Her dreams feature 'dark, glowering landscapes peopled with ominous unrecognizable figures' (*JP* 49) in contrast to Harold's dreams of literary figures and vivid backgrounds. She tries to increase her ability to dream by reading – 'seized by a kind of ravenous hysteria' – everything she can, from novels to magazines to the 'instructions on soap-flake boxes' (*JP* 53). The words stubbornly refuse to convert to pictures in her imagination and she is forced to resort to television to 'lull her into a rhythmic trance' (*JP* 54). Plath does not specify the programmes and that is probably deliberate. It does not matter what Agnes watches, as she only uses it in an attempt to occupy her mind. The television only has to be 'on' to create an effect. Rolf B. Meyersohn wrote in 1956 that 'viewers seem to be entertained by the glow and the flow, regardless of whether it presents a commercial, a second-rate comic or an ancient western. Television succeeds "because it is there".'[27]

Plath's use of colour throughout 'The Wishing Box' recalls Esther's ambivalent attitude towards Technicolor films in *The Bell Jar* and further separates Agnes's visits to the cinema (where films could be shown in colour) from the black-and-white programmes displayed on the television at home. She recalls dreams from her childhood, featuring 'magic glass-blades [. . .] one red, one blue, one silver'; wearing 'red-and-white striped mittens' and catching 'turquoise-blue sulfa gum' (*JP* 50). The television gives her the ability to include colour in her daytime imagination, 'with a certain malicious satisfaction' (*JP* 54), where the cinema had not, as if the lack of colour on screen forces the mind to create it.

The combination of television and sherry has given her a 'visionary' release in her waking state but ironically do not help the dreams as even the ability to fall asleep eventually eludes her. Her realisation that there is no escape from her mind's 'perfect vacancy' leads to an overdose. Domesticity – with its isolation and numbness – is the cause of Agnes's suicide. In death, she is somewhat victorious. 'Her tranquil features were set in a slight, secret smile of triumph, as if, in some far country unattainable to mortal men, she were, at last, waltzing with the dark, red-caped prince of her early dreams' (*JP* 55). Agnes is finally free and able to dream. The end of the story seems to prefigure one of Plath's last poems, 'Edge', in which 'The woman is perfected. / Her dead / Body wears the smile of accomplishment' (*CP* 272).

During this period, mothers (and to a lesser extent, fathers) were bombarded with parenting guides in magazines and in book form on appropriate media and activities for children. In 1954, although articles on the subject appeared as early as 1948, psychiatrist Fredric Wertham published *Seduction of the Innocent*, which warned of the threat comic books posed to the developing minds of children, writing that 'the visual immediacy of comics left children vulnerable to their unsavoury content'.[28] Wertham's fear of comic books because of their visual impact can only have been furthered by the popularity of television and its ability to actualise fictional and real events. Voicing just such a fear, Margaret Mead later wrote of her worry for children growing up where 'radio and television and comics and the threat of the atomic bomb are every day realities'.[29] As television viewing became more widespread, there were growing anxieties about its power to influence children, exposing them to inappropriate programming and adult themes. A cartoon in a 1950 issue of *Ladies' Home Journal* suggests a typical scenario. The magazine showed a little slumped girl on an ottoman, suffering from a new disease called 'telebugeye'. According to the caption, the child was a 'pale, weak, stupid looking creature' who grew bugeyed from sitting and watching television for too long.[30]

Plath would have been influenced by opinions such as these, and no doubt felt watching television was an inappropriate activity for her children. In a letter to her mother in 1951, she writes that she and Marcia Brown talked about 'how horrible a fate television is for children' (*LV1* 273). Certainly, Ted Hughes was critical of its effects on children. In 1957 while living in the United States, he wrote a letter to his brother in England regarding his children: 'How is your nursery for books? Let the two amuse themselves – don't kill them with TV. It's terrifying to see this American race turning into gaping automata – audiences, consumers, "Show me, amuse me, feed me"' (*LTH* 114). However, just as Plath became aware of the power of television as a medium she also discovered that television programmes were a source of fascination for children. In a journal fragment in 1962 she describes taking her daughter Frieda to the house of a neighbour where the 'TV set [is] blaring. Frieda cried, startled. Then fascinated. A closeup of a dumptruck emptying rocks. "Ohhh"' (*J* 667).

Plath's awareness of the power that televisual images have on children is reflected in some of her poems in which the speakers discuss the experiences they wish their children to have. For example, in 'For a Fatherless Son', the speaker describes 'an absence' like 'color gone' (*CP* 205), and in 'Balloons', there is much delight in the 'globes of thin air, red, green' (*CP* 271). This theme is most striking in 'Child'. The opening of the poem 'Your clear eye is the one absolutely beautiful thing. / I want to fill it with color and ducks' (*CP* 265) emphasises the speaker's desire to introduce the child to the world. The child's eye is 'clear', thus unburdened with impurities and pollution of the world. Clearness also suggests an emptiness that the speaker needs to 'fill'. As the 'one absolutely beautiful thing' it signifies uniqueness and elucidates the individual importance of the child. The speaker wishes to provide the child with a world of colour and this is likely to be a response to the black-and-white world of television. The majority of programming in the 1950s and early 1960s was in black-and-white and colour TV sets were very rare. A lack of colour in the world suggests a grey and dull existence and as the speaker in Plath's 'The Thin People' indicates, 'gray people' are 'meagre of dimension' (*CP* 64). Thus, the grey, microscopic world of television cannot match up to the tangible world full of beautiful colour and 'ducks'.

In the penultimate stanza, the eye is a 'little stalk without wrinkle' (*CP* 265) which is clearly a reference to the youth of the child but the unusual description of the eye as a stalk accentuates the significance of sight and visual stimulus. A stalk is the support structure for either a plant or a human organ and therefore the metaphor of eye as stalk means that the eye will sustain the child, providing it with the necessary support for the child to thrive. Therefore, the speaker needs to carefully control the images that the child sees in order to ensure a healthy and creative development. These images should be 'grand and classical', an allusion to 'high' culture; not the perceived 'low' of the television.

The poem ends with the antithesis of these 'grand' visuals. The 'troublous wringing of hands' (*CP* 265) indicates some kind of human worry or suffering and the 'dark ceiling' suggests a closing-in of blackness and claustrophobia. There is no star, which represents not only a lack of light but also potentially the death of the world. These are the images that the speaker wishes to protect the child from, but this ending suggests a sense of inevitability and that this task is an impossibility. Referring back to Mead's concern that children would be exposed to the everyday reality of the threat of the bomb through cultural mediums as well as to other horrors in the world, this poem succinctly reflects the fear of a child's loss of innocence. It also supports a contemporary dread that the influence of the television would overpower the authority of the parent who wishes to control what their children saw.

The development of television in the 1950s is an important context to the work of Sylvia Plath. Despite her ambivalence to the medium, her prose and poetry demonstrate awareness of, and an engagement with, contemporaneous debates about privacy, suburbia and children as related to television. There is further research to be developed here; for reasons of space I have had to omit the fascinating 'Hospital Notes' from 1958, which show the relationship between television and mental illness and how Plath used these in her writing. Further questions of television and gender, and television and confessional poetry, are also crucial in examining Plath's work, and open up new avenues of exploration.

Notes

1. All citations from *The Letters of Sylvia Plath: Volume 1 (1940–1956)* refer to the UK edition published by Faber and Faber.
2. Spigel, *Welcome to the Dreamhouse*, 193.
3. Brain, *The Other Sylvia Plath*, 118.
4. Peel, *Writing Back*, 29.
5. Rees-Jones, *Consorting with Angels*, 105.
6. Rose, *The Haunting of Sylvia Plath*, 23.
7. Elliott, 'Introduction', 3.
8. All citations from *The Bell Jar* within this chapter refer to the 1996 Faber and Faber edition.
9. Bayley, 'Sublime Encounters in Sylvia Plath's Tree Poems', 101–2.
10. Brain, *The Other Sylvia Plath*, 37.
11. Lipstiz, *Class and Culture in Cold War America*, 185.
12. Halliwell, *American Culture in the 1950s*, 147.
13. Keats, *The Crack in the Picture Window*, 28.

14. Spigel, *Welcome to the Dreamhouse*, 128.
15. Keats, *The Crack in the Picture Window*, 70.
16. Nelson, *Pursuing Privacy*, 167.
17. Bryant, 'Everyday Ariel', 132.
18. Spigel, *Welcome to the Dreamhouse*, 49.
19. Stevenson, quoted in Susan Van Dyne, *Revising Life*, 133.
20. All citations from *Johnny Panic* refer to the UK edition published by Faber and Faber.
21. *Ladies' Home Journal* (*LHJ*), February 1955, 95.
22. *LHJ*, January 1955, 97.
23. *LHJ*, February 1955, 95.
24. Gitlin, *Watching Television*, 3.
25. *LHJ*, February 1965, 110.
26. *LHJ*, February 1965, 110.
27. Meyershon, 'Social Research in Television', 347.
28. Wertham, *Seduction of the Innocent*, 377.
29. Mead, quoted in Spigel, *Make Room for TV*, 385.
30. Spigel, *Welcome to the Dreamhouse*, 193.

CHAPTER 15

Plath and Art

Jane Hedley

When a poem engages with a work of visual art, whether to describe, address or 'envoice' it, we call that poem 'ekphrastic' – from a Greek verb that means 'speak out' or 'tell in full'. At a minimum, poetic ekphrasis is descriptive and interpretive: the poem explains what the visual work is about and may engage its formal properties, as well. The work of visual art cannot speak; the poem speaks on its behalf. W. H. Auden's 'Musée des Beaux Arts', an often-cited example of poetic ekphrasis, explains what Pieter Brueghel is implicitly 'telling' us about suffering in having depicted a scene from classical mythology in a particular way. Keats's 'Ode on a Grecian Urn', even while professing to have fallen under the spell of the urn's provocative silence, famously concludes with its supposed message for humankind – 'to whom thou *sayest*, / "Beauty is truth, truth beauty"' (my emphasis). Theorists including W. J. T. Mitchell, Wendy Steiner and James Heffernan have suggested that ekphrastic poems are implicitly rivalrous; the poet envies, or feels threatened by, the painting's wordless immediacy.[1] Others have suggested instead that the poet seeks to befriend the painting, striving for a 'perfect receptiveness' to what it is 'trying to say'.[2] In a book-length study aptly entitled *Museum of Words*, James Heffernan points out that the ekphrastic lyric 'springs from the museum', where paintings and other works of visual art are presented as 'self-sufficient icon[s]', each 'set [. . .] off for contemplation or veneration in its own framed and labelled space'.[3] In the United States ekphrastic poetry could also be said to spring from the undergraduate classroom – the art history classroom, where 'art in the dark' courses deliver up their own museum of visual icons, and the creative writing classroom, where ekphrasis has been a standard exercise for apprentice poets since the 1950s.

Sylvia Plath's considerable knowledge of modern art can be traced not only to art history courses – especially the one she audited with Priscilla Van der Poel in 1958, while teaching for a year in the English department at Smith College – but also to the study she had made of painting and drawing as a fledgling artist, from an early age. In *Eye Rhymes: Sylvia Plath's Art of the Visual*, Kathleen Connors and Sally Bayley have reproduced, from the Plath collections at Smith and at Indiana University, a number of the paintings and drawings Plath made for private teachers and in studio art classes. Essays by Connors, Bayley and others present this material from many angles, including the poet's commentary on her own creative process. She had a strongly visual imagination; Frieda Hughes's introduction to a book of her drawings quotes her saying, in an interview, 'my inspiration is paintings and not music when I go to some other art form . . .' (*SPD* viii). This is borne out by a number of poems, both early and late in her all-too-brief career, whose subject is poetic inspiration and/or the creative process and whose starting-point is either a work of visual art – as in 'Conversation Among the Ruins' (1956), 'Yadwigha, on a Red Couch Among Lilies' (1958) and 'Perseus: The Triumph of Wit Over Suffering' (also 1958) – or a scene from nature that is treated quasi-ekphrastically, as if it were a painting: 'Black Rook in Rainy Weather' (1956), 'Poppies in October' (1962), 'Man in Black' (1959).

Even after Plath decided to become a writer rather than a commercial artist, it is clear that, as her daughter puts it, visual art continued to be 'an important element of my mother's life' (*SPD* vi). In the journals she kept during her Fulbright year at Cambridge she often describes her surroundings with a self-consciously painterly eye: 'Noticed rooks squatting black in snow-white fen, gray skies, black trees, mallard-green water. Impressed' (*J* 203). On a train journey through France she invokes the visual vocabularies of particular modern painters: the stars against the night sky, she writes, are 'growing to look like Van Gogh stars. And quarries, steep like a cubist painting in blocks . . .' (*J 548*). Ted Hughes recalls, in the *Birthday Letters* poem 'Your Paris', that when they visited Paris on their honeymoon the city that was for him still deeply scarred by the Nazi Occupation was for her the city of the French Impressionists, of Picasso and Toulouse-Lautrec: naïvely oblivious of its recent political history, she '[c]alled [him] Aristide Bruant and wanted / To draw *les toits*' (*BL* 36).

Plath and Hughes also spent part of their honeymoon in the small Spanish town of Benidorm, where Plath made a series of pencil-drawings that were subsequently published in a travel piece for the *Christian Science Monitor*. 'I feel', said Plath to her mother about these drawings in a letter cited by Kathleen Connors, 'I'm developing a kind of primitive style of my own which I am very fond of. Wait till you see.'[4] In the context of modernist painting, 'primitive' is a capacious (albeit problematic) term for works that draw inspiration from the art of non-Western, pre-industrial

societies and from self-taught 'outsider' artists whose work is admired for
its supposed honesty and spontaneity. Sally Bayley reports that Plath's
college art notebooks, both from courses and museum trips, 'are filled with
commentary on Rousseau's jungle scapes, Picasso's African figures and
masks, the colors and forms of Van Gogh and Matisse'.[5] Looking at slides
of African masks during one of Van der Poel's lectures in 1958, she is
inspired to project her own future as an artist under the sign of 'The
Earthenware Head'. An artist friend at Cambridge had made a terracotta
model of her head whose 'spite-set ape of her look' she found off-putting,
and wanted to be rid of; two years later, however, under the influence of
Van der Poel's course, the earthenware head becomes a 'terrible and holy
token of identity'. 'Rough, crude, powerful and radiant', it will 'release'
her, she hopes, into 'cadences and rhythms of speech to set world-fabrics in
motion' (*J* 332–3).

A month later, another journal entry proclaims with great excitement
that after having been invited to submit an ekphrastic poem to the journal
Art News she has written eight new poems in as many days: 'deep visions of
queer and terrible and exotic worlds' (*J* 358). The poems she lists as having
come to her in this way include four ekphrases of drawings and paintings
by Paul Klee, two of paintings by Henri Rousseau, and two by Giorgio de
Chirico. 'I've discovered my deepest source of inspiration, which is art', she
writes to her mother: 'the art of primitives like Henri Rousseau, Gauguin,
Paul Klee, and de Chirico'.[6] Her repeated references to world-making in
this context are significant: whereas mirroring, a term she might have used
but didn't, would connote a realistic depiction of 'things as they are',
world-making implies the creation of an alternative reality that is sufficient
unto itself, 'perceived in a final atmosphere', as Wallace Stevens puts it in
his quasi-ekphrastic manifesto for modernism, 'The Man with the Blue
Guitar'.[7]

The deeply three-dimensional 'worlds' of de Chirico's early, 'metaphysical' phase had an especially powerful appeal for Plath, as Christina
Britzolakis explains in her essay for the *Eye Rhymes* volume. Plath had
found her way to de Chirico before taking Van der Poel's course; her
Collected Poems begins in 1956 with an off-rhyme sonnet inspired by
a painting of his. In that poem we find Plath reading herself into the
painting, using its *mise-en-scène* to depict her explosive first meeting with
Hughes as an artistic and psychological crisis: amidst the ruins of
a 'bankrupt estate', the poem's speaker remains outwardly 'composed'
but is inwardly wondering 'What ceremony of words can patch the
havoc' (*CP* 21). Whereas other ekphrastic poems of hers stand back from

the work in question, addressing or describing it from a safe distance ('How this tart fable instructs / And mocks', begins her ekphrasis of a drawing by Paul Klee [*CP* 81]), de Chirico gave her access to a space she could move into and inhabit – a first-person space, albeit a space of self-estrangement. In 'The Disquieting Muses', arguably the best and certainly the best known of the eight ekphrastic poems she produced so close together in the spring of 1958, a daughter confides to her mother that 'the kingdom you bore me to' is the landscape of de Chirico's painting of the same name, where a setting sun that 'never brightens or goes down' casts long, sinister shadows and a trio of surreal godmothers 'stand their vigil in gowns of stone' (*CP* 76). In 'The Colossus', written a year later, a daughter speaks of having spent a lifetime trying to mend the enormous broken statue of her father, a hopeless task that holds her prisoner while '[a] blue sky out of the Oresteia / Arches above us' (*CP* 129). 'The Colossus' is not based on any particular painting, but strongly recalls de Chirico's 'poetic of ruins and fragments' and the 'silent, evacuated' spaces of his 'metaphysical' period.[8] In 'Edge', one of the last poems Plath wrote before taking her own life in 1963, the woman who lies atop her own sarcophagus, 'perfected' in death, is reminiscent of de Chirico's painting of a recumbent statue of 'Ariadne, deserted, asleep'. Plath had written about this haunting sculptural image in her journal in 1958 (*CP* 272; *J* 355). In these paintings of de Chirico's, time is suspended, not only in the usual sense that the visual medium stills the life depicted in it but also insofar as their 'kingdom' is both a contemporary space and a space of mythic grandeur, 'peopled' for the most part by statues and ruins. The sense of arrested life becomes even eerier in the poems that inhabit these spaces, whose speakers are seemingly bereft of the capacity to experience time as movement or change.

In an important article published in 1988, Leonard Scigaj argues that Plath had an equally strong affinity for the 'comic expressionism' of Paul Klee. Her suicide notwithstanding, Scigaj finds that Plath shared Klee's 'optimism toward human survival powers', a stance he finds clearly adumbrated in another of the ekphrastic poems she produced in the spring of 1958: 'Perseus, the Triumph of Wit over Suffering'. As Plath had learned from Klee's own commentary on this etching of Perseus with the head of Medusa, he had sought to transform the classical hero's warrior-prowess into a feat of psychic or spiritual resiliency. On the face of Klee's 'new' Perseus, whose head and shoulders only are depicted in three-quarters profile, 'a laugh is mingled with the deep lines of pain and finally gains the upper hand'.[9] Medusa's head, suspended alongside Perseus' in two-dimensional profile, has been divested of its snaky locks, except for a single snake-braid that hisses impotently downward into the empty space beneath. According to Plath's ekphrastic tribute, which astutely captures the implicit message of the etching, Perseus' triumph resides in his capacity to 'outface the gorgon-grimace / Of human agony' with a 'fun-house mirror that turns the tragic muse / To the beheaded head of a sullen doll' (*CP* 83). As I have argued elsewhere,[10] we would do well to read Plath's later 'confessional' poems in the light of this poem's artistic credo; when we do, poems like 'Daddy', 'Lady Lazarus' and 'Medusa' appear both wittier and stagier than they were taken to be by their earliest readers. The suffering on display in these poems may well be Plath's, and as such real enough, but the poems' performance of it is comically excessive and outlandish. These are poems Plath rightly predicted would 'make my name' (*LH* 468), but that she called 'light verse'[11] when she read them aloud to the critic Al Alvarez.

What did it really mean to say, as Plath said of herself, that her 'deepest source of inspiration' was the work of modern artists like de Chirico and Klee? Scigaj goes to meet this question by pointing out that her formation as a poet under the aegis of the New Criticism had made her especially receptive to the formalist aesthetic of modern art. 'Plath's New Critical art is in some respects the exact equivalent', he suggests, of Klee's 'expressionist formalism': 'both add the illusion of a third dimension', not – or not only – by building it into the depicted landscape (as de Chirico did), but 'by dramatizing the contradictory nature of experience, at the same time that these contradictions are reconciled and transmuted into new unities by the imagination'.[12] In a telling analogy between poems and paintings that Scigaj cites from a 1961 radio broadcast, Plath explains that 'just as a painting can recreate, by illusion, the dimension it loses by being confined to canvas, so a poem, by its own system of illusions, can set up a rich and apparently living world within its particular limits'.[13] The aesthetic properties that the poem and the painting crucially share, from the perspective of this analogy between them, are complexity, boundedness and self-sufficiency. They are in the business not of mirroring but of worldmaking, and their worlds come alive by incorporating tensions and contradictions, irony and paradox. A poem, insisted Cleanth Brooks, one of the foremost exponents of what came to be called the New Criticism, is not a paraphrasable statement but an intricate verbal structure whose complexities of both sound and sense a successful reading will unpack and reckon with, as he himself does in a series of close readings of single poems in *The Well Wrought Urn*. Plath had been given *Understanding Poetry*, a textbook-cum-anthology edited by Brooks and Robert Penn Warren that codified and taught this approach to literary study, as a book prize in the ninth grade. During her undergraduate years at Smith she also owned a copy of *The Well Wrought Urn* and her underlinings suggest, according to Scigaj, that she read it from cover to cover. 'The truth which the poet utters can be approached only in terms of paradox',[14] Brooks notoriously insisted, and many of Plath's poems are begotten by just such an understanding of the poet's task and challenge.

A good example is her 1959 poem 'Medallion', whose quasi-ekphrastic description of a dead snake bristles with metaphors that insist on its deadness while at the same time conferring upon it an eerie posthumous aliveness. Encountered in the grounds at Yaddo, where she and Hughes were doing a residency, the dead snake's 'unhinged' jaw makes it appear to be grinning at her, its laugh 'perfected' by the 'flung brick' that must have killed it earlier that day. Maggots are at work inside its belly; the snake thus appears still to be actively engaged in predation and digestion. This is emphatically not the anthropomorphised talking snake of a biblical encounter that also took place in a garden: in 'Medallion' the snake's aliveness is a function of its deadness, which the poem does not shrink from taking on board. Death and life chase each other in a circle in its densely metaphoric descriptions; art and nature become inextricable as the poetess studies the snake with a *sang-froid* that matches its own. 'Knifelike, he was chaste enough, / Pure death's-metal' (*CP* 125): subtly personified throughout the poem, the snake becomes capable of savouring his own transformation into a medallion, a dead but also living work of art.

Plath's 'formation as a poet coincides', affirms Christina Britzolakis, 'with the point at which modernism began, in the 1950s, to be canonized and institutionalized within the American academy'.[15] The modernist poet who taught her the most about how to approach a poet's task with a painterly eye was probably Wallace Stevens, a connoisseur of modern art who also, according to Bonnie Costello, had a lifelong habit of 'imagining the world in aesthetic and compositional terms'.[16] For Stevens, says Costello, 'painting seemed to typify the power of the imagination and its role in an often desolate world'. Although he 'almost never describes a work of art or responds to it directly', he 'keeps an association with painting constantly before the reader' of his poems.[17] Thus, for example, 'Thirteen Ways of Looking at a Blackbird' delivers 'a serial equivalent to cubism's multiple perspectives'; 'Anecdote of the Jar', which Costello reads as a modernist response to Keats's 'Ode on a Grecian Urn', may well have been inspired by the 'ready-mades' of Marcel Duchamp.[18] As a college student Plath owned a copy of Stevens's *Collected Poems* in which, as Scigaj attests, she 'underlined almost every passage concerning the imagination'.[19] Stevens's influence is most apparent in poems of hers that celebrate the imagination's power to construct 'a rich and apparently living world' that both is and is not the world of things as they are.

'Man in Black' is such a poem, and so is 'Poppies in October'. In the former, as in Stevens's 'Idea of Order at Key West', a turbulent seascape is mastered, its chaotic energies contained and organised, by an anonymous human figure, seen from a distance, who becomes the scene's 'fixed vortex' (*CP* 120) as he strides out to the edge of the ocean and stands there, his commanding stillness thrown into sharp relief against the plunging grey tumult of water and wind. Ted Hughes recognised himself in this black-clad figure and was unnerved by the poem, which he read as having proleptically cast him as a father-substitute in the family romance that would culminate in Plath's suicide ('Black Coat', *BL* 102–3). The poem can accommodate, but it does not invite, that kind of reading: its manifest subject is abstract and self-reflexive, a demonstration of the imagination's power to 'take dominion everywhere' as per Stevens's 'Anecdote of the Jar'.[20] The poet eschews 'I'-reference entirely, yet clearly she is the only begetter of her poem's powerful description, which unspools as a single sentence through seven stanzas of *terza rima*. The man in black has his entrance delayed until the last line of the fifth stanza, where he is summoned onto the scene by a poetic apostrophe that enlists her visionary powers and asserts her prerogative of world-making (*CP* 119–20).

In 'Poppies in October' the poet's own visionary powers are again her subject: on an overcast, smoggy London morning the poppies' out-of-season brilliance fills her with pain and wonder. A streetful of faceless, dull-eyed bureaucrats making their way to work is impervious to a vision that comes to her – and her alone – with violent urgency. The poppies' astonishing redness connects them to a mysterious woman in an ambulance whose open heart '*blooms* through her coat' (my emphasis), a metaphorical exchange of properties that raises the stakes of the poet's astonishment. She has been chosen to receive this vision, and yet it renders her baffled and helpless: 'what am I', she cries, at the poem's anguished climax, that these reddest of flowers should have sought her out to waylay her with their wounded and wounding display.

This poem's ultimate triumph, says one of its best readers, Helen Vendler, is to have 'succeed[ed] in containing life and death within a single steadfast gaze'. The poppies 'create around themselves a paradoxical environment, composed of a forest of frost that breathes death, and a dawn of cornflowers that breathes renewal'.[21] And whereas a disturbing quasi-humanity is predicated of the poppies – by the end of the poem they have mouths of their own with which to 'cry open' – their human interlocutors, including the poet herself, have had *their* personhood grotesquely diminished. From a New Critical perspective this poem thus speaks the language of paradox. At the same time it satisfies another famous New Critical dictate, in that it gives its readers no incentive whatever to commit the intentional fallacy. We are not going to want to reply, to its speaker's anguished question: 'why you, of course, are Sylvia Plath, living on your own in London with two small children, and you are clearly at the end of your tether'. That may indeed be *who* she is, but *what* she is is a poet. As such, she has been gifted with an aesthetic experience of such transcendent intensity that it has estranged her not only from other people but in some measure, as Vendler also suggests, from her own humanity.

Classical rhetoricians did not limit the scope of ekphrasis to 'the poetic description of a pictorial or sculptural work of art', as Ruth Webb pointed out in 1988 in an essay on ekphrasis for the journal *Word and Image*; descriptions of persons, places and events might also be termed *ekphraseis* if they appealed strongly to 'the mind's eye'.[22] Modern critics have narrowed the term's use, but Fan Jinghua suggests, in his essay for the *Eye Rhymes* volume, that this original, broader understanding of ekphrasis is especially helpful where Plath is concerned. Her later poems, says Fan, 'demonstrate an internalized principle of visual thinking, . . . freed from any dependence on specific visual art techniques or artworks'.[23] Late poems like 'Edge' and 'Poppies in October' bear this out, and they also demonstrate Plath's internalisation of a New Critical aesthetic. A poem's boundedness, its self-sufficiency, its complexity and its hospitality towards paradox are the hallmarks of that aesthetic, which, notwithstanding the explicitly personal subject matter of many of Plath's later poems, sustained her right through to the end of her career.

Notes

1. See Hedley, *In the Frame*, 22–4.
2. See for example Kirchwey, 'Women Look at Women', 93.
3. Heffernan, *Museum of Words*, 138–9.
4. Cited in Connors, 'Living Color', 101.
5. Bayley, 'Sylvia Plath and the Costume of Femininity', 204.
6. Cited in Scigaj, 'The Painterly Plath', 235.
7. Stevens, *The Collected Poems*, 168. This poem was strongly influenced by Picasso, although Stevens insisted that he had no particular painting of Picasso's in mind. And indeed in 'The Old Guitarist' the painting from

Picasso's 'blue period' that is likeliest to have inspired 'The Man with the Blue Guitar', the only thing in the painting that is *not* blue is the guitar itself.

 8. Britzolakis, 'Conversation Amongst the Ruins', 169.
 9. Cited in Scigaj, 'The Painterly Plath', 243.
10. See Hedley, 'Plath's Ekphrastic Impulse', 97–8.
11. Alvarez, 'Prologue', 31.
12. Scigaj, 'The Painterly Plath', 241.
13. Cited in Scigaj, 'The Painterly Plath', 227.
14. Brooks, *The Well Wrought Urn*, 3.
15. Britzolakis, 'Conversation amongst the Ruins', 169.
16. Costello, 'Effects of an Analogy', 165.
17. Costello, 'Effects of an Analogy', 169.
18. Costello, 'Effects of an Analogy', 168–9.
19. Scigaj, 'The Painterly Plath', 230.
20. Stevens, *The Collected Poems*, 76.
21. Vendler, *Last Looks, Last Books*, 68.
22. Webb, '*Ekphrasis* Ancient and Modern', 11–12.
23. Jinghua, 'Plath's Visual Poetics', 221.

PART IV

Sexual and Gender Contexts

CHAPTER 16

'Minor Scandal': Lesbian Writing Contexts for The Bell Jar

Beatrice Hitchman

A few blocks from *Mademoiselle* HQ, where Esther Greenwood is feeling unsure of herself, a group of women know exactly what they are doing in New York. The summer of 1953 was queer and sultry in more ways than one, and the lesbian bars of Greenwich Village were doing a roaring trade. Since the 1930s, the West Village had been a centre for lesbian bar culture, and a haven for women seeking to understand their sexuality. Mona's, on West 3rd St, had been founded in the early 1940s, and remained highly popular, but by the 1950s the Sea Colony nightclub on 52nd and 8th was the 'pre-eminent lesbian hangout',[1] attracting a dancing crowd on Wednesday and Saturday nights. For Joan Nestle, the bars provided a welcome escape from day-to-day heterosexist living; of the 1950s, she writes: 'we needed the Lesbian air of the Sea Colony to breathe the life we could not anywhere else'.[2] Two blocks south, the Bagatelle at 86 University Place attracted an African-American crowd. A young Audre Lorde, visiting in 1954, reported that it 'smelled like plastic and blue glass and beer and lots of good-looking young women'.[3] Lorde became a regular customer, although she was always too shy to dance. Meanwhile, upstate, a group of women were forming a sea colony of their own, at the beach resort of Cherry Grove on Fire Island. Founded in 1945, Cherry Grove was like a 'very private gay country club'[4]: a mostly white, mostly upper-class group of women living in the same small community. Audrey Hartmann, a visitor to the colony, described it as a pastoral lesbian Mecca:

> The houses were all gas-lamps, charming little houses [...] it was so wooded, and so beautiful, a canopy of trees wherever you'd walk, and you could look in the windows and I remember seeing women by candlelight sitting there, and thinking 'Oh, I wish this were I!' I so well remember that [...] I just said 'I *have* to come back and live here.'[5]

This feeling of homecoming was shared by Peter Worth, a woman who had escaped Nazi Germany and then Occupied France, and who settled at

Cherry Grove: '. . . *finally* I am in the majority – ah! This was my world and the other world was not real.'[6]

These idyllic-sounding 'zones of belonging', so very necessary to the emotional health of their clientele, operated in a political atmosphere of the utmost hostility. Although Cherry Grove largely escaped police surveillance, some women were still arrested for indecent conduct, and the community's only social space, Duffy's hotel, was reliant on the friendliness of its owner, Edward Duffy.[7] It was illegal to run a lesbian bar, and to dance with persons of the same gender, so the Sea Colony was forced to develop a clever system. If a policeman came calling, a red light was flicked on and off, and couples in the back room would have time to separate into appropriate pairings. Nevertheless, raids often included the use of police dogs and sexual handling: one bargoer describes being pushed up against the wall of the Sea Colony ('Oh, you think you're a man. Well, let's see what you've got here.').[8] The Daughters of Bilitis, a lesbian cultural organisation formed in the early 1950s, published a guide on to how to respond if a woman was arrested and forced to spend a night in the cells.[9] As one participant in a lesbian oral history project writes of the atmosphere of the 1950s, 'We were all terrified in those days.'[10]

It is more common to read *The Bell Jar* as an outraged response to heterosexism than as a lesbian plot. Yet the text is unusual, for literary fiction of the time, in containing an overtly lesbian character in Esther's friend Joan Gilling, who creates a 'minor scandal' (*BJ* 210) at college and later sleeps with a fellow female patient at the hospital where they are interned. Like many lesbian characters in literature, Joan commits suicide at the end of the story. In this respect, we could argue that *The Bell Jar* is a classic 'lesbian panic' plot, as defined by Patricia Juliana Smith:

> Typically, a female character, fearing discovery of her covert or unarticulated lesbian desires [. . .] lashes out directly or indirectly at another woman, resulting in emotional or physical harm to herself or others. This destructive reaction may be as sensational as suicide or homicide, or as subtle and vague as a general neurasthenised malaise.[11]

Although Esther is not responsible for Joan's suicide, we recall her neurotic response to discovering Joan in bed with another woman ('You make me want to puke!') (*BJ* 211). It is also difficult not to feel, as Tracy Brain has argued, *The Bell Jar*'s spooky doubling with *Mrs Dalloway*, with Joan as the counterpart to Sally Seton.[12] We might also note, alongside hoogland, the 'unmistakably erotic' terms in which Doreen is described, and which cause uncomfortable feelings that Esther purges via hot baths.[13] Running behind the narrative of failed heterosexuality, we can therefore sense a second story about lesbian sexuality. Esther's fictional life on N52nd Street and the real-world, crowded bar at the Sea Colony begin to seem part of the same spectrum.

What cultural narratives nuanced Plath's portrayal of lesbian sexuality in *The Bell Jar*? Alongside the discourse of political violence written on the lesbian body, we find, of course, various ways of (secretly) speaking of lesbianism specific to the 1950s. Strict forms of censorship meant that what was written about lesbianism was controlled – but, paradoxically, the scene of reading was also, for many lesbians, the scene of coming-to-consciousness. As Meredith Miller notes, 'respondents to oral history surveys, when asked about the process of lesbian identification, rarely fail to mention the printed word'.[14] This chapter considers what discourse – political, medical, psychological, fictional or a mixture of them all – was produced and consumed about lesbian sexualities at the time of the fictional setting of *The Bell Jar*. In other words, what might Plath have known of such secret lives?

*

Esther Greenwood twice undergoes electro-convulsive therapy as treatment for her mental health issues (*BJ* 138, 205). The first, 'unmodified', the kind that is 'associated with a significant rate of bone fracture',[15] is delivered without anaesthetic. Yet, as her psychiatrist states, 'If it's done properly, it's like going to sleep' (*BJ* 182). The violence of the (two) electric current(s), and the unconscious state after treatment, link Esther in the text to the communist spy Ethel Rosenberg, who famously received two doses of electricity during her execution.[16] The electric current also references the psychiatric treatment of homosexuals, of which hospitalisation and ECT were the gold standard.[17]

Cold War paranoia of the early 1950s implicitly linked communism with dissident sexual identity, with communist witch-hunts mirrored by purges of suspected homosexuals. Between 1947 and 1950, 4,954 men and women were dismissed from the armed forces and civilian agencies for their alleged homosexuality;[18] the Head of the Washington Vice Squad wanted to form a 'lesbian squad' to 'rout out the females'.[19] By 1951, federal agencies had begun to use lie detectors to determine sexuality in 'loyalty' investigations, just as they would with suspected spies.[20] Meanwhile, in psychiatric circles, lesbianism was viewed, just like communism, as a refusal to integrate with productive American capitalism. Sexual object choice, curiously, takes a back seat: W. Bertram Wolfe argued that 'lesbian love [. . .] represents an evasion of the responsibilities of marriage and motherhood'.[21] Frank Caprio's *Female Homosexuality*, published in 1954, ascribed lesbianism to 'emotional immaturity in their attitude towards men, sex and marriage';[22] Caprio also suspected that lesbians who were married to men 'had established communist-like networks'[23] with which to communicate. As late as 1959, the psychiatrist Richard Robertiello wrote an account of successfully converting a lesbian patient, Connie, to heterosexuality. This was accomplished by emphasising her duties as a good American homemaker, with the sexual component seamlessly elided: 'She said she was thinking how nice it would be to get into a domestic life again. She spoke of getting a rotisserie.'[24]

Discussion around the topic of lesbianism was lively: there were hundreds of books and articles available, as the psychiatric community struggled to understand homosexuality. For women realising their own lesbian desire in the 1950s, this produced a useful, unforeseen effect. Psychological literature could be mined for information, however skewed. Esther tells us:

> I had bought a few paperbacks on abnormal psychology at the drug store [...] The only thing I could read, beside the scandal sheets, were these abnormal psychology books. It was as if some slim opening had been left, so I could learn all I needed to know [...] (*BJ* 153).

What Esther says about researching her own psychological problems, might equally apply to lesbian readers, right down to the furtive 'drug store'[25] purchase of scandalous books.

Two landmark studies, published in 1953 and 1957, marked the beginning of a shift in psychiatric attitudes away from the pathologisation of homosexuality. The first of these was Dr Alfred Kinsey's second book, *Sexual Behavior in the Human Female*, which followed on from his 1948 investigation into male sexuality. Kinsey found that 28 per cent of females had had 'an erotic response' to other females, and 20 per cent had had 'some homosexual experience'.[26] Such large percentages suggested that lesbianism could not be dismissed as an unusual psychiatric disorder.

The second study was Dr Evelyn Hooker's *The Adjustment of the Male Overt Homosexual*. Hooker recruited thirty homosexual subjects and thirty heterosexual subjects, and asked them to perform in several tests, including the Rorschach ink-blot. The results were then blinded and given to consulting psychiatrists to assess. The psychiatrists were unable to tell which blot tests belonged to which group simply by looking; where pathology was 'revealed' in the subjects, it was spread equally across heterosexual and homosexual populations.[27] In previous work, psychiatrists had been falsely led to believe that all homosexuals had mental health issues, because the homosexuals whom they saw were self-selecting, presenting with psychological distress due to other conditions. For example, Irving Bieber's study of 200 homosexual and heterosexual partners failed to mention that twenty-six of the homosexual subjects were also schizophrenic.[28]

Simple and elegant, Hooker's work confirmed that correlation did not equal causation. Although Hooker was unable to carry out a parallel study involving lesbians – in case she herself were suspected of lesbianism[29] – her contribution changed the attitudes of psychiatrists:

> I'm thinking of a young woman who came up to me and said that when her parents discovered she was a lesbian, they put her in a psychiatric hospital. The standard procedure for treating homosexuals in that hospital was electroshock therapy. Her psychiatrist was familiar with my work, and he was able to keep them from giving it to her.[30]

The Bell Jar arrives at an interesting time, with the early 1950s marking a shift in how lesbianism was viewed in psychiatric terms: for the first time, one could view homosexuality not as pathology but as within normal boundaries. It may be possible to see this shift echoed in Esther's ambivalence around Joan, as her conversations with Dr Nolan in the latter part of the novel become more sensitively questioning:

> 'I don't see what women see in other women. . . . What does
>   a woman see in a woman that she can't see in a man?'
> 'Tenderness.'
> That shut me up.   (*BJ* 210)

*

The Well of Loneliness was first published in England in 1928; in the United States, in 1929. In the UK, the book was immediately subject to an obscenity trial on publication. Jonathan Cape packaged the novel at a high price point and with an expensive dust jacket,[31] in order to show that the book was 'literature', but to no avail: it was banned anyway. In the United States, however, where there was also an obscenity trial, the book's status as 'high culture' and 'of literary merit' was taken into account, and the court found that *The Well* could not be considered pornographic material.

Whether or not Plath read *The Well of Loneliness*, what we can be sure of is how deeply the novel permeated the public consciousness. Ironically, the trial cemented *The Well*'s status as cult fiction, and the book sold 20,000 copies in its first month on the American market.[32] The publicity around the trial also meant that the 'deviant' content could not be elided: for the first time, lesbians were directed to a literary work about themselves. Oral histories make clear that even until the 1960s, *The Well of Loneliness* remained the *ur*-text for American lesbians hoping to see themselves reflected in print. 'I cried my eyes out over it', says one respondent, 'I thought it was a marvelous book.'[33] Another writes:

> *The Well* opened the door for a lot of people, including me. I read that book and found that I was coming home. I recognised myself in the characters, and I also recognised the emotions that were so beautifully written there.[34]

Radclyffe Hall herself narrowly escaped becoming part of lesbian slang: a movement formed to replace 'the inelegant word *butch*' with the word 'Clyffe' to designate masculine-presenting women.[35] Such was the book's ubiquity that the Daughters of Bilitis called their magazine *The Ladder* – because it was designed to help others climb out of the well.[36] In *The Bell Jar*, Esther's first psychiatrist shares the surname of *The Well of Loneliness's* protagonist, Dr Gordon, who has eyelashes 'so long and thick they looked artificial' and 'features [. . .] so perfect they were almost pretty' (*BJ* 123). For some lesbians, *The Well* really was a kind of medicine.

   The aristocratic, mannish lesbian heroine of *The Well of Loneliness* finds certain echoes in Joan Gilling. Linda Wagner-Martin notes that the characterisation of Joan lets Plath explore not only the theme of the 'double', but also of 'the gifted and wealthy eastern woman'.[37] An outdoorsy sportswoman like Stephen Gordon, a 'champion horse-jumper at the annual college gymkhana' (*BJ* 190), Joan also shares Stephen's chivalric code. When Esther is taken to hospital, Joan stands 'rigid as a soldier' next to her during the examination, 'holding my hand, for her sake or mine I could not tell' (*BJ* 222). Like Esther, Joan is a product of a women's college. In the public imagination, an association between female-only colleges and lesbianism began as early as 1902, when the sexologist Havelock Ellis referred to them as 'the great breeding ground'.[38]

   This pattern of thinking continued into the 1950s. In 1955, the dean of UCLA lamented 'the attraction of colleges, both public and private, for overt, hardened homosexuals'.[39] In 1951, Dr Carl Binger, head of the Mellon Foundation at Vassar, resigned because of his concerns over 'sexual development of undergraduates in an atmosphere of supervision by matriarchy';[40] in 1948, he had told an undergraduate who was sent to him on suspicion of lesbianism not to worry about being sent down, because to expel her would also require 'the expulsion of 10% of the student body'.[41] His resignation made the front page of *The New York Times*.

Esther recounts a 'minor scandal' in which two girls 'started seeing too much of each other' (*BJ* 210). The way she tells of their discovery ('Milly was sitting on the chair and Theodora was lying on the bed, and Milly was stroking Theodora's hair') (*BJ* 210) and her own confused reaction, recalls one Vassar student's story of lesbians being found together in their college rooms:

> A freshman [. . .] knocked, and when there was no answer, opened the door. Seeing them on the couch she said, 'Oh, I'm *terribly* sorry – I didn't know you were busy!'[42]

Just like Vassar, which educated Elizabeth Bishop, Esther's college has a 'famous woman poet' who 'lives with another woman' and sports a 'cropped Dutch cut' (*BJ* 210). It is reasonable to assume that Plath, who attended Smith, would have been exposed to some of the same lesbian communities as the characters she writes about in *The Bell Jar*.

*

The year of *The Bell Jar*, 1953, was also the year in which the Gathings Committee, which had been formed to investigate what proportion of current literary works were 'obscene', published its report. One of the genres most clearly in its sights was lesbian pulp, which since 1950 had exploded in popularity. Priced at 25 cents and presented in garish dust jackets, retailed through drugstores and petrol stations, the pulps were marketed in exactly the opposite way to *The Well of Loneliness*, to enormous effect. Pulp author Vin Packer's *Spring Fire*, published in 1952, sold more than 1.5 million copies; Tereska Torres sold 2 million copies of *Women's Barracks* in the United States between 1950 and 1955: the same number as Khaled Hosseini's bestseller *The Kite Runner*, except that the population of the United States at the time was only 55–60 per cent of today's figure;[43] and Ann Bannon's *Odd Girl Out* was the second best-selling paperback original of 1957.[44]

Also available were non-fiction lesbian pulps, marketed as 'popular sexology'. Presenting factual case studies in the lurid detail and tone of pulp fiction, this subgenre's foremost author was Ann Aldrich, whose books included *We Walk Alone* (1955), *We, Too, Must Love* (1958), *We Two Won't Last* (1963) and *Take a Lesbian to Lunch* (1972). *We Walk Alone* was one of the bestselling titles for 1955,[45] and its author became a national celebrity in the lesbian subculture, though one whose identity was intriguingly complex, because Ann Aldrich and the aforementioned Vin Packer were both pseudonyms for the writer Marijane Meaker.[46]

These texts occupy, as Kaye Mitchell indicates, an 'uneasy position both within and without the sexological framework'.[47] By presenting life-stories in a fictional narrative framework, she retains an ironic position to formal psychology. In some ways, this simply recognised a contested border country between fact and fictional narratives of lesbianism: the psychologist Frank Caprio borrowed from 'case histories' from true-confession magazines such as *Life Romances* and *My Confession* in order to show lesbians as pathological.[48] And in *The Lesbian in Our Society* (1962) by W. D. Sprague, it was claimed, entirely fictionally, that one in four women had tried lesbianism 'since moving to the suburbs'.[49]

For lesbians, the pulps – particularly the fiction – were a way towards finding a community. Often, books sketched a virtual map of the bars in Greenwich Village;[50] but they were also important psychically – 'signs of a secret history of readers'.[51] Carol Seajay talks about finding a pulp novel for the first time: 'I was thrilled by what I read: that we could support ourselves and make our lives together, and that there were many women like us'.[52] Yet, the enormous sales figures indicate that it was not only lesbians who formed the buying audience: pulps were read by heterosexuals and homosexuals alike.

The Gathings Committee report prompted publishers to remain conservative in the sexual content of the pulps, and also in storyline. In particular, the endings of the stories should underline the tragic consequences of living outside heterosexuality:[53] either the lesbian character should die at the end or renounce her lesbianism. Thus *Spring Fire* ends with one protagonist becoming psychotic, whilst her lover returns to loving men. Seajay was so familiar with, and so tired of, the typically unhappy ending that she would read only as far as the last twenty pages, 'to avoid sharing the lesbian protagonist's inevitable tragic end'.[54] Given the 1950s writing of unhappy endings for lesbian characters, it isn't surprising to find Joan committing suicide at the end of *The Bell Jar*. Throughout the novel, Esther and Joan have been drawn into an uneasy relationship: 'It was as if we had been forced together by some overwhelming circumstance, like war or plague, and shared a world of our own' (*BJ* 215). Esther reluctantly accepts that Joan is here to stay, in spite of her attempts to dissolve the partnership: 'In spite of my profound reservations, I thought that I would always treasure Joan' (*BJ* 215). After this relationship-building, culminating in Joan rescuing Esther from bleeding to death, the novel's ending functions almost like a gloss on lesbian pulp fiction. Just as Esther is taking her first (albeit disastrous) step into heterosexual sex, Joan commits suicide. Where Esther represents the partner who turns away from lesbianism, Joan is the partner who, heartbroken, kills herself.

*

Eve Sedgwick has argued that the trope of *coming-out* only comes into force in the aftermath of the 1969 Stonewall riots.[55] Given this, it is hard to say that lesbian rights in the 1950s were an 'articulated politics of representation'.[56] Whilst, in the opinion of one commentator, 'the 1950s were perhaps the worst time in history for women to love women'[57] ('We were all terrified in those days'),[58] we nonetheless find the beginnings of a distinctive subculture ('I was thrilled by what I read')[59] and the start of a move towards the normalisation of homosexuality. Although political repressions were still widespread, at all levels of discourse, lesbianism was widely discussed in forms from scientific journals to popular paperbacks. Obsessive policing of the site of sexuality, and an obsessive need for censorship, exerted a paradoxical effect, in which what is repressed seeps through the Foucauldian grid. Indeed, as Mitchell argues, we can find a lot of 'queerness' in the disparity of experience, and the lack of coherence in lesbian texts.[60] Ellen Lewin further notes that the era complicates our understandings of what being 'in the closet' means. The women she interviewed saw their sexuality as a complex open secret, cut across by various codes: not to be talked about, but nevertheless available information to the sensitive ear.[61] As one African-American gay oral history respondent, Paul Phillips, neatly summarises: 'If somebody asks me, depending upon who it is, of course, I'll tell them.'[62]

The Bell Jar shares this incoherent position. On the one hand, we find the typical structures of lesbian panic: the doubling of heroines, the hospitalisation and death of the only lesbian character, which seems to be responding to the archetypal lesbian-pulp plot of the 1950s. But Esther pathologises Joan's illness, instead of her sexuality; she responds with incomprehension, but not judgement, to the idea of two women seeking tenderness together. If Joan's suicide is part of what liberates Esther ('... after Joan's death Nurse Kennedy had moved somewhere else and left no trace. I was perfectly free') (*BJ* 232), her funeral also gives Esther an experience of meaning:

> There would be a black, six-foot-deep gap hacked in the hard ground. That shadow would marry this shadow, and the peculiar, yellowish soil of our locality seal the wound in the whiteness, and yet another snowfall erase the traces of newness in Joan's grave (*BJ* 232).

Recalling the epiphanic ending of Joyce's *The Dead*,[63] snow begins to smooth out the unevenness of Esther's recent experience, including, perhaps, the psychic 'wound' left by her depression and hospitalisation. Whilst 'that shadow would marry this shadow' refers to the oncoming darkness in the graveyard, the verb 'marry' is significant, as is the offhand tone of 'this' and 'that': it is suggested that shadows of any persuasion may marry each other, with gender and sexuality not seen to be of any great importance. In *The Bell Jar*, Plath was able to draw on an evolving history of sexuality, with its simultaneous repressions and liberatory possibilities. Lesbian sexuality becomes that marvellously contradictory phrase, a 'minor scandal', rather than a major one.

Notes

1. Hurewitz, *Stepping Out*, 54.
2. Hurewitz, *Stepping Out*, 89.
3. Hurewitz, *Stepping Out*, 91.
4. Newton, 'The "Fun Gay Ladies"', 156.
5. Newton, 'The "Fun Gay Ladies"', 145.
6. Newton, 'The "Fun Gay Ladies"', 146.
7. Newton, 'The "Fun Gay Ladies"', 149–50.
8. Hurewitz, *Stepping Out*, 90.
9. Streitmatter, *Unspeakable*, 22.
10. Faderman, *Odd Girls*, 139.
11. Smith, *Lesbian Panic*, 2.
12. Brain, *The Other Sylvia Plath*, 149.
13. hoogland, '(Sub)textual Configurations', 294.
14. Miller, 'Secret Agents', 54.
15. Kellner, 'Electroconvulsive Therapy', 4.
16. Peel, *Writing Back*, 69.
17. Marcus, *Making History*, 25.
18. Faderman, *Odd Girls*, 140.
19. Faderman, *Odd Girls*, 143.
20. Faderman, *Odd Girls*, 142.
21. Penn, 'The Meanings of Lesbianism', 193.
22. Littauer, 'Someone to Love', 70.
23. Gutterman, 'Another Enemy Within', 480.
24. Penn, 'The Meanings of Lesbianism', 196.
25. For a discussion of sites of purchase of lesbian texts in the 1950s, see Miller, 'Secret Agents', 37–58; and Gallo, 'No Secret Anymore', 44.
26. Miller, *Out of the Past*, 250.
27. Miller, *Out of the Past*, 263.
28. Miller, *Out of the Past*, 248.

29. Marcus, *Making History*, 21.
30. Marcus, *Making History*, 25.
31. Miller, 'Secret Agents', 42.
32. Innes, *The Lesbian Menace*, 15.
33. Marcus, *Making History*, 69.
34. Marcus, *Making History*, 71.
35. Faderman, *Odd Girls*, 173.
36. Streitmatter, *Unspeakable*, 22.
37. Wagner-Martin, *The Bell Jar: A Novel of the Fifties*, 65.
38. Innes, *The Lesbian Menace*, 36.
39. Faderman, *Odd Girls*, 145.
40. MacKay (ed.), *Wolf Girls*, 16.
41. MacKay (ed.), *Wolf Girls*, 41.
42. MacKay (ed.), *Wolf Girls*, 12.
43. Seajay, 'Essay: Pulp and Circumstance', 18–19.
44. Miller, 'Secret Agents', 46.
45. Aldrich, *We, Too, Must Love*, 165.
46. Aldrich, *We, Too, Must Love*, 160.
47. Mitchell, 'Who is She?', 158.
48. Faderman, *Odd Girls*, 136.
49. Gutterman, 'Another Enemy Within', 482.
50. Gallo, 'No Secret Anymore', 44.
51. Foote, 'Deviant Classics', 178.
52. Seajay, 'Essay: Pulp and Circumstance', 18.
53. Alexander, Meem and Gibson (eds.), *Finding Out*, 232.
54. Foote, 'Deviant Classics', 176.
55. Sedgwick, *Epistemology of the Closet*, 15.
56. Mitchell, 'Who is She?', 152.
57. Faderman, *Odd Girls*, 175.
58. Faderman, *Odd Girls*, 139.
59. Seajay, 'Essay: Pulp and Circumstance', 18.
60. Mitchell, 'Who is She?', 152.
61. Kennedy, 'But We Would Never Talk About It', 16.
62. Marcus, *Making History*, 87.
63. See Joyce, *Dubliners* (Penguin 1992 edition), 224–5: '[. . .] snow was general all over Ireland. It was falling on every part of the dark central plain, on the treeless hills, falling softly upon the Bog of Allen [. . .] It was falling, too, upon every part of the lonely churchyard on the hill where Michael Furey lay buried.'

'Woman-haters Were Like Gods': The Bell Jar and Violence Against Women in 1950s America

Kate Harding

That Betty Friedan's *The Feminine Mystique* and Sylvia Plath's *The Bell Jar* were both published in 1963, the same year Plath committed suicide, has been remarked upon by many a writer,[1] but it is worth briefly connecting those dots once more. All of us who read *The Bell Jar* today do so through a post-Friedan lens, with a feminist historical perspective denied to its author and her protagonist, Esther Greenwood. Neva Nelson, a colleague of Plath's at *Mademoiselle* magazine during the summer out of which *The Bell Jar* emerged, says of their college-aged cohort, 'We were all immature adolescents —products of the middle 1950s, pre-Pill, pre-*Feminine Mystique*— expected to do something extraordinary, but left with the ambiguity of the female role, with its stress on home and family.'[2]

To Plath, the 1950s were not a brief, backward moment between the Second World War and the Age of Aquarius, but her day-to-day lived experience of the adult world, with no end in sight and few with whom to commiserate. Before Friedan's now-classic book arrived, women of her class nursing ambitions beyond housewifery generally did so alone. Feminist scholar Susan Brownmiller writes of that era, 'Femininity was a challenge thrown down to the female sex, a challenge no proud, self-respecting young woman could afford to ignore, particularly one with enormous ambition that she nursed in secret, alternately feeding or starving its inchoate life in tremendous confusion.'[3] Although proud, self-respecting women of lower socioeconomic status would remain in the workforce out of necessity, Sylvia Plath and Esther Greenwood entered adulthood at a moment that was peculiarly hostile to career-oriented, white, educated women. In *A Strange Stirring: The Feminine Mystique and American Women at the Dawn of the 1960s*, Stephanie Coontz writes, 'A half century after they read the book, many of the women I talked to could still recall the desperation they had felt in the late 1950s and early

1960s, and their wave of relief when Friedan told them they were not alone and they were not crazy.'[4]

Set ten years pre-*Mystique*, *The Bell Jar* is one version of what going 'crazy' looked like for a young woman resisting society's demands that she diminish her ambitions and desires to an appropriately feminine size. (Mid-century slang for weight-loss dieting makes it a perfect metaphor for this spiritual self-annihilation: Esther notes, 'Almost everybody I met in New York was trying to reduce.' [*BJ* 25].) The boundaries of femininity for Esther and her contemporaries are enforced – both symbolically and literally – throughout the novel by increasingly harsh punishments for the characters, from physical illness to attempted rape to electric shock treatment and death. In this chapter, I will focus on instances of sexual and gendered violence enacted upon and around Esther, and how, in the context of 1953 New York and New England, these experiences penalise her specifically by stripping her of any pretensions to masculine independence, reinforcing her femininity while simultaneously defining it as a cause of pain and vulnerability.

My conceptualisation of sexual violence as both punishing and inscribing femininity has its foundations in Sharon Marcus's 1992 essay 'Fighting Bodies, Fighting Words: A Theory and Politics of Rape Prevention'. Writes Marcus:

> Masculine power and feminine powerlessness neither simply precede nor cause rape; rather, rape is one of culture's many modes of feminizing women. A rapist chooses his target because he recognizes her to be a woman, but a rapist also strives to imprint the gender identity of 'feminine victim' on his target. A rape act thus imposes as well as presupposes misogynist inequalities; rape is not only scripted—it also scripts.[5]

Thinking of sexual violence in this way, as the expression of a 'rape script', allows us to understand that the gender roles Esther struggles against are redefined by sexual violence, even as they also predicate it. If Esther's central dilemma is the tension between her desire for a masculine type of independence and the unchangeable fact of her female body, her attempted rape by the 'woman-hater' (*BJ* 106). Marco is traumatic not only because of the straightforward violence, but because it is the single most *feminising* experience the protagonist has that summer. All of the previous month's accomplishments – living on her own, doing a job that uses her intelligence, socialising on her own terms rather than her mother's or supervisors', even walking miles alone at night – have erected a shaky structure of masculine possibility in Esther's young mind, but Marco takes a wrecking ball to it.

In 1949, Simone de Beauvoir writes in *The Second Sex*, 'No biological, psychic, or economic destiny defines the figure that the human female takes on in society; it is civilization as a whole that elaborates this intermediary product between the male and the eunuch that is called feminine.'[6] Even more than the expectation that she wear white gloves to work or feel grateful that a future doctor wishes to marry her, the sexual assault forces Esther to identify as a member of the so-called weaker sex.

*

Primary sources on 1950s American attitudes towards what today we call 'sexual assault' are scant. Like the feminine drudgery Friedan describes in *The Feminine Mystique*, it existed as a widespread problem with no name. The crime of rape – defined as 'carnal knowledge of a woman forcibly against her will' – existed as a felony on the books in all the (then) 48 states, but a 1951 study found little agreement among state legislatures as to its seriousness.[7] In New Jersey, Pennsylvania and Vermont, it was possible to be convicted of rape and receive only a monetary fine as a sentence, while in Louisiana and North Carolina, conviction carried a mandatory death sentence.[8] (Those states with the harshest penalties were arguably motivated more by racism than a commitment to women's safety; the vast majority executed were African American men convicted of raping white women, as a campaign by the NAACP's Legal Defense Fund would document in 1966.)[9] Meanwhile, sodomy was illegal in all but two states, while adultery and fornication were still criminalised in many. 'Much of our sex law is incomplete and lacking reality', writes Robert Bensing, author of 'A Comparative Study of American Sex Statutes' (1951), who notes that a reasonable person is likely to feel 'utter bewilderment at the crazy-quilt legislation that has been produced by the state legislatures'.

It wasn't until the feminist movement of the 1960s and 1970s that legislators were pushed to write clearer definitions and consider consent – as opposed to a man's good name, a woman's perceived virtue or the marital status of the parties involved – as the salient difference between sex and sexual violence. In the meantime, once again, Plath and her characters were stuck living in a time just before their problems were given names, faces and voices. Although the first Kinsey Report, *Sexual Behavior in the Human Male*, was published in 1948, the companion study of female sexual behaviour was not made available until 1953, the same year Esther encounters her 'woman-hater'. In between, writes Viola Klein in

1950, American women were expected to choose between being 'the woman to whom sex is chiefly a means to produce children, and the woman who seeks it for the sake of the pleasure it affords her by itself'.[10] Klein adds, 'In either case, her relationship to the opposite sex is the focal point from which her personality is viewed . . .'[11]

Esther Greenwood is confronted with how sharply one of her male contemporaries – 'the only boy I ever actually discussed going to bed with' (*BJ* 78) – makes this distinction. Eric, who lost his virginity to a sex worker, has no interest in combining sex with love, because 'it would be spoiled by thinking this woman too was just an animal like the rest . . . He'd go to a whore if he had to and keep the woman he loved free of all that dirty business' (*BJ* 79). Esther herself reifies a version of this dichotomy when she contrasts her fellow *Ladies' Day* guest editors Betsy and Doreen. The latter, who dresses to emphasise her sexuality and prioritises parties over work, represents to Esther 'a whole life of marvelous, elaborate decadence that attracted me like a magnet' (*BJ* 5). But Betsy – whom Doreen nicknames 'Pollyanna Cowgirl' (*BJ* 6) – makes Esther feel safe, virtuous and bored.

In her journals, we see Plath frequently agonising over this impossible choice between the two sexual roles available to women of her class and generation. 'And yet does it not all come again to the fact that it is a man's world?' she asks. 'For if a man chooses to be promiscuous, he may still aesthetically turn up his nose at promiscuity. He may still demand a woman be faithful to him, to save him from his own lust. But women have lust, too. Why should they be relegated to the position of custodian of emotions, watcher of the infants, feeder of soul, body and pride of man?' (*J* 71).

Still, the reality of being 'a female always in danger' is never far from her mind. During a blind date with a man named Bill, who demands sex with increasingly frightening intensity, Plath thinks to herself while pinned, 'This is the one time your innocence won't help you' (*J* 36). She averts the crisis by shaking him and screaming at him, 'I hate you. Damn you. Just because you're a boy. Just because you're never worried about having babies!' then stops, admitting that she wants to consent and only feels she must not because of the critical voices telling her a good girl wouldn't. 'You want him, yet you remember: "Once a woman has intercourse she isn't satisfied." "You need time and security for full pleasure." "You'll be finished at Smith"' (*J* 36).

This episode – itself written in the manner of a short story or novel, with dialogue and extra attention to style – has echoes in at least two scenes in *The Bell Jar*. Marco's attempted rape of Esther and the scene in which she learns that her sometime boyfriend, Buddy Willard, is not a virgin. Her rage over the latter revelation is not so much because Buddy lied to her, but because he had the freedom to act on his sexual desires while feigning continued innocence, a path not available to women. 'I couldn't stand the idea of a woman having to have a single pure life and a man being able to have a double life, one pure and one not' (*BJ* 81). (In her journal, Plath quips, 'I am not yet the smart woman who can keep her reputation and be a highclass whore on the side' [*J* 141].)

The earlier part of the episode with Bill, however, reads unsettlingly like the attempted rape scene in *The Bell Jar*, beginning with Esther pinned on the ground by an aggressive man. In this case, the thought running through her head is, 'It's happening. If I just lie here and do nothing it will happen' (*BJ* 81).

Plath leaves us to wonder *what*, exactly, Esther believes to be happening – that she is finally going to have sex for the first time, or that she is about to be raped? To the contemporary feminist reader, the difference between the two is vast and crucial. For Esther, however, coming into womanhood two decades before the term 'acquaintance rape' was coined, there may be substantially more overlap between how she conceives of those two options. What she wants – whether she consents – is of no more importance to society at large than it is to Marco.

An earlier scene with Doreen in the slick radio personality Lenny's apartment underscores how differently the twenty-first-century reader and Esther perceive the threat of sexual violence. This much older man has picked up two young women, brought them home and plied them with alcohol. Doreen even says to Esther, 'Stick around, will you? I wouldn't have a chance if he tried anything funny' (*BJ* 15). But between her drunkenness and her attraction to Lenny, Doreen giggles as she says it, as though sexual assault is quite literally their euphemism for it: something funny. Some time later, while watching Lenny lift Doreen onto his shoulder, Esther notices 'in the routine way you notice the color of somebody's eyes, that Doreen's breasts had popped out of her dress' (*BJ* 17). Doreen is described as 'thrashing' and 'screeching', as Lenny tries to bite her hip, but rather than express concern for her clearly intoxicated friend, Esther takes the opportunity to leave. Hours later, Doreen comes to Esther's door, too drunk to stand upright, and asks to be let in. When Doreen vomits, Esther turns her back, shuts her door.

Although Doreen continues to date Lenny, it is far from clear that the events of their first night together would meet contemporary standards for consent, if only based on the degree of Doreen's inebriation. But for

Esther, steeped in 1950s sexual mores that cast Doreen as a loose woman who was asking for it the second she entered Lenny's home, the only question is whether it is socially safe to be around such a bad influence. She sublimates the loneliness and jealousy she feels watching Lenny and Doreen become physically intimate (*BJ* 16) into a high-minded rejection of her friend's licentiousness:

> I made a decision about Doreen that night. I decided I would watch her and listen to what she said, but deep down I would have nothing at all to do with her. Deep down, I would be loyal to Betsy and her innocent friends. It was Betsy I resembled at heart (*BJ* 23).

Esther feels shame not for abandoning a friend who specifically asked her to help avoid 'anything funny', but for being observed with such a friend at all.

The night maid who delivers Doreen to Esther's door looks 'stern and hardworking and moral as an old-style European immigrant', which makes the protagonist want to 'run after her and tell her I had nothing to do with Doreen' (*BJ* 21). Helen Meyer Hacker, writing in 1951, explains that it is common among members of oppressed minority groups to internalise society's judgments this way, regardless of whether the individuals involved recognise themselves as minorities:

> From those, to us, deluded creatures who confessed to witchcraft to modern sophisticates who speak disparagingly of the cattiness and disloyalty of women, women reveal their introjection of prevailing attitudes toward them. Like those minority groups whose self-castigation outdoes dominant group derision of them, women frequently exceed men in the violence of their vituperations of their sex. They are more severe in moral judgments, especially in sexual matters.[12]

Eventually, Esther reconciles with Doreen, only to be set up on a date with the 'woman-hater' who will echo those moral judgments as he tries to rape her.

Even as she resists his violent intentions, Esther is reminded by Marco's words that society derogates women who dress attractively, drink alcohol and end up alone with men:

> Marco set his teeth to the strap at my shoulder and tore my sheath to the waist. I saw the glimmer of bare skin, like a pale veil separating two bloody-minded adversaries.
> 'Slut!'
> The word hissed by my ear.
> 'Slut!' (*BJ* 109).

The third 'slut' Marco spits at her prompts Esther to break the script, using the distinctly feminine weapon of a high-heeled shoe. After gouging his leg with the heel, she punches him in the face and, the attack aborted, begins to cry.

The power in this scene changes hands a few more times before she gets away. He marks her face with a streak of the blood coming from his nose and demands the return of a diamond stick pin he gave her earlier in the evening. She pretends not to know where it is, and thinks of what she might buy with a diamond that size. He puts his hands on her again, and threatens to break her neck if she doesn't return the jewel. She admits that it's in her purse, lost 'somewhere in the muck', and leaves him searching for it on his hands and knees. At the end of all that, Marco is the one left in the dark and the mud, his nose bloodied by a woman he believed he could conquer.

It might be a triumphant moment for Esther, an assertion of her strength and independence despite being a young woman thrown to the ground by a misogynist brute, if only she didn't have to find a ride home. Returning to the party in search of Doreen, Esther takes on the shame that ought to belong to Marco. 'I kept to the fringe of the shadows so nobody would notice the grass plastered to my dress and shoes, and with my black stole I covered my shoulders and bare breasts' (*BJ* 110). Her successful fight against the woman-hater becomes meaningless as she recognises how she must appear to other people: literally and figuratively, a ruined woman.

*

The mores that damned Esther whether she did or she didn't were influenced by a number of misogynistic cultural influences that flourished in the 1950s United States. There was an advertising industry that told young women the right lipstick could help them integrate their sexual selves – 'tease and temptress, siren and gamin, dynamic and demure'[13] promised one Revlon ad – while telling older ones that 'the really crucial function, the really important function women serve as housewives is *to buy more things for the house*'.[14] Women's magazines and television 'portrayed the postwar housewife as the happiest person on the planet',[15] which meant many women not flush with domestic fulfilment felt somehow inadequate. And the advent of *Playboy* magazine in 1953 brought pornography into the mainstream despite its 'distortion of female sexuality, and its light-hearted treatment of rape, child molestation, battering, and sexual harassment.'[16]

Not coincidentally, advertising, mass media and pornography all are also pillars of what feminists would begin in the 1970s to call 'rape culture', a set of cherished myths and stereotypes that work to exonerate sexually violent men and blame their victims. Brownmiller, in her landmark 1975 book *Against Our Will: Men, Women and Rape*, calls these 'the deadly male myths of rape, the distorted proverbs that govern female sexuality'.[17]

For Brownmiller, the core argument of these myths is that women secretly want to be raped, and that they cannot in fact be raped against their will. Essentially, they boil down to what Marco says as he dabs his bloody nose with a handkerchief: 'Sluts, sluts, sluts. Yes or no, it is all the same' (*BJ* 109). 'There is good reason for men to hold tenaciously to the notion that "All women want to be raped,"' writes Brownmiller. 'Because rape is an act that men do in the name of masculinity, it is in their interest to believe that women also want rape done, in the name of femininity.'[18]

Feminists from Friedan on would lay much of the blame for this sort of thinking at the feet of Sigmund Freud, who in 1953 was still (Kinsey reports notwithstanding) just about the only game in town where popular discussions of human sexuality were concerned. Although the feminist arguments against Freudian theory are by this point well-rehearsed, while looking at the context of 1950s attitudes towards sex and sexual violence, it is worth revisiting a few that pertain specifically to women's dehumanisation and abuse by men. 'The feminine mystique derived its power from Freudian thought',[19] writes Friedan. 'The fact is that to Freud, even more than to the magazine editor on Madison Avenue today, women were a strange, inferior, less-than-human species.' Echoing Klein, she adds, 'He saw them as childlike dolls, who existed in terms only of man's love, to love man and serve his needs.'[20]

In *The Bell Jar*, Buddy Willard's mother, Esther's nemesis, expresses a similar sentiment: 'What a man is is an arrow into the future and what a woman is is the place the arrow shoots off from' (*BJ* 72). Never mind that Esther hates 'the idea of serving men in any way' (*BJ* 76) and would prefer 'change and excitement and to shoot off in all directions myself, like the colored arrows from a Fourth of July rocket' (*BJ* 83). Two decades before *Against Our Will* would help mainstream audiences conceptualise rape as a systemic means of oppression, Freud's popular ideas about female sexuality were reinforcing the virgin/whore dichotomy that vexed both Plath and Esther. We know from her journals and letters that Plath read Freud and engaged with his ideas from college throughout her short adulthood.[21] Stephanie Coontz notes that 'Studies of postwar culture show that Freudian notions of sexual difference permeated popular culture, becoming a major explanatory device for human behavior in movies, magazines, and news stories.'[22] Although there were 'sharp critiques of Freudian antifeminism found in magazines of the late 1940s', they 'had faded by the early 1950s'.[23] Once again, Plath had the terrible luck to come of age between those earlier thinkers and the second wave of feminism, which would produce a large body of criticism in response to the father of psychoanalysis.

'Freud did not accept his [female] patient's symptoms as evidence of a justified dissatisfaction with the limiting circumstances imposed on them by society, but as symptomatic of an independent and universal feminine tendency',[24] writes Kate Millett in 1970. 'He named this tendency "penis envy," traced its origin to childhood experience and based his theory of the psychology of women upon it . . .'[25] In other words, Freud reduced an understandable envy of masculine independence, freedom and authority to a strictly genital concern.

Anthropologist Peggy Reeves Sanday notes that Freud reframed what would now be seen unequivocally as sexual assault as 'acceptable seduction' when described by his female patients. Poor Dora, despite slapping and verbally rejecting her father's friend Herr K., is told she has 'displaced her Oedipal love for her father onto him'.[26] And that's not the worst of it:

> Most startling and pertinent to American thought with respect to rape in Freud's thinking is the underlying proposition that renders women responsible both for male arousal and aggression on the one hand and her own subordination on the other. To become a true woman, it seems, a woman must conspire in her own rape.[27]

Plath's journals show her struggling with the cognitive dissonance arising from this paradoxical definition of femininity: being complicit in an act defined by lack of consent.

Although she wishes not to be 'accused of sentimentality or emotionalism or feminine tactics' (J 58) and deplores 'feminine burbling' (J 159) she describes herself as 'at bottom, simple, credulous, feminine & loving to be mastered' (J 355). And yet, even this desire to be mastered must not be expressed with too much relish, lest she tip over into the masculine territory of open desire. 'Oh, I would like to get in a car and be driven off into the mountains to a cabin on a wind-howling hill and be raped in a huge lust like a cave woman, fighting, screaming, biting in a ferocious ecstasy of orgasm', she writes in her journal, then sarcastically replies to herself, 'That sounds nice, doesn't it? Really delicate and feminine' (J 168).

The inherent contradiction of a rape fantasy – to desire it is to make it something other than rape – is framed here as a war between the feminine and masculine in Plath's mind. To fight, scream and bite in ecstasy is to regress to the status of cave woman, as unrefined an image of womanhood as one can muster; in order to be 'really delicate and feminine' by modern standards, it follows that one must meekly submit to being raped, neither enjoying it nor fighting back. Any sexual agency at all must be punished either by physical pain or reclassification as a masculine, and therefore unappealing, woman (like Esther's doomed lesbian friend/double Joan).

As Iris Jamahl Dunkle notes, '*The Bell Jar* is filled with examples of women paying for their un-feminine appetites and sexuality', from food poisoning to romantic rejection to electrocution, in the case of Ethel Rosenberg.[28] It is perhaps no wonder, then, that Plath's vision of Esther's first experience with sexual intercourse is, in some ways, just as violent and disturbing as the attempted rape. Although Esther gladly consents to sex and is excited by the possibility that she will feel profoundly changed by it, she instead feels only a 'sharp, startlingly bad pain' (*BJ* 229) and starts haemorrhaging severely. She begins her evening as a diaphragm-equipped modern woman, grateful for the freedom birth control affords her – 'freedom from fear, freedom from marrying the wrong person, like Buddy Willard, just because of sex' (*BJ* 223) – and ends it feeling like a character in one of many Victorian novels 'where woman after woman died, palely and nobly, in torrents of blood, after a difficult childbirth' (*BJ* 232).

No matter how fervently Esther wishes to be her own person acting on her own desires, American society in 1953 continually reminds her that her lot in life is submission and passivity. As Plath herself wrote in her *Journals*, in July of 1951:

> Being born a woman is my awful tragedy. From the moment I was conceived I was doomed to sprout breasts and ovaries rather than penis and scrotum; to have my whole circle of action, thought and feeling rigidly circumscribed by my inescapable femininity. Yes, my consuming desire to mingle with road crews, sailors and soldiers, bar room reg-ulars – to be a part of a scene, anonymous, listening, recording – all is spoiled by the fact that I am a girl, a female always in danger of assault and battery (*J* 77).

What Esther wants is immaterial when weighed against the fact of a female body: *Yes or no, it is all the same.*

Notes

1. Coontz, *A Strange Stirring*, 245.
2. Winder, *Pain, Parties, Work*, 246.
3. Brownmiller, *Femininity*, 14.
4. Coontz, *A Strange Stirring*, xx.
5. Marcus, 'Fighting Bodies, Fighting Words', 391.
6. Beauvoir, *The Second Sex*, 283.
7. Bensing, 'A Comparative Study of American Sex Statutes', 58.
8. Bensing, 'A Comparative Study of American Sex Statutes', 58.
9. McGuire, *At the Dark End of the Street*, 198.
10. Klein, 'The Stereotype of Femininity', 4.
11. Klein, 'The Stereotype of Femininity', 4.
12. Hacker, 'Women as a Minority Group', 61.
13. Winder, *Pain, Parties, Work*, 149.
14. Friedan, *The Feminine Mystique*, 173.
15. Coontz, *A Strange Stirring*, 22.
16. Bronstein, *Battling Pornography*, 255.
17. Brownmiller, *Against Our Will*, 312.
18. Brownmiller, *Against Our Will*, 312.
19. Friedan, *The Feminine Mystique*, 86.
20. Friedan, *The Feminine Mystique*, 90.
21. See for instance: *J* 86, 308, 449; *LH* 107, 146; *LVi* 598, 669, 838, 866, 1003.
22. Coontz, *A Strange Stirring*, 69.
23. Coontz, *A Strange Stirring*, 66.
24. Millett, *Sexual Politics*, 253.
25. Millett, *Sexual Politics*, 253.
26. Sanday, *A Woman Scorned*, 131.
27. Sanday, *A Woman Scorned*, 129.
28. Dunkle, 'Cultural and Historical Context', 71.

CHAPTER 18

Plath and the Culture of Hygiene

Laura Perry

'Pureness was the great issue', recalls Esther Greenwood in *The Bell Jar* (91). Drawing upon recent scholarly research into the racialised dimensions of modern hygiene, as well as historical and archival research into the rhetoric of mid-century advertisements, this chapter argues that Plath's concern with purity and cleanliness is a complex, racially coded engagement with a global culture of hygiene. Plath's recurring images of hygiene consumer culture (from a 'clear / Cellophane I cannot crack' to the 'gluepots and pails of Lysol') (*CP* 266, 129) emerge from sexual, racial and national containment during the Cold War years. Plath's poetics of hygiene engages in conversation with a transatlantic discourse about hygiene evident in postwar advertisements and US and UK government publications that trafficked in mid-century anxieties about biological containment, sexual purity and interracial contact. Plath links hygiene to gender, geopolitics and poetic form throughout her writings, and, thus, this attention to hygiene in Plath serves to reframe her search for transcendental purity ('my selves dissolving') (*CP* 232) by showing how this purity is embodied and historically located. As Plath writes, 'the times are tidy' (*CP* 107).

Concepts of hygiene and purity are rhetorically essential to policing racial lines and national boundaries. When Plath put pen to paper, she did so after several decades of eugenic propagandising that led to biological violence against millions worldwide and after a subsequent collective forgetting of the American origins of the eugenic ideals at the heart of the Nazi project.[1] Eugenic ideology may have reached its peak in the United States in the early twentieth century, but the racist fears fomented by eugenic thought persisted long after the government and private institutions that once supported eugenic projects had publicly disavowed them. As one example, many eugenic concerns about racial purity were translated into a sanitised, supposedly neutral concern about the harmful impact of nuclear radiation on the human genome.[2] Advertisements touting the sparkling cleanliness of post-war kitchens used racialised language to portray the new modern domesticity as a crucial bulwark against supposed encroachments on white families, white neighbourhoods and white wealth.[3] Xenophobic, dehumanising language stoked anxieties about infection, contagion and contact that needed to be addressed on both the national and individual level. Edwin Black details in his history of American eugenics and its supporters how 'American eugenicists saw mankind as a biological cesspool.... America's elite were describing the socially worthless and ancestrally unfit as "bacteria," "vermin," "mongrels" and "subhuman".'[4] To think and write about cleanliness is, thus, necessarily also to think and write about attempts to define and police national boundaries as well as the vulnerable bodies within them.[5] As Anne McClintock writes in *Imperial Leather*, connecting colonial cultural products with imperial projects: 'The poetics of cleanliness is a poetics of social discipline. Purification rituals prepare the body as a terrain of meaning, organizing flows of value across the self and the community and demarcating boundaries between one community and another.'[6] In other words, what takes place in the kitchen and the bathroom is shaped by cultural and political forces.[7] Notions of domesticity are intimately entangled with notions of racial and sexual purity, an influence evident in the phrase chosen by Harvard anthropologist E. A. Hooton to describe what he saw as the crucial eugenic project ahead of the United States in the twentieth century: 'biological housekeeping'.[8]

Plath's ambivalence about the cleanliness and purity promised by the modern wonders of mid-twentieth-century domesticity is evident throughout her writings, particularly in the way she connects hygiene with different forms of oppression and policing. She repeatedly foregrounds how a hygienic cultural turn may be anathema to poetic practice, detailing her resistance to a moment in which 'history's beaten the hazard' (*CP* 107). Describing an unsuccessful batch of poems, she writes of feeling: 'as if little hygienic transparent lids shut out the seethe and deep-grounded swell of my experience' (*J* 501). While Plath claims that hygiene, sanitation and sterility are opposed to successful poetic practice, she paradoxically returns again and again to these subjects within her poems and writing. In the 1960 poem 'Magi', Plath presents this hygiene as racialised and gendered. The poem begins by describing 'abstracts' that have a 'whiteness' that 'bears no relation to laundry' but is instead a whiteness associated with 'the Good, the True – // Salutary and pure' (CP 148). Here, as elsewhere, Plath's descriptions of domestic habits of cleanliness like laundry and boiled water make visible the intimate connection between those daily material purities and the abstract purities of a racial ideology that associates whiteness with cleanliness. The lines that follow conjure up the long history of religious and philosophical policing of the gendered, physical body in figures and phrases that explicitly yoke purity with dullness, and oppose it to the female speaker's flourishing.

These hygienic abstractions return in Plath's play *Three Women*, where Plath connects conceptual purity with construction and bureaucracy, providing a spatial infrastructure for these abstract purities. In other words, Plath does not present decontextualised or transcendent images, but rather points out how an abstraction like purity can become, like a bulldozer or a guillotine, an instrument of the state. One of the titular three women, describes 'cold angels' that echo the 'dull angels / . . . Salutary and pure' of 'Magi:'

> I watched the men walk about me in the office.
> They were so flat!
> There was something about them like cardboard, and now
>   I had caught it,
> That flat, flat, flatness from which ideas, destructions,
> Bulldozers, guillotines, white chambers of shrieks proceed,
> Endlessly proceed – and the cold angels, the abstractions.[9]

Here, Plath begins to describe a patriarchal project that, in its abstraction, links mass production (cardboard, bulldozers), bureaucracy (the office) and the atrocities of war (guillotines, white chambers of shrieks).

Her use of Holocaust imagery has sparked criticism, but this reference seems markedly different from Plath's more self-referential turns to the events of the Second World War in 'Lady Lazarus' and 'Daddy'. Rather, her expansive analogy between 'the office' and 'chambers of shrieks' connects these spaces in order to suggest an ideological link by way of flatness, akin to Hannah Arendt's phrase 'the banality of evil' in its focus on narrative and tone. Plath goes on:

> Governments, parliaments, societies,
> The faceless faces of important men.
> It is these men I mind:
>
> . . .
>
> 'Let us make a heaven,' they say.
> 'Let us flatten and launder the grossness from these
> souls.'[10]

The implied connection becomes clear, as 'governments, parliaments, societies' declare hygiene a state project and, in a gendered labour inversion, work to 'launder the grossness from these souls'. In these lines, Plath invokes the 'biological housekeeping'[11] of eugenic ideologies and presents it as a transatlantic anxiety that drives both parliaments and societies at large. These hygienic assumptions are rhetorical, happening and taking root in language and propagating through literary, legal and popular texts.

Plath's invocations of purity connect body with culture, inviting us to consider how ideas of what makes a clean body are gendered and policed by institutions and norms. Her interest in purity includes her expansive and rigorous critique of mid-century gender norms and expectations, as in Esther's explanation of sexual purity in *The Bell Jar*, cited in the first sentence of this chapter.[12] Hygiene helps to define gender roles and family structures, as in 'The Colossus', where purity becomes a patriarchal project, as the speaker describes carefully cleaning a large paternal statue, 'scaling little ladders with gluepots and pails of Lysol' (*CP* 129). Lysol is a particularly resonant agent of 'biological housekeeping', not only because it was initially marketed as a douche, but also because, as Lysol advertisements reminded consumers, hygiene and national defense are united: 'like a good housekeeper, Uncle Sam disinfects and deodorizes as he cleans'.[13] This is a collision of anxieties that Plath returns to time and again, tracing a through-line from personal hygiene to Cold War containment and geopolitics.

In 1956's 'Tale of a Tub', Plath's speaker begins by seemingly buying into the promise of modern sanitation and order. Her speaker compares the dangers 'bred' by the 'familiar tub' in decades past with how modern 'water faucets spawn no danger' (*CP* 25). Another version of her claim that 'history's beaten the hazard', these lines ostensibly refer to water purification. Yet this is not about whether water is potable, but about breeding, spawning, dangers to come and the 1930s (a timeframe made explicit by the speaker's mention of 'Twenty years ago'). Again, Plath makes historical links by way of sanitation and purity. She goes on to depict what could be a restful scene of bathing (limbs, under water) and fiction ('dreams') interrupted by 'absolute fact':

> absolute fact
> intrudes even when the revolted eye
> is closed; the tub exists behind our back:
> its glittering surfaces are blank and true   (*CP* 25).

The site of sanitation becomes one of confinement ('the shape that shuts us in') and purity that, even at this site of intimate, immediate, embodied cleansing, 'exists behind our back' and exceeds the bodily context. The close of the poem rejects both nostalgia and optimism, ending instead in an apocalyptic image that foregrounds how purity is contextual and historical, formed by 'the navel of this present waste' (*CP* 25).

Plath's 'hospital poems', the label many critics use for her non-sequential but recurrent poems set in wards, rooms and operating theatres, are another recognisable constellation in which she works out these ideas. In many poems, Plath could be a contributor to the 'Third Book of Fear', as she describes in 'Johnny Panic and the Bible of Dreams', her short hospital story where a germophobe's dreams form the basis for 'Chapter Nine of Dirt, Disease, and General Decay' (*JP* 159).[14] In 'Johnny Panic', Plath's narrator views consciousness as unclean, framing the physical body using images that echo mid-century rhetoric about decaying urban land-scapes and the white sanctum of suburban pastoralism:

> It's into this lake people's minds run at night, brooks and gutter trickles to one borderless common reservoir. It bears no resemblance to those pure sparkling-blue sources of drinking water the suburbs guard more jealously than the Hope diamond in the middle of pine woods and barbed fences. It's the sewage farm of the ages, transparence aside (*JP* 159).

In this spatial arrangement, the 'borderless common reservoir' becomes the 'sewage farm of the ages'.

Yet what this description also points out is how borders are more rhetorical than physical, as the suburbanites with 'barbed fences' and 'pure', sanitary drinking water remain implicated and contaminated by this 'common reservoir' in which we all swim. This purity would have had an apparent racial cast to it in a national culture where, for example, the *Christian Observer* referred to immigrants moving into American neighbourhoods as 'like sediment in the water'.[15] The cleanliness of the suburban landscape was and remains a racialised project supported by government action and funding. As Carl Zimring notes in *Clean and White*:

> American sanitation systems; zoning boards; real estate practices; federal, state, and municipal governments; and makers and marketers of cleaning products have all worked with an understanding of hygiene that assumes that 'white people' are clean, and 'non-white people' are less than clean.[16]

Plath's figures of purity implicitly address this mid-century conflation of hygiene and the racist politics of advertisements and suburban real estate.

The Bell Jar includes meditations on 'the celestially white kitchens of *Ladies' Day*' magazine (*BJ* 53) and 'the white, shining, identical clap-board houses with their interstices of well-groomed green proceeded past, one bar after another in a large but escape-proof cage' (*BJ* 128). Plath takes up this conflation – between clean and white – and employs it in writing that makes connections across bodily boundaries and the larger terrain of national and international conflicts. When Plath writes about dirt, dust, stickiness, pus, sewage, garbage and the inextricable accompanying host of 'celestially white kitchens' and 'bright, white, sterile cubicle[s]' and 'white, shining, identical clapboard houses with their interstices of well-groomed green', the language she uses depends on the cultural power of hygiene as an agent in enforcing national and racial boundaries. In Plath, hygiene not only divides up a geographical landscape but also polices the human body. Her shifting notions of purity help put in context the mid-century injunction to 'master the surface' (as she describes her own ambition in a journal entry that elides the distinction between personal hygiene and poetic practice).[17] Though she writes her brother from across the pond, 'How I miss our American hygiene, preventative and wise',[18] Plath's poems make connections between hygiene and other cultural and legal forces of sexism and racism. Purity is not neutral.

Plath repeatedly returns to sanitary spaces like hospitals, but also to the material culture of hygiene and the products that make tangible these cultural anxieties. Plath's use of cellophane, for example, speaks to the collision of containment narratives, biological purity and poetic form in the face of the new technological modern hygiene of post-war domesticity.[19] Cellophane's role allows us to think through the link between visibility and hygiene in modern domesticity. Consider the rhetoric in DuPont cellophane ads from the 1940s and 1950s, which would have appeared in magazines like the *Ladies' Home Journal* and *Ladies' Day*, which Plath read:

> Let the strange hands grab and paw ... Dust, dirt and the germs on inquisitive hands are *kept out* by ... Cellophane. It keeps out *foreign odors* too.
> ... Dust is the drab veil that smothers clear, lovely color. The dirtiest dirt, ground so fine that you can't even see its true ugliness. In smoky cities, it's a powdered mass of acids that eat fabrics. It's a magic carpet for *billions* of germs ...
> ... Strange hands. Inquisitive hands. Dirty hands. Touching, feeling, examining the things *you* buy in stores. Your sure protection against *hands-across-the-counter* is tough, clear, germproof Cellophane.[20]

As these anxieties about 'strange hands', 'foreign odors', 'smoky cities', the invasion of 'hands-across-the-counter' and the germ-filled 'magic

carpet' suggest, the cultural force of cellophane was rhetorically connected to mid-century worries about containment, contamination and
the imagined encroachment of dirty, unclean bodies into public and
private spaces.[21]

This reframing of cellophane's glamour helps cast Plath's poetic
figures in a new light. In a draft of 'The Babysitters' still entitled, at
this point, 'Madonna (of the Refrigerator)', 'gilded cellophane' promises glamour yoked to a national regime of appearances – where
a 'tan' echoes the packaging of cellophane:

> Tan and American, seen through the gilded cellophane
> that takes the place of Dutch veneer.[22]

In packaging skin in cellophane, Plath invites considerations of the
marketing of human flesh, the racial politics of skin color.[23] Plath
implicitly links Americanness with modernisation, 'taking the place of
Dutch veneer', but with reservations. The clear plasticity of cellophane
simultaneously invokes surveillance, glamour and hygiene – an intimate
distance that emphasises both visuality and materiality, a form that is
meant to disappear but, particularly in its initial emergence, became the
focus. This understanding of cellophane unifies containment narratives,
surveillance and hygiene – a trinity that reveals the importance of biological containment (purity) to containment narratives and the nuclear
family.[24]

In 'Paralytic' (*CP* 266–7), Plath connects the domestic cleanliness of
cellophane with the medical hygiene of national projects, by inverting
interiors and exteriors in her attention to various containers (lungs,
dust bags, breasts, eggs, worlds, photographs, water, flowers and, of
course, cellophane). In 'Paralytic', the male speaker (a rarity in Plath),
is simultaneously domesticated and medicalised – he is a vacuum
cleaner under cellophane ('Dust bags' for lungs, under 'A clear /
Cellophane I cannot crack') as well as a patient with an iron lung
and an oxygen tent. On the one hand, this is a scene of claustrophobia,
and the failure of hermitically sealed isolation to support poetic production, where 'selves dissolving' dissolve into dust bags rather than
a transcendent purity.[25] On the other hand, the lines 'Dead egg, I lie /
Whole / on a whole world I cannot touch', particularly in the context
of cellophane, invite comparisons between the medicalised, domesticated patient under cellophane and the biological products of industrial agriculture, under cellophane. Inverting the expected relationship
between a human observer and cellophane, that of consumer and

product, here the speaker is inside the cellophane, inside the egg shell, and sanitised and under surveillance as a piece of meat. Plath likewise conflates medicalised human bodies and animal byproducts again in another hospital poem, 'The Surgeon at 2 a.m.', in which she describes an amputated limb as a 'pathological salami'.

With these comparisons, Plath extends purity to yet another context: the animal body. With the advent of modernised processing, packaging and preservation, particularly in the post-war era, poultry and bypro-ducts production – the business of making eggs and salamis – trans-formed more radically than perhaps any other sector of food production. Hygiene, in the form of antibiotics, power-washing and packaging (new artificial casings, like cellophane and others), worked to substantially alter the materiality of the animal body as experienced by modern consumers.[26] In positioning speakers as a 'pathological salami' and a 'dead egg, whole' 'unable to touch the whole world', Plath brings together human and non-human subjects under a shared regime of hygiene and surveillance. These domestic forms of purity – clean laun-dry, sanitised meat – call to mind the same mid-century anxieties about meat-packing, biological containment and consumer safety aroused by the 'strange' and 'foreign' threats of DuPont Cellophane advertisements. Her depictions of purity invoke the purity of eugenics, stretching across borders and re-emerging in chronologies that reject collective forgetting, sexual purity as a national project, municipal purity and neighbourhood hygiene as a white supremacist, government-enforced project, and, here, another international form of hygiene and purity: agricultural.

Plath is not the first poet to be drawn to hygiene and its attendant cultural signifiers and tropes. As Robin G. Schulze argues in *The Degenerate Muse*, Plath's poetic forebears Marianne Moore and Ezra Pound found the relationship between fears of racial and cultural decline and poetic practice an important and driving concern. Because artists are so often charged with degeneracy, poets have an intimate connection to the concept. As Schulze describes, Moore and Pound 'struggled to write in ways that would not be perceived as unhealthy by their countrymen', which meant, particularly in Pound's case, 'posing as a patient rather than a doctor'.[27] Where Pound's interests in degen-eration and hygiene were, Schulze argues, 'part of what led him to appreciate Mussolini's fascist program in the 1920s and 30s',[28] for Plath, years later, a focus on hygiene would be part of connecting a series of cultural fixations and historical atrocities. In Plath's repeated invocations of cleanliness across domestic and statist projects, she underscores the persistence of an ideology of purity and the cultural power of hygiene.

Notes

1. For more on eugenics in the United States, see Black, *War against the Weak*. As Black details, eugenics and sanitation were deeply intertwined. Many leading eugenicists were students of earlier sanitation movements concerned with germs and disease, one reason why the terms 'eugenics' and 'race hygiene' were often used interchangeably (*War against the Weak*, 262). See also Bruinius, *Better for All*.
2. Kühl, *For the Betterment*, 147.
3. See, among others, Baldwin, *The Racial Imaginary*, and Harris, *Little White Houses*.
4. Black, *War against the Weak*, 235, 258.
5. As Mary Douglas writes in *Purity and Danger*, 'the mistake is to treat bodily margins in isolation from all other margins' (122).
6. McClintock, *Imperial Leather*, 226.
7. The influence of cultural, political and racial ideologies on notions of purity and hygiene extends to spaces beyond the kitchen and the bathroom, of course. For example, one of Plath's first acts after setting foot in her college campus was to take the required 'hygiene exam', an institutional articulation of purity that she described in a September 1950 letter to her mother as 'peculiar' and surprisingly unscientific: 'Technical questions were few and far between' (*LV1* 175).
8. Quoted in Bruinius, *Better for All*, 239.
9. Plath, *Three Women*, 9.
10. Plath, *Three Women*, 12.
11. E. A. Hooton, quoted in Bruinius, *Better for All*, 239.
12. Feminine purity was increasingly biological as well as behavioural, evident in what US historian Elaine Tyler May calls in *Homeward Bound* 'wartime purity crusades . . . a revision of the germ theory: germs were not responsible for spreading disease, "promiscuous" women were' (*Homeward Bound*, 69). Propaganda warned 'she may look clean – but . . .' (*Homeward Bound*, 70).
13. Lysol advertisement, 35.
14. Citations are from the 1977 Faber and Faber edition.
15. Quoted in Schulze, *The Degenerate Muse*, 16.
16. Zimring, *Clean and White*, 217.
17. In Plath's *Journals*: 'My face I know not. . . . exuding soft spots of pus, points of dirt, hard kernels of impurity . . . The surface texture of life can be dead, was dead for me. My voice halted, my skin felt the pounds & pounds pressure of other I's on every inch, wrinkled, puckered, sank in on itself. Now to grow out. To suck up & master the surface' (*J* 306).
18. 1956 Plath letter, quoted in Brain, *The Other Sylvia Plath*, 57.

200 LAURA PERRY

19. For more on Plath's environmentalism, see Brain (*The Other Sylvia Plath*), Knickerbocker (*Ecopoetics*), Peel (*Writing Back*). Brain reads Plath's bodily boundaries as cultural spaces, where 'the permutation and poisoning of the human body by toxic chemicals and pollutants' and 'material interpenetrations mirror the ideas of cultural movement and permeability that are also important in Plath's work' (*The Other Sylvia Plath* 85).

20. Fenichell, *Plastic*, 115.

21. See the Hagley Library's fascinating archive of digitised DuPont Cellophane advertisements from the early twentieth century: www.hagley.org/research/digital-exhibits/packaging/polymers.

22. Connors, 'Madonna (of the Refrigerator)', 136.

23. In one particularly strange crossover between Plath's poetic project and its critical afterlife, Elizabeth Winder, a biographer of Plath's, claims in *Pain, Parties, Work* that Plath's skin 'has been described as waxen or looking like wet cellophane' (47).

24. For an overview of literary responses to Cold War-era geopolitics, see, for example, Davidson (*Guys Like Us*), Nadel (*Containment Culture*), Nelson (*Pursuing Privacy*). Davidson and Nelson discuss Plath at length.

25. As Judith Brown notes in *Glamour in Six Dimensions*, this is also where Plath recasts Gertrude Stein's icy modernist flatness as a stifling project (168).

26. Horowitz, *Putting Meat on the American Table*, 129–52.

27. Schulze, *The Degenerate Muse*, 35.

28. Schulze, *The Degenerate Muse*, 234.

PART V

Political and Religious Contexts

CHAPTER 19

The Bell Jar, *the Rosenbergs and the Problem of the Enemy Within*

Robin Peel

The execution of Julius and Ethel Rosenberg forms the famous first sentence of *The Bell Jar*, and its significance has long been recognised and debated. As the event fades further into history the extraordinary impact on the collective psyche of 1950s American Cold War hysteria can easily be forgotten, as it seems to be forgotten by Plath's narrator once she has returned from New York to Massachusetts. Here I will argue that the Rosenbergs cast a shadow across the whole novel, with their electrocution for espionage serving an important metonymic function. The trial and 1953 execution represent a Cold War anxiety that had surfaced in Plath's 1958 short story 'Johnny Panic' in which the female narrator's illicit copying of confidential documents is punished by ECT, and in a British spy trial as Plath began writing her novel. In 1953 the fate of Ethel Rosenberg, who before her arrest had seemed to be a conventional 1950s wife and mother, suggested the terrible fate of those who heroically refused to conform. The Rosenberg trial mirrors the insider-outsider dialectic of Plath's novel and provides a counterpoint to the absurd paradox of *self*-destruction.

The Bell Jar's account of 1953 New York and Massachusetts was written in London in 1961. Alan Nadel notes that this eight-year interval witnessed a change to the Cold War 'story of containment ... [which] derived its logic from the rigid major premise that the world was divided into two monolithic camps, one dedicated to promoting ... capitalism, democracy and [Judeo-Christian] religion, and one seeking to destroy the ideological amalgamation by any means.'[1] By the mid-1960s the logic of such *containment* had been exploded. *The Bell Jar* is one of the first novels to view 1950s events from this revised, droll perspective.

Ted Hughes declared 1961 the most terrifying of years. Plath composed the novel against the background of the disastrous Bay of Pigs invasion of Cuba and the later Berlin Wall military stand-offs. As Plath started writing, in March 1961 a couple known as Peter and Helen Kroger, two spies with links to the Rosenbergs, were appearing at the Old Bailey in London in the headline-making Portland Spy Ring trial. The Krogers were actually Morris and Lona Cohen, who, it later emerged, had fled New York soon after the Rosenbergs' arrest in 1950. Lona appears to have been a courier who passed on secrets from Los Alamos to the Soviet Union. She probably had contact with Ethel's brother, David Greenglass.

But first, a word of explanation. In her 2006 essay on the reception of *The Bell Jar*, Janet Badia[2] considers how what Plath herself described to a friend as an 'amateur novel' and to her mother as merely 'a potboiler and just practice' (*LH* 468, 477) has become a cult novel that now features in cartoons, contemporary films and high school syllabuses. It is part of popular culture, as the latest film version confirms. Plath was alert to a market in which Mary Jane Ward's successful 1946 novel *The Snake Pit* inspired a successful 1948 film. In 1959, Plath wrote in her journal, 'Must get out SNAKE PIT. There is an increasing market for mental-hospital stuff. I am a fool if I don't relive, recreate it' (*J* 495). *The Ha-Ha*, Jennifer Dawson's well-received 1961 novel about an Oxbridge student who has a breakdown and receives treatment in an institution, received favourable reviews. For some readers *The Bell Jar* is either the slight apprenticeship, poet's notebook novel that Plath told her mother it was, or a callow novel popular because it trades on the experiences of young women who suffer teenage depression and the trauma of mental hospital life. It would be foolish to deny these elements in the novel's reputation, but though it might have started out as a money-earner that exploited the appetite created by the earlier success of fiction by J. D. Salinger and Shirley Jackson, it is a significant work that insightfully captures the 1950s conformist pressures on Americans, particularly young American women.

But how important are the deaths of the Rosenbergs to this novel? Early critics often considered their significance marginal.[3] 'The Rosenbergs are in no way part of the story',[4] wrote Elizabeth Hardwick in 1974, allocating them a limited metaphorical function. *The Bell Jar* might open with the sentence 'It was a queer, sultry summer, the summer they executed the Rosenbergs' followed later on this first page with Esther's comment that 'I kept hearing about the Rosenbergs over the radio and at the office' but the narrator herself admits that 'although she couldn't get them out of my mind' the incident 'had nothing to do with me' (*BJ* 1).[5] Esther suggests that it is the idea of being electrocuted, 'being burned alive all along your nerves' that haunted her, and her obsession with their imminent deaths, like her obsession with the cadavers she was shown by Buddy Willard, is a symptom of her own personal psychological decline and disintegration.

After all, this novel originally had the title 'Diary of a Suicide' and much early criticism read it as a transparently autobiographical work, concerned primarily with the depression that led to Plath's own suicide attempt in 1953. If critics mentioned Plath's employment of political and historical events such as the Rosenbergs' execution, it was disparagingly. Plath was appropriating their deaths gratuitously and for effect, a charge that had been levelled by Alvarez at Plath's use in her 'Ariel' poetry of the atom bomb dropped on Japan[6] and in Steiner's remark about Plath's 'subtle larceny'[7] of the Holocaust. Opening her novel with the Rosenbergs – and then seemingly dropping them – looked similarly meretricious.

A closer examination, however, confirms that spying, surveillance and punishment inform much of Plath's writing after 1958. 'Johnny Panic', can be read as a story of espionage, in which the narrator (a deliberate conflation of hospital employee and patient) reads and copies out secret information, is intercepted and taken to the punishment room to receive electric shock treatment anticipating the 'spying' and 'punishment' in *The Bell Jar*. Esther Greenwood spies on Dodo Conway when she hears Dodo's pram on the sidewalk. She spies through the Venetian blind in the bathroom on Olga, the 'Slavic lady' (*BJ* 239) who calls on Irwin. She observes those who spy on her, whether it is Mrs Tomolillo in the hospital, or the nosey neighbour Mrs Ockenden. Esther spends a great deal of time looking, studying and scrutinising. 'I liked looking on at other people', she says (*BJ* 13), but like the Rosenbergs, is bewildered by what feels like inexplicable retribution. 'I wondered what terrible thing it was that I had done' (*BJ* 152) she declares, after her first, abortive ECT treatment. In their prison letters to one another the Rosenbergs find their arrest, sentence and betrayal by close and trusted individuals inexplicable. David Greenglass betrayed his sister Ethel, who also felt betrayed by her mother. Esther feels betrayed by Buddy Willard and Dr Nolan. Buddy pretended to be sexually innocent, but then confesses to an affair, while trusted Dr Nolan fails to prepare Esther for her hospital ECT treatment.

The Rosenbergs reappear briefly in Chapter 9, when Hilda comments on their imminent execution. Hilda is, in Macpherson's words, 'Plath's symbol for McCarthyism's captive citizen'[8] when she says in a sentence repeated three times by Esther, with the second in italics '*I'm so glad they're going to die*' (*BJ* 104). The Rosenbergs are not named again, but this is a pivotal chapter, after which Esther's rebellious cynicism hardens into a quest for death, which promises an escape from otherwise intractable, overpowering forces. Esther returns to the suburbs still streaked with Marco's blood on her cheeks, and sinks into a suffocating depression. 'A summer calm laid its soothing hand over everything, like death' (*BJ* 119). Esther's great fear is that she is a fraud. Her creative writing professor wrote 'Factitious' on her story 'The Big Weekend'. She consults her dictionary: 'Factitious, artificial, sham' (*BJ* 155). In contrast, the Rosenbergs' deaths secured them *authenticity*. Esther systematically embarks on a quest to achieve this authenticity. Her failed and painful ECT treatment, overseen by Dr Gordon, accelerates Esther to attempt suicide, emulating the Rosenbergs' martyrdom.

Ethel and Julius Rosenberg were executed for the crime of conspiracy in passing information about the atomic bomb to the Soviet Union, information that supposedly allowed the United States' Cold War enemy to carry out a successful test in 1949. They were arrested in 1950 and tried and found guilty in 1951. The trail leading to their arrest began with Klaus Fuchs, a German-born Englishman who was found guilty of spying for the Soviet Union. His courier was Harry Gold, who identified David Greenglass as another source of information about the Los Alamos research into atomic bomb making. Under interrogation David Greenglass, who had worked as a mechanic at the Los Alamos bomb project, implicated Julius and Ethel, largely it seems to secure his own survival and that of his wife Ruth. Following his arrest in 1950 he gave evidence that Julius had recruited him and encouraged him to pass on sketches (crude sketches) of the atomic bomb to him; his own sister Ethel had typed up the reports. Ethel seems to have been arrested largely to exert pressure on her husband. David Greenglass did not serve his full sentence, but was released from prison in November 1960, just before Plath started work on *The Bell Jar*. His release is mentioned in *The Times* report of the last day of the Portland Spy Ring trial in March 1961.

Is Esther's name an allusion to Esther Ethel Greenglass Rosenberg? Possibly not, as Plath's maternal grandmother was Aurelia Greenwood Schober and Plath changed the name of her protagonist Victoria Lucas to Esther Greenwood quite late in the publication negotiations. But both Esther and Ethel initially conform to 1950s gender norms that shaped American women's appearance and role in society. The conformist woman paid great attention to her looks, was deferential to men and expected to be devoted wife, homemaker and mother. Following her experience as guest editor at *Ladies' Day,* a magazine devoted to *image,* Esther internalises during an empty domestic summer of introspection the totalitarian banality of this power. Macpherson notes the parallel between this self-surveillance and the tyranny of McCarthyism's anti-communism, noting drolly that the 'Hoover in every home'[9] is the FBI chief as much as it is a home-cleaning appliance. Macpherson describes J. Edgar Hoover as a social hygienist, for whom failure to be anything but a strident anti-communist, just like a woman's failure to clean, was evidence that that the suspect individual is in reality an enemy within. Communism is likened to an infectious disease. No-one is immune. In the novel the conventional male Buddy Willard contracts TB, which, he remarks, is 'like living with a bomb in your lung' (*BJ* 92). Esther is haunted by the Rosenbergs partly because they represent that rejection of the norm, and are prepared to die for their beliefs. Esther's feeling that marriage and motherhood ensured that women 'went about numb as a slave in some private, totalitarian state' (*BJ* 89) partly echoes Ethel's assertion that their execution would make them the 'first victims of American Fascism'.[10]

In 1959 Nixon and Khrushchev had engaged in the famous 'kitchen debate' at the American exhibition in Moscow. Nixon boasted that American superiority was reflected in the American kitchen with its labour-saving washing machines. Nixon's model of the good life assumed the role of woman as homemaker, and consumer goods as the real weapons in the Cold War, a subject discussed in Elaine Tyler May's insightful 1988 study of containment and American families in the Cold War era. May describes how 'containment' became the means to ensure American survival and success.[11] The kitchen is one such place of containment and Esther notes its place in the commercial culture. '*Ladies' Day* – the big women's magazine that features lush double-page spreads of technicolour meals, with a different theme and locale each month – we had been shown around the endless glossy kitchens' (*BJ* 26–7). Nuclear weapons needed to be contained in the hands of the US, and sexuality contained by a family centred norm. The *Ladies' Day* food testing kitchen is staffed by women in 'hygienic white smocks, neat hair nets and flawless make-up of a uniform peach-pie colour' (*BJ* 26).

The distancing of time (1961 looking back to 1953) and place (looking back to the Cold War United States from Cold War Europe) is mirrored in *The Bell Jar*'s internal retrospection, as the narrator Esther is writing from a position of recovery recalling a period that ends with a tentative and uncertain survival. Yet, as Tim Kendall points out,[12] there is no explanation of how the journey was made from fragile solitary woman to Esther's apparently happy motherhood. Images of babies in *The Bell Jar* are frequently unsettling. In the moment before Esther breaks her leg, pressed by Buddy into trying a ski slope that is beyond her ability, she likens herself to 'the white sweet baby cradled in its mother's belly' (*BJ* 102). Later Esther imagines herself as a baby, taking hot milk after her reaction, 'tasting it luxuriously, the way a baby tastes its mother' (*BJ* 213). There are false babies. Esther becomes increasingly fat as a consequence of the course of insulin injections she has at Caplan and notes: 'I looked just as if I were going to have a baby' (*BJ* 203). But the 'Children made me sick' ('*made*' not 'make') response to Dodo Conway's multiple children, is the older Esther performing her younger voice, her Caulfield voice.

The conflation of Eisenhower and babyhood makes a sharp political point. Eisenhower had been elected president in 1952 and again in 1956. It was Eisenhower who refused to override the Rosenberg court's verdict and judge's death penalty. The decision to deny clemency was made public on 11 February 1953, exactly ten years before Plath's own death. In a letter written that same day, Julius Rosenberg wrote that 'this harsh and cruel decision was sired in madness'.[13] Eisenhower's domed head, central to Plath's 1960 Cold War collage, is twice associated with dead or doomed children. When Esther visits Buddy at the sanatorium, she tells us: 'On a low coffee-table lay a few wilted numbers of *Time* and *Life*. I flipped to the middle of the nearest magazine. The face of Eisenhower beamed up at me, bald and blank as the face of a foetus in a bottle' (*BJ* 93). The Eisenhower-faced baby has a happier context among the pictures in *Baby Talk*, which Esther peruses, ironically, while she is waiting to be measured for a contraceptive device. But even here Esther thinks of the 'anxious and unsettling world' (*BJ* 234) in which they will grow up. The Rosenberg letters show how the couple agonised over the consequences of their deaths on their own young children. But, Julius writes, '(a)s long as we do the right thing by our children and the good people of the world, nothing else matters'.[14]

Plath's 1958 journal speaks of the nightmare of 'Joan of Arc's face, as she feels the fire and the world blurs out in a smoke, a pall of horror' (*J* 386). On learning that Judge Kaufman refused to alter the death sentence, Ethel Rosenberg likens herself to Joan in Shaw's play *Saint Joan*. Judge Kaufman will be like Shaw's prosecutor who knows that while Joan will go to heaven he will go to hell. Plath, however, is driven to judge and punish *herself* and her anxieties are displaced into metaphors of mental and physical oblitera-tion, the bell jar and burning. In the end, it is her 'double', Joan Gilling, who dies. Joan is not electrocuted, or burned, but found hanged. The Rosenbergs, like Esther, are masquerading insiders who reject American ideology. This partly explains why they haunt Esther, who evolves from insider into traumatised outsider. Notorious 1953 essays by Leslie Fiedler and Robert Warshow derided the myth of the Rosenbergs' martyrdom, arguing that the Rosenbergs were shallow frauds.

There are other parallels. Like Esther, the institutionalised Ethel banished her mother. Astonishingly, Mrs Greenglass had begged Ethel to *support* David's damning testimony. '(F)or Hoover, Ethel's refusal to see her mother was . . . evidence of a betrayal of her role as a good daughter'.[15] The FBI was able to characterise Ethel as an unnatural mother because of this strained relationship and the fact that she would not confess for the sake of her children. An FBI psychological profile concluded that 'Julius is the slave and his wife Ethel the master'.[16] Like Esther's sexual assertiveness, this represented a dangerous subversion of 1950s gender norms. At the end of Plath's novel Buddy is physically weak. When his car needs to be dug out of a snowdrift Esther notes 'Buddy . . . let me do most of the work' (*BJ* 251). Contemporary anxieties about Ethel are evident in the description by eyewitness reporter Bob Considine of Ethel's electrocution: 'Ethel wore a Mona Lisa smile . . . (and) as the torrent of electricity swept through her body . . . I had the startled feeling that she would break those bonds and come charging across the floor, wielding those tight little fists.'[17] Carmichael argues, 'It is clear that the level of discourse has changed from one of public and institutional rationalization to one of primitive fears and fantasies of the woman out of bounds.'[18]

Marie Ashe goes further, claiming that Ethel and Esther face an identical sense of failure as 'proper' women and that this is what drives them towards radical vindicating actions.[19] On the day after her husband was arrested, Ethel was photographed and interviewed by reporters in her kitchen. A month later she herself was arrested. Ashe argues that Ethel Rosenberg assumed the role of heroic martyr precisely because she identified with late 1940s and early 1950s images of womanhood, involving caring mother and homemaking wife of the kind that appeared in glossy advertisements in American magazines, but fell short of this ideal. As a consequence, if she could not succeed as the perfect woman, she would triumph as a Joan of Arc martyr. Similarly, Esther, who discovers in New York that she is at odds with the 1950s ideal of womanhood (she mocks the advertisements showing the happy housewife in her gleaming kitchen), after failing to destroy herself, seeks resurrection through submission to ECT. Only through extreme resolution and action can both women defy a senseless world. This is a seductive reading of the parallel between the Rosenberg events and *The Bell Jar*, but it requires us to ignore the difference between two different kinds of politics. Ethel dies; Esther not only survives, she succeeds as both writer and mother.

In the kitchen photograph taken just before her arrest Ethel stands drying the dishes, looking unglamorous beside the battered rubbish bin.

In contrast, glossy advertisements in the *Life* magazines that Plath leafed through in her small London apartment seemed to show how magical the American dream could become. By 1961 it was clear that the United States was winning the kitchen war, but the Soviet model of womanhood rejected *homemaking*. Esther sits with Constantin in a plush United Nations auditorium 'next to a stern, muscular Russian girl with no make-up, who is a simultaneous interpreter like Constantin' (*BJ* 78). This was not the domestic woman praised by Nixon in the kitchen debate, but a woman speaking in two languages, two codes, two voices. Esther wishes she could crawl inside this woman and do what she is doing, 'barking out one idiom after the other' (*BJ* 78). *The Bell Jar* voice is a prolonged experiment in idiom.

Hilda's culturally ventriloquised callous Rosenberg remark reminds Esther of a dibbuk's voice. Ethel was almost certainly arrested in the belief that she would possess her husband, forcing him to speak. But there was no last-minute confession from either Rosenberg, to either the world or the officiating rabbi. At their execution, special FBI personnel were on standby ready to intervene and interrupt the executions if either of them spoke. They said nothing.

Esther speaks unstoppably in Plath's novel, but in a sardonic, cynical and detached voice. It is not the voice Plath used in her 1953 journal, where she expresses excitement about the guest editorship and New York, and neither is it the voice of the older, wiser Esther, mother of a baby. Her voice, like that in Kafka, deliberately 'defamiliarizes the world'.[20] Tracy Brain has shown how earlier drafts of the novel indicate the strong case for regarding Esther as an unreliable narrator.[21] We should not accept at face value Esther's comment that the Rosenbergs had nothing to do with her. Ethel's voice, whether speaking in court, or in her prison letters to Julius, was attacked by commentators, who declared it empty or contrived. Plath's decision to have as narrator an adult woman writing in the persona of a senior student enforces the simultaneous political engagement and detachment that has troubled some readers.

Ethel is condemned partly because she refused to be defined by mother-hood. Esther's alignment is more equivocal. She aligns herself with con-ventional heterosexuality, as demanded by Red Scare homophobia. Although she will not be like Dodo Conway, the servant of her womb, she rejects the childless professionalism of the lesbian poet at her college. Esther leaves the asylum; Ethel never left the prison alive. Ethel and Esther succeed in their own terms, but at a considerable price. Ethel refused to be saved through confession; for her electrocution is more valiant than the compromised life. Esther is briefly attracted to the heroic authenticity of death secured by the appropriately named 'Red-mountain' Rosenbergs. Suicide, too, could be a political act. F. O. Matthiessen, the Harvard scholar who represented the East Coast establishment that McCarthy loathed, had jumped to his death from a Boston hotel window on 1 April 1950, leaving a note that included the sentence 'As a Christian and a socialist believing in international peace, I find myself terribly oppressed by the present tensions.'[22] But after her own failed suicide attempt Esther contemplates her own rebirth. She accepts ECT in return for a second chance.

The novel ends with Esther about to be discharged from the asylum. It is a moment both banal and profound. As Esther enters the judicial interview room, she senses rebirth, but feels like a 'retreaded' tyre (*BJ* 257). Unlike Joan, who has just been buried in their hometown, Esther will return to college. Unlike Ethel Rosenberg whose silence meant an acceptance of death, Esther has chosen life. Ethel entered the electrocution chamber and said nothing of consequence. Esther is silent only *about* her interrogation. But in returning to the college in which the 'girls sat under bell jars of a sort' (*BJ* 251) like the inmates at Belsize, she knows this might be a temporary reprieve. She is rejoining conventional society, but as Buddy implies, who will marry a woman who has been in an asylum? Esther knows that 'To the person in the bell jar, blank and stopped as a dead baby, the world itself is the bad dream' (*BJ* 250). But we know that Esther has a living baby, and quite possibly, the husband Buddy thinks will be denied her. The Rosenbergs bravely accepted electrocution as the price for their beliefs. Esther has taken her own kind of punishment, involving incarceration and electric shock treatment, and she has now written the account we are now reading as a book. There is more than one route to immortality.

In the closing scenes, the earlier Rosenberg references are not forgotten. The summer heat in which they were sacrificially 'burned' has been replaced by the cold of January, symbolic, perhaps, of the Cold War, for Plath's writing fuses private life and public events. Eight years on from 1953, the Cold War continued and another spy trial, fears about the radioactive contamination of cows' milk and nuclear Armageddon meant that the political atmosphere continued to crackle like a Geiger counter. By the early 1960s, however, the absurdity of 1950s containment, conformity and conservatism could now be the subject of dark humour, as it is in the black comedy of *Catch-22* (1961) and the film *Dr Strangelove* (1964), so different in tone from the 1958 novel on which it is based. *The Bell Jar* anticipates many later novels in its sardonic reading of 1950s containment, including the death of the Rosenbergs. Unlike Ethel, Esther *is* prepared to answer the board's questions to secure her release. Together, the assertive dismissal of Buddy and Irwin, the callous treatment of transgressive Joan, and the conformist straightened stockings worn for the 'hearing' make Esther's 'recovery' more like betrayal and capitulation. But the narrative is teasingly ambiguous to the end. Esther is dressed in clothes reminiscent of the ones she once threw over the balcony, but it is a flamboyant *red* suit she is wearing.

Notes

1. Nadel, *Containment Culture*, 7.
2. See Badia, '*The Bell Jar* and Other Prose'.
3. Janet Salter, one of Plath's friends at Smith, believes that Plath simply used the Rosenbergs as a device to set the novel in time. This was something that the professor in the creative writing course they both took as Juniors had stressed to them. [Email from JSR to RP October 2017.] Coincidentally [though the name is common], Janet Salter later married a Rosenberg.
4. Hardwick, 'On Sylvia Plath', 113.
5. Citations from *The Bell Jar* in this chapter refer to the 1986 Faber and Faber edition.
6. Alvarez, *Savage God*, 15.
7. Steiner, 'Dying is an Art' in *Language and Silence*, 330.
8. Macpherson, *Reflecting on* The Bell Jar, 35.
9. Macpherson, *Reflecting on* The Bell Jar, 1.
10. Rosenberg, *The Rosenberg Letters*, 170.
11. May, *Homeward Bound*, 10–29.
12. Kendall, *Sylvia Plath*, 57.
13. Rosenberg, *The Rosenberg Letters*, 120.
14. Rosenberg, *The Rosenberg Letters*, 124.
15. Carmichael, *Framing History*, 103.
16. Carmichael, *Framing History*, 103.
17. Considine, *Its All News to Me*, 170–2.
18. Carmichael, *Framing History*, 106.
19. Ashe, '*The Bell Jar* and the Ghost', 218.
20. Scholes, 'Esther Came Back', 7.
21. Brain, *The Other Sylvia Plath*, 153–5.
22. Stern, *F.O. Matthiessen: Christian Socialist as Critic*, 31.

CHAPTER 20

Religious Contexts for Plath's Work

Gail Crowther

Sylvia Plath was raised within the Unitarian faith and, as such, was brought up rejecting the soteriological doctrines of original sin, predestination and atonement. Although she studied religion throughout her school and college education, as she grew older, Plath moved into, and maintained, a position of reluctant atheism. Towards the end of her life in an exchange of letters with an Assumptionist priest, Father Michael Carey, she aptly described her longing for, yet inability to embrace, any religious belief. In a letter to him written on 21 November 1962 she writes, 'I am myself, ironically, an atheist. And like a certain sort of atheist, my poems are God-obsessed, priest-obsessed. Full of Marys, Christs and nuns' (*LV2* 917).

This struggle manifested itself in her later work in two distinct ways, which this chapter will explore in more detail. First, perhaps influenced by an upbringing that rejected Trinitarianism, she expressed anger and ridicule towards the Judaic and Christian concepts of the divine. In some cases this anger is used to appropriate male biblical figures and re-gender their story ('Lady Lazarus'). In other cases, she mocked the grandiose claims of God ('Years'). The result is to subvert male power and demonstrate a bold irreverence that Cheryl A. Hemmerle argues blurs the boundary between the sacred and the profane.

Having disrupted this patrilineage, Plath switches her focus to Marian notions of love, care and redemption. By filling her poems with 'Marys', Plath demonstrates through her speakers a yearning for some kind of existential hope. Yet even this longing for maternal redemption fails, as Mary is ultimately regarded as a loving but ineffectual mediatrix ('The Moon and the Yew Tree', 'Finisterre').

This chapter will draw together Plath's ambivalent response to religion and highlight how the context of her religious upbringing lay at the root of her theological discontent. By exploring poems and extracts from her journals and letters, we can see that Plath remained engaged with religion throughout her life. Eventually, however, she rejected any message of theological hope or comfort. Her final poem dealing with religious imagery was written ten days before her death. 'Mystic' asks the powerful question 'Once one has seen God, what is the remedy?' (*CP* 268). Rather than addressing the potentially messianic moment, Plath's speaker descends into a spiral of doubt until even a seemingly miraculous moment is thrown into uncertainty; 'Does the sea / Remember the walker upon it?' (*CP* 269). In the end, redemption does not come from a religious figure or context, but rather the everyday events of the sun flooding into a morning room, of children leaping in their cots. It is the humdrum happenings of the here and now that ensures 'the heart has not stopped' and the overblown promises of eternal life are rejected as vacuous and boring.

Plath's parents had mixed religious upbringings. Her father, Otto Plath, was raised with the intention of his becoming a minister. In the introduction to *Letters Home*, Aurelia Plath informs us that Otto was sent to college at the expense of his grandparents on the understanding that he would afterwards prepare himself for the Lutheran ministry. He lasted only six months during which time he suffered 'agonising self-doubt and self-evaluation' (*LH* 9). By the time he was a young adult he had become an atheist with his name struck from the pages of the family bible and ostracised for the rest of his life. Aurelia Plath was brought up a Catholic but by the time she met Otto, she was a practising Methodist. Following the death of her husband in 1940, the family moved inland from Winthrop to Wellesley and started attending the local Unitarian church.

Strands of Unitarian thinking can be detected in Plath's work from when she was a young child right through to the end of her life. Most notably Unitarianism rejects certain Western Christian doctrines such as predestination, original sin and the Trinity. Stressing the humanity of Christ, rather than his divinity, Unitarians believe in the moral authority of Christ's teaching, which can happily coexist alongside philosophy, science and 'rational' thought. This multidisciplinary approach to creating an ethical framework for life seems to have remained with Plath throughout her life. Indeed, in a letter to Father Michael Carey written on 21 November 1962, Plath demonstrates how this belief system seeped into her work. She writes, 'Theology and philosophy fascinate me, and my next book will have a long bit about a priest in a cassock' (*LV2* 917). Although Plath does not name this book, at the time she was collecting her autumn poems into the collection that would eventually become *Ariel* and so it is likely she is referring to her poem 'Berck-Plage' here.

The Unitarian rejection of the triune God also impacted on Plath's theological beliefs. When she moved to Devon in 1961 she decided the best way to 'grow' into the community was to attend the local Anglican church, which happened to be just the other side of her garden wall. However, she had certain reservations that led her to contact the rector. In a letter to her mother on 13 October she writes, 'he came and said he'd go through the creed and order of service with me, but that I'd be welcome (I'm afraid I could never stomach the Trinity and all that!) to come in the spirit of my own Unitarian beliefs' (*LH* 432). Plath's beliefs, however, are rooted in scholarship, morality and philosophy. As a young woman her journals are full of her struggle, wanting to believe but not quite being able to. At age 18, she wrote bluntly, 'You don't believe in God, or a life-after-death, so you can't hope for sugar plums when your non-existent soul rises' (*J* 63). Later that same year she laments '(Oh the grimness of atheism!)' (*J* 102). At times of despair, she desperately wants to believe but ultimately decries 'I talk to God but the sky is empty ...' (*J* 199). Luke Ferretter supports this view when he writes, 'even in these moments when it seems she most wants to, Plath never allows herself to believe in God'.[1] Despite this, Plath did study and read sections of the Bible, finding certain comfort from the words: 'Am reading the book of Job: great peace derived of therefrom. Shall read the Bible: symbolic meaning, even though the belief in a moral God-structured universe not there. Live As If it were? A great device' (*J* 462). This seemingly contradictory position resurfaces on and off. When she became a mother herself she decided to get her children baptised and while living in Devon planned to send her daughter Frieda to Sunday School, explaining to Aurelia Plath that 'I am sure as she starts thinking for herself she will drift away from the church, but I know how incredibly powerful the words of that little Christian prayer, "God is my help in every need", which you taught us has been at odd moments of my life, so I think it will do her good to feel part of this spiritual community. I must say I think I'm a pagan-Unitarian at best!' (*LH* 433). That said, the symbolic and powerful figure-heads of Christianity were never far away.

God often appears in Plath's poems as either an absence or as an object of scorn. A 1956 poem 'Soliloquy of the Solipsist' removes God from the picture entirely and the speaker becomes the centre and meaning of the whole universe, holding the ultimate powers of creation and destruction. She tells us, for instance, that she has 'Absolute power / To boycott color and forbid any flower' (*CP* 37–8). The responsibility for being lies firmly with humanity here. There is no room or place for a creator God.

Six years later, in her 1962 poem 'Years', Plath ridicules and mocks the notion of an eternal, unchanging God. Furthermore, the idea that a deity in 'bright stupid confetti' can in some way bestow eternal life is not only scorned but actively seen as undesirable ('Eternity bores me') (*CP* 255). Cheryl A. Hemmerle argues that the poems Plath wrote in the last two weeks of her life successfully play around with the notion of the sacred and the profane. By this she defines these two positions as the sacred being concerned with religious rites and that which is holy and cherished, whereas the profane is connected to the secular and shows disrespect for sacred things. Hemmerle asserts that Plath introduces an element of fluidity and the 'erasure of duality' in dealing with these elements, which are usually regarded as coexisting in some form of dualistic relationship; in doing so, she creates a 'valuable complexity of meaning and understanding embodied in shared symbols or totems alongside mundane individual concerns'.[2] Hemmerle singles out the last two weeks of Plath's work because of the shift in tone and different style of writing that saw Plath herself distinguish this final work as something completely different. However, I wonder if, using Hemmerle's framework, we can adapt this idea to earlier poems that also seem to confound and complicate our understanding of the sacred and the profane. In 'Years', we have the existing figure of an eternal God (sacred symbol) alongside an individual concern (or lack thereof) for eternal life (profane). The shift between the two positions is interwoven in such a way that any demarcation becomes a little blurry and difficult to define. The grandiose claims of God are exposed as somewhat overblown and as readers we, too, are thrown into an exhilarating position of swaying between the sacred and profane.

Another tactic Plath employs to reject certain Christian theologies is to appropriate male biblical figures and re-gender their stories. Although predating second-wave feminism, Plath pre-empted some of the conservative and liberal feminist approaches to reclaiming Christianity from its patrilineal heritage. By erasing male figures and replacing them with female versions, and versions who are more powerful, she disrupts the traditional theological power relations. The most infamous example of this can be found in the poem 'Lady Lazarus'. In the Bible, the male figure, Lazarus of Bethany, is fairly benign. Usually regarded as the brother of the sisters Mary and Martha, Lazarus takes ill and dies. He is then placed in a tomb where he lies mouldering for four days. When Jesus arrives in Bethany and finds that Lazarus is dead, he goes to the tomb, rolls away the stone and tells Lazarus to come out. Lazarus duly appears, still wrapped in his grave clothes, seemingly brought back from the dead by a miracle carried out by Jesus.

This is a story that had already fascinated Plath for many years. In 1956 she wrote in her journal how strongly she identified with the figure of Lazarus, having survived her first suicide attempt three years previously: 'I feel like Lazarus: that story has such fascination. Being dead I rose up again ...' (*J* 199). The appropriation of this story by Plath's narrator in 'Lady Lazarus' subverts the entire episode. First, the re-gendering of the story is relevant, mainly because one of the purposes of the resurrection of Lady Lazarus is to become a dangerous figure towards men; 'I eat men like air' she concludes. However, she needs no miraculous prayer or messianic godhead to bring her back from her deaths – she is able to do that all by herself. Echoing Lazarus's four days in the tomb, Lady Lazarus also returns worse for wear from the grave, but firmly asserts her gender: 'And I a smiling woman' (*CP* 244). Ultimately though, despite the smiles, Lady Lazarus is so fearsome that even the most unlikely characters of 'God' and 'Lucifer' need to take care: 'Beware' (*CP* 246). The final image of the red-haired, resurrected woman rising from the ash has become perhaps one of the most striking in twentieth-century literature.

In some ways we can see Plath's Unitarian beliefs lurking behind this rewriting of the story. Christ loses his divinity and power, God loses the ability to decide or grant predestination and the traditional doctrines of sacrifice and atonement become invalid. Lady Lazarus has her own free will and her own moral authority. Everyone else needs to be very careful. This poem also allows us to once again slip between the boundaries of the sacred and profane, as with the proximity of references to God and Lucifer. A biblical figure and a miraculous healing is overwritten by the secular, by a woman who needs no external masculine force to rescue her. She can take care of herself and furthermore boasts about her ability to cheat death and be utterly unreliant on anyone or anything, and she does it 'exceptionally' (*CP* 245).

This disruption of traditional Christian patrilineage either by absence, scorn or re-gendering highlights the ways in which Plath found it almost impossible to follow any form of traditional theology. Luke Ferretter argues that 'Plath is a poet of the death of God. While she finds belief in God attractive she does not share it.'[3] However, Plath did remain a reluctant atheist all of her life, never believing, never quite wanting to give up on the possibility of believing. A fine example of how Plath negotiated this paradox can be seen in her identification with Mary, the Mother of Christ. Many of Plath's later poems refer to, or yearn for, Marian notions of love, care and redemption. Yet Mary remains a kindly but inadequate mediatrix. In fact, in some cases she does not even listen at all.

The poem 'Finisterre', written in 1961, describes a scene on the French coast of Brittany. A statue of Our Lady of the Shipwrecked looks out to sea. At Mary's feet a 'marble sailor kneels', and a marble, black-garbed 'peasant woman' kneels in turn to him. Mary seems indifferent to the two figures who have come to pray to her, a beautiful but detached figure whose lips are 'sweet with divinity', who 'does not hear what the sailor or the peasant is saying' and is 'in love with the beautiful formlessness of the sea' (*CP* 170). This idea of the sweet, loving but distracted mother is a recurring theme in Plath's final poems. It does not, however, stop Plath's speakers wanting more, or even in some cases identifying with the difficult role of being the mother of a son in a cruel and heartless world.

'The Moon and the Yew Tree', written shortly after 'Finisterre', is another poem in which Mary appears as a benevolent but ineffectual figure. Unlike the coast at Finisterre where the hypnotic sea distracts Mary, the night-time setting of the moon and the yew tree is altogether bleaker. The speaker describes a landscape of despair in which she cannot find her symbolic or literal way. Rather than turning to Mary for maternal comfort, the speaker claims 'The moon is my mother. She is not sweet like Mary.' Despite this sweetness, Plath's speaker cannot believe in or accept any form of love from Mary and her desire for this remains an unfulfilled yearning, 'How I would like to believe in tenderness.' Instead, inside the silent church the plaster-blue saints, 'stiff with holiness' (*CP* 173), loom over the cold pews. Religion offers no answers, the moon remains oblivious, and ultimately the speaker is left with a message of blackness and silence.

In November 1962, Plath sent a typescript of her poem 'Mary's Song' to Father Michael Carey with the authorial comment, 'I think I will send you a poem of my own, very rough, but about the Christ-ness in all martyrs, and written by a mother of a son' (*LV2* 917). It is significant that although Plath stresses the role of Christ here, the poem is named after and spoken from the point of view of Mary. Here the position of the speaker switches. Rather than yearning for maternal love to come her way (as in 'The Moon and the Yew Tree'), she identifies with Mary as the mother of a son in an uncaring and torturous world. One theme established immediately in the first line is that of sacrifice in the image of the crackling Sunday lamb. But the poem extends the image of the fire cooking the lamb to spread across Europe and the ovens that reduced so many Jewish people to ash. The glowing ovens instil fear in the heart of the mother who feels, like Mary, it is her own son that will pay the ultimate sacrifice, 'O golden child the world will kill and eat' (*CP* 257). This maternal fear for her son appeared repeatedly in Plath's poems and can be found in 'For a Fatherless Son', 'By Candlelight' and 'Nick and the

Candlestick'. So, too, Plath worried for her daughter, with the speaker of 'Magi' replacing the three wise men leaning over Christ's crib, with abstracts of Good, Truth, Love and Evil bending over her daughter's. Worriedly, the speaker asks: 'What girl ever flourished in such company?' (*CP* 148).

A question like this raises the issue of meaning and redemption in a seemingly godless world. In keeping with her Unitarian beliefs, Plath appears to reject the idea of atonement, sacrifice and eternal life/damnation. In 1959 she wrote in her journal, 'Sitting here on a blue clear cold morning, Easter, I believe, and the risen Christ meaning only a parable of human renewal and nothing of immortality' (*J* 475). Constance Scheerer argues that Plath 'seeks redemption elsewhere and in a different form'. She suggests that in some of Plath's 'simpler nature poems' there is some kind of hope, and that poems dealing with the mother/child relationship 'hint at a similar transforming power'.[4] Undoubtedly, some of Plath's poems appear to offer no hope at all. 'The Moon and the Yew Tree', as we have already discussed, results in a silent and black hopelessness. The final line of 'Berck-Plage', as the speaker's neighbour is lowered into a red-earthed grave, offers a similar world-view: 'There is no hope, it is given up' (*CP* 201). In one of Plath's last poems, 'Sheep in Fog', the final stanza was altered two weeks before her death. The changes brought about a desolate outlook. The speaker is riding on her horse as the morning around her blackens. She regards the distant 'fields' as a gateway to a bleak version of 'heaven' that is 'Starless and fatherless, a dark water' (*CP* 262).

This despondency, however, is countered in other poems, where Plath's redemption appears to come from those things around her in her day-to-day life. It is the familiarity of the mundane – love, children, her garden, even the domestic – that offers comfort and hope. 'By Candlelight' sees the speaker nursing a crying infant. As the mother rocks her child, it is the small candlestick of Hercules hefting the world on his back that 'keeps the sky at bay' (*CP* 237). Similarly, in 'Nick and the Candlestick', the speaker addresses her infant son 'O love, how did you get here?' (*CP* 241) and in the final stanza her own son usurps the role of the infant Christ:

> You are the one
> Solid the spaces lean on, envious.
> You are the baby in the barn. (*CP* 242)

In 'Mystic' Plath's speaker speculates as to what the remedy may be when one has been seized up by God (and by implication the religious rites and beliefs associated with this). A series of questions follow: is the remedy the pill of the communion tablet? Memory? Looking for the face of Christ in everyday life? These musings culminate in the incisive question, 'Is there no great love, only tenderness?', recalling 'The Moon and the Yew Tree''s expression of desire for that same tenderness. In the end, redemption comes from the early-morning city coming to life: 'The chimneys of the city breathe, the window sweats, / The children leap in their cots' (*CP* 269).

Although Plath ultimately rejected many traditional Christian doctrines, we can equally see how her Unitarian beliefs formed a context for much of her work. While she remained at best ambivalent to religion, she was never indifferent, writing: 'I know & feel & have lived so much: and am so wise, yes, in living for my age; having blasted through conventional morality, and come to my own morality. Which is the commitment to body & mind: to faith in battering out a good life. No God, but the sun anyway' (*J* 269). Plath took comfort from certain ideals, and remained engaged with biblical texts, but in the end she created her own moral framework.

Notes

1. Ferretter, 'What Girl Ever Flourished', 103.
2. Hemmerle, 'That Still, Blue, Almost Eternal Hour', 274.
3. Ferretter, 'What Girl Ever Flourished', 113.
4. Scheerer, 'The Deathly Paradise of Sylvia Plath', 477.

CHAPTER 21

Plath and Nature

Richard Kerridge

On 25 July 1958, Sylvia Plath wrote to her mother:

> ... I am becoming more and more desirous of being an amateur naturalist. Do you remember if we have any little books on recognizing wild flowers, birds, or animals in Northern America? I am reading some Penguin books about 'Man and the Vertebrates' and 'The Personality of Animals' and also the delightful book *The Sea Around Us*, by Rachel Carson. Ted's reading her *Under the Sea Wind*, which he says is also fine. Do read these if you haven't already; they are poetically written and magnificently informative (*LH* 345).

The works mentioned here were not recent publications. *Man and the Vertebrates*, by the American palaeontologist A. S. Romer, was first published in 1933. The Personality of Animals, by the British experimental zoologist H. Munro Fox, appeared in 1940. Carson's *The Sea Around Us* dated from 1951, but *Under the Sea Wind* was older, having been published in 1941.

The first three of these works were what we would now call non-fiction in the popular science genre – that is, books of direct explanation. *Under the Sea Wind*, in contrast, conveyed the natural history information by telling the stories of a succession of animal protagonists: a black skimmer, a sanderling, a mackerel, an eel and a sea-trout. Carson names these characters, and some of the other creatures they encounter. She tells their stories in third-person narrative that moves between indirect representation of the animal-character's viewpoint and wider perspectives. Once or twice, briefly, the viewpoints of human beings are introduced. All this is very much in the manner of the animal novels of Henry Williamson, author of *Tarka the Otter*, whose influence Carson acknowledged, and whose work Hughes loved.

Plath clearly did not have a sustained interest in becoming an amateur naturalist. She found intense theatrical, symbolic and poetic meaning in the animals and places she encountered, and described them with vividness and often precision, but her curiosity was not usually very scientific. For example, in her journal and in a letter, she describes a baby bird fallen from the nest that she and Hughes found and attempted to nurture but eventually decided they had to kill, since it was slowly dying. They found the bird on 3 July 1958, three weeks before the letter quoted above, and on 8 July Hughes carried out the mercy-killing, using a hose attached to a gas ring. Plath's descriptions have a fascinated directness. 'Every moment I expected the breath in its scrawny chest to stop. But no. [...] As we came up the stairs the bird squawked piteously & opened its yellow froggish beak wide as itself, so its head wasn't visible behind the forked-tongued opening' (*J* 400). Sometimes these descriptions have a cartoonish quality, in the concentration on facial features and highly dramatic movements. Plath combines this cartoonishness with close and unsparing description of bodies, often violently distressed, bedraggled, hungry, dirty, incontinent or dead. These two approaches were important components of the mythopoetic style that Hughes was later to develop in *Crow*.

But it is remarkable that neither Plath nor Hughes seems to have seriously attempted to identify the species of the bird, which would have been an immediate question for any birdwatcher or naturalist. In her letter, Plath does say that it 'looked like a baby starling, with funny furry eyebrows' (*LH* 347) (that cartoonish touch again), but the identification is never pursued or confirmed, even after Plath and Hughes have revisited the tree and caught a glimpse of one of the likely parents: 'a small brownish birdface looked, then vanished' (*J* 403). Plath is much more intent upon the unnerving phenomenological experience of the encounter with the bird ('his scrabble in the box, [...] his pin-feather wings against the cardboard sides') (*J* 402), and upon seeing the creature as suggestive symbol or metaphor. First, the bird is an allegorical personification of the general life-impulse: 'However small, it is an extension of life, of sensibility & identity' (*J* 402). Then, immediately, it makes Plath think of a human baby and her feelings about the prospect of caring for one of her own.

These features are consistent through the many encounters with wild creatures recorded in the journals and letters. Plath rarely sets out on an expedition with the specific intention of searching for a wild animal, but her imagination is frequently seized by glimpses that take her by surprise or dead creatures that lie in her path. An unidentified black frog makes her think of obsidian carvings. A skate caught by Hughes has a 'foul-lipped face'. Toadstools as large as oranges fist themselves up through the soil. Two dead moles in the road have 'white, clawlike hands' with 'human palms' (*J* 402, 493, 515, 520). Again, Plath shows little interest in identifying species or looking up the natural history of what she sees. Perhaps this is partly because she wishes to preserve the intensity of the moment of encounter with something unexpected. She dramatises herself in these moments as a kind of ingénue, startled by the grotesque newness of what she sees and also by a strange feeling of recognition, as if an intimate fact about human life has been laid bare. Plath may have felt that scientific identification would weaken this effect by introducing a tone of knowing-ness and confidence, though some nature writers, including Carson and Williamson, have combined the two styles.

Occasionally, however, Plath clearly did go to natural history books for information about something she had seen. In the journals, between 1956 and 1958, there are extensive notes upon starfish of various kinds, including Latin species-names and other scientific terms, and references to several books (*J* 584–6). But this is exceptional, and, as it turned out, the *Collected Poems* has only one mention of starfish, despite the abundance of other sea and shoreline creatures such as crabs, oysters, octopuses, mussels and gulls. 'The body of a starfish can grow back its arms / And newts are prodigal in legs' (*CP* 184) says one of the speakers in the verse drama *Three Women*, who then expresses a grieving hope that she, too, will be prodigal, perhaps in regenerating what has been lost, perhaps in letting it go, perhaps both. She has suffered a miscarriage. Plath mentions in her journal notes the capacity of starfish to grow replacement arms, and this readily symbolic ability also features, briefly, in the autobiographical fragment 'Ocean 1212-W', but apart from these two instances the information she gathered did not find its way into any of her published work, except subliminally, perhaps. I wonder, for instance, whether the white cave-newts in 'Nick and the Candlestick' were prompted into poetic life by a photograph of a cave salamander in Romer's *Man and the Vertebrates* (mentioned in the above-cited letter to her mother).

Plath's anthropomorphism turns wild nature – especially helpless infant creatures, remorseless hunters, devouring mouths and exposed corpses – into a theatre of elemental life, strongly suggestive of the human life that modern civilisation conceals. That combination of cartoonish anthropo-morphism and precisely observed detail enables her to create an area of overlap between the otherness of non-human species and their function as indirect representations of human life – a function that is possible because of the sudden, surprising resemblances to human features that occur in the midst of non-human otherness. The tiny palms of the dead moles' hands are a touching example, and the sight of these two corpses surely provided the central image for the poem 'Blue Moles', published in 1959, a poem that continually finds disturbing glimpses of the human in non-human phenomena. Another striking example of this technique, as Plath later honed it for the poems, comes in the 1962 poem 'Berck-Plage', when the seaweed is suddenly 'hairy as privates' (*CP* 197).

Her interest in wild nature, then, was primarily in using animals, plants and landscapes to flush out elusive and elemental human meaning, rather than in scientific understanding. Profoundly influenced by D. H. Lawrence's animal and flower poems, and of course profoundly influencing each other, Plath and Hughes, in their different ways, sought to endow the familiar wild creatures around them with poetic meaning of an elemental and archetypal kind, without losing the intensity of the personal reaction in its particular moment. They sought to connect symbolic, metaphorical, cosmic and mythical meaning to wildlife and landscapes that people encountered in their ordinary lives. These literary and cultural aims were bound to have a complicated and ambivalent relationship with scientific natural history. Sometimes the relationship was creative, enabling the poets to find new symbolic meaning that spoke immediately to other powerful experiences, as with the ability of starfish and newts to regenerate limbs. Poetry in this sort of relationship with science might wrest wild nature away from the colonial tradition and from mere nostalgia for the pre-industrial past. Encounters with wildlife might begin to have some centrality in modern culture, and poetry itself might command more attention in turn. Such a renewed sense of wild nature's meaning would go well with the environmental concern that was beginning to emerge from ecological science.

But the poetry needed also to push against some attitudes common in scientific culture. There was often an undiscriminating dismissiveness towards anthropomorphism, for example. Such attitudes made the two kinds of writing difficult to combine, and there was a pervasive idea that the scientific and literary cultures were fundamentally separate and often necessarily antagonistic. It was widely assumed that the arts and sciences appealed to radically different abilities and temperaments, and in British sixth-form and university education it was normal for pupils to specialise in either the sciences or the humanities. In 1959, C. P. Snow gave his controversial Rede Lecture on 'The Two Cultures and the Scientific Revolution', arguing, in technocratic and positivist vein, that the split was a serious impediment to economic growth (which he took to be an unqualified good), and blaming the influence of literary intellectuals, whose attitudes Snow characterised as Luddite. F. R. Leavis's retort, a polemical rejection of the reductiveness of these technocratic values, came in 1962.

Despite this culture of polarisation, and though Plath's work made only limited direct use of scientific natural history, the concepts that were dominant in zoology and ecological science at the time form an important part of her historical context, along with the recent literary traditions of nature writing, and the changing attitudes to wild nature in popular culture. The books she mentioned in that letter in 1958 were by that time somewhat out of date, as we have seen, but they had been influential works of popular science, appearing in Pelican editions and going through numerous reprints in the 1940s and 1950s. One of the shifts taking place in that period was a change of emphasis from the structural anatomical study of species, orders and classes of species to a more ecological perspective, more concerned with the relationships of species to their changing environments, and the coevolutionary effects of species on each other. *Man and the Vertebrates*, Romer's title, exemplifies this shift.

In his narrative of vertebrate evolution, Romer uses a rhetoric that now seems remote and sinister, but lingered in popular assumptions long after it had been superseded in scientific writing. 'The amphibians', he says, 'are a defeated group.' He talks of 'the reason for amphibian failure and reptilian success' (this supposedly unsuccessful class of animals includes the newts with their ability to grow new limbs). They have failed because the 'amphibian is still chained to the water'.[1] It is a strange idea. Amphibians are found in large numbers and great diversity of species across the world. In what respect have they failed? It is true that more recent events have shown that, in the context of global warming and the spreading of fungal infections due to the globalisation of trade, amphibians, with their highly permeable skins, are especially vulnerable. Some have become extinct. But any rhetoric of the success or failure of species applied in this context would simply absolve human beings of responsibility.

Romer's vocabulary here seems to come from the days when social Darwinism was proposed as a naturalising justification for capitalist competition and colonialism. This is also true of the terms 'degenerate' and 'primitive', used repeatedly by Romer. These terms retain something of the assumption that evolution is qualitative development, a progression from lower to higher, from simplicity to sophistication. In the case of the amphibians, Romer's suggestion is that the anatomy of these creatures constitutes an arrested stage, or that they are even in a process of reversion. He constructs a momentary time-lapse drama, in which their evolutionary history becomes a surrender. Demoralised, the amphibians just give up the effort:

> [I]t is not to be wondered at that among the salamanders, and apparently among many extinct groups as well, there are numerous types which have (so to speak) given up the struggle and have slumped back, reverting to a permanent life in the water and a life-long retention of water-breathing.[2]

It seems funny now, this taken-for-granted assumption that land-life is superior to water-life, and that any evolutionary move to a niche resembling an earlier niche must be seen as regression and failure.

But the idea of evolution as qualitative progression was extremely pervasive and lingering, as was the merging of evolutionary narrative with a confidently technocratic story of human progress. 'Primitive' and 'degenerate' were terms that had featured in colonial and Nazi rhetoric, and, after the Second World War, as the process of decolonisation was beginning, this history overshadowed any more neutral and technical sense the words might have had. Later ecological writing dispensed with the concept or implication of qualitative progression in evolution, while the emerging environmentalism brought a profound challenge to technocratic narratives of progress.

Plath's writing did not engage directly with controversies in ecological science, but, as part of a description of her context, it is worth outlining the major shifts that were taking place in the way ecology was seen as working. These shifts had implications for the symbolic and poetic meaning of wild nature, as well as for environmental policy, and ideas often persist in public culture long after science has changed them and moved on. One of the most important of these is the concept of nature's 'balance', which in the 1950s and 1960s was going through a process of scientific challenge and modification, even as it was being taken up by environmentalists as a model that seemed helpful to their cause.

The notion that there is a balance of nature that we disturb at our peril derives from the concept of the ecological 'climax', which became a dominant paradigm after the First World War. Frederic Clements developed the theory from his study of plant succession, the order in which plants establish themselves on land where climatic or other disruption has removed the previous cover. Clements found that disturbed areas were colonised first by a few 'pioneer' species and then by others able to take advantage of the conditions the pioneers had created. The arrival of other life forms took the same pattern, in which each stage was called a 'sere', until a 'climax' condition was reached in which all the established species had stabilised in their various niches and relations of interdependency. After each local disturbance, the same order of succession would take place, culminating in the same climax conditions. Within each climatic area there was one dominant pattern of species that constituted the climax condition, though other formations, subclimaxes, could be found locally. This version of the climax theory is usually called 'monoclimax', and has been largely superseded by 'polyclimax', which recognises that climax (nowadays more cautiously called 'late succession') will in most areas consist of a variety of local formations. Clements went so far as to describe the biotic community – the combination of all the life forms that made up the climax condition – as a 'superorganism', whose growth, reaction to disturbance and power of recovery resembled those of an individual plant or animal.

In part, the popular idea of the 'balance' of nature derives from this 'climax' theory, though 'balance' also means something simpler – the fluctuating relationship between predator and prey populations, for example, such as to maintain the presence of each and the environments they mutually create for long periods of time. This idea of 'balance' has older origins, too. One reason for its persistence is that it chimes with a vestigial Natural Theology. Traces of the idea of nature as morally coherent survive in the notion that each creature has been provided with a secure niche. Such cultural traditions may have been involved, to some extent, in the formation of the models themselves. This possibility reveals how science always has a cultural situatedness, present at the origin of any scientific theory, and also how the accounts of nature given by science and by artistic and religious traditions tend to become intertwined.

Several perceived shortcomings undermined 'climax' as an orthodoxy. Critics noted that habitats more often consisted of numerous patches or belts in which different species were dominant than of clearly demarcated 'communities'. Patterns of arrival, dominance and disappearance were much more fluctuating and unpredictable than Clements's order of succession had allowed. Even the modified principle of 'polyclimax' did not fully account for these variations. Succession could be retrogressive as well as progressive. Some species were not members of the 'community' but made only a temporary difference as they passed through. These observations did not entirely dispose of the climax idea, but they called for a more complex model.

In 1935, A. G. Tansley introduced the word 'ecosystem' as a corrective. He wanted a new term that would encompass not only this 'biotic community', but also the other factors such as climate and soil composition.

'Ecosystem' was a word that would emphasise the role of all the elements in producing and maintaining each other, and thus constituting an environment. The system was the totality of these relationships. Boundaries were marked by abrupt changes of climate, geology and species, zones of transition by mixtures of one community with another. Tansley's departure from the rigid model of climax enabled him to take account of flow through the system as well as function within it, and also to acknowledge the role of human activity, with all its technological innovations, as a dynamic ecological factor rather than a mere disrupter of the climax condition:

> It is obvious that modern civilised man upsets the 'natural' ecosystems or 'biotic communities' on a very large scale. But it would be difficult, not to say impossible, to draw a natural line between the activities of the human tribes which presumably fitted into and formed parts of 'biotic communities' and the destructive human activities of the modern world. Is man part of 'nature' or not?[3]

Our activities disrupt natural environments but are themselves natural and to be counted as new ecological factors. Sometimes we are in, sometimes out.

The historian of ecology Donald Worster puts it like this:

> But then, beginning in the 1940s, while Clements and his ideas were still in the ascendant, a few scientists began trying to speak a new vocabulary. Words like 'energy flow' and 'trophic levels' and 'ecosystem' appeared in the leading journals, and they indicated a view of nature shaped more by physics than botany. Within another decade or two nature came to be widely seen as a flow of energy and nutrients through a physical or thermodynamic system.[4]

Nature seen in this way is a continuous process from which it is well-nigh impossible to detach particular species.

As biologist Daniel Botkin has said more recently:

> We are accustomed to thinking of life as a characteristic of individual organisms. Individuals are alive, but an individual cannot sustain life. Life is sustained only by a group of organisms of many species – and their environment, making together a network of living and nonliving parts that can maintain the flow of energy and the cycling of chemical elements that, in turn, support life.[5]

Ecology's broad cultural mission has always been to persuade us to see things in such holistic terms. But the model has limitations from an environmentalist perspective. It does not necessarily promote biodiversity. As long as the flow of energy is efficient, in the sense that little is wasted, the system functions healthily whether there are many species or few. A monoculture may indeed be more 'efficient', in terms of pure energy transfer, than a highly diverse ecosystem. Intensive farming could, from this point of view, be seen as a triumph of applied ecology (which is how its early champions saw it). This Janus-face of ecological science – its aspect as penetrative control, and its aspect as concerned awareness of the intricate vulnerability of the unbounded system – begins to register in Plath's poetry.

While these conceptual shifts in scientific natural history were taking place, new literary, social and technological contexts for the love of wild nature were also emerging. The inter-war years had been a period of great popularity for literary nature writing, much of it associated with the rural revivalist movement, preoccupied with searching for enclaves that offered contact with the deep past, and shelter from mass-democratic industrial modernity. These desires had been strong cultural currents before the First World War, evident in the nature writing and topographical writing of Richard Jefferies, W. H. Hudson and Edward Thomas. D. H. Lawrence's animal poems, published soon after the war, also sought contact with the pre-modern past, but for Lawrence it was a much deeper past and much more enduring. His mythopoetic nature writing, later to be very important to Plath and Hughes, expressed much greater confidence that 'life's unfathomable dawn' and 'the primeval rudiments of life'[6] ('Tortoise Shout', 1920) were still present and potent, and manifest when one looked poetically at wild creatures. It seems likely that here is one origin of the 'extension of life, of sensibility & identity' (*J* 402) that Plath saw in the struggling baby bird.

After 1918, and through the 1920s and 1930s, the desire for enclaves of escape from modernity became deeply involved with traumatised reaction to the war. Henry Williamson, a war veteran himself, was a leading figure in rural revivalism and an exemplar of this combination. The disastrous political trajectory that led him to become a proselytising member of Sir Oswald Mosley's British Union of Fascists was his own, but had enough roots in the fear of modernity that was characteristic of rural revivalism to raise questions about the dangers of these attitudes. After the Second World War, this association of literary nature writing with a need to seek refuge from urban modernity and its crowds continued to be part of the genre's appeal but also called for a reinvention, or cultural repositioning. In the 1940s and 1950s, the literary genre – as opposed to the popular science books, field guides and narratives of zoological expeditions – became relatively unfashionable, at a time when popular enthusiasm for natural history was taking new forms.

One theory about the popularity of nature writing in the interwar period identifies a process that extended into Plath's writing lifetime, and in which Hughes was a leader. The postcolonial critic Jed Esty, in his book *A Shrinking Island* (2004), interprets the rural revivalism and enthusiasm for wild nature of the 1930s as a sometimes subliminal anticipation of the end of empire. As it began to seem likely that the wild environments and charismatic wildlife of Asia and Africa, which had featured in so many colonial adventure stories, would soon cease to be available in quite the same way as territory for fantasy and the natural sublime, an impulse arose to 're-enchant' the home territory of Britain, both as a site for anthropological exploration and an environment for encounters with wild nature. Esty calls this impulse the 're-substitution of England's own fetishized or primitivized past for the vanishing pleasures of colonial exoticism',[7] and the finding of new depth of significance in Britain's wild animals played a part.

In the 1950s and early 1960s, Hughes's poems restored intense and cosmic meaning to the wild animals that the general public in Britain could easily encounter – the fox, the pike, the thrush and the crow. Some details in Hughes's work seem to confirm Esty's thesis. In 'Pike', Hughes describes the stripes on the pike's body as 'green tigering the gold' (*TH:CP* 84). Tigers, the most blazingly savage of the wild creatures of the empire, and the most prestigious trophies for colonial hunters, have been relocated to ordinary British rivers and canals. Hughes was not afraid to avow Williamson as an influence. The main difference in their poetics of natural history is that Williamson sought wildness in rural places remote from the urban centres, and in ritualistic rural pursuits such as otter-hunting, whereas Hughes, at least in his early work, sought it in much more populated places, the territory of common experience.

During the Second World War, an attitude was developing that prepared the way for this emphasis in Hughes's work. The association of the love of wild nature with an anti-modern reclusive spirit was challenged by a new emphasis on wildlife and landscape as the shared possession of the whole population, part of what they were fighting for, and part of the life they would deserve to enjoy after their sacrifices. In 1940, the ornithologist James Fisher, who was to become an editor of the important Collins New Naturalist series of substantial natural history books for the general reader, expressed this view in the preface to his book *Watching Birds*:

Birds are part of the heritage we are fighting for. After this war ordinary people are going to have a better time than they have had; they are going to get about more; they will have time to rest from their tremendous tasks; many will get the opportunity, hitherto sought in vain, of watching wild creatures and making discoveries about them.[8]

These sentiments were in tune with the welfare state ethos. A culture of popular natural history was emerging that partook of that spirit.

'The point', said George Orwell, in his essay 'Some Thoughts on the Common Toad' (1946), 'is that the pleasures of spring are available to everybody, and cost nothing.' He went on to say that it was 'a rather pleasing thought' that none of the million birds in his part of the centre of London paid 'a halfpenny of rent'.[9] Orwell's emphasis on wild nature as available to all at no charge calls to mind the political context that produced two years later the launch of the National Health Service, which was to figure importantly in Plath's life in England, and to which she makes numerous references in her letters and journals.

By the late 1950s, this social democratic vision of the love of nature was becoming intertwined with new forms of consumerism resulting from two immensely transformative developments. Popular car ownership made excursions into wild nature more easily available as a leisure activity than ever before, as Fisher had predicted, while mass access to television brought exotic wild nature into ordinary homes as dramatic spectacle. Wildlife documentaries quickly became one of the new medium's most popular genres and they have been so ever since. Plath came to Britain from a country where these developments had begun sooner, and where – in contrast to the British sense of post-imperial retrenchment diagnosed by Esty – there was a national culture of technologically empowered expansionist confidence.

Amanda Hagood has observed that Rachel Carson's *The Sea Around Us*, while beginning to nurture in its readers the new sense of environmental concern, also emerged from, and appealed to, this confidence:

> But she also worked against the background of the United States' growing geopolitical expansion into the world's oceans—and with it, the assumption that the sea was a virtually unlimited resource, as well as a readily available dumping ground, for the growth of American industries. These contrasting ways of imagining the ocean suggest a remarkable paradox: for many of Carson's mid-century readers, wonder for the sea occupied the same emotional spectrum as an imperialist impulse to exploit its once-impenetrable reaches.[10]

Plath's short story 'The 59th Bear', about the car tours of Yellowstone National Park that by this time were a well-established part of the national tourist industry, introduces an ominous sense of impending catastrophic consequence that has both proto-feminist and proto-environmentalist elements.

'Waking in Winter', similarly, connects the experience of setting off on a car journey to a seaside resort with insidious deadly pollution: the lawns are green because they are poisoned and still, and the car and its occupants are drinking that poison. In 'Elm', the tree's deep taproot connects it to the whole global ecosystem, encompassing oceans, skies, polluted rain and the terrible overload of foreboding knowledge in tree and human protagonist alike, as receptive systems. Tracy Brain has identified in some of Plath's late poems a response to Carson's environmental warnings in *Silent Spring*, the book widely regarded as having launched the contemporary environmental movement. In this chapter, I have sketched the culture of scientific and popular natural history in which Plath was making this intervention.

Notes

1. Romer, *Man and the Vertebrates*, 51.
2. Romer, *Man and the Vertebrates*, 44–5.
3. Tansley, 'The Use and Abuse', 64.
4. Worster, *Nature's Economy*, 159.
5. Botkin, *Discordant Harmonies*, 7.
6. Lawrence, *The Complete Poems*, 296, 297.
7. Esty, *A Shrinking Island*, 41.
8. Marren, *The New Naturalists*, 27.
9. Orwell, *Essays*, 361.
10. Hagood, 'Wonders with the Sea', 60.

CHAPTER 22

Plath and War

Cornelia Pearsall

War occupied Sylvia Plath's attention from at least early adolescence to the end of her life. Writing on Christmas Eve, 1950, to a young German correspondent named Hans-Joachim Neupert, she describes her first semester at Smith College, with its courses and 'dances and parties on weekends'. She continues, 'but this war-scare bothers me so much that I can never completely forget myself in artificial gaiety'. Plath in this letter writes of the Korean War (1950–3) and 'the A-Bomb' (*LV1* 250–1).[1] Some months before, she had published an article with her high-school classmate Perry Norton, 'Youth's Plea for World Peace', in the *Christian Science Monitor*, as she mentions in a previous letter to Neupert. Their goal, they declared in the article, was 'to speak out concerning the President's direction to the Atomic Energy Commission to continue its work on the hydrogen bomb'. This sense of the immanence of war as a persistent backbeat to the rhythms of her life, '[a]lways in the background', as she tells Neupert, only intensified (*LV1* 251). Eleven years later, in December 1961, she writes to her mother, Aurelia Plath, to explain her failure to write: 'The reason I haven't written for so long is probably quite silly, but I got so awfully depressed two weeks ago by reading two issues of *The Nation*.' Referring to Fred J. Cook's recent essay, 'Juggernaut, the Warfare State' and a related article on nuclear fallout, Plath emphasises their evidentiary power. '[F]actual, documented, and true', the claims were so compelling she 'simply couldn't sleep for nights with all the warlike talk in the papers'. She states, 'I am very much behind the nuclear disarmers here' (*LH* 437–8), but Aurelia Plath would already have known this from her daughter's prior letters, describing, for instance, Plath's attendance at a Campaign for Nuclear Disarmament rally in Trafalgar Square in April 1960 with newborn Frieda in her arms.[2] Although reading about war incapacitates her writing in winter 1961, it appears in the period before her death in February 1963 to have fuelled it: war and its representations inform some of Plath's most powerful and canonical poems.

The inescapable force of 'some war or other', (*CP* 248) as a clause in Plath's poem 'Getting There' puts it, exerts its pull in her poetry and fiction as well as her letters and journals. Repeating the word three times – 'wars, wars, wars' (*CP* 222) – the speaker of 'Daddy' similarly announces its inexorable nature. These lines both connect and confound a plurality of military engagements, as if to suggest that there are few if any distinctions among them: how to distinguish 'wars' from 'wars' and still more and other 'wars'? The repetition suggests a transhistorical or even ahistorical approach to this subject, of a piece with her assemblage of a range of military-historical associations in a range of poems. Stephen Gould Axelrod notes in 'Cut', for example, the poem's adumbration of 'a history of political violence in references to Pilgrims, Indians, Redcoats, Saboteurs, Kamikazes, Klansmen, and Soviets'.[3] Armies, conflicts, nations, places, politics, tactics and wounds all cohere about the figure of the poet's own wound, activated by and interacting with her 'thumb stump' with what Susan Van Dyne calls the poem's 'metaphoric audacity'.[4] Wars war against one another in Plath's later poems, figuring forms of enduring and seemingly unstoppable strife. Her reflective and reflexive referentiality can function at once to contextualise and decontextualise, both connecting to and estranging the military conflicts to which they refer.

Although conceptually drawn to inexorable recurrences of war, however, Plath also took a highly specific interest in particular historical and contemporary conflicts. These wars extend across chronological and geographical spans. They call out from 'the mouths of Thermopylae' (*CP* 254) in 'Letter in November', extending from her own boots in the same poem, 'My Wellingtons', (*CP* 253) to the 'Waterloo, Waterloo, Napoleon' (*CP* 216) figures marching across 'The Swarm'. Still more multifarious are her allusions to the First and Second World Wars, and most controversially, to the Holocaust and Hiroshima. In her letters to Neupert, Plath writes directly of the Korean War ('As for the Korean situation, I feel ill every time I read about it', she tells him in summer 1950 [*LVI* 168]) and still more of the escalating Cold War and threat of thermonuclear annihilation, aspects of which she tracked assiduously then and in the years to come. Plath brought intellectual curiosity and political commitment to her study of war, and its operations in her poetry were not simply reactive or reportorial but generative in sometimes seemingly contradictory and invariably complex ways.

Between 1947 and 1952, from adolescence to the first half of her Smith College career, spanning the ages from fifteen to nineteen, Plath wrote some eighteen letters to Hans-Joachim Neupert, of Grebenhain, West

Germany. This international epistolary exchange was initially sponsored by Wilbury Crockett, Plath's English teacher at Bradford Senior High School, in Wellesley, Massachusetts. The course of countless such cross-cultural epistolary assignments is to fizzle out after a few exchanges, so it is a testament to the relationship that this one extended so far beyond its schoolroom origins. At some point after her daughter's death, Neupert sent photocopies of these letters to Aurelia Plath, who donated them to Smith College in 1983. Little is known of Neupert and nothing is known about whether this is the extent of a correspondence of which Plath scholars have not yet taken full account. These provide a rare glimpse of a period in her life, particularly before she started college, when there are relatively few letters, and, I think, crucial contextualisation for later writings.[5] War is the inescapable context of this friendship. Plath's letters to Germany are particularly valuable for their articulation of her formative thinking on the subject of war and her insistent curiosity about that country, interrelated topics to which she (and, one may extrapolate from her responses, he) returns again and again, in a probing five-year conversation regarding wars past, present and future, in and beyond the European theatre.

More and More Historical

Introducing herself in her first letter to Hans-Joachim Neupert, Plath informs him, 'we study your country in our history classes' (*LV1* 87). Although simply stated, perhaps deliberately as she begins to gauge his fluency in English – which from the start she praises – her declaration also raises at the outset the framing of Germany as an object of study, acknowledging at once a bridge ('we study') and a divide ('your country') between them. I would emphasise that when Plath refers to history, in these letters and elsewhere, she tends to signify military history. In late October 1962, some fifteen years after her correspondence with Neupert began and during an extraordinarily productive period for her work, Plath tells Peter Orr in an interview for his BBC series *The Poet Speaks*:

> I am not a historian, but I find myself being more and more fascinated by history and now I find myself reading more and more about history. I am very interested in Napoleon, at the present: I'm very interested in battles, in wars, in Gallipoli, the First World War and so on, and I think that as I age I am becoming more and more historical. I certainly wasn't at all in my early twenties.[6]

Deliberating on history, Plath stresses temporal immediacy ('at the present') while also contrasting her past ('I certainly wasn't at all') with her future ('I am becoming more and more'). She twice repeats 'I am very interested', perhaps the stammer of someone accustoming herself to interviews, but also placing deliberate emphasis on the sustained and serious nature of this interest; in these few sentences, she repeats the phrase 'more and more' three times. Plath states that she 'certainly wasn't all' interested in history in her 'early twenties', which we should understand to mean that it had not engaged her *poetically*; other than occasional studies (most notably 'The Thin People', a 1957 poem concerning Holocaust victims), her poetry did not engage in a sustained way with representations of war until late in her life. She had, however, commenced her formal study of the First World War (the conflict she specifies to Orr) in her early teens. The Sylvia Plath Collection at Smith College holds her 1946 report from Phillips Junior High School on the war, the year after the conclusion of the Second World War and before she began writing to Hans-Joachim Neupert. Titled, dramatically and sardonically if not particularly originally, 'A War to end Wars', the report is the product of an eighth-grade overachiever, running to nineteen short chapters and close to forty pages, comprehensively reviewing political background and specific battles, for which she produced detailed maps showing particular manoeuvres, as in the map titled 'Final Thrusts of the First World War'. It concluded with a few First World War poems, accompanied by her illustrations, including John MacCrae's 'In Flanders Fields'.

That Plath threw herself into this project with particular fervour is evident from its title-page, which features a watercolour, presumably a self-portrait, of a girl with dark blonde, shoulder-length hair clasped in a red bow, sitting in an angular chair before an angular table set on a round rag rug, reading a book whose pages seem almost to be turning themselves.[7] Her head rests on the crook of her arm, but her mind is clearly restless, as thought-bubbles float out from behind her hair, leading to one large bubble with an image of a soldier blasting a howitzer's bright-red fire into fields, where figures run headlong in the blue distance. As the gunner rises out of the trench, another man's body hangs into it, straddling it, legs akimbo. Where his face should be there is only red blood, dripping into the trench, in counterpoint to the red flare exploding out of it. The thirteen-year-old student dramatises her engagement with the Great War; her research project is an act of imaginative projection. Producing this document the year after the end of the Second World War, she is remote from the First World War generationally and geographically, and yet there it hovers above her head. Plath received an A+ in red ink, with the underlined sole comment 'Excellent!', a satisfying if succinct assessment that must have rung as a commendation of her affective as well as academic work.

Although Plath in her interview with Peter Orr describes herself as not 'at all' interested in martial subjects in her 'early twenties', by the later years of that decade she had again returned to intellectual engagement with the subject of war, writing in a letter of 16 August 1960 to her mother: 'As you were reading your World War II book about Auschwitz, I was finishing Allan Moorehead's *Gallipoli*: absolutely fascinating and terrifying.' As with her First World War report, Plath attests to an experiential relation with the battle about which she reads, explaining, 'Ted's father fought at Gallipoli, and a diary in a breast pocket stopped a bullet, so I feel incalculably lucky as I read of the mammoth, pointless slaughters that he survived and fathered the one husband I could imagine' (*LH* 390–1). War and its effects engage Plath's imagination with a sense of vivid immediacy and relevance to her own domestic life, as they had in the training grounds of her eighth-grade report on the Great War, informing her later observation to Orr that 'personal experience . . . should be *relevant*, and relevant to the larger things, the bigger things such as Hiroshima and Dachau and so on'.[8] The 'pointless slaughters' of Gallipoli are associated pointedly with the very existence of Ted Hughes, 'the one husband I could imagine', a making intimate of 'the larger things, the bigger things' that she would explore intensively in late poems aggressively juxtaposing the martial and the marital.

'I Thought Every German Was You'

'There is so much I want to know about Germany!' So Plath exclaims to Neupert in a letter of 14 April 1949; it is a refrain of hers throughout the five years of their correspondence. In early letters to him her requests are somewhat formal, as on 14 June 1948 when, after describing for him local activities such as ping-pong and baby-sitting, she states rather stiffly, 'I will like very much to hear about Germany in your next letter. Would you like to compare some of our ideas about religion, war, or life or science?' (*LV1*). Only a few months later her tone is already lighter – 'There are so many things I want to ask you!' – and yet her subject matter is weightier, as she unleashes a series of pressing questions, culminating in, 'Do you "worry" about Russia as many of us do?' (*LV1* 136). That the majority of Plath's letters to him make reference to Germany is not surprising given the roots of their relationship in post-war American-German exchange. But what did 'German' signify in the course of their correspondence, and after? As a start: a geographical region, a history, a language, two world wars, divided nations, her friend, and, in the terminology of 'Lady Lazarus', 'Herr Enemy' (*CP* 246).

Plath's questions concerning the German view of American militarism intensified after she entered college. A letter to Neupert in the autumn of her second year at Smith conveys the urgency of her curiosity, asking, 'What is the opinion of your young German friends of the battle going on in Korea? Whose side do they take?' (*LV1* 397). Neupert is not alone in serving as a potential informant regarding war and its effects. The previous winter, Plath went on a date with a Marine named Bill who had been wounded in the Korean War. In her account of the evening in her journal, she initially portrays her intensive interrogative mode somewhat comically: 'Tell me,' she says to Bill, '"About the war." "Where were you hurt?" . . . "What's it like to fight? to kill someone?" "Your curiosity is aflame,"' she writes, observing herself as closely as she observes him. Bill, meanwhile, 'nonchalant' and laconic, later in the evening sexually assaults her (*J* 41). Plath in a different register reports on the incident in a letter to her mother, and in still another register in a 1952 short story entitled 'Brief Encounter'.[9] We might even hear its faint echo in *The Bell Jar*, in Esther Greenwood's still briefer encounter with a sailor she meets on Boston Common, who, unlike Bill, 'looked Nordic and virginal' (*BJ* 133).[10]

In an early letter to Neupert of 14 June 1948, after detailing for him information about 'American youth', she asks, 'Have I told you that my Father was born in Germany? He came to America as a boy and worked until he became a professor of German and Biology at Boston University' (*LV1* 110). Plath affirms the strength of this familial connection repeatedly, as on 10 October 1949 when she writes, 'I feel a strong kinship for anything German. I think it is the most beautiful language in the world, and whenever I meet anyone with a German name or German traits, I have a sudden secret warmth. Austria too, I love!' (*LV1* 153). Drawing her German father and Austrian mother into an expansive love, Plath in another letter of 1949 extends that warmth to anyone of Teutonic nationality, reflecting, 'I wonder [. . .] what makes us like certain things and fear others? [. . .] For instance, when I meet someone here who has a German background, I immediately say to myself inside, "Hmmm, must be a nice person." I have a partiality – for no good reason except that I, too, have a German background' (*LV1* 151).

Plath in these reflections draws Neupert himself into a circle of 'kinship' and what she considers an instinctive affection, a 'sudden secret warmth'.

Her repeated professions of 'partiality', the immediacy of the assumption 'must be a nice person', the exclamations of 'love': these may read simply as an extension of the hand of international friendship. They may also strike readers, however, as contradicting her later, fiercer, lyric situating of German language, locations and persons – in the abstract and as individuals – in martial contexts. She writes to Neupert that his is the 'most beautiful language in the world'. Her own interest in learning German may predate this correspondence but the relationship must surely have compounded a linguistic desire that dogged her for years. Source of a scourge of self-goading and self-loathing, 'Plath's passionate desire to learn German and her constant failure to do so', Jacqueline Rose observes, 'is one of the refrains of both her journals and her letters home.'[11] The language is presented far less positively in the poem 'Daddy', the 'German tongue' (*CP* 222) deemed a 'language obscene'. The poem's speaker describes being 'scared', of 'your Luftwaffe, your gobbledygoo' (*CP* 223). Jacqueline Rose defines *gobbledygoo* as 'clichés and childish nonsense',[12] although the line's grammatical construction suggests the word may also serve as a modifier to the terrifyingly meaningful name of the German Air Force, the 'Luftwaffe', and we might hear as well in the word an aesthetic assessment of the language's sound. 'Daddy', called by Ann Keniston one of Plath's 'so-called Holocaust poems'[13] presents a *summa* of Nazi-related terminology, each word powerfully resonant: Dachau, Auschwitz, Belsen, Luftwaffe, Aryan, swastika, fascist, *Mein Kampf.*

Plath writes often to Neupert of her longing to visit Germany, regretting particularly her inability, due to its unaffordability, to join a student summer trip there led by Wilbury Crockett; her late poem 'Mary's Song' depicts the land as at once devastated and destructive: 'burnt-out / Germany' (*CP* 257). She acknowledges to Neupert a kind of blanket affection for 'anyone with a German name or German traits' (*LV1* 153). 'The Munich Mannequins' portrays a different kind of highly generalised depiction of and attitude towards 'The thick Germans slumbering in their bottomless Stolz' (*CP* 263). Plath generally writes familiarly to Neupert, calling him 'Hans' and addressing a 'you' that assumes companionable relationality, seemingly unlike the apostrophised 'you' figured as German ('Panzer-man, panzer-man, O *you*') (*CP* 223) who stalks and is staked in 'Daddy'. Plath's use of the second-person singular in her late poetry presents as complex and shifting a set of constructions as the 'I' who addresses him, her or them: variously, father, husband, rival, baby or reader, to name a few of the options of address.

'I thought every German was you' (*CP* 223), declares the speaker in 'Daddy', but the disturbing connotations of the poetry's voicing of unspeakable associations do not appear to have characterised her relationship with Neupert. Her German correspondent seems to have been for Plath an utterly likeable friend, and their inviting, sociable correspondence one of the least complicated relationships of her life – and yet nevertheless intersecting with some of the most pressing complexities of her art, especially in its representations of war. The frequency and vehemence of Plath's philo-German declarations to Neupert suggest their authenticity, as the frequency and vehemence of what might be considered anti-German allusions in her late poems suggest theirs. Authenticity may be less at stake, though, than an authorial distinction between writing to a pen-pal and writing a poem. In this light, the contradiction is not at all surprising: though in each case inflected by her absorption in the subject of war and its histories, she is writing in different genres for different audiences at different periods in her life and her times. These contextual distinctions thus highlight the provisional and contingent category of context itself throughout Plath's writing.

I would argue nevertheless that these distinctions are consonant rather than contradictory. Plath's Teutonic representations counterbalance rather than countermand each other. Germans are either the most appealing or appalling of people; they 'must be' either 'nice' or Nazis. Both are more multifaceted views than they might initially seem, each nuanced rather than negated by the other, and consonant in that in either case a particular nation and its people are singled out, collectively, as special or exceptional, in relation to militarism and to her own identity in relation to militarism. Plath's German preoccupation highlights some of the complexities of national identity and nationalism that in the poet's time, as now, in various manifestations can underwrite war. This takes us some distance towards understanding the functions for this poet of the thick referentiality, and relationality, of 'wars' and 'wars' and 'wars'. The 'Hiroshima ash' (*CP* 231) of 'Fever 103°', floating through the late poems like other manifestations of violence that radiate out in this work, represents the kinds of devastations wrought on and by the nation-state that Plath critiques, actively and passionately, from the start of her correspondence with her German friend.

'A Great Help Toward Peace'

On the Fourth of July, 1949, Sylvia Plath took time out from American Independence Day celebrations to write to Hans-Joachim Neupert, describing the national holiday. 'I always await your mail very eagerly, and read your letters with great delight', she writes, thanking him also for a booklet he had sent her about Germany. In January of that year Plath had herself sent him a pamphlet: a 'little folder that tells about a World Federalist Group which seems to have the right idea of world peace' (*LVi* 141). Founded in the late 1930s and established more formally in the late 1940s, this organisation seeks to create international mechanisms to prevent future world wars. That Plath was aware of and indeed promoting this relatively new global organisation to her German friend indicates how engaged she was in anti-war enterprises and activism, and how relevant to this she considered their correspondence. In the letter enclosing the pamphlet, she wrote to Neupert: 'I think that corresponding, the way we are doing, is a great help toward peace. I consider you as a special friend, and I do not think of Germany as a cold, impersonal nation, but rather I think of Germany as made up of a lot of Hans-Joachims, all willing to be friends if only we will get to know them better' (*LVi* 141).

Plath's peopling of Neupert's nation with proliferations of himself illuminates her broader concern about the future of war – its representation and still more, its prevention. 'You know what a pacifist I am!', she declares to him – not for the first time, as she acknowledges – in the last letter we have of hers addressed to Neupert (*LVi* 433). In this profoundly formative correspondence, Plath articulates a pacifism that accords consistently with similar statements throughout her prose writings, an ideological commitment notable for its informed seriousness. The correspondence challenges us as well to consider more fully the ways in which her poems representing war, in their ferocity of military engagement, are also, or even actually, poems working 'toward peace'.

Notes

1. I am grateful to my colleague Karen Kukil for bringing these letters to my attention.
2. Plath's 1960 collage of Cold War images (featuring a picture of Eisenhower with a fighter jet across his head aiming for a woman's belly) also indicates her prior concern (*SMITH*; reproduced in Connors and Bayley (eds.), *Eye Rhymes*, Plate 37).
3. Axelrod, 'Plath and Torture', 73.
4. Van Dyne, *Revising Life*, 147.
5. Tracy Brain notes that *Letters Home* begins 27 September 1950, with the first letter Plath wrote from Smith College; still extant are some early cards and letters, including those written home from summer camp in 1945–8 (Brain,

'Sylvia Plath's Letters and Journals', 140). In addition to her letters home, Plath in college entered into what one biographer calls 'passionate correspondence' with several male friends and boyfriends: 'to all her male admirers she wrote voluminously' (Stevenson, *Bitter Fame*, Houghton Mifflin edition, 39). The Neupert letters augment the epistolary record, then, and perhaps also serve as a precursor to Plath's substantial correspondence with other peers, male and female.

6. Orr, *The Poet Speaks*, 169.

7. Langdon Hammer in 'Plath at War' insightfully examines the 'related, gendered positions' of these figures in their dialectical relation of 'attlefield and home', with particular attention to the implications of the rag rug that weaves together various associations (148).

8. Orr, *The Poet Speaks*, 169–70.

9. See *LH* 62–3, for her account to Aurelia Plath. See Ooms, 'I'm Willing' (33–40) for an analysis of the 'striking reimagining of her date with Bill' (39) in her unpublished February 1952 short story in the Lilly Library, Indiana University.

10. All citations from *The Bell Jar* refer to the 1999 Harper Perennial Classics Edition.

11. Rose, *The Haunting*, 227.

12. Rose, *The Haunting*, 232.

13. Keniston, 'Holocaust Again', 140.

PART VI

Biographical Contexts

CHAPTER 23

Plath's Journals

Sally Bayley

In October 1952, shortly before her twenty-first birthday, a maudlin Sylvia Plath makes a brief reference in her journal to the following passage from Virginia Woolf's novel *To the Lighthouse*:

> But there was a force working; something not highly conscious; something that leered, something that lurched; something not inspired to go about its work with dignified ritual or solemn chanting. Mrs. McNab groaned; Mrs. Bast creaked.[1]

Plath's note, placed carefully inside Woolfian parentheses, reads as a proleptic epigraph for what she fears might be her own fate, a life curtailed by domestic drudgery:

> So much working, reading, thinking, living to do. A lifetime is not long enough. Nor youth to old age long enough. Immortality and permanence be damned. Sure I want them, but they are nonexistent, and won't matter when I rot underground. All I want to say is: I made the best of a mediocre job. It was a good fight while it lasted. And so life goes on. (Mrs McNab: 'There was a force working.') (*J* 149).

Mrs McNab is Plath's literary shorthand for what she fears will be her future self. At the same time, Woolf's groaning charwoman represents an unruly and unconscious life force that Plath associates with literary creation; and so she tucks Mrs McNab at the bottom of her entry as a reminder of that working force she wishes to harness. Her journal, she implies, will help bring about her own version of Mrs McNab.

For the purpose of this chapter, I'd like to take Plath's reference to Mrs McNab and her 'working force' as a metaphor for what Plath hopes to achieve within her journal. Limiting my discussion mainly to the intense period of Plath's late teenage years and early adulthood, from November 1949 to the winter of 1952, the first three years of her college career, I will trace Plath's emerging relationship to her journal persona and creed.

But let me first explain Mrs McNab in her original context. Within the life of Woolf's novel, Mrs McNab is charwoman to the Ramsay family.

After the death of Mrs Ramsay (the novel's emotional centre), Mrs McNab
is sent to restore the neglected holiday home in the Isle of Skye to proper
use. Mrs McNab is a restorer of order; she carries with her a 'leering' and
'lurching' energy, a crude form of physical life that gets done the difficult
job of clearing out a home abandoned to grief. As such, she is an effective
metaphor for the emotional and creative spring cleaning Plath carries out
inside her journals.

But what do we know of Mrs McNab? According to her snobby
narrator, she is a lower-class woman who generates a drunken sort of
visceral energy. McNab drinks because her life has been hard – she has
lost children – and in her role as hired help, she is also Woolf's unconsciously feeling, perpetual mourner. And yet, Mrs McNab's real life
matters little; in the novel's scheme of things, she is pure symbol, the living
embodiment of what Woolf calls 'Time Passing' with all of its unacknow-
ledged and wasted moments of being. At the same time, Mrs McNab is
restorative; she is an essential life force and reformer of spaces – rooms –
wrecked by grief.

It is this sort of invigorating, unconscious energy that Plath looks to in
her journal. Depression or a desultory mood is the enemy of creative
inspiration. And so Mrs McNab's point of arrival is timely: she appears
in the middle of a series of very depressed journal entries. For some
months, Plath has been considering the span of her 'lifetime', from
youth to old age, and what she might achieve. Her verdict is not all
positive. Just before she summons Mrs McNab, Plath is reflecting upon
the inadequacy of a single mortal life: 'A lifetime is not long enough'
(*J* 149).

Aged twenty and a sophomore at the elite, all-female Smith College,
Plath is in acute existential crisis. She is contemplating her past and her
future with ferocious, critical intensity. But in the world of her journal, this
is regular business. Her journal exists to uphold one recurring thought
structure, one primal drama. It is the same metaphysical crisis that Hamlet
faces: whether or not he can bear the world in all of its compromised forms.
Plath loops around and around a similar theoretical question; she picks at
the same wound. Can she go on living knowing, as she does, that her
choices are limited by an unimaginative culture?

We see this in her habit of hovering over herself in the conditional
mood; 'what if' is her preferred mode of thinking:

> I wonder if art divorced from normal and conventional living is as vital as art
> combined with living: in a word, would marriage sap my creative energy and

annihilate my desire for written and pictorial expression which increases with this depth of unsatisfied emotion ... or would I achieve a fuller expression in art as well as in the creation of children? ... Am I strong enough to do both well? (*J* 55–6).

But the conclusions to these contingent thoughts are not always encouraging. Such questions bring more crises, which in turn, produce more stalemating questions. Either she must do something sensational, she concludes, or she might as well give in to the throes of despondency and depression. If she continues to live, how will she manage to harness the overwhelming possibilities of her creative life? How will she avoid the domestic fate of a Mrs McNab and still generate the life force she associates with her literary foremother, Virginia Woolf, and Woolf's artist-representative, Lily Briscoe?

Plath regards her journal as a space for generating a creative will-to-power that will allow her to transcend more enervating forms of life. Her diary's special commission is to interrupt daily life with its restricting errands and exigencies. Just as Mrs McNab enters into the Ramsay home to 'tear[ing] the veil of silence', so Plath's journal will pull her away from the undignified business of 'limitations'. Limitations are those cultural restrictions – marriage, children – she associates with the death of the creative life.

All such limitations must be swept away:

And there it is: when asked what role I will plan to fill, I say 'What do you mean role? I plan not to step into a part on marrying – but to go on living as an intelligent mature being, growing and learning as I always have. No shift, no radical change in life habits.' (*J* 105 [underlining is Plath's])

Her journal, then, will creatively disrupt and override the negative effects of an oppressive cultural conformity. This, in essence, is Plath's journal creed: a belief system as ambitious as the one she holds for life.

And yet, as Woolf cruelly reminds us, Mrs. McNab's lurching work is not dignified or solemn. Plath's journaling follows a similar sort of clumsy pattern as she veers towards and then away from her ideal self. But unlike Mrs. McNab, young Plath *does* turn (as I will show) to the solemn language of ritual and religion in an effort to summon a higher creative power. Plath longs to make sense of the rush of feeling and frustration that arises when she considers matters of life over death. Her journal habit allows her to dwell, as Emily Dickinson put it, in imaginative possibility:[2] to prepare for a bolder and better life ahead; to play at God with all the grandiloquent rhetoric of her journaling ancestors.

II

Diaries and journals generate particular habits of self-address and self-understanding. How you speak to yourself inside your journal sets the tone for the way in which you understand yourself in the world. Journals build ego, says Plath's fellow diarist and contemporary, Susan Sontag, in an entry entitled 'On Keeping a Journal', written on 31 December 1957, when Sontag was twenty-four. But the budding ego of the journal-writer is quite another self, a distinct alter-ego:

> In the journal I do not just express myself more openly than I could do to any person; I create myself. The journal is a vehicle for my sense of selfhood. It represents me emotionally and spiritually independent. There (alas) it does not simply record my actual, daily life but rather – it many cases – offers an alternative to it.[3]

Sontag remains clear-eyed about the role of the diary in her own life; she realises that any diary writing forces an absurd split between the life led within the diary – a life often grossly distorted, exaggerated and sulky in the face of the world – and the more gracious and forgiving person living without: 'There is often a contradiction between the meaning of our actions towards a person and what we say we feel towards that person in a journal', she confesses.[4]

A journal, in other words, encourages the hypocrite in us. It frees us from the necessities of daily life where we regularly swallow our words, bite our tongues and generally try to behave ourselves. Self-censorship is a large part of being socially acceptable. The diary allows us to indulge the weaker parts of our ego; and so it is that the diary persona is often poorly socialised, rude, veering like an adolescent between overly sincere and insincere poses.

For the young Sylvia Plath, her younger journals, or diaries as she calls them, are an essential part of her ego development and journal credo. In the weeks following on from her seventeenth birthday, Plath recommits to her diary religion. Her diary, she theatrically declares, will help her contain the experience of 'rapture'; it will relieve some of the overwhelming sensations that come with being seventeen.

> 13 NOVEMBER: As of today I have decided to keep a diary again – just a place where I can write my thoughts and opinions when I have a moment. Somehow I have to keep and hold the rapture of being seventeen. Every day is so precious, I feel infinitely sad at the thought of all this time melting farther and farther away from me as I grow older. Now, now is the perfect time of my life.[5]

Between childhood and young womanhood, Plath is intoxicated by the idea of herself; for now, she wants nothing more than to hold onto that dramatic moment of pure, operatic self-emergence.

'Now' is the moment of her subject's nativity. 'Now' is pure 'I' and 'Me': undiluted teenage egoism. Her diary, she declares, will attach her to pure selfhood: an invulnerable, meaningful self, filled to the brim with significance. 'Now' is the extended moment of this rapturous state of being. But as John Beer has noted, Plath's experience of being was typically more mobile than static: mercurial, shifting and changing. Her mobile personality made her difficult to pin down. But a mobile and malleable selfhood was Plath's applied poetics for living. Aged eighteen, and in the mode of philosopher-poet, she passionately declares: 'With me, the present is forever, and forever is always shifting, flowing, melting. This second is life.' Plath's journal-confession broaches the real limitations of the journal form, which is, that no diarist can quite capture life unfolding in the present tense. Always there is a lag between the living and the recording. Still, Plath's diary promises a close approximation; a holding space for the 'continuous quicksand' of living sensations (*J* 9). Her diary will move her through the shifting territories of mood and circumstance; that mosaic of conflicting voices that reaches, as a poem does, for a persistent thread of meaning.

Beer quotes Plath's contemporary Clarissa Roche at length on these fragmented constituents of Plath's 'uncompleted' self: 'Like fragments of mercury racing and quivering toward a center to settle in a self-contained mass, the myriad ramifications of her personality sought a focal point.'[6] As such, her journal entries often read as shouting matches with her several selves; a frustrated series of pointed rhetorical questions she throws at herself like knives. What have other women done to free themselves from such terrible choices, she asks herself? How can she avoid joining the destructive circle of several female literary ancestors? How can she avoid the fate of Virginia Woolf? Plath's solution is simply to press on: to produce more words.[7]

In her mature poetry, this uncentred and incomplete subject is attached to verbs of disintegration and formlessness. 'Melting' is the verb Plath vividly applies in 'Lady Lazarus', who describes herself as 'The pure gold baby // That melts to a shriek' (*CP* 246). At the heart of this image is the painful substitution of a melting body for the sake of an emerging voice. Pure voice comes at the price of surrendering the body. We see this costly substitution throughout 'Ariel': in the 'substanceless blue / Pour of tor and distances' where 'Pour' turns into a noun; or in the figure of Godiva that

'unpeel[s]'; and in the cry of the child that 'Melts' (*CP* 239). Plath's mature
self resists substance and instead embraces an alchemical state of *prima
materia* or formlessness.

It is this unformed self that leads her into such quick adoptions of other
literary lives. We see this most obviously in her appropriation of Woolf's
domestic life for her own literary fantasy. Nearly eight years later, in
February 1957, and now a Fulbright scholar at Newnham College,
Cambridge, England, Plath reattaches herself to her literary foremother,
Virginia Woolf, through her diary. Blindsided by the details of her own
literary efforts, she writes over the biography of her literary foremother,
revising Woolf's daily life in 1941 and drawing it into a version of her own.
Consequently, her summary of Woolf's habit of breaking off from writing to
cook in response to literary rejection is a deceptive synopsis of the main thrust
of *A Writer's Diary*:

> I pick up the blessed diary of Virginia Woolf which I bought with a battery
> of her novels saturday with Ted. And she works off her depression over
> rejections from Harper's (no less! - - - and I can hardly believe the Big Ones
> get rejected, too!) by cleaning out the kitchen. And cooks haddock & sausage
> (*J* 269).

Plath's summary of Woolf's daily life is misleading; her recreation of Woolf
at fifty-nine is also inaccurate. In place of the desperate and despondent
Woolf she creates a blithe individual more akin to Plath's own ideal self
than the historical Virginia Woolf. To be more precise, the entry Plath cites
comes at the end of Woolf's life and at a very fragile moment in English
history.

On Sunday 8 March 1941, Woolf's writing is punctuated – you might say
paralysed – by fear of German invasion. Her homes in London have been
reduced to rubble. If you read Woolf's entries from 1941 you quickly see
that, at this most desperate moment, she can respond only in stunted
telegraphic fragments. 'We live without a future' she writes hopelessly on
26 January 1941. By March of that year she is desperately trying to secure an
order of 'occupation' to daily life. Her diary writing is nothing more than
a catalogue of banal fragments, a scrappy list of instructions on the basic
mechanisms of survival:

> I will go down with my colours flying. This I see verges on introspection; but
> doesn't quite fall in. Suppose I bought a ticket at the Museum: biked in daily
> and read history. Suppose I selected one dominant figure in every age and wrote
> round and about. Occupation is essential. And now with some pleasure I find
> that it's seven: and must cook dinner. Haddock and sausage meat. I think it is

true that one gains a certain hold on sausage and haddock by writing them down.[8]

Plath's account of Woolf's life says more about Plath herself than it does about Virginia Woolf. Woolf is not energetically cleaning out the kitchen; she is urging herself to get some dinner on now that she has dragged herself to the end of another day. Woolf's diary entry is a bleak note from a war survivor and a pending suicide.

III

A few weeks after her Mrs McNab entry and her twentieth birthday, Plath again tries to set down the rituals of her journal life. Her focus is still the looming past and pressing future, and her task, she tells herself, is to remember what she has lost and what she might lose again: 'Recall, remember: please do not die again. Let there be continuity at least – a core of consistency – even if your philosophy must always be a moving dynamic dialectic' (*J* 154).

Repeated self-recollection and self-reprimand are part of what Plath terms her 'dynamic dialectic'. When those efforts run out, and in order to keep the story of herself moving, she must transfer her story elsewhere, towards a Christian fairy tale where she imagines herself as 'The girl who died. And was resurrected. Children. Witches. Magic Symbols' (*J* 154). Suddenly her journal takes on a shamanic urgency, the 'rough magic' of Shakespeare's magus, Prospero,[9] and part of what John Beer has recognised as Plath's struggle to unite her 'vegetative existence' – the life of the body – alongside her simmering 'intelligent consciousness':[10]

> Tomorrow I will curse the dawn, but there will be other, earlier nights, and the dawns will be laid out in alarms and raw bells and sirens. Now a love, a faith, an affirmation is conceived in me like an embryo. The gestation may be a while in producing, but the fertilization has come to pass (*J* 154).

Plath's urgent 'now' is the dynamic force behind this new self-reckoning. 'Now' forcefully pushes her journal persona into the realm of spiritual mantra and spells. 'Now' is her vigorous effort to produce some sort of magical intervention that will rip open the present moment and inject it with more meaning. It is what Plath calls, in a January 1953 journal entry, her 'mental magic' (*J* 158): the creative interruption of the ordinary by way of the imagination.

In its imitation of a spellbook, Plath's journal recalls sixteen-year-old Ralph Waldo Emerson's incantatory imperatives to witches and fairies as he initiates his first journal persona, grandly entitled 'The Wide World':

> O ye witches assist me! Enliven or horrify some midnight lubrication or dream ... to supply this reservoir when other resources fail ... Spirits of Earth, Air, Fire, Water, wherever ye glow, whatsoever you patronise, who-ever you inspire, hallow, hallow, this devoted paper – Dedicated & Signed Jan 25, 1820.[11]

Emerson's journal spell is a magician's will-to-power reminiscent of Shakespeare's muscle-flexing magus, Prospero. Twenty-year-old Plath asserts the same dramatic rites to summon a new form of life that will resuscitate her flagging ego. Her entry imitates Emerson's incantatory self-creation, the tradition of the transcendental journalist playing at God.[12]

Plath borrows from Emerson's grandiose modes of self-creation and self-projection. As a student at Harvard University in 1820, Emerson writes, as Plath does, towards his future self. For this, he needs more creative space, and so he turns his journal into a grand horizon, an imaginative line between here and there, then and now. His journal will help him 'talk & write & think out'[13] what cannot be expressed in daily life because there is so little room. Space is essential to Emerson's journal creed. His young self demands space to stretch out and be. Emerson is an ambitious young man; he would like, he thinks, to enjoy something of infinity before he dies.

Emerson's journal will bridge the gap between the visible and invisible world, between God and himself, between God and his imperious 'me':

> Who is he that shall control me? Why may I not act & speak & write & think with entire freedom? What am I to the Universe, or, the Universe, what is it to me? Who hath forged the chains of wrong and right, of Opinion and Custom? And must I wear them?[14]

Emerson's journaling self demands unbounded imaginative and social freedom. Within the security of his journal, the journalist can devise his own rhetorical and symbolic structures. If we read this statement closely we see that, grammatically speaking, Emerson's 'I' and 'me' surround a conjured 'Universe'; in other words, the Universe is the object around which both the 'I', as speaking subject, and the 'me', as reflexive object, circulate. But 'me' has another role: it keeps the world apart. Me is the self that creates a vital barrier between the self in private (the 'I') and the wide world: 'I see the world, human, brute and inanimate nature,—I am in the midst of them, but not of them; I hear the song of the storm ... I see cities and nations and witness passions . . . but I partake it not . . . I disclaim them all.'[15]

In order to vitiate the effects of social conventions, Emerson suggests, the private self must fashion a second self. For Plath, this second self should exist alongside her daily self whilst holding some stake in the supernatural; a self that will live and move alongside the sexually vital, ambitious college girl tearing home on her bike: 'Tonight, biking home toward midnight, talking to myself, sense of trap, of time, rolled the stone of inertia away from the tomb' (*J* 154). Above all, Plath's journal persona offers her sight of a second life and recognisable myth of self-resurrection and reconstitution, accelerating her 'now' into Emerson's infinity through the act of being reborn, the rolling away of the stone. This divine alter ego will enter into her mature poems as the 'Godiva' (*CP* 239) who will ascend in 'Ariel' and as the 'walking miracle' (*CP* 244) of 'Lady Lazarus'.

But as with Emerson's journal persona, there are more relatives to be found. The Plath who pedals home at midnight is also a relative of teenage Virginia Woolf's (then Virginia Stephen's) journal persona, Miss Jan, who is first born on 3 January 1897, a few weeks before Woolf's fifteenth birthday. Both are divine chaperones of the everyday world. But Plath is critical of Woolf's journal aesthetic; she finds her literary foremother too 'ephemeral'. She will correct this, and in her writing life, of which her journal writing was a crucially propulsive form, she will 'speak [her] deep self' (*J* 286). The life of the creative mind will lead the life of the body. If we think back to Mrs McNab, our working metaphor for Plath's journal credo, then Plath's deeper or deepest self is that lurching unconscious force that promises to roll away 'the stone of inertia' (*J* 154) from the entrance to her creative life.

Notes

1. Woolf, *To the Lighthouse*, 158.
2. Dickinson, *The Poems of Emily Dickinson*, no. 466.
3. Sontag, *Reborn*, 166–7.
4. Sontag, *Reborn*, 164–5.
5. Quoted in Connors, 'Living Color', 69.
6. Beer, *Post-Romantic Consciousness*, 157.
7. Bayley, *The Private Life of the Diary*, 12–13.
8. Woolf, *A Writer's Diary*, 345.
9. Shakespeare, *The Tempest*, 5.1.38–55.
10. Beer, *Post-Romantic Consciousness*, 144.
11. Emerson, *Selected Journals*, vol. I, 1.

12. Plath studied and annotated the works of Emerson as a student at Smith College: fcaw.library.umass.edu/F/?func=direct&doc_number=010268851& doc_library=FCL01.
13. Emerson, *Selected Journals*, vol. I, 1–2.
14. Emerson, *Selected Journals*, vol. I, 91.
15. Emerson, *Selected Journals*, vol. I, 91.

CHAPTER 24

Plath's Teaching and the Shaping of Her Work

Amanda Golden

Sylvia Plath herself may have steered critics away from investigating the unwieldy sheaf of notes that she prepared to teach first-year English at Smith College from 1957 to 1958.[1] Her letters and journals impress upon readers that she was overwhelmed with reading, outlining and preparing her classes, and would have rather devoted the time to her writing.[2] Had she not left them at home before departing for England in late 1959, however, she may have recycled these meticulous notes, often on pink Smith memorandum paper, for her writing. The topics Plath addressed, her interpretations of passages and her overview lectures bear the influence of her careful work, not only selecting texts and topics but also reading recent criticism. Plath's teaching materials shed light on the ways that her voice as a teacher developed alongside her voice as a writer. Her pedagogy blended impersonality and philology, emulating the modern writers whom she taught and teaching her students to be as thorough as she may have once been. Modelling these strategies sharpened her own gaze, and, even as she denied it, filtered into her poetry and prose.

Contexts

Over coffee in Cambridge during the spring of Plath's first year as a Fulbright Scholar at Newnham College, Mary Ellen Chase mentioned the possibility of Plath's returning to teach at Smith (*LV1* 1194). After receiving a position the following year, Plath prepared her course, selecting predominately texts she had encountered at Smith and Cambridge, as well as poets she had read on her own (*LH* 318).[3] The department outlined a structure for English 11, including the genres of texts to cover, the length of writing assignments and the types of assignments, including research skills.[4] It was a rigorous course, teaching students not to be satisfied with 'the slipshod, the half-done',[5] and Smith's austerity shaped these expectations. In returning to Smith,

Plath would have wanted to prove herself, as a teacher, and as one who continued to be worthy of the praise she once received. Her teaching notes indicate the extent to which she continued to study, immersing herself in the aspects of the texts she would emphasise, reading widely in the criticism and incorporating this research in her notes.

In Smith's *Hamper* yearbook from 1953, Plath stands in the back row of the English department faculty photograph (*J* Plate 16). Looking closely, one can see what may be a hint of the bold necklace Plath wore when photographed by Rollie McKenna the following year.[6] This flourish reflects the fact that despite the overall impression of darkly dressed professional convention that Plath conveys in the image, she also went against the grain. Her grim expression, however, is keeping with a student's memory that Mrs Hughes 'rarely cracked a smile'.[7] Judging from the photograph, neither it seems did many of her colleagues, who appear stern and formally dressed. Even as it contained several women, the faculty cautioned students against sounding too girlish. The English 11 Handbook that Plath had received during her first year of college warned against the 'Feminine Demonstrative' in which 'The indiscriminate use of *so* as an intensive . . . gives an effect of "schoolgirl gush" and is called in derision the "feminine demonstrative". *Examples* "She was so sweet". "There is some-thing so beautiful and so awe inspiring about a snow-capped mountain."'[8] While concision makes for more effective writers, the gendered terms of this example are also indicative of the ways that the field was still driven by a sense of masculinity that resonated with the coldness of the texts Plath taught and emulated.

Plath crafted a formidable course. Beginning the term with William James's *Varieties of Religious Experience*, she proceeded to the stories of Nathaniel Hawthorne, Henry James, D. H. Lawrence and James Joyce, including 'The Dead'. She taught two novels, Fyodor Dostoevsky's *Crime and Punishment* and Joyce's *A Portrait of the Artist as a Young Man*, before a tragedy unit including Aristotle's *Poetics*, *Oedipus Rex*, *Antigone*, the plays of Webster and Tourneur, August Strindberg and Henrik Ibsen. She closed the term with the poetry of T. S. Eliot, W. B. Yeats, W. H. Auden, Dylan Thomas, Gerard Manley Hopkins, e. e. cummings, John Crowe Ransom and Edith Sitwell. Because Plath prepared such detailed teaching materials, working alongside and annotating the books in her personal library, we can watch as she blends texts and interpretations she had encountered as a student with others she had read since, gaining a new sense of the ways that her gaze as a writer was entangled with her reading.

English 11 acclimatised students to college writing while also introducing them to 'literary forms and the techniques of criticism'.[9] Preparing for this task, Plath annotated Gilbert Highet's *The Art of Teaching* (1954). Near the close of his book, Highet finds that 'Real teaching' – and Plath seizes upon his conclusion with her underlining – 'culminates in a conversation, an actual change of the pupil's mind'.[10] The English 11 Handbook similarly advised students to engage with others' ideas as part of developing their own: 'We must certainly *begin*, as critics, with our own genuine and firsthand impressions, and we must certainly *end* with our own well-defined and disciplined tastes—our own, and not someone else's, however learned or authoritative.'[11] Smith's expectations would have framed those Plath held for her students and for herself. As Langdon Hammer points out, 'Plath conceived of the female professional as a kind of student.'[12] By comparing her teaching notes with her student notebooks and annotated books, we can better understand the ways that she approached the role of teacher, expanding upon the strategies that had brought her success as a student. Part of Plath's student-writer identity rests upon the fact that she does not appear to have made as bold a distinction as other readers may make between her independent reading and her student reading. The attitude that Plath brings to the margins of her reading reflects her sizing up texts with the gaze of both a critical and a creative writer.[13]

Plath spent the fall of 1953 at McLean Hospital. A copy of Edmund Wilson's *Axel's Castle* was waiting for her when she returned home for Christmas. A gift from Gordon Lameyer, Plath's former boyfriend with whom she shared an interest in Joyce, the book's arrival meant that she could return to the modern writers whom she admired (*LV1* 651, 652 *n*). With exuberant, snarky marginalia, Plath joins Wilson in his assessment of the field. When he offers that 'Milton's poetic reputation has sunk', Plath voices her relief in the margin.[14] She adds more marginal applause when, speaking of Gertrude Stein, Wilson remarks, 'one should not talk about "nonsense" until one has decided what "sense" consists of'.[15] The edge in Plath voice avoids the sentimental, blending poise and exclamation. She sustains this enthusiasm throughout what may have been multiple readings of Wilson's book, noting her strong approval beside his connection between James's and Eliot's lifeless protagonists.[16] She later draws on this connection in her own teaching notes.[17]

Margins provided spaces for Plath to collect ideas and interpretations, and her student books include points from her teachers and secondary sources. We can tell this by comparing the annotations in Plath's own copies of Virginia Woolf's *To the Lighthouse* and Joyce's *A Portrait of the*

Artist as a Young Man, now in the Stuart A. Rose Manuscript, Archives, and Rare Book Library at Emory University, with her teacher Elizabeth Drew's notes for the lectures she prepared, now in the Smith College Archives.[18] While we cannot know whether Drew shared her written notes with Plath, or Plath reconstructed them after hearing Drew's lectures, the shared ground between Plath's notes and Drew's reveals what Plath gleaned from her former teacher. On the second page of Drew's lecture notes on Joyce's *Portrait of the Artist*, she objects to an interpretation of the novel in which Icarus is the 'eternal symbol of artist'.[19] Plath made a similar note in her copy of *Portrait of the Artist*. Perhaps while listening in class, Plath rejected the conviction, in an overview that opens her copy of the novel, that 'Icarus is the eternal symbol of the artist' (Plath's underlining), writing a single-syllable rebuttal beside it.[20] When she returns to teach, Plath's student notes and copy of Drew's *T. S. Eliot: The Design of His Poetry* (1949) become texts upon which she relies.[21]

From teaching research methods to demonstrating close reading, Plath's manner in the classroom mirrored the impersonal strategies of the modern writers whom she taught. On Saint Patrick's Day during her junior year of college, Plath had visited Northampton's Hampshire Bookshop, bringing home a copy of *Dubliners* (*LVI* 587–8). Her underlining in Padriac Colum's Introduction reflects the ways that Joyce offers his characters without commentary. With regard to 'Ivy Day in the Committee Room', she underlined Colum's observation that 'Joyce is letting us look at a happening through his eyes while making no comment. Hence the feeling of detachment that is in these stories'.[22] The style of Plath's teaching, like that of her earlier poetry, takes on this distance. Her close readings keep to aesthetic and formal commentary, sizing and dividing up texts into sections and parts, itemising themes and listing issues.[23] As one of her students remembers, in class Plath was 'focusing always on what an author was saying and how he was saying it'.[24] This concentration echoes the philological work she taught students to pursue and reflects the ways that language could linger in her memory.

When she introduced Joyce's *Dubliners* in her teaching notes, Plath recounted his inspiration for the final scene of 'The Dead', repeating Hugh Kenner's explanation that Joyce looked into a snow globe 'containing floating crystals & murmuring "Yes, snow is general all over Ireland".'[25] The final moments of 'The Dead' speak to Gabriel Conroy's bewilderment in realising that he has never understood what he thought he did. Plath underlines the following in Colum's Introduction: 'in "The Dead" a man whom he had never known and of whom he might never have heard, recalled from the dead by a song, makes a husband realize that there is a portion of his wife's life in which he has no part'.[26] Plath in turn uses *The Bell Jar* to explore how one's sense of reality can be overturned. The academic success on which Esther Greenwood had depended is rendered meaningless. She adapts Joyce's trope as well, as snow surrounds Buddy Willard's asylum (*BJ* 87)[27] and covers the hospital (*BJ 236*), dramatising various ways that both sites capture a state of 'paralysis', the lifelessness that Joyce and his critics identified in *Dubliners* and Plath stressed as she taught the stories in it.[28]

Including the story of Joyce's snow globe in her teaching notes would also help students begin to make sense of 'The Dead'. In addition to following the example of critics like Kenner who turned to this anecdote to explain how Joyce came to imagine the story and to help readers understand it, introducing this backstory in her class would similarly mean making the unclear less so. Plath had flagged Highet's advice to seek out material that would make concepts clearer and more engaging. Marking the page by turning down the corner, Plath underlined and drew a star beside Highet's point that 'The good teacher is an interesting man or woman.'[29] Engaging students meant bringing new life to one's subject. She noted Highet's recommendations, underlining the following passage:

> Most teaching, is done by talking. If your mind is full of lively awareness of the world, you will never be at a loss for new points of view on your subject. ... Much teaching consists in explaining. We explain the unknown by the known, the vague by the vivid.[30]

Scouring criticism as Plath did, we can see her seeking new ways to explain what texts mean.[31] And we will see that neither the strategies Plath used nor the images she introduced were limited to her teaching.

Years later, to illustrate the difference between poetry and fiction writing, Plath remembers another snow globe in 'A Comparison' (1962). Here, she recalls 'those round glass Victorian paperweights[.] ... This sort of paperweight is a clear globe, self-complete, very pure, with a forest or village or family group within it. You turn it upside down, then back. It snows. Everything is changed in a minute' (*JP* 62–3).[32] This example helps Plath to demonstrate the ability of the poem, as opposed to the novel, to quickly capture such shifts in perspective. As the world of a snow globe is altered, those on the inside and the outside see it differently.

Armed with Poetry

In her teaching notes on Henry James's 'The Pupil', Plath plans a lesson in which students will define terms from the story using the *Oxford English Dictionary*, assess James's use of French words by consulting Fowler's *Dictionary of Modern English Usage*, and compile relevant details from the *Dictionary of American Biography*. This assignment complies with Smith College's suggestion (without specifying what texts to use) that instructors teach library research by asking students to consult the *Oxford English Dictionary* and other possible resources.[33] Developing an ear for James's language would have also improved their reading of poetry. According to her teaching notes, Plath and her students consulted Elizabeth Drew's *Poetic Patterns: A Note on Versification*.[34] After stating the poem's message, students were to address how the poet achieves it, considering the poem's 'Patterns of symbols and images' and its language, investigating various meanings, including unusual or unclear words, and allusions.[35] She followed these facets with scansion and metre, rhyme scheme and sound. This taxonomy is not surprising, but Plath's delineation of it gives us a sense of her voice as a teacher and the structure she brought to her pedagogy. The role of philological research in the papers students wrote would also have heightened Plath's attention to certain words on which the students focused.

By the end of the term, Plath's students successfully demonstrated skills that she had taught them. In her notes for their final class session, she commended their essays' careful treatment of Marianne Moore's '*kok-saghyz*-stalks' in 'Nevertheless',[36] the 'dominant letter X', in Wallace Stevens's 'The Motive for Metaphor',[37] and 'the transmogrifying bee' in Ransom's 'Janet Waking'.[38] These references invite different kinds of interpretive work attending to their meaning, appearance and sound. Writing about Moore's '*kok-saghyz*-stalks' meant investigating the role of these dandelion stems of Russian origin and the rubber they yielded.[39] In a different fashion, 'the dominant letter X' refers to the final line of Stevens's poem 'The Motive for Metaphor', 'The vital, arrogant, fatal, dominant X', opposed to 'The A B C of being'[40] with which he closed the penultimate stanza. By contrast, in Ransom's 'Janet Waking', students would need to define transmogrifying, learning of the bee's metamorphosis. The sting of Ransom's bee alters the course of the poem, ending the life of Janet's hen, and in the poem's final lines she learns 'how deep / Was that forgetful kingdom of death'.[41] In each instance, we can also see parallels in

Plath's own poetics, from her lifelong interest in bees to the gravity and dramatic impact of each poem.

On her final day of class, Plath arrived at Seelye Hall, '[a]rmed with various poems by Ransom, cummings & Sitwell' (*J* 388).[42] (Plath was also 'armed' when she 'loaded arms' with Woolf novels the previous year in the Cambridge bookstore, Bowes & Bowes [*J* 271].) On that last day at Smith, according to her teaching notes, Plath had selected more poems than she could probably cover, indicating that she would teach Elizabeth Bishop's 'The Fish' and Richard Wilbur's 'Potato', 'If time'. This selection of poets was strong in a range of ways, from formality to humour to playfulness. The idea of being 'armed with poetry', however, perhaps takes most profound shape in Moore's poetry, particularly in her 'armoured' animals like 'The Pangolin' and 'The Armadillo'.[43] In 'Nevertheless', Moore selects animals and fruit with tough exteriors, such as the 'hedgehog' and 'prickley-pear' (161),[44] and the poem articulates a fighting spirit: 'The weak overcomes its / menace, the strong over- / comes itself. What is there / like fortitude' (161–2).[45] Assigning this poem, Plath also speaks to the strength she has marshalled over the course of the term. It is telling, too, that 'Nevertheless' contains 'barbed wire',[46] as it is not only a metaphor for Plath's obstacles in teaching, but it also will accompany the weaponry that Plath brings to such late poems as 'Cut' and 'Daddy'.

In April 1958, Plath told Lee Anderson during their interview in Springfield, Massachusetts that 'the kind of analysis I do with my classes is somehow inimical to the sort of work I do by myself'.[47] Plath here revises an earlier comment from Anthony Hecht's contribution to 'Poets on Campus' while she was a Guest Editor at *Mademoiselle*. In Plath's copy of the magazine, she underlined Hecht's response that 'Teaching and writing are not inimical.'[48] While she reverses the meaning of Hecht's phrase, the language of her complaint paradoxically becomes a part of her poetry, describing the scene to which the protagonist returns as 'inimical' in her 1958 poem 'Green Rock, Winthrop Bay' (*CP* 105). In this instance and so many others, we can see that while Plath was drained of energy during her teaching year, it still had an irrevocable impact on her attention to language, her sense of clarity and her imagination.

Notes

1. Sylvia Plath, 'Cambridge, Newnham college; Teaching year at Smith', box 13, f. 10, *LILLY*; The materials in this box will be referred to in this chapter, and in any subsequent end notes, as 'Teaching Notes'.

2. See also Golden, *Annotating Modernism*; and Golden, 'Sylvia Plath's Teaching Syllabus'.

3. There is a copy of this list, dated 5/28/58 in the English Department files. *SMITH*. Even as it is the end of her teaching year, the information appears consistent with much of Plath's course.

4. English Department Papers, 1957–58, *SMITH*. This may date from the end of Plath's teaching year as the list of books includes a handwritten date of 5/28/58.

5. English Department Papers, 1957–58, *SMITH*.

6. McKenna, 'Sylvia Plath'. Karen V. Kukil considered this necklace in her presentation at the Sylvia Plath 75th Year Symposium, Oxford University, 2007.

7. Bartlett Nodelman and Golden, 'Recollections of Mrs. Hughes's Student', 127.

8. *English 11 Handbook: 1950–1951* (Smith College, 1944), *LILLY*.

9. English Department Papers, 1957–58, Smith.

10. Highet, *The Art of Teaching*, 249. *LILLY*.

11. *English 11 Handbook: 1950–1951* (Smith College, 1944), 8. This recommendation also resembles what Plath learned as a student of creative writing at Smith, that, as Langdon Hammer puts it, 'you must express yourself; you must master formulas to do so'. Hammer, 'Plath's Lives', 83.

12. Hammer, 'Plath's Lives', 66.

13. Considering H. J. Jackson's work in *Marginalia*, Richard Oram points out (Oram, *Collecting, Curating*, 5) that 'Jackson maintains that writers' dialogue with a text is a form of creative expression'.

14. Wilson, *Axel's Castle*, 116. *SMITH*.

15. Wilson, *Axel's Castle*, 244. *SMITH*.

16. Wilson, *Axel's Castle*, 102. *SMITH*.

17. See Golden, *Annotating Modernism*, for further treatment of Plath's teaching of Eliot and James.

18. Elizabeth A. Drew Papers, Box 770.1: folder 19: 'The Novel II'. *SMITH*.

19. Drew crossed out this statement in her notes, but it is not clear when she did so. Drew, Box 770.1: folder 19: 'The Novel II'. *SMITH*.

20. Plath's copy begins with an 'About this Book' sketch that is not attributed to an author. Joyce, *Portrait of the Artist*. *EMORY*.

21. See Golden, *Annotating Modernism* for further consideration of Plath's teaching of Eliot.

22. Colum, 'Introduction', xi. *SMITH*.

23. Teaching Notes.

24. Nodelman and Golden, 'Recollection', 131.

25. Joyce quoted by Kenner, *Dublin's Joyce*, 68.

26. Colum, 'Introduction', xii.

27. All citations from *The Bell Jar* refer to the 1999 edition published by HarperCollins.

28. In her teaching notes, Plath repeated Joyce's explanation of Dublin as 'the centre of paralysis'. Joyce quoted by Kenner, *Dublin's Joyce*, 48.

29. Highet, *The Art of Teaching*, 51. *LILLY.*

30. Highet, *The Art of Teaching*, 51. *LILLY.* Underlining is Plath's.

31. See also Golden's discussion of Plath's teaching of D. H. Lawrence's 'The Blind Man' in the afterword to 'Recollections of Mrs. Hughes's Student', 136–7.

32. All citations from *Johnny Panic and the Bible of Dreams* refer to the edition published by Harper & Row.

33. Second page of course list and outline, dated 5/28/58, English Department files, *SMITH.*

34. The pamphlet I have accessed remains in the files of Katherine Gee Hornbeak, instructor of freshman English, with whom Plath shared an office during her teaching year at Smith. Katherine Gee Hornbeak, Series IV: 'Lecture and Research Notes', box 6, folder 2: 'Lecture Notes for English 11-Notes, etc.' c. 1954., *SMITH.* There is not specific copyright information. The bottom of the first page reads, 'From MAJOR BRITISH WRITERS edited by G. B. Harrison, copyright, 1954, by Harcourt, Brace and Company, Inc.'

35. Teaching Notes [Plath's underling].

36. Moore, *New Collected Poems*, 161.

37. Stevens, *Collected Poems*, 288.

38. Ransom, 'Janet Waking'.

39. *OED* 'A kind of dandelion, *Taraxacum koksaghyz*, whose roots contain a latex used for making rubber. **1932** *Bull. Rubber Growers' Assoc.* Sept. 534 The Kak-Saugyiz, gave a material with even more resilience, but it has a lower content of caoutchouc. **1945** K. E. KNORR *World Rubber* x. 182 Experiments with *kok-saghyz*, the Russian dandelion, and *Cryptostegia* were soon abandoned'. www.oed.com/. Accessed 17 February 2009.

40. Stevens, *Collected Poems*, 288.

41. Ransom, 'Janet Waking'.

42. Marsha Bryant has addressed Plath's reading of Sitwell in Bryant, 'Queen Bees'.

43. See Quinn, 'The Artist as Armored Animal'.

44. Moore, *New Collected Poems*, 161.

45. Moore, *New Collected Poems*, 161–2.

46. Moore, *New Collected Poems*, 161.

47. Sylvia Plath, interview with Lee Anderson, Springfield, Massachusetts, 18 April 1958, Recording. *SMITH.*

48. Reproduced in Hammer, 'Plath's Lives', 62.

CHAPTER 25

Electroshock Therapy and Plath's Convulsive Poetics

Anita Helle

In an era prior to informed consent, Sylvia Plath was shattered by what she described as a 'rather brief and traumatic experience' of 'badly-given shock treatments'.[1] Plath was twenty. Aurelia Plath's notes indicate that this took place without adequate benefit of relaxants and anaesthesia, at a private hospital in Carlisle, Massachusetts. Months later, at the end of 1953, she received insulin and further electroshock therapy at McLean Hospital in Belmont. The earlier set of treatments were worse than the last, although even at McLean's, Plath writes about electroshock with an 'ugh'.

Readers and scholars have readily empathised with this moment in Plath's biography. Electroshock treatment has been regarded as a traumatic kernel whose gaps and lacunae became available as literary subject matter between 1958 and 1960, with poems of oracular possession such as 'Hanging Man' and 'Poem for a Birthday'.[2] Whether the emphasis is laid on suicide or aesthetic triumph, the teleological arc of the over-determined narrative is best exemplified by Anne Stevenson's expansive claim in *Bitter Fame: A Life of Sylvia Plath*, that electroshock was the 'menace behind nearly everything [Plath] ever wrote',[3] and by another critic's more recent assertion that electroshock 'would forever re-wire Plath's sense of identity'.[4] Of course, as Tracy Brain, Marjorie Perloff and Jacqueline Rose have in various ways observed, we now know that had Plath's *Bell Jar* remained in circulation under Plath's pseudonym Victoria Lucas, and/or if Hughes's version of the *Ariel* poems had not come into print so soon after Plath's death, marketers of Plath's books might not have found profit in advertising the most sensational aspects of the story (one Turkish translation of *The Bell Jar* blatantly features a head pinned between electrodes on its jacket).[5]

Recent biographers have made a few new discoveries, but have not done much to fill out cultural or historical contexts. Plath's psychiatrists have been named. Connie Kirk draws on Plath's calendar to more precisely date the initial round of shock treatments on 29 July 1953 at the private outpatient clinic.[6] Biographies such as Elizabeth Winder's *Pain, Parties, Work* have been more expressly interested in Plath and trauma without, however, incorporating insights about literary style from the field of critical trauma studies, which might lead us to considering temporal dislocations, repetitions, silences, ocular disturbances.[7] Bob Fournier's clinical biography, *Trauma and the Golden Lady*, draws from in-house interviews at Valleyhead, including one official's perspective that the hospital had 'developed a reputation as a popular site, perhaps too popular' for outpatient electroshock, and that physicians who oversaw shock treatment were doctors who travelled from other hospitals, informally known as 'the shockers'.[8] Abigail Cheever persuasively argues that since the millennium, the autobiographical confessional narrative of Plath's depression and treatment is more often read through pharmacological narratives such as *Prozac Nation*, in which the depressed person is a special kind of citizen, 'a self who somehow lacks the capacity to be a self'; by extension, even in a post-confessional environment, Plath's biographical narrative seems an especially over-determined case of repeating an origin story of pain.[9]

To be sure, historical and discursive contexts of electroshock have been retroactively applied to events of 1953, reframing or confirming cultural expectations. Between the 1960s and the 1990s, Plath's autobiographical confessional breakdown story became an open subtext for social movements. By the 1970s, an anti-psychiatry movement had marched onto the pages of feminist criticism in works such as Phyllis Chesler's *Women and Madness*; R. D. Laing's *The Divided Self* had rendered the 'madness' that electroshock proposed to cure as a cultural symptom of the patient's alienation in language from the physician's ideal of normality. New evidence about the special hazards of bilateral electroshock for creative writers came to light in the 1970s, 1980s and 1990s through biographies of figures such Ernest Hemingway, Antonin Artaud and Paul Celan[10] – namely, that beyond retrograde amnesia, there was the risk of damage to speech-centres at the frontal temporal lobes.

As the celebrated film *One Flew Over the Cuckoo's Nest*, based on the 1962 novel by Ken Kesey, and the publication of Michel Foucault's *Madness and Civilization* (published in 1961 and first translated into English in 1964) popularised the view of clinical shock as a means of social control, new ethical and political questions were raised. These included questions about whether family members who aided in treatment should be subject to exculpation or exoneration. An interview conducted around the time that Aurelia Schober Plath cooperated with Rose Leiman Goldemberg on the American Place Theater production of the play

Letters Home in 1979, Aurelia Plath expressed remorse about Plath's initial outpatient treatment and concern that even the new dramatic portrayal, in which lines of overlapping dialogue between mother and daughter were written to emphasise the empathy and mutuality, might never exonerate the view of the mother as the 'ogre' responsible for the tragic wound of electroshock.[11] By 1993, when Adrienne Rich in *What is Found There: Notebooks on Poetry and Politics* wrote that US entry into the Persian Gulf War 'bestowed electroshock' on a 'chronically depressive nation', the biographical subtext had been thoroughly incorporated into a critical social narrative of mass behavioural engineering of the national body electric, where, I would contend, Plath's figurations of electricity and the shocks of modernity began, long before she had ECT.[12]

So what new questions, alternative perspectives and counterpoints does a material aesthetics of electricity offer? For one thing, as the examples above indicate, the *cultural* ground of electroshock's social and historical meanings has long been dynamic and shifting. This has to do not only with changing social attitudes but also with the labile metaphorical possibilities of *electricity* and *shock* that have provided ample ground for literary figuration. Often seen as a master-trope of metaphor, the word *electric (Grk: Elektron)* was used by Francis Bacon to characterise the transformative action of materials such as amber and metals, especially copper, in attracting other objects.[13] From Mary Shelley's *Frankenstein* to Ted Hughes's late theory of style as an 'electrograph' of 'the writer's whole sensibility' through an epigenetic trace in language,[14] cultural associations with electricity and electroshock have been fraught with themes of guilt and self-knowledge, moral recrimination and scenarios of death and rebirth. More recently, scholars such as Paul Gilmore, Jennifer Lieberman and Carolyn Thomas de la Peña have supposed that 'a language of electricity' in modern literary texts constitutes what Gilmore terms a 'strain of romanticism on both sides of the Atlantic' well into the 1950s,[15] distilling cultural anxieties associated with rapidly expanding distribution networks of electricity grids, mass systems of communication and accelerated consumerism dependent on electricity.

The new, two-volume *Letters of Sylvia Plath* adds to the biographical account of Plath's treatment provided in *Letters Home*, although on the narrow subject of electroshock the news is less than might have been anticipated. In part, this is understandable, given that Plath did not immediately have words for what she had gone through at Valleyhead or at McLean's, and was eager to return to collegiate 'normality'. In the Talcott Parsons era, the job of the physician was to tell the patient what to do, and the job of the patient was to apply mental hygiene and do anything needed to get well, including bringing a positive attitude.[16] In letters, Plath refers to her own strategies for self-protection. In a letter to Gordon Lameyer of January 1954, she notes that she had just emerged from a rather 'singular experience', and reflects on the need to 'play parts', her smile being only a 'protective and camouflaging mask'.[17] We learn that, upon returning to Smith, Plath confided details of her experience to a few close friends, including Jane Truslow, who 'had shock at Baldpate', to Jane V. Anderson, the model for her character of Joan Gilling in *The Bell Jar*, and to Marcia Brown, whose mother had been briefly institutionalised.[18]

Earlier letters also reveal another pattern that is echoed in her short fiction and collage scrapbook – well before electroshock: a fascination with electricity as an aspect of culture that might be mythologised and mystified as well as critiqued. In a poem entitled 'I Am an American', folded into a letter that Plath wrote to Melvin Woody after her first year at Smith, the speaker sees herself as created by a collective national body – or 'belly' – electric. Its first lines, 'We all know we are created equal: / All conceived in the hot blood belly/ of the twentieth century turbine',[19] offers a 1950s take on Henry Adams's 'The Dynamo and the Virgin' (1900); it also provides a sexualised cyborgian image of violent human coupling that relies on appropriating the female body. In the letter, Plath introduces her poem with invective: 'I too get seething mad at civilization, dogma, prejudice' (*LV1* 346). In satirical fashion, the poem goes on to link electricity to other material currencies – the postal system, the monetary system and consumer products ('the Bendix' vacuum cleaner), all of which stamp out individuality. In its catalogue form, and its two parallel symmetrical stanzas, Plath's poem can be read as a response to the popular schoolroom classic of the same title, 'I Am an American' (1916) by Russian Jewish poet Elias Lieberman, a patriotic poem well known to New Englanders. Lieberman's poem equates assimilation with technological progress and the modern electrified city: 'As each new star in the nation's flag / Keen eyes of mine foresaw her greater glory / . . . the man-hives of her billion wired cities.'[20]

If Plath used electricity to materialise the national body electric – or 'belly' electric – in 'I Am an American', she could also idealise the materiality of language in textual exchanges. In a remarkable letter of Joycean wordplay responding to a thick missive from Gordon Lameyer, written during the first month of her return from McLean, Plath comments on the 'mystic electric current of understanding' that emerges from riffing on great works in the British tradition, an interest she and Lameyer shared. Plath writes, 'And why should I quote? Speak in other voices?

Because, like the archetypal wanderer, I am part of all that I have met, and all that I have seen is part of me, and there is a mystic electric current of understanding . . . that runs through all the subjective worlds we two share fragments of.'[21] The letters also offer glimpses of a more intimate, shared language between Plath and Hughes, in which electric shock could be filtered through Plath's hyperbolic dark humour. Writing one Sunday in October of her fall semester alone at Cambridge (Sunday was a day of 'no mail'), the yawning distance of intimacy between them prompts Plath to conjure what she admits is an exaggerated, 'hellish' scenario: 'I get these electric shocks of knowing how I miss you.'[22] In the same month, Hughes's letters imagine their distance on terms that parallel hers: 'sitting around in a daze of shock' and with 'incomplete brain surgery'.[23] This is a language of electricity, electroshock and surgery that Hughes will return to in *Birthday Letters*.

By the time Plath's signed on for her stint as a medical secretary in the Adult Psychiatric Clinic in October and November of 1958, she already saw hospitals as electrified cities, with cell-like cubicles and bureaucratic regimes, wired devices and power grids, operations that go on in relative ignorance of the often-secretive, subliminal imaginings of humans in their midst. As is well known, 'The Daughters of Blossom Street' was originally entitled 'This Earth our Hospital'. Plath's story paces off a geospatial imaginary that is made more vivid by visiting the site. Massachusetts General looks in one direction towards Blossom Street, the location of the morgue in the story, and to Boston Common on another side, twin poles in the story's theme of wished-for individual and communal redemption. As in a later poem, 'Berck-Plage', the dialectic between malignancy and hope in 'The Daughters of Blossom Street' is animated by oblique allusions to that most 'electrical' of all Eliot poems, 'East Coker', in which an 'electric heat / hypnotizes' and 'fancy lights' seductively 'risk enchantment', even as they threaten to suffocate and sap vitality.[24] Plath notes in her journals at the time that she was 'jam full of Eliot titles' (*J* 489). It is interesting to speculate as to why, in her *Journals*, Plath insists that 'This Earth Our Hospital', represents an 'advance' from her earlier hospital story, 'Johnny Panic and the Bible of Dreams'. She liked the former so much, in fact, that while waiting to see if *The Atlantic* would take it, she muses that it 'should be a Best American Short Story' (*J* 489). In any case, in 'This Earth Our Hospital' the apocalyptic events touched off by an electrical storm and its disruptions are not spuriously dramatic: the electrical atmospherics and the electrical things in the story are well integrated with the affects and sensations of characters, a putative community of women who huddle together as a hurricane bears down. As in the type of Frank O'Connor short stories Plath thought she should write, the characters are, as O'Connor recommends, 'submerged populations' floating in separate spot-lit zones.[25]

As in Eliot's poem, an 'electric heat' in 'The Daughters of Blossom Street' fuses the animalistic with the human and mechanical into a thick compound. Electricity is outside, in a naturally occurring form, and inside the hospital's power grids: heat melts the starch in the blouse at the narrator's armpit and clings to the damp cement walls of the hospital's basement tunnels; but it is not outside the discourse of power and power lines. Lights from the downed power lines in the electrical storm fail and flicker off and on at critical moments in the plot, evoking the lack of saving insight on the part of her characters as well as the absence of redemptive sources. The story's electrical sensations, anticipating the later 'Berck-Plage', mirror the purgatorial atmosphere of Eliot's poem in which 'the whole earth is our hospital / endowed by a millionaire', with no Christ-like 'wounded surgeons' capable of 'plying the redemptive steel' that might cure the disease of mortality at its centre.[26] When the storm threatens to blow everything up, 'shaking [the Clinic] to its roots', Plath's narrative relies on *film noir* lighting effects: characters take on semblances of the automatons they have become in their bureaucratic roles, 'wax dummies', figures 'flattened back against the wall' (*JP* 124–5). In the maelstrom of uncertainty, panic is imaged as a 'galloping hysteria', the collapse of a system. In the aftermath of a power failure, 'we [the lowly assistants] have to feel our way along the walls in the semi-dark. Everywhere doctors and interns are snapping out orders, nurses gliding by white as ghosts in their uniforms, and stretchers with people bundled on them – groaning, or crying' (*JP* 129). A semblance of relief is offered in one scene when the hospital's back-up generator apparently takes over, and four copper lights in a formal meeting room burn more steadily; but these lights only cast theatrically distancing effects. In Plath's 'Hospital Notes', she was sufficiently impressed by the details of the Hunnewell Meeting Room that she makes detailed notes about four lights that had been installed to modernise the space (*J* 627).[27] Unsurprisingly, then, when the women carry on with their bureaucratic reporting on the dead from within the sealed-off room, they are worse, not better off. Sepia portraits of the Civil War surgeons whose faces line the walls of the Hunnewell Room are emblems of paternal failure. The instruments gleaming in the glass cabinets above the women's heads under the light of the copper bowls cast no more than a simulacrum of their faces on the dark, coffin-like wooden table, which the narrator tells us is so 'polished you can see your face in it' (*JP* 117). In this story, as in 'Johnny Panic and the Bible of Dreams', the hospital is more than just a 'hive with its billion wires'. It is a place where lines of force and power are sufficiently part of an administrative apparatus that only armoured characters are visible, notably the 'tinted blonde chignon' of the supervisor, whose head gleams under the copper lights like a 'cap of mail' (*JP* 118).

In 'Johnny Panic and the Bible of Dreams', Plath's electrified hospital is also a media-wired environment. It has been too easy to over-focus on the dream of 'one great brotherhood' (*JP* 155) that doesn't pan out in this story, or the seemingly biographical narrative of electroshock in its ending, with its 'metal box covered with dials and gauges', which seems to be 'eyeing me, copper-head ugly' (*JP* 165). But there is another layer to this story, another electric box at its centre, in the shape of a transcribing machine that sits on the narrator's desk, and which she terms an 'audiograph' (*JP* 156). Plath's precise use of this term makes it possible to identify the device as the Gray Audograph, or 'soundscript' machine, an electronic transcription device commonly used in medical secretarial settings from the 1940s to the 1970s.[28] As a black box, the dictating machine uncannily resembles the electroshock machine in form if not function: it is portable, metal, about the same size as electroshock boxes of the era, and emits a red fluorescent signal. The cover of the user manual portrays a preternatural blonde with headphones piping sound from the mouth of the handsome doctor to the secretary's ears. One advert for the machine from 1953 features a sound track from a popular dance-band record that hit the top of the charts in the late 1950s with a schmaltzy lyric ('It's cherry pink and apple blossom white when true love comes your way ... the poets say'). In another advert, a doctor in the upper right-hand corner of the ad is speaking directly into the ear of the medical secretary at the lower right, advertising 'a perfect partnership' ('Gray Audograph').

Alan Ramón Clinton brings a fresh critical lens to 'Johnny Panic and the Bible of Dreams' by considering the fate of the poet-dreamer as one writing under media conditions, or *into* media conditions of what some media theorists have termed 'electracy'.[29] He rightly notes that the dream transcription from the sound text is an impossible archival project, because dreams occupy the realm of the imaginary, while the discourse of health and happiness, the discourse of the hospital, occupies the realm of the symbolic.[30] As long as she is merely transcribing dreams, the narrator is bound to a bibliographic method, and therefore to 'dream connoisseurship' (*JP* 153). Transcribing sound-text from a dictaphone clearly is antithetical to the poet's vocation as the dreamer of dreams, yet the situation is integral to the story. Ramón Clinton does not comment upon another reason for the narrator's desire to compulsively record her made-up dreams in alternative notebooks: that is, the darkly gendered and intimate associations of the dictaphone with the fabrication of workplace romance. In addition, the narrator wants to capture 'unfinished messages' from the 'great I Am' (*JP* 155), a comically expressed yearning for greater meaning. The distance between the desire of the dreamer who hopes to impossibly transcribe and collect dreams stands in opposition to the physician's worldly cure. This desire is further frustrated by the dreamer's realisation of an architectonic dream of dreams in which she would fashion an autotelic reservoir of narratives that will fail.

We read about this failure through the narrator's other aerial flights, over the illuminated city, and, in mock-Icarian fashion (powered by a helicopter) over 'Lake Nightmare' and the 'Bog of Madness'. These aerial views also fail to offer unmediated transparency, revealing only 'dark masses moving and heaving', and 'figuring out the wheel and the alphabet', earlier phases of media archaeology (*JP* 154). It is the dream of the pieceworker at the fluorescent factory, another worker who lives and burns in the hum of an electronic environment, which most closely mirrors the narrator's plight. The narrator is exquisitely attuned to her electrified environment, and to what Tracy Brain describes as the ill effects of toxic environments.[31] She, too, works under 'ice-bright florescence that makes the skin look green and all the pink and red flushes dead black-purple' (*JP* 157). What the narrator learns from the fluorescent worker's dream is that: he was 'scared blue he'd only go to hell' when it turns out he was 'only afraid of the dark', (*JP* 157), but the narrator's concerns are not so easily dismissible.

Although Esther Greenwood's dramatic episode of electroshock in *The Bell Jar* is often read as a literal rendering of Plath's electroshock experience, Plath's narrative in *The Bell Jar* incorporates multiple narratives of electrification from myth, science and modern cinema. As Luke Ferretter notes, *The Bell Jar* is pre-scripted by journalistic and cinematic influences that were part of Plath's cultural vocabulary prior to her electroshock experience.[32] When Plath writes the 'drubbing' or convulsive scene of electroshock, she equates the sharp intake of breath that precedes convulsive seizure by drawing from mythologies of oracular possession and poetic seizure. She attributes sounds and lights that electroshock boxes don't actually emit – 'Whee-ee-ee-ee-ee-ee' and 'air crackling with blue light' (*BJ* 117). In these images, William Blake meets Carl Jung: the iconographic representation of blue light is reminiscent of Blake's *A Vision of the Last*

Judgement, in which blue colouration charges the moment of explosion with an overwhelming power.[33] Plath's more immediate source for these images would likely have been Jung's *The Archetypes and the Collective Unconscious*, which comments on flashes of lightning as a symbol used by Paracelsus to suggest a sudden, unexpected and overpowering change of psychic conditions.[34] The sudden plunge into the unconscious rendered through this imagery and sonic effects precipitates the memory of a second electrical 'shock', a memory critical to Esther's narrative, but a puzzle to critics who pass over it. Awakening from shock, Esther recalls having been shocked by the fuzzy or frayed cord of a lamp belonging to her father's study, when she attempts to move it from the side of her mother's bed. The explicit description of the copper shade 'surmounting' (*BJ* 118) the bulb is sexual, and the cord itself, the umbilicus tying her to her mother, reiterates the daughter's desire to separate from her mother, as well as Esther's identification of male figures with powers of sex and language. As in a dream the second shock is predicate to the first. The 'old metal floor lamp' (*BJ* 118) confirms the tawdriness that class-conscious Esther associates with her familial background by contrast to the glamorous world of *Mademoiselle*.

Tawdriness was a staple of the artificial lighting effects Plath adopted from the film noir cinema style and from *The Snake Pit* (1948), a film that made a 'deep impression' on Plath and which she must have seen shortly after it came out (*LVi* 657). The film's director, Anatole Litvak, and the co-author of its screen play, Millen Brand, have both been linked to the development of *noir* cinema in its classic era 1930–60.[35] According to film historian Patrick Keating, references to indirect lighting and explicit reference to the iconographic signs of light (lamps, shades, bulbs) could bring a sense of wonder or alienation to technological achievements and ideas of modern progress. Within the diegesis, the varying intensities and degrees of electrical illumination became the signature style of *film noir* in establishing character (typically dopplegangers, detectives, femmes fatales), mapping space and colouring ideological perspectives.[36] Plath's cinematic viewing habits (which included Hitchcock films) included another forerunner of *film noir* style, the German expressionist film *The Cabinet of Dr. Caligari* (1920), which she immediately grasped as material for themes of the novel she was writing at the time she saw the film in Cambridge. In a letter to her mother, Plath comments that the 'jagged black-and-white sets grow out of states of mind and everywhere there is a subtle reversal between the worlds of sanity and insanity. Really Weird and haunting' (*LVi* 1002). In *The Snake Pit*, the *noir* lighting style applies primarily to depictions of the asylum ward, where the inmates are seen only in pools of shadow, denoting their subordinate status, and are uttering nonsense syllables.

In *The Bell Jar*, Plath strategic use of light effects comments directly on a range of subjects, the contrast between glamour and affluence as well as the contrast between city and suburbs, and exterior/subterranean perspectives on the electric shock clinic. The 'celestially white kitchens' of Ladies' Day are 'photographed under brilliant lights' (*BJ* 21); for a claustrophobic effect, 'glittering white torture chamber tiles' bounce light back in the Ladies' Day bathroom where Esther retreats when she is poisoned at the luncheon (*BJ* 36). Doreen, the Marilyn-like fashion doll, is more recognisably both sinister and the glamorous type of femme fatale because her glamour has grown into a second skin – her gown sticks to her skin by 'some kind of electricity' (*BJ* 4). Esther begins to know she is sick once she's home and even the clothes she is wearing are 'unfamiliar'. She tells us, 'The skirt was a green dirndl skirt with tiny black, white and electric blue shapes swarming across it, and it stuck out like a lampshade' (*BJ* 92). Perhaps the most compelling use of *film noir* lighting – a departure from *film noir*'s portrayals of suburbs as brightly lit places, are the pools of shadow – 'full bosomy elms made a tunnel of shade' (*BJ* 107) that mark Esther's passage back from Dr Gordon's office through the tunnels and elms of suburbia.

Plath's writing of electroshock may be read as part of what Tim Armstrong characterises as modernism's desire to 'intervene in the body' to render the body modern through biomedical, behavioural and technological means.[37] Electroshock may have provided Plath with a storehouse of images of bodily disruption, metaphors and plot kernels. But when we consider Plath's multiple narratives of electricity and electric shock in broader cultural contexts, they contribute to a mesh of affects and sensations, ideas and things that are by no means reducible to biography.

Notes

1. Letter to Eddie Cohen, 28 December 1953, *LV1*, 655.
2. Middlebrook, *Her Husband*, 110–11.
3. Stevenson, *Bitter Fame*, 47.
4. Clinton, 'Sylvia Plath and Electracy', 60–71.
5. See Brain, *The Other Sylvia Plath*, 8–10. For the cover of the Turkish edition (1975), see Temple, 'A Fifty-Year Visual History'.
6. Kirk, *Sylvia Plath*, 76.

ANITA HELLE

7. Winder, *Pain, Parties, Work*.
8. Fournier, *Trauma and the Golden Lady*, 118.
9. Farland, 'Sylvia Plath's Anti-Psychiatry Movement', 256; Cheever, *Real Phonies*, 95.
10. See, for example, Felsteiner, *Paul Celan*.
11. Robertson, 'To Sylvia Plath's Mother'.
12. Rich, *What Is Found There*, 15.
13. Bacon, *Novum Organum*, 457.
14. Letter to Tom Paulin, 6 August 1998, *LTH*, 727.
15. Gilmore, *Aesthetic Materialism*; Lieberman, *Electricity in American Life and Letters*; Thomas, *Body Electric*.
16. Fox, *Sociology of Medicine*, 17–25.
17. Letter to Gordon Lameyer, 10 January 1954, *LV1*, 661.
18. Letter to Jane V. Anderson, 25 February 1954, *LV1*, 695.
19. Letter to Melvin Woody, 22 June 1951, *LV1*, 345–7.
20. Lieberman, 'I Am an American', *Paved Streets*. See suzyred.com/american .html. Retrieved 15 June 2017.
21. Letter to Gordon Lameyer, 21 February 1954, *LV1* 691.
22. Letter to Ted Hughes, 21 October 1956, *LV1* 1319.
23. Letter to Sylvia Plath, 3 October 1956, *LTH* 55.
24. Eliot, *The Poems of T. S. Eliot*, 188.
25. O'Connor, 'The Lonely Voice', *Short Story Theories*, 85–7.
26. Eliot, *The Poems of T.S. Eliot*, 190. See Gilbert, 'On the Beach with Sylvia Plath', 121–38.
27. Plath underscored basic elements in her *Merriam Webster Dictionary*; she would have been aware of the definition of copper as 'one of the best conductors of electricity', www.merriam-webster.com/dictionary/copper.
28. Please see obsoletemedia.org/audograph/ and www.youtube.com/watch?v= wyMoH11-rjs. Retrieved 1 October 2017.
29. Clinton, 'Electracy', 60. On 'electracy', see Ulmer, *Internet Invention*.
30. Clinton, 'Electracy', 60.
31. Brain, *The Other Sylvia Plath*, 93–7.
32. Ferretter, *Sylvia Plath's Fiction*, 49.
33. Blake, *The Paintings and Drawings*, 826.
34. Jung, *The Archetypes and the Collective Unconscious*, 303.
35. Spicer and Hanson, *A Companion to Film Noir*, 101.
36. Keating, 'Film Noir and the Culture of Electric Light', esp. 68–70.
37. Armstrong, *Modernism, Technology, and the Body*, 6.

CHAPTER 26

Plath's Scrapbooks

Peter K. Steinberg

In *Scrapbooks: An American History*, Jessica Helfand asserts that people keep scrapbooks 'to try to capture those few mesmerizing years when we were here, alive, and alert and, in a million small ways, bearing witness'.[1] The bulk of Sylvia Plath's autobiographical writing exists in her diaries, journals and letters and covers a wide sweep of years from 1940 to February 1963. This essay focuses on the two scrapbooks Plath created to document her high school and college years as a late teenager into her early twenties during the time she resided in or visited Massachusetts, New York and other New England locations. Helfand remarks that the 'study of scrapbooks is complicated and messy and far from complete: as material artifacts, they're basically an untamed species'.[2] This chapter highlights the ways Plath's scrapbooks support her journals and letters, and how they fill in various gaps in her private writings. Such an intertextual reading has the potential to broaden our appreciation of Plath's development as a person and a writer.

Plath learned the importance of documentation, specifically self-documentation, at an early age, seeing the practice modelled by her mother. Aurelia Plath kept a very detailed 'Baby Book' for the first three years of her daughter's life. In blue ink on the title page, she names herself as the author of this record.[3] Plath's first retained writings date to 1937 (poetry), 1940 (letters) and 1944 (diaries). Plath combined words and drawings in each of these mediums of expression from the outset. Scholars approach Plath's poetry and prose differently to her letters, diaries and journals. Whatever she created, she focused her work for its specific audience. The scrapbook is no different a category of document with regard to the concerted effort she put into its construction. Helfand astutely writes: 'To read another person's scrapbook is to acquire a body of knowledge about an entirely different time and place.'[4] Plath's scrapbooks show how engaged she was in the social customs of the late 1940s and early 1950s.

Danille Elise Christensen determined that 'as a private autobiographical practice' the rampancy of scrapbook-keeping in the nineteenth and twentieth centuries is 'so ubiquitous as to be off critical radar screens'.[5] Plath's scrapbooks are heavily used documents by visitors to the Lilly Library; however, they have a relatively low profile on 'critical radar screens', as they are not frequently cited in scholarship. The near-omission is surprising, given the fact that the scrapbooks are fascinating in and of themselves, and offer a fresh overview of the many memorable experiences that otherwise may not receive the attention they deserve, biographically or otherwise.

On 1 February 1947, Plath wrote in her diary that she went to the Book Stall in Wellesley, Massachusetts, and purchased a 'much-longed-for' red scrapbook. Once home, she taped photographs of herself and her childhood friends on the first pages and composed a 'running account' of her life to that point. The next day she continued writing about her experiences and pasting more photographs onto the early pages. The constructed story that these first pages tell brings its potential viewers up-to-date with her life as a then fourteen-year-old. But Plath was not a novice scrapbooker. In 1944 she maintained scrapbooks for pressed flowers and movie-star pictures. In her diary on 23 January 1945, she noted that she had started a compilation of poems, stories and pictures into a 'booklet' she titled 'From Sylvia's Scrapbook'.[6]

In their seminal essay 'Scrapbooks as Cultural Texts: An American Art of Memory', Tamar Katriel and Thomas Farrell contend that the scrapbook is a 'genre of self' and 'an established mode of self-narration'. Finding the art of scrapbooking to be 'performative', they define the items used by the creator as 'memory objects', which are used in the act of a 'social construction of the self'.[7] As is evident from Plath's diary comments, from the beginning her scrapbooks depict what Katriel and Farrell define as 'the experience of growing up as a fun-filled journey through episodic time'.[8] The decisions Plath made on what to include, and by default what she chose to exclude, exhibit similar care in its creative process as she used in her creative writings. The 'memory objects' and narratives therefore articulate 'an authentic value judgment at the very time of inclusion'.[9]

It is difficult to determine Plath's practice for updating her scrapbook. It was most likely done every few months. Her diary ritual took care of her daily experiences, and during the school year her energies were devoted largely, in theory, to her studies. But the scrapbook functions in a similar fashion to the diary as a 'commemorative' text, allowing its maker to look back to 'get some sense of who [she] was'.[10] However, diaries and scrapbooks 'provide different contexts and forms of self-narration'. On their differences, Katriel and Farrell argue that diaries are 'introspective', serving 'as self-contained texts', and are intended to be read. As opposed to diaries, scrapbooks 'provide a look at the self from the outside', are 'only skeletal texts' and are ultimately 'performed'.[11]

Many Plath scholars, such as Tracy Brain, Anita Helle, Jo Gill and Diane Middlebrook, have remarked on what can be termed a performative aspect in Plath's letters and adult journal writing. Plath employed different voices to entertain her many letter recipients as she performed many roles: daughter, sister, niece, grandchild, friend, lover and writer, to name several. While the addressee was the main audience, Plath was aware that her letters might be shared, and often advocated this – especially in her family. Middlebrook argues that in her journals Plath's 'most frequent aim was to compose passages that might someday find their home in a certain kind of novel'.[12] Brain agrees: 'Plath used her journals as a writer's notebook where she tried out various tones and emotions. As journals so often are for writers, Plath's were a place to play with and store material that she would later use.'[13] Helle praises Plath's 'fierce dedication to particularity, and her near-empirical habits of observation'.[14]

Plath experimented with various ways of capturing her lived and observed world and did so with the understanding that certain writings were more private. Jo Gill writes, 'Rather as in *Letters Home*, the *Journals* provide Plath with the opportunity to scrutinise herself, to identify, castigate and correct her failings . . . The self that Plath finds or constructs is often found to be at fault and must repeatedly be criticised and punished'.[15] Early passages from her first years at Smith College predominate with second-person singular pronoun 'you' entries, as though Plath was attempting to write outside of her self.[16] Gill succinctly summarises the issue of Plath's audience: 'If *Letters Home* represents an attempt to persuade the mother of the stability of Plath's position and the validity of her decisions she has made, then the *Journals* arguably represent an attempt to persuade and reassure the self.'[17]

Plath's diaries and journals were not always private, however. During her first suicide attempt in August 1953, *The Boston Post* reported, 'The mother of Sylvia Plath, 20, missing Smith College senior, said last night that her daughter had been "writing despondently in her diary since about July 1" and had voiced the opinion that she was losing her creative ability in writing.'[18] After her death, Plath's childhood diaries covering the years 1944 to 1951 remained in the Wellesley house until Mrs Plath sold them to the Lilly Library in 1977. Aurelia Plath clearly read them, as they are littered with her commentary and explanatory notes.

Plath's scrapbooks, though, are a hybrid. Ostensibly created to record personal memories and milestones, these documents were designed for exhibition to friends, roommates and housemates – and to dates. In a letter to her mother, Plath describes part of a date she had that weekend, the young man 'had pictures & scrapbooks of his girl – a Smith girl spending her Junior year abroad – around the room' (*LV1* 203). Later in life when she lived in North Tawton, following a visit to the Billyealds in Winkleigh Plath remarked in her typed notes on neighbours that 'At the end of the afternoon, [Mrs Billyeald] brought out her scrapbook of her life in British Guiana' and Plath found it to be 'An astounding document' (*J* 660). Plath's are too.

Plath's high school scrapbook and the subsequent Smith College volume are housed at the Lilly Library, Indiana University at Bloomington. Both scrapbooks have come unbound as a result of handling by researchers and years of use. The photographs are stored largely on their own in separate folders from the scrapbook pages on which they originally appeared. The general procedure in the reading room is that you look at a page, put the page away and then look at the photographs; or vice versa. As a researcher, there is a significant loss of context in our inability to view the pages as Plath herself built them. However, four pages of the first scrapbook were reproduced in *Letters Home* (two pages for the endpapers and another two pages as an in-text illustration in Aurelia Plath's long introduction). At present, this is the closest experience available in approaching a facsimile of the original, though still highly imperfect.[19]

I conducted a review and analysis of the items in both scrapbooks from 2015 to 2016.[20] There are 287 total items in the high school scrapbook that I assigned into three fairly broad categories.[21] There are 133 photographs, 106 attachments and 40 clippings. There are also eight missing items: five photographs, two attachments and one clipping.[22] Three pages are blank (12, 58 and 66). This first scrapbook includes Plath's first year as a student at Smith College. In the Smith College scrapbook, there are 319 total items that comprise 58 photographs, 233 attachments and 28 clippings.[23] Due to the use and the disbanding, and a presumed, unfortunate carelessness by some researchers, several items were located in the wrong place.[24] As such, it remains slightly unclear but there may be two missing photographs and two missing attachments.[25] There were four blank pages (1, 2, 87 and 88).

High School Scrapbook

If we take self-photographs as a barometer, it appears that Sylvia Plath was less self-conscious in her high school scrapbook than she was subsequently in her second scrapbook from Smith (and later in life). Starting at the age of fourteen, Plath was in a period of adolescence that found a unique pleasure in both childhood and contemporary photographs of the self. Photography itself was becoming more pervasive at the time Plath started to scrapbook. This is likely to be why she puts fewer photographs of herself in the second scrapbook documenting her time at Smith (36) than the first that reflected her time in high school (54). The photographs show Plath in a variety of settings in Jamaica Plain, Winthrop, Wellesley and other locations, at school, at summer camps and at Smith College. There are photographs of friends, as well, who feature in her diaries – making it pleasant to put faces to names.

This scrapbook further traces Plath's indoctrination into social events, from playing sports to dating. She began a practice of saving ticket stubs for movies, plays and other events. She saved dance cards, pressed flowers, programmes and newspapers as evidence of her new experiences. On page 21, Plath pasted in a souvenir photograph from The King Philip, a club on Lake Pearl in Wrentham, Massachusetts. The photograph shows Plath with a large smile, enjoying herself while on a triple date. Plath's 'Record of Summer Dates, 9 June– 2 August 1949' provides some details of this night from 6 July 1949, thereby giving us a small backstory to the image. During an intermission from the dancing, the group went to the bar and had their photograph taken; Plath vowed to keep a copy as a souvenir.[26]

Plath's dating life dominates the end of her high school scrapbook. Her boyfriend Bob Reideman receives most attention. Towards the end of her first year at Smith College, her lifelong friend Marcia Brown enters, as well as Richard Norton, who was a serious yet contentious boyfriend. These two acquaintances link the two scrapbooks.

The last six pages of Plath's high school scrapbook capture Plath's creative and professional endeavours. Plath pasted clippings of her published prose and poems from *The Philippian* (junior high school), *The Bradford* (high school) and the *Christian Science Monitor*.[27] In some instances, Plath's scrapbooking has saved the only known copy of her publications.

On page 64, Plath pasted down ten of her alleged fifty rejection letters from *Seventeen* magazine, commenting, like countless other writers, that she could have papered her walls with them. Plath saved a writing aptitude review dated 27 October 1948, her sixteenth birthday. Her reviewer wrote that although 'Miss Plath muffed the peak of drama' she 'is an interesting person with real possibilities. She thinks straight. Chooses words skillfully [*sic.*] from good vocabulary. Writes with pleasing touch that a little well-directed practice would shape into rigorous finished style.'

Smith College Scrapbook

Shortly after a cartoon was published about Plath in the *Peoria Star* on 23 January 1951, Plath wrote home to her mother: 'I think I shall start a new scrapbook about myself, what with all my little attempts at writing being blown up rather out of proportion' (*LV1* 289). This became her Smith College scrapbook. Christensen posits that 'Scrapbook makers readily acknowledge that they live differently than they did before they began scrapbooking.'[28] The Smith scrapbook looks quite different to the first one and shows how, according to Christensen, scrapbooking 'enhanced' an 'ability to recognize and enjoy "moments" as they're happening'.[29] We can conclude that the practice of compiling her first scrapbook enabled Plath to construct her second in a slightly different way. There are more total items (319 versus 287) and 75 fewer photographs (133 versus 58). Interestingly, though there are fewer photographs the ones included tend to depict Plath herself more than others.[30] The focus of Plath's Smith scrapbook is socialising, as there are 127 more 'attachments' commemorating plays and movies (ticket stubs, as well as cast lists and covers that she snipped from theatre programmes), restaurants (menus, napkins and matchbook covers) and correspondence (notes, postcards and telegrams), to name a few of the ephemera she saved. Periodically, Plath sent items home in letters to her mother in the hope she would 'save' them 'for my scrapbook' (*LV1* 492). Plath kept a 'box of "scrapbook" material' atop her bookcase in her Wellesley bedroom and asked her mother to look through it and send along some items for her dormitory room at Smith (*LV1* 503). Plath's pocket calendars occasionally record when she scrapbooked, such as on the eve of returning for her senior year at Smith on 19 September 1954 and from 22 to 25 June 1955.

The diverse nature of Plath's personal materials means that, ideally, these different sources materials should be read in combination. In addition to writing letters and journal entries almost daily, she concurrently maintained at least one calendar. Her wall and pocket calendars, maintained from January 1951 to October 1956, are particularly useful in tracking the minutiae of her life experiences while at college and as a graduate student.[31] While these calendars largely offer a redundancy of information on her obligations, frequently they do register complementary data.

The period of Plath's recovery from her first suicide attempt is thin in life-writing and self-documentation. There are no entries in her calendars from 18 August 1953 to 30 June 1954. Likewise, there are no journals from 14 July 1953 to 21 November 1955. There are only ten known letters during her hospitalisation and up to her resumption of studies at Smith with the start of classes on 1 February 1954. Plath's scrapbooks, however, dedicate fifty pages to the time covering her guest editorship at *Mademoiselle* through her graduation from Smith. Plath reflected that June 1953 was characterised by four fantastic weeks in New York City.[32] We take Plath at her word, here, but Christensen indicates the scrapbooker participates in 'selective reshaping' of events; that 'the life as lived and the life as retrospectively fabricated become inseparably intertwined'. As if quoting Plath's later view of the poet and her craft, Christensen declares that scrapbooking takes 'control ... mastery ... retrospective and prospective'.[33] Plath's candour at the aftermath of her month in New York has a literary bent, referring to a time of black desolation and disenchantment.[34] She dedicates just the one page to the autumn of 1953, which suggests that there was little more to say and even less printed matter to paste down.

Therefore, in the absence of her private journals and pocket calendars, Plath's Smith College scrapbook serves as a bridge between what she wrote in letters from summer 1953 until her summer school calendar begins on 1 July 1954, when the daily register of her activities recommences. The importance of this interval is vital to understanding how Plath changed after her suicide attempt and during her recuperation. She returned to Smith College to begin her studies and picked up on her previously active social life by attending events in and around campus, and 'getting back in Circulation' so far as dating was concerned (*LVi* 703). She took a reduced course schedule to ease back into the rigours of academic life. Possibly as a result, her experiences turned more robust. In the first week she attended a Smith College Religious Association forum entitled 'Search For Meaning: Why Are We Here? Where Are We Going?' In late March, Plath triumphantly revisited New York during her spring vacation. Shortly afterwards, she met Richard Sassoon, and concurrently maintained relationships with Gordon Lameyer, George Gebauer, J. Melvin Woody and Philip McCurdy. That June, Plath witnessed her original class graduate from Smith and attended the wedding of her best college friend, Marcia Brown. Her scrapbook records it all with commentary, along with souvenir matchbook covers, menus and napkins from restaurants. As with her high school scrapbook, Plath's last pages in the Smith one conclude with some literary mementos such as clippings and award notifications from varied contests such as the Glascock Poetry competition, the Christophers and *Vogue*'s Prix de Paris.

Sylvia Plath's scrapbooks offer a wealth of text and souvenirs of her life from the mid-1930s to June 1955. Plath saved ephemera as a way to document her experiences as a young American woman and employed it as a way to recall the peoples, meals, cities and much more. No biographical examination of Plath's life is complete without consulting these precious, fragile documents. They offer Plath's view of herself in a different yet complementary way to her diaries, journals, pocket calendars and letters. This is especially true for a select period in the late 1940s, as well as July 1953 to June 1954, when there are no journals or other simultaneously created autobiographical writing.

Notes

1. Helfand, *Scrapbooks*, 171.
2. Helfand, *Scrapbooks*, 177.
3. Plath, Aurelia. 'Baby Book'. *LILLY*, Box 14, Folder 4. Plath mss II.
4. Helfand, *Scrapbooks*, 175.
5. Christensen, 'Look at Us Now!', 176.
6. The location of this scrapbook is unknown. Two days later, on 14 January 1945, Plath lists the title as just 'Sylvia's Scrapbook'. However, Plath made another 'Sylvia's Scrapbook' of poems and pictures in 1947 (Box 8, Folder 6, Plath mss. II, *LILLY*). In addition to a photo album documentary of her travels with Ted Hughes, Plath compiled scrapbooks of her own publications and reviews, as well as those of Ted Hughes, from 1956 through 1962, which are held by Emory University and Smith College, respectively.
7. Katriel and Farrell, 'Scrapbooks as Cultural Texts', 2.
8. Katriel and Farrell, 'Scrapbooks as Cultural Texts', 7.
9. Katriel and Farrell, 'Scrapbooks as Cultural Texts', 8. These 'memory objects' likely enabled Plath to tell more to the people she showed the scrapbooks to, if she shared them around. The objects thus served as a memory trigger and added another possible narrative strain to what she chose to write about each item on the scrapbook page itself.
10. Katriel and Farrell, 'Scrapbooks as Cultural Texts', 8.
11. Katriel and Farrell, 'Scrapbooks as Cultural Texts', 9.
12. Middlebrook, *Her Husband*, 15.
13. Brain, 'Plath's Letters and Journals', 143.
14. Helle, 'Reading the Paratexts of Plath's *Unabridged Journals*', 96.
15. Gill, *Cambridge Introduction*, 106.
16. For example, in entries numbered 41 to 46, Plath writes 'you' a total of 172 times: (#41 [19], #42 [3], #43 [12], #44 [29], #45 [106] and #46 [3]).
17. Gill, *Cambridge Introduction*, 107.
18. 'Missing Smith Girl', 1.

19. See *LH* 26–7 for the in-text facsimiles. Depicted are pages 2 and 31 with no indication that the pages are not sequential. It should be pointed out, too, that both pages are doctored, with some content having been removed. Similarly, the endpapers reproduce pages 3 (left-hand side) and 1 (right-hand side).

20. In a visit made in March 2015, I was given permission to reassemble the scrapbooks by placing the loose items in their original place and to photograph the pages.

21. A full catalogue of Plath's High School scrapbook is on my Sylvia Plath Info Blog: sylviaplathinfo.blogspot.com/2017/05/sylvia-plaths-high-school-scrapbook.html. Accessed 1 May 2017.

22. Based on Plath's on-page captions, missing from the high school scrapbook are photographs of Otto Plath, Ruth Geisel, Sylvia Plath with braids, Sylvia Plath shovelling snow and an art exhibit featuring Plath's work; attachments of a Christmas card and *The Bradford* newspaper from 27 October 1949; and a clipping of 'Funny Faces' (Plath's first published drawing).

23. A full catalogue of Plath's Smith College scrapbook is on my Sylvia Plath Info Blog: sylviaplathinfo.blogspot.com/2017/06/sylvia-plaths-smith-college-scrapbook.html. Accessed 10 June 2017.

24. This was not realised until after the pages were photographed when I catalogued the scrapbooks in the spring of 2016.

25. Again, based on the captions, the missing photographs in the Smith College scrapbook are of Richard Norton, and of Plath interviewing Elizabeth Bowen. The missing attachments are from a spring visit to New York City in March 1954 and an item from Smith College commencement, June 1955.

26. *LILLY*. Box 7, Folder 4, page 13. Plath mss II.

27. One piece, entitled 'Bradford Editors Attend Boston Tea Party!!', appears to be in the font and layout of *The Bradford* and won Plath $10 in a Boston Globe contest, but was not found in a review of *The Bradford*'s archive at Wellesley High School.

28. Christensen, 'Look at Us Now!', 195.

29. Christensen, 'Look at Us Now!', 197.

30. Plath is depicted in 41 per cent of the photographs in her high school scrapbook and in 62 per cent of her Smith scrapbook.

31. There is a curious absence of calendars from late 1956 through 1961, and 1963. Plath's October 1956–July 1957 pocket calendar records sporadic activities from 30 November 1956 through July 1957. In this calendar, there is evidence of use through 1958.

32. Smith Scrapbook, 38.

33. Christensen, 'Look at Us Now!', 197.

34. Smith Scrapbook, 42.

CHAPTER 27

Beyond Letters Home: Plath's Unabridged Correspondence

Karen V. Kukil

From Letters Home to The Letters of Sylvia Plath

As early as 28 May 1968, Olwyn Hughes began pressuring Aurelia Plath to give Ted Hughes her blessing to publish *The Bell Jar* in the United States. Despite Aurelia's well-documented resistance (she 'had blocked an American edition'[1]), *The Bell Jar* was finally published by Harper & Row, in 1971.

Aurelia vowed to counteract *The Bell Jar* through a project of her own, and *Letters Home* was published in 1975. Critical response largely confirmed Ted Hughes's prophetic warning that the 'emphasis' in *Letters Home* on Plath's 'joyful excitements' would 'produce the opposite effect' (*LTH* 352) of the antidote to *The Bell Jar* that Aurelia hoped for. Moreover, reviewers were not pleased by the extensive deletions,[2] a problem that Aurelia had foreseen with her original desire to publish the letters in two volumes, rather than the one to which the publisher restricted her. In 1976, the editor of *Letters Home*, Frances McCullough, tried to justify the deletions, explaining also that many were made by Ted Hughes in order to protect the feelings of the real people Plath was discussing.[3]

Now, thanks to Frieda Hughes, who owns copyright to her mother's correspondence, we finally have a full edition of Plath's letters. *The Letters of Sylvia Plath*, with Volume I published in 2017 and Volume II the following year, provides a myriad of perspectives previously unavailable. There are more than 1,400 letters, including every (extant) word Plath sent to her mother, and new letters to more than 140 additional correspondents. Transcriptions are as faithful as possible to the original documents. They give us direct access to Plath's vibrant epistolary voice and record a remarkably candid autobiography. More than 3,600 factual footnotes and a full chronology provide context and a detailed index completes each volume.

Beyond her letters home to family, Plath wrote to a wide array of business, literary and personal contacts. As a result, Plath's epistolary style is as varied as her contacts and equally entertaining. This kaleidoscope of voices provides another key to understanding Plath's complex and multifaceted personality. Within this trove of letters, the influences of popular culture and homages to other writers abound, anchoring Plath to specific times and places. At the heart of her correspondence is her dedication to the creative process and her focus on current projects. Read in conjunction with the unabridged *Journals of Sylvia Plath,* these letters provide a deeper insight into one of the most innovative, bold and resilient writers of the twentieth century.

This chapter provides an intellectual, cultural and personal biography of Sylvia Plath via the first volume of her letters. It traces the larger contours of the themes and concerns that preoccupy her, situating these important strands of her thoughts within clear temporal periods. Thereby, it establishes the key contexts out of which the writing emerges, and from which it may be better understood.

Childhood

None of Plath's early childhood letters were published in *Letters Home.* It is worth pausing to observe their value in documenting Plath's early development as a poet, prose writer, journalist, artist, public speaker, peace activist, voracious reader, fashion designer, musician (piano, viola), athlete (tennis, hiking, swimming and rowing), stamp collector, budding feminist and active Unitarian. She is curious about other cultures and yearns for first-hand experience. Her detailed correspondence during high school with her German pen pal, Hans Joachim Neupert, reveals Plath's social consciousness at a very early age. The childhood letters and postcards are written in cursive and are often illustrated with drawings. After July 1946 Plath types some of her subsequent letters.

Smith College

During Plath's undergraduate years, we witness her development as a proud intellectual, sensual woman, and creative writer and artist. The letters from this period are particularly significant, given what they reveal about the context out of which *The Bell Jar* emerged. Plath's first semester at Smith College (September–December 1950) is documented in almost daily postcards to her mother, which give us a glimpse of American social customs and daily life at a women's college.

Plath learns to keep disappointments and news of her frequent sinusitis attacks to herself in 1951 because she does not want to burden her mother, who is in poor health. She is more candid in letters to her housemates from Smith College, including Ann Davidow-Goodman and Marcia Brown Stern, who remain her lifelong correspondents. She begins to navigate the world and learn adult independence. She does not want to sink into the track she was born into by marrying a doctor and 'leaving the world untried' (*LVI* 372). In addition to succeeding academically, she publishes short stories in *Seventeen*, writes and illustrates articles for the *Christian Science Monitor* and begins a career as a journalist by writing press releases about lectures and other political events at Smith College. After writing a paper on Edith Sitwell's poetry, her own near rhymes become more original and nuanced (*LVI* 396). Books, theatre and clothes are her 'few cardinal weaknesses' (*LVI* 406). She even masters the domestic arts as a mother's helper for a wealthy family in Swampscott, Massachusetts. For relaxation during these summer months, she sketches landscapes and completes portraits in pastels and watercolours. She also learns to harness her wit and humour to describe difficult situations, such as an unsuccessful conversation with her boyfriend, Dick Norton, which was 'as decisive as John James Audubon trying to converse with a Dovetailed Kingfisher' (*LVI* 369).

As a sophomore her writing career achieves a new level after winning the *Mademoiselle* fiction contest with her short story 'Sunday at the Mintons'. As a result, she receives encouragement from Knopf editor Harold Strauss and is greatly admired by her friends and professors. Listing her published work in the *Christian Science Monitor, Seventeen* and *Mademoiselle*, Plath discovers to her surprise that she has earned almost $700 in three years. At Smith College, Plath is elected to Alpha-Phi Kappa Psi for her creative writing ability and at this point decides to major in English. She religiously reads newspapers for her government course and covers a wide variety of lectures for Press Board, including speeches by Reinhold Niebuhr, Robert Frost, Senator Joseph McCarthy and Ogden Nash. Plath discovers that she is more politically liberal than her mother, who votes for General Dwight D. Eisenhower in the November 1952 presidential election.

Plath spreads herself too thin by editing the *Smith Review*, serving as secretary to the Honor Board, teaching art to local children at the People's Institute in Northampton, Massachusetts, and organising the decorations for college dances. She eventually learns to limit her extracurricular activities. She gains self-confidence by learning to drive, travelling alone to New York City, and dating a variety of men, from Hungarian Attila Kassay to Detroit Tigers' pitcher Myron Lotz. She samples all kinds of culture from ballet (*Swan Lake*) to theatre (*The Glass Menagerie*). Plath even confronts her worst fears by visiting the Northampton State Hospital: 'I want so badly to <u>learn</u> about <u>why</u> and <u>how</u> people cross the borderline between sanity & insanity' (*LVi* 536).

Many of these college letters are written in blue ink on blue laid paper. Some are typed on Smith College letterhead. Plath's epistolary style is influenced by the modern authors she reads. She drops all her capitals in imitation of e. e. cummings (*LVi* 429). She tries to capture vernacular speech in letters to close friends. Whenever possible, she frugally uses scraps of paper at hand, such as letterhead from the Belmont Hotel in West Harwich, Massachusetts, and recycled personalised postcards from Haven House after she moves to Lawrence House, a cheaper cooperative house at Smith College.

Plath wrote a variety of letters during her junior year at college – 'all sorts, all sizes: contrite, gay, loving, consolatory' (*LVi* 569). She dated Myron Lotz and wrote 'Mad Girl's Love Song' about him. Lotz influenced her interest in abnormal psychology. Plath noted, 'I am getting more proficient with the singing uncrowded lyric line, instead of the static adjectival smothered thought I am usually guilty of' (*LVi* 575). Gordon Lameyer was a Joyce enthusiast who inspired Plath to audit a course at Smith taught by Elizabeth Drew. Ray Wunderlich was in medical school at Columbia and took Plath to cultural events in New York City, including *Camino Real*: 'the most stimulating, thought-provoking, artistic play I've ever seen in my life!' (*LVi* 611). At Smith Plath studied Chaucer, Milton and modern poetry with relish and railed against a required course in science.

Plath's spring semester at Smith during her junior year was particularly stimulating. Robert Gorham Davis directed her creative writing and W. H. Auden critiqued her poetry. Plath told her brother, 'I found my God in Auden' (*LVi* 589). In addition to Auden readings, she heard Dylan Thomas on 20 May 1953 at Amherst College. As a correspondent for the *Daily Hampshire Gazette* she earned $170 and contemplated a career in journalism. Plath won two writing prizes and was elected to edit the *Smith Review* during her senior year. *Harper's* paid her $100 for three poems, which, in Plath's mind, inaugurated her adult publications.

Plath felt like Cinderella winning the *Mademoiselle* contest. She interviewed Elizabeth Bowen and wrote a two-page spread on five young male teacher-poets, including Richard Wilbur. Most of Plath's source material for *The Bell Jar* is contained in her June correspondence from New York, including meeting disc jockey Art Ford and dating simultaneous interpreter for the United Nations Igor Karmiloff. Plath was clearly overwhelmed by her experience in New York, which made her realise how young and inexperienced she was in the ways of the world. She secured a scholarship to summer school at Harvard, but did not attend when she was not accepted to Frank O'Connor's writing course. He thought she was too advanced for his course. Her summer job at Newton-Wellesley Hospital depressed her: 'I never realized or paused to think about the side of the world where the people are reaching the other end of the line: senility, even death' (*LVI* 645). She suffered from insomnia and 'became immune to increased doses of sleeping pills', 'underwent a rather brief and traumatic experience of badly-given shock treatments' at an outpatient clinic and decided to commit suicide because 'it would be more merciful and inexpensive to my family' (LVI 655). After her unsuccessful suicide attempt, Plath slowly recovered at McLean Hospital even though she underwent 'insulin shock' and 'electric (ugh) shock therapy' (*LVI* 657).

When Plath returns to Smith College as a junior instead of a senior in January 1954, she expects all sorts of problems, but is met with 'love and warmth' (*LVI* 686). Throughout the year, she nurtures and develops her 'newfound independence and self-reliance' (*LVI* 793). Her letters are philosophical and introspective during this period. Plath tries to integrate the various aspects of her personality: 'the serious creator, the strong honest out-door type that scorns persiflage, the urbane and seductive partygoer'; 'the eggs-and-bacon-and-coffee girl in a housecoat who can also exist somehow on olives, roquefort and daiquiris while clad in black velvet, and make a switch to a tanned saltwater and sunworshipping pagan' (*LVI* 661–2). The latter brings to mind the dream-girl of a woman's magazine, and it is noteworthy that for Plath this wasn't inimical to the more serious facets of her identity and cultural values.

During the first half of the year, Plath dyes her hair platinum blond and concentrates on getting back into social circulation, dating seven boys in four weeks. She auditions Gordon Lameyer as a possible future husband, wanting a good provider, intellectual companion and a good lover. Above all, she needs a mate with whom she can be in the same room and write. Plath also dates and corresponds with close friend Phil McCurdy; Richard Sassoon, who looks like an absinthe addict; and spars verbally about sex and literature with Sassoon's roommate at Yale, Melvin Woody. She reassesses Eddie Cohen, an early friend, who is not complex enough,

Myron Lotz, who is too materialistic, and Dick Norton, who seems 'to have shrunk' (*LVI* 769). Living on her own in Cambridge, Massachusetts, while studying German at summer school, she also dates various professors at Harvard.

Plath systematically embraces and delights in life: flying in planes (her 'Icarian lust' [*LVI* 832]), experiencing New York City (lectures, plays, movies, museums, restaurants) and even going skiing with Amherst graduate Jon Rosenthal after telling him: 'I have a very attractive, but nervous mother, whom I see as little as possible' (*LVI* 849). She also admits to Phil McCurdy that she has 'shocking feelings' (*LVI* 687) about her mother, which she explores in biweekly meetings with her psychiatrist from McLean, Ruth Beuscher, who is now, Plath says, 'one of my best friends' (*LVI* 715).

During her fall 1954 semester at Smith, Plath dyes her hair a shade that is closer to her natural brown to look more studious, applies for a Fulbright to attend either Oxford or Cambridge and focuses on her studies. She continues to study German to meet graduate requirements and by the end of the year successfully translates 'Ein Prophet' by Rainer Maria Rilke with his exact 'rhyme scheme and rhythm' (*LVI* 845). She is a 'bibliomaniac' (*LVI* 727) and voracious reader, underlining her texts in black ink. The location of each annotated volume from her personal library mentioned in her correspondence is identified in the footnotes of the *Letters*. She reads Sigmund Freud, James Frazer and Carl Jung for her thesis on 'the recurrence of the split personality' in Fyodor Dostoevsky (*LVI* 740), focusing on 'doubles, twins, mirror images' (*LVI* 822). Plath is a chameleon in the photographs from this period. Photographs 'are not ME' she tells Gordon Lameyer. The sole 'virtue of my face is that it is extremely mobile' (*LVI* 778).

Plath submits very little new material for publication in 1954, pouring her creativity instead into her letters, which are 'close to talking' (*LVI* 660). She is candid with Jane Anderson about her breakdown and experiences at McLean Hospital in 1953: 'I have somewhat of a personalized understanding of the sensations and physical and mental states one experiences previous to the act' of suicide (*LVI* 695). Going forward, she is determined to condition herself to 'hear, and not just listen; to see, and not just look; to communicate, and not just talk; to feel, and not just touch' (*LVI* 681). After meeting Alfred Kazin, she begins writing short stories again and hopes one day to publish in the *New Yorker*. The secret of being a creative writer, she tells her mother, 'is not to talk, but to do it, no matter how bad or even mediocre it is' (*LVI* 827).

Plath turns her attention to international subjects in 1955 (*LV1* 892). Inspired by Alfred Kazin, Plath concentrates on her writing and continues to draft short stories, including 'Platinum Summer' and the 'Smoky Blue Piano' for the *Ladies' Home Journal*. By the end of her senior year, after handing in a 'batch of poems each week' (*LV1* 855) to her special studies professor, Alfred Young Fisher, she produces a book manuscript – 'Circus in Three Rings' – of sixty poems, which she hopes eventually to edit for the Borestone Mountain and Yale Series of Younger Poets contests. She ties for first prize at the Irene Glascock Poetry Contest with enthusiastic support from John Ciardi and also meets Wallace Fowlie and Marianne Moore. Altogether she earns $465 in prizes and awards for the year and eventually publishes poems in the *Atlantic, Mademoiselle, Nation* and the *New Orleans Poetry Journal*. Extracurricular assignments include an article for *Mademoiselle* on Smith's symposium 'The American Novel at Mid-Century' with Alfred Kazin, Saul Bellow and Brendan Gill. Plath realises that 'writing is the first love' of her life (*LV1* 880).

Through Alfred Kazin she meets and dates Peter Davison, who is an editor at Harcourt, Brace and then at the Harvard University Press. He is well connected and social, 'playing on the keyboard of people like an organ' (*LV1* 950). Richard Sassoon continues to treat her to cultural weekends in New York City, eating gourmet French meals and seeing Japanese movies (*Gate of Hell*), Russian drama (*The Dybbuk*, about the soul of one dead before his time) and silent French films (*The Passion of Joan of Arc*). She becomes reacquainted with Braque and Picasso at the Museum of Modern Art and writes poems, including 'Three Caryatids without a Portico', about sculpture and paintings she sees at the Whitney Museum. She notes that she must learn to get over her habit of 'impressionistic, indescriminate [sic] gush' (*LV1* 952).

Plath's female friendships are equally strong and long-lasting. She tells newly married Enid Mark, her former co-editor of the *Smith Review*: I am 'the sort who can somehow always pick up a friendship that was very dear, no matter how long the time, nor how wide the space between' (*LV1* 866).

Rejections are particularly difficult for Plath to process, such as losing the Woodrow Wilson Fellowship. She tells Gordon Lameyer: 'it is a black month in the sense that a hideous committee of 4 smug men interviewed me at harvard for a national teaching scholarship (ww) and found me wanting because I was a woman' (*LV1* 894). Fearing she would not get into the University of Cambridge or win a Fulbright, she considers teaching for one year at the American School in Tangier, Morocco, sternly telling her mother: 'do not get blind with anger ... I would like you to appreciate my aims and attempts, even if you do not personally agree with them' (*LVi* 892–3). These exchanges do not appear in *Letters Home*. Four days later she writes to Ruth Cohen, the Principal of Newnham College, accepting her 'offer of admission' to Cambridge (*LVi* 897) and also is awarded a Fulbright on 21 May 1955. Before leaving for Europe, Plath takes dancing lessons for the crossing on the *Queen Elizabeth* so that she can express all the life inside her 'in rhythm and patterns' (*LVi* 957).

Newnham College, Cambridge

Plath's Cambridge letters chronicle developments in her intellectual, cultural and personal life that are foundational contexts for the writing.

She loves the lectures and readings, but quickly realises that her 'kind of vital intellectual curiosity could never be happy in the grubbing detail of a phd thesis', telling her mother, 'I will never be an academic scholar' (*LVi* 1006). Plath joins the Amateur Dramatic Club, playing a 'mad poetess' and meeting 'as large a cross-section of people' as possible (*LVi* 998). As soon as she arrives at Newnham College, she submits her poetry to the *London Magazine* and *Chequer* and starts to write 'a few articles on the atmosphere' at Cambridge with a sketch or two for the *Christian Science Monitor* (*LVi* 978). She decorates her room at Whitstead with two bookcases of colourful volumes, reproductions of Braque paintings, a tea set from Holland and sherry glasses from Sweden with which to entertain the British men she meets. She enjoys plays such as *Waiting for Godot* and experimental movies that shock one into 'new awareness of the world by breaking up the conventional patterns and re-molding them into something fresh and strange' (*LVi* 1003). She spends her Christmas vacation in Paris, escorted by American writer friend Nathaniel LaMar and Richard Sassoon, who is now at the Sorbonne. She writes to British friend J. Mallory Wober that she feels like 'a kind of feminine ulysses, wandering between the scylla of big ben and the charybdis of the eiffel tower' (*LVi* 1046). Paris is 'one colossal surrealistic dream' (*LVi* 1064).

In 1956 Sylvia Plath finally finds her life partner, discovers her mature writing voice and starts 'living from the center' (*LVi* 1252).

Plath begins the New Year in the south of France with Richard Sassoon, then sketches and writes about the Matisse Chapel in Vence. Later, she tells Elinor Friedman Klein that she wishes to hell she 'would meet some other man who could break richard's image & free' her (*LVi* 1132). Travelling to Germany and Italy in the spring with Gordon Lameyer, who is now just a friend, also proves to be a mistake. Many of the Oxbridge Englishmen

Plath dates 'think women become unfeminine when they have ideas & opinions' (*LVi* 1156) and consider Plath 'as a 2nd Virginia Woolf' (*LVi* 1144).

Plath longs for a soulmate who can accept all her 'knowing and laughing and force and writing to the hilt' (*LVi* 1164). She finds him in Ted Hughes, whom she meets at a publishing party for *Saint Botolph's Review*. She tells her mother that she has 'fallen terribly in love, which can only lead to great hurt' (*LVi* 1161). Hughes is 'a brilliant poet' (*LVi* 1200), but is 'arrogant, used to walking over women like a blast of Jove's lightning'. 'He is a breaker of things and people' (*LVi* 1166). She tells her brother that she is in love with the only man in the world who is her match. 'He has done nothing but write, rave, work and desert women for 10 years' (*LVi* 1174). Plath is amazed that she can work with Hughes in the same room and writes poems 'which make the rest look like baby-talk' (*LVi* 1179). With Hughes's support, she now faces 'those 6 terrible months at McLean' (*LVi* 1176) that enable her to write prose with 'realistic detailed descriptions of psychological states' (*LVi* 1292). Hughes reads her work in his strong voice, is her best critic, as she is his, often encouraging him to find alternative words (*LVi* 1280). Plath becomes Hughes's literary agent and starts to send batches of his poems out to American magazines. They spend as much time as they can together through the spring. These candid early assessments of Hughes do not appear in *Letters Home*. Plath begins her relationship with Hughes with her eyes open, hoping, as she tells her brother, to 'make him kind' and 'a little more caring of people' (*LVi* 1174). According to Plath, Hughes tells her that she has 'saved him from being ruthless, cynical, cruel and a warped hermit' (*LVi* 1189).

Plath's spring term at Cambridge is rewarding academically too. Dr Dorothea Krook, her brilliant, beautiful, young supervisor in philosophy is 'a blessed change from the majority of newnham grotesque dons who are relics from the victorian era when a woman had to sacrifice all claims to femininity & family to be a scholar!' (*LVi* 1153). Plath gives up acting for writing, contributing articles to *Varsity*, the Cambridge weekly undergraduate newspaper. One assignment sends her to a caviar-and-vodka reception for Bulganin and Khrushchev at Claridge's in London. Plath's Fulbright is renewed on 13 March 1956. She plans to buy an Olivetti typewriter in London when her mother visits in June and vows to be 'one of the few women poets in the world who is fully a rejoicing woman, not a bitter or frustrated or warped man-imitator' (*LVi* 1200). She also plans to write short stories about her time in England and weave them together into a novel, *Hill of Leopards*, which she later retitles *Falcon Yard*.

Plath's health continues to torment her. She wonders 'how one head can manufacture so continually such green guck' (*LVi* 1125). Over the winter she visits the casualty ward where a splinter is removed from her eye and often suffers from insomnia and nightmares. After she meets Hughes, however, her health improves. Hughes often hypnotises her and she wakes up 'refreshed and fine and relaxed' (*LVi* 1220). As long as she and Hughes are together, Plath says, she 'can bear anything in the world' (*LVi* 1235).

When Plath returns to Cambridge in the fall of 1956, after her secret marriage and their honeymoon in Spain, Hughes lives and works in London. Her sixteen love letters to him over this period express distress over the separation, though his visits and letters sustain her. Envisaging their future archive, she tells him to date his letters so that when they are famous their letters will be 'dove-tail-able' (*LVi* 1281).

After much deliberation, Plath and Hughes decide to announce their marriage to the Fulbright Committee and live together during Plath's last semester at Cambridge. Plath devotes herself to her studies and to marketing their creative writing. By the fall, the *Atlantic* publishes 'Pursuit', the first poem Plath writes after meeting Hughes, and *Poetry* accepts six of Plath's new poems 'glorifying love and Ted' (*LVi* 1259). Even her articles and sketches of Benidorm, Spain, are purchased by the *Christian Science Monitor*. Plath tells Hughes they shall be living proof that 'great writing comes from a pure, faithfull, [sic] joyous creative bed' (*LVi* 1268).

Plath types multiple copies of Hughes's poems and children's fables to send out to her American contacts, including editor Peter Davison. She organises Hughes's first book of poems, *The Hawk in the Rain*, for Harper's First Publication Contest. She also prepares Hughes for his debut reading for the BBC by sending him 'to an American-trained dentist' (*LVi* 1231) and ordering him a suit and tweed jacket on her Fulbright grant money. Everything she does is 'to please him and make him proud' (*LVi* 1262). She thinks of him as 'a kind of genius' (*LVi* 1275) and looks forward to taking him to America, where he 'will be reverenced properly' (*LVi* 1316).

Hughes teaches her to read tarot cards (*LVi* 1306) and they explore goddess lore together (*LVi* 1197). After hiking to Top Withens in Yorkshire and rereading *Wuthering Heights*, she exclaims: 'we are a happy Heathcliffe [sic] and Cathy' (*LVi* 1243). She can't believe that anybody ever loved like they do and predicts: 'We will burn love to death all our long lives' (*LVi* 1298).

From Black-and-White to Full Colour

Reading the 1,330 pages of volume I of the *Letters of Sylvia Plath* after 240 pages in the first half of *Letters Home* allows us to experience Plath's world in full colour after a black-and-white preview. We can now appreciate Plath's full-throttled embrace of life and the extraordinary talents, ambition, love and dreams that she brought to the beginning of her marriage. Although volume II provides a bleaker ending to her life with Hughes, there is no greater satisfaction for an editor than to release a great writer from the muzzle of competing family interests and allow her to tell her own story, in her own words, at her own pace; and in the process open up a world of new scholarship.

Notes

1. See for instance Locke, 'The Last Word'.
2. See for instance Jong, 'Letters Focus Exquisite Rage'.
3. McCullough, 'Anyone Who Remembers'. The tensions between Aurelia Plath and Ted Hughes over *Letters Home* are recounted by him in *LTH* 351–3 (16 July 1974) and 364–5 (3 April 1975).

PART VII

Plath and Place

CHAPTER 28

'A Certain Minor Light': Plath in Brontë Country

Sarah Corbett

Although Sylvia Plath visited West Yorkshire, the birthplace of Ted Hughes, only a handful of times – on visits to Ted Hughes's parent's house after her wedding and on subsequent Christmases – her response to the powerful and often threatening natural and human landscape that formed both the writings of Emily Brontë and the poetry of Ted Hughes was profound. The person/persona in Sylvia Plath's 1957 poem, 'Hardcastle Crags', on a night walk to Hebden Bridge's famous landmark, turns before, 'the weight / Of stones and hills of stones could break / Her' (*CP* 63). The poem captures an atmosphere of fear and loneliness that were Plath's own, perhaps, but one that can also be located in the landscape and in the human architectural response to it: those 'dark, dwarfed cottages' of the 'black / Stone-built town' (*CP* 62). These West Yorkshire interludes show Plath making use of an ambivalent energy in the landscape to mirror her self/psyche, and in the handful of poems discussed here Plath can be heard sounding out a Hughesian strain of voice against the rumoured ghosts and angels of her own emergent poetics.

To fully understand these 'West Yorkshire' poems it is essential also to take account of the particular landscape that produced them, especially the Calder and the Worth valleys, a triangle of about twenty square miles that reaches between the village of Heptonstall, the market town of Hebden Bridge, the hamlet of Mytholmroyd and over the back of the hill about ten miles as the crow flies, to Haworth, home of the Brontës. There is something unique and distinct about this place: high, wild wind-blown moorland and deep wooded river valleys set on millstone grit, the carboniferous rock that gives the area its distinctive black winter mantle. The 'black stones' that occur and reoccur in these poems are blackened not by centuries of soot as might be assumed, but by a natural process of oxidisation; their unremitting 'blackness' emerges from within their very nature rather than being externally created, an essence that mirrors the landscape they are set within. This harsh, demanding place provokes a powerfully ambivalent response in Plath just as it provokes an ambivalent response in many of its inhabitants, incomer or native. Hughes identifies how this, his native landscape, is one where, 'The people are not detached enough from the stone, as if they were only half-born from the earth, and the graves are too near the surface.' Yorkshire, Britain's largest county, is as diverse as it is wide, but there is nowhere else in Yorkshire that is quite like the Calder Valley.

As would be expected of such a sensitised conductor as Plath, she picked up on this particularity straight away, at first thrilled by the austere beauty, 'an incredible, wild, green landscape [. . .] with amazing deep-creviced valleys feathered with trees' (*LH* 268), whilst immediately alert to the darker currents brought by the 'wicked north wind' to a place high, spare and lonely where the sun is often only out 'by a miracle' (*LH* 268–9). On a visit in June 1957, before Sylvia and Ted left for the United States, despite a landscape where 'the view of spaces' is 'like anything I've seen in my life' (*LH* 317), the cold rainy week that precedes it requires a coal fire, where Sylvia can be found, 'toasting my toes' (*LH* 317). This is a place that can be deceptively idyllic one moment, coldly inhospitable the next, and the poems, rather than the *Letters Home*, attest to how Plath responds fully to the mercurial nature of a place that surely mirrors her own.

Plath's practised, close-crafted poetics seems particularly suited to this landscape, the words as masterfully knocked and tapped into place as a dry-stone wall. The first handful of 'West Yorkshire' poems, such as 'November Graveyard', 'Black Rook in Rainy Weather' and 'Hardcastle Crags' are evidence of Plath's gift of mimicry, as well as her ability to push her poetic intelligence outwards to greet the world as it comes to meet her. In 'November Graveyard', the speaker is, like a ventriloquist, throwing a voice, and anyone familiar with the West Yorkshire accent, in particular that of the Calder and Worth Valleys, will hear the vowel-heavy foreshortening in a stare that 'stands stubborn' *(CP* 56). The word 'dour' in the poem is especially Northern, both in idiom and suggestiveness, and the repetition of 'grass' and 'grassiness' only really works with the tight Northern 'a', chiming as it does with the short, hard 'a's in 'hardhearted' earlier in the line. Anyone who has heard a recording of Ted Hughes cannot fail to hear the long o's that rhyme 'moor' with 'stare' (the West Yorkshire 'o' contains to the ear its own 'u', making moor, mouer, and no, nouer) or the 'ow's and 'oo's and 'ars' that patter through the poem like ghosts, like the wind itself. The poem is an aural conduit for a place and a people entrenched and defined by a particular landscape, each vowel leaning back into the previous one in a pattern of assonance that makes a grave and yard of the space of the poem that is not unlike the steep-sided glacial rifts of the Calder Valley itself.

Plath studs the poem 'November Graveyard' with Yorkshire words – 'stubborn', 'skinflint', 'dour', 'foist' – words that call up a parody of Yorkshire-ness that is no less affectionate than it is tongue-in-cheek; the 'hard-hearted emerald' is after all in the poem acknowledged to lie hidden within the grass. Indeed, the idea of a 'hidden gem' might even have summed up the austere beauty of the moorland village of Heptonstall, where the Hughes family was living in 1956. The house was the Beacon, a square, black stone house that stands in its own garden a little out of the village on the wind-whipped moor-top road to Slack and Blackshaw Head. Plath's first visit to the Beacon took place in September 1956, after returning from honeymooning with Ted in Benidorm, but the poem is set in November, when she would have been back in Cambridge. Plath spent her first Christmas as a married woman at the Beacon, so it's possible that she is amalgamating first impressions with a second, more wintry and undoubtedly less sympathetic one. When the bright, mid-Atlantic voice slips in in the midst of the poem, it is the voice that might conjure a 'fictive vein', acknowledging its outsider status, its role as commentator on this 'essential landscape' at which the onlooker can only 'stare, stare' (*CP* 56).

The 1957 sonnet 'Mayflower' reuses the word 'dour', for 'dour skies' and the poem's 'black winter', 'Assault of snow-flawed winds' and 'steepled wood' (*CP* 60) recall the Calder Valley to those who know it intimately. Due to the nature of soil, rock and stone particular to this region the moors in winter can look black at a distance, and the woods climb near-vertical hillsides. Also familiar is the ever-welcome 'white bloom' of the mayflower, the small white flowers of the may tree, or Hawthorn, that signal the beginning of summer. There's a Yorkshire saying often misinterpreted, 'never cast a clout until the may is out' ('clout' is Yorkshire idiom for clothes). Misread this to mean the month of May and you might easily get caught out without a coat freezing in a sudden turn of wind or rain; the small white five-starred may flower ('the may') can come as late as June, as it did in the cold spring of 2015.

'Mayflowers' is a poem that deftly brings together the two developing aspects of Plath's sense of belonging: to the New World, where she comes from, and the old one, where she now finds herself and where she is to remain. However, the poem, looking outwards, reverses this poetic homecoming. The image of the mayflower conjures the pagan fertility ceremony of Beltane, held at the beginning of May, and brings to mind weddings and couplings, here the coupling of Britain and

America, of Plath and Hughes. Plath not only adopts Britain as her home, but as is evident in the 1961 BBC interview, 'Two of a Kind', she has already begun to pick up Hughes's particular accent: that long 'leigh' at the end of a word such as Italy or that pure West Yorkshire 'Realeigh' (really) exactly mirrors Hughes's own; it is a very place-specific idiom you will only hear in Calderdale.

'Black Rook in Rainy Weather' can be considered the second of the West Yorkshire poems. The poem borrows from what might be seen as an emerging Yorkshire word-hoard – 'black', 'dull', 'flare', 'haul', 'stubborn' – where the shortened northern vowel dominates the sound pattern, but is more conversant than its predecessor, exploring an idea and developing it. There is still the element of mimicry, her 'rook' standing in perhaps for Hughes's hawk from his seminal poem 'The Hawk in the Rain', and a tightly rhymed yet limber and elastic five-line stanza form that she will make use of again with greater effect in 'Hardcastle Crags'; the turn to the self, the lyric 'I', is noticeably present, and gives the poem a foreshadowing of the *Ariel* voice that will in a few years make far greater demands of its reader and its material, demanding, 'some backtalk / From the mute sky' (*CP* 57). However, the speaker is content for now with 'A certain minor light (that) may still / Lean incandescent // Out of kitchen table or chair' (*CP* 57).

What is this 'minor light'? Is it perhaps a rendering of Keats's negative capability, in Plath's poem become the space where the material world meets the metaphysical one; an ur-place where poetry does its work, and the inspiration for poetry is to be garnered? The 1957 poem 'The Great Carbuncle' revisits the argument of 'Black Rook' but condenses it more successfully around one central event and image: walkers cresting the moor, 'In a light neither of dawn / Nor nightfall, our hands, faces / Lucent as porcelain' (*CP* 72). Ted Hughes's note to the poem tells us usefully that 'the great carbuncle' is, 'An odd phenomenon sometimes observed in high moorland for half an hour or so at evening, when the hands and faces of people seem to become luminous' (*CP* 276). But it is not necessary to know this in order to appreciate the beauty of the poem; there is an ease of diction and rhythm here, something of that idiom of direct speech that will come to signify her most mature poetic voice, yet one that lends this poem an intimacy and warmth. The poem transforms what might be a lucid yet graspable experience into something utterly beyond the ordinary, reusing the motif of tables and chairs from 'Black Rook in Rainy Weather', where angels are also to be found floating, siting the extraordinary moment of vision within the everyday.

In the first West Yorkshire poems 'November Graveyard' and 'Black Rook in Rainy Weather', we can see Plath starting to work out this idea of moments of radiance or rapture: ghosts or angels suddenly appearing from this mute, dour landscape like annunciations, bringing poems or glimpses into the moment of inspiration that allows a poem to come into being; there's something about this landscape, it seems, as she encounters it in these poems, that provokes this insight. In 'November Graveyard', the landscape, become uncanny, appears to conjure ghosts to haunt the moor. Another famous literary ghost surely hovers behind Plath's 'vision' here: that of Catherine Earnshaw tapping at the locked casement window in *Wuthering Heights*. A journal entry the following summer whilst Plath is in the United States recalls the configuration of death and angels in the poem 'Black Rook in Rainy Weather': 'Writing breaks open the vaults of the dead and the skies behind which the prophesying angels hide' (*J* 286). 'Black Rook in Rainy Weather' locates the writing self in the landscape, but in a landscape populated by supernatural forces that bring inspiration to the poet ready and willing to take notice of the message or gift. These are poems, then, in which Plath is recognising the source of her poetic inspiration and locating it within in a tradition that embraces the mid-eighteenth-century romanticism of Emily Brontë tied to the mid-twentieth-century romanticism of Ted Hughes, extended into a neo-paganism that takes account of the psychic forces redolent in the landscape that she was rapidly becoming open to.

Plath responded strongly to the English landscape, and its flora and fauna found its way very quickly into her poems. She wrote detailed descriptions of Cambridge and of the surrounding Fens in her journals and a poem from 1955, 'Winter Landscape with Rooks', set in the Fens, appears to pre-empt the darker, more complex response to landscape that was to appear in her West Yorkshire poems. It is important to note that Plath calls this early Cambridge poem a 'psychic landscape' (*CP* 275): it is the symbolic nature of the landscape that matters to Plath, how it provides a mirror for the inner workings of the self – the mind, the imagination, the psyche and that 'deep self' she was, in her writing, really concerned with. What Jacqueline Rose noted in *The Haunting of Sylvia Plath* (1991) is how in Plath's landscape poems 'the problem is not just something from which she is in danger but something which she is in danger of responding to'.[2] Tim Kendall has noticed how '"Hardcastle Crags" discovers a malevolence in the natural world which Plath's later poems set themselves the task of assimilating.'[3] The character in the poem retreats in the face of the 'looming', almost primordial presence in the landscape, but in the last West

Yorkshire poem, 'Wuthering Heights', the danger is that if the speaker
looks too closely at the 'roots of the heather', they will, 'invite me / To
whiten my bones among them' (*CP* 167).

'The Snowman on the Moor' records an argument or lovers' tiff. The
female speaker walks angrily out of the house, 'Still ringing with bruit of
insults and dishonours' (*CP* 58). A reader would be forgiven for reading an
autobiographical note here, but it is perhaps more instructive to recall the
scene in *Wuthering Heights* where Cathy is telling Nelly why she cannot
marry Heathcliff and Heathcliff, listening at the door, runs raging and
heartbroken onto the rain-soaked moor at night and disappears before he is
able to hear what follows: Cathy's declaration of undying love for
Heathcliff. Of course the poem is not a rewriting of this scene, but it is
redolent of the presence and influence of Emily Brontë's novel that must
have been at work in Plath's unconscious at this time. It is on her first visit
to the Beacon that Plath rereads *Wuthering Heights*, 'I really *felt* it this time'
(*LH* 270), she says in one of her *Letters Home*. The opening lines of
'stalemated armies' is suggestive of Angria, the imaginary world the
Brontë children created. On her visit to the museum, Plath was fascinated
by the Brontë children's 'books in microscopic script' (*J* 581), makes
detailed notes for the story 'All the Dead Dears' that draws on the
'drama of Cathy and Heathcliffe' (*J* 580), and uses the same name as
Brontë for her narrator, 'Nellie'. 'I wish you could see your daughter
now, a veritable convert to the Brontë clan' she reports cheerily to her
mother (*LH* 268).

If Plath is reimagining the Cathy/Heathcliff scene in 'The Snowman on
the Moor', the female figure in the poem becomes Heathcliff-like, stalking
'intractable as a driven ghost // Across moor snows / Pocked by rook-claw
and rabbit-track' (*CP* 58). It is 'she' who breaks the stalemate and rushes
out onto the moor, becoming the primary agent, however briefly, in the
drama of the poem. If, in poems such as 'November Graveyard' and 'Black
Rook in Rainy Weather', Plath is trying on a Hughesian persona, however
much set at a critical or satirical angle, here she is attempting to throw this
off under the influence of a female writing tradition embodied by Emily
Brontë, one that continues in Plath's day as it did in Brontë's to demand
such risk and force. The landscape is both dreadful and frightening, its
essence embodied in the terrifying figure of a giant who has walked straight
out of the Middle English poem *Sir Gawain and the Green Knight* to
become the snowman of the title. As in the next West Yorkshire poem,
'Hardcastle Crags', the female figure turns home. This is not so much
a defeat as common sense: to be out at night and lost in such a landscape is

to risk not returning at all. After all, it was the West Yorkshire weather that did for Emily and her sisters.

'Hardcastle Crags' is set at night under a full moon, in summer, suggested by the fields full of grass and the cows in the meadows. A lone woman sets out to walk, we assume by the title of the poem, to Hardcastle Crags, a woodland set in a deep valley between Heptonstall and Hebden Bridge. We're never told why she is walking at night, alone, to the woods – on some quest for poetic inspiration, or, perhaps she is a kind of Red Riding Hood – but the point of the poem is that she never gets there; she doesn't get much beyond the edge of the village and the surrounding fields. This is no benevolent landscape. The grasses 'seethe'; the mist that rises from the valley is ghoulish. The landscape is a medusa, turning everything in it to stone, the poem returning endlessly to a nightmarish vision where the grass is 'a moon-bound sea' that 'Moves on its root', the 'long wind' pares 'her person down', and her head is a pumpkin carved for Halloween (*CP* 62/63). The landscape is ancient, pre-human, and the human figure of the woman is at such risk that her only sensible response is to retreat under the threat of a landscape powerful enough 'to snuff the quick / Of her small heat out' (*CP* 63). The figure in the poem might well be a stranger, naive enough to venture out unawares at night on a romantic quest, excited at first by the echoes her feet strike from the street, but wise enough to recognise the malevolence in a power far greater than herself.

Plath wrote two poems about Top Withens, the fabled inspiration for the setting of Emily Brontë's *Wuthering Heights*. What remains – and what Plath would have seen – a few miles' walk outside Haworth over rough moorland that is now a well-trodden path signposted for tourists in several languages, is hardly impressive, a tumbledown ruin half sunk into the moor side. But it is the landscape that surrounds it that is impressive, where 'There is no life higher than the grasstops' (*CP* 167). This is not a human place, but one where demons might exist reflected in the eyes of sheep as unsettling as fairy-tale grandmothers in 'disguise', and horizons 'dissolve' like a series of mirages. Plath is, in this final West Yorkshire poem, not only recognising a chthonic terror in the natural world that reflects her own internal demons, but entering into this horror, 'the one upright / Among all horizontals' (*CP* 168). This is not the longed-for communion of 'I am Vertical', written several months earlier, where the speaker 'shall be useful when I lie down finally' (*CP* 162), but as if the speaker has been turned to stone and is as locked into the landscape as the decaying farmhouse.

As Tim Kendall points out, Plath's 'exploration of the relationship between the individual and the natural world is fundamental to the development of her mature voice'.[4] This is an exploration that takes root, and then takes flight, after she visits the landscape of West Yorkshire and the Calder Valley. 'The Rabbit Catcher' begins in 'A place of force' (*CP* 193) that is perhaps as much the scabrous moor of Withens or the Beacon as it is the moorland of Devon or Cornwall. It takes us to the 'only one place to get to. / Simmering, perfumed, / The paths narrowed into the hollow.' (*CP* 193) and in so doing echoes an incident that took place on Plath's very first post-honeymoon visit to Calderdale in a way that suggests the origins of the poem:

> Last night Ted and I hiked out at sunset to stalk rabbits in a fairy-tale wood, falling almost perpendicularly to a river valley below [. . .] Ted, a dead-eye marksman, shot a beautiful silken rabbit, but it was a doe with young, and I didn't have the heart to take it home to make a stew of it . . . (*LH* 269).

Even Plath's cheery *Letters Home* voice cannot completely eradicate the note of warning, one that takes on full symbolic power in the later poem. Plath writes home after her first visit to West Yorkshire how 'I never thought I could like any country as well as the ocean, but these moors are really even better, with the great luminous emerald lights changing always' (*LH* 270); is the snowman of 'The Snowman on the Moor' an unconscious precursor to the less easily vanquished Daddy? Plath 'tries out', parodies and ultimately finds wanting the 'Yorkshire' voice that can be associated with Ted Hughes in order to reach the clear pure notes of her mature poems. Perhaps it is first here, in the Calder Valley, that she meets, confronts and eventually assimilates an external landscape with an inner 'psychic landscape', into a place from where the *Ariel* poems can themselves emerge.

That Sylvia Plath is now buried in the very graveyard she describes in 'November Graveyard' hardly needs mentioning but is difficult to ignore. The grave has become something of a place of pilgrimage but is largely, and thankfully, no longer the site of the vandalism and controversy that attended it in the 1970s and 1980s, when the grave was desecrated several times. The town of Hebden Bridge, these days a lively, open-minded and open-hearted place populated by diverse communities as well as many poets and artists, has become associated with Sylvia Plath and she with it in ways that show a new readership ready to leave behind an obsession with her biography and the manner of her early death and start to celebrate the legacy of her work. Recently a life-sized piece of graffiti appeared on the side of the 'Shoulder of Mutton' pub in the centre of the town, showing Plath as a young woman in a 1950s swing skirt leaning against a bicycle. The image is witty and optimistic, showing her as she might have appeared, perhaps, in her first days at Cambridge, but her face and posture full of knowing and self-possession, as if she has returned to begin again with all she has learned.

Notes

1. Hughes, quoted in Wagner, *Ariel's Gift*, 34.
2. Rose, *The Haunting*, 133.
3. Kendall, *Sylvia Plath*, 30.
4. Kendall, *Sylvia Plath*, 31.

CHAPTER 29

Plath in London

Elaine Feinstein

Sylvia Plath returned to London in the autumn of 1962, determined to make a new life in the literary world. She'd felt intellectually isolated in North Tawton, and knew it would be easier to pick up freelance work in London. It was a shrewd decision, yet it took courage. All her friends in that world had been made at Ted's side and he had now reached a level of fame that made it natural for him to be photographed at a Faber and Faber party, alongside W. H. Auden, T. S. Eliot and Louis MacNeice. Plath was not yet recognised as a writer of comparable significance. As she wrote to her mother on 9 October 1962, 'I shall hear of Ted all my life, of his success, his genius . . . . I must make a life all my own as fast as I can' (*LH* 465).

Al Alvarez recalls how,[1] only a month before her death, Karl Miller, then Literary Editor of *The New Statesman*,[2] told him that he had received a 'whole wedge' of Plath's new poems, but taken none of them: '. . . They are too extreme for my taste.'[3] Miller feared Plath was mentally ill, and made some effort to contact her through friends,[4] but clearly did not recognise the poems as among the most remarkable of the time.

Plath wanted to make a dedication to writing central to her life. As she wrote memorably in 'Stings', in the first week of October: 'I / Have a self to recover, a queen. / Is she dead, is she sleeping? / Where has she been, / With her lion-red body, her wings of glass?' (*CP* 215).

Moving involved many practical difficulties. A flat big enough for herself, the children and an au pair to give Plath time to write, would be hard to find, and expensive to rent in the area she knew best. Plath had a car, however, and she was not penniless. Ted had made over to her all the money that remained in their account, and taken a loan for himself from his Aunt Hilda. They remained in touch, though Sylvia kept up a brittle cheerfulness, which convinced Ted that she was happy with the situation.

It was Suzette Macedo who invited Sylvia to stay with her in London so she could look for a place to live. Sylvia left the children in Court Green with a nanny while she did so.

Suzette and Helder Macedo had met Sylvia in 1960 at a party in the house of their South African friends Sylvester and Jenny Stein. Helder Macedo was a Portuguese poet. Suzette, who had grown up in Martinique, then a Portuguese colony, was working on the poetry of W. B. Yeats. Both Macedos had been very impressed with Ted, and Suzette took Sylvia at first for a wife who had 'no thought of a separate career for herself',[5] before discovering she had written poems under the name of Plath. Both women shared a passion for Yeats.

For Sylvia, staying with the Macedos was convenient and friendly, but stressful, because she well knew Suzette was a close friend of Assia Wevill,[6] the woman who had precipitated the break-up of her marriage. Assia's beauty, sophistication, glamorous clothes and well-paid job in advertising had impressed the whole circle of Plath's London acquaintance. Suzette herself was 'almost in love with her'.[7] Alvarez is a dissenting voice. He thought Assia 'vain and predatory' and declared she 'would have had a Russian peasant shape if she had grown older'.[8]

It was in part because Sylvia knew how close Suzette was to Assia that she preserved such an obstinate insistence that she was completely happy to be separated from Ted. When Helder Macedo tried to persuade her that she should be less precipitate about seeking a divorce, Sylvia shrugged away the advice, just as she ignored Suzette's opinion that Assia was far from sure she wanted to leave her husband, David. Suzette soon realised that Sylvia's composure was a pretence; the first night she slept in their flat Suzette heard weeping from Sylvia's room: it was Sylvia sobbing in her sleep.[9]

Sylvia knew that the Macedos had a wide circle of literary friends and wanted to be introduced to them, so Suzette took her to meet Doris Lessing, but Doris did not take to Sylvia's 'gushing' enthusiasm for museums and art galleries.[10] Sylvia's manner may have masked an uncertainty in the presence of a successful novelist since Sylvia hoped to earn her living by writing novels herself. Whatever it was, Doris asked Suzette not to bring Sylvia again.

From Suzette, Sylvia heard that Ted and Assia were going away to Spain together and it angered her. Her reaction was to write David Wevill – who so far knew nothing about his wife's affair – telling him of it. Assia had elaborately arranged for her sister to cover for her, and now asked Helder Macedo to go round and comfort David. He found Wevill lying on a couch, prostrate with grief; he had driven a fist through a door in his fury, and put a knife into Assia's favourite handbag.

Ted had for some time been enjoying his new freedom, staying at first on couches in friends' flats. When Dido Merwin returned to London to look after her mother's flat she offered him a perch there, in a pleasant room with a desk and a telephone in Cleveland Street, W1. Since October he had been enjoying 'the single life' as he was writing to Bill Merwin in the States and his brother in Australia.

Suzette soon came to realise that Sylvia needed more emotional support than she could offer, and suggested she visit her own GP, Dr Horder. On a visit to Dr Horder Sylvia came by chance on a maisonette to let in a house on Fitzroy Road, NW3, which had a blue plaque on its wall to proclaim W. B. Yeats had once occupied it. This seemed a miraculous sign, and Sylvia acted quickly. At the estate agent's, she discovered there was another person interested in the property, and that she would have to put down a year's rent in advance to secure the lease. It was Ted who helped her find the money she needed to do that. There were references to be taken up, and some suspense; a single woman whose income depended on freelance writing cannot have seemed a financially reliable tenant.

Sometime before the move to London Sylvia decided to dress herself for the city. She went to a shop in Exeter selling Jaeger clothes and bought a 'gorgeous camel suit ... and matching camel sweater, a black sweater, black and heavenly blue tweed skirt, dark-green cardigan, red wool skirt' (*LH* 480),[11] and had her hair cut more fashionably. It made her feel ready for London. She spoke with some excitement to Suzette Macedo of setting up a literary salon.

The flat was completely unfurnished. Sylvia had to arrange for the connection of gas and electricity, and the installation of a gas stove. She bought simple unpainted furniture from John Lewis, borrowed a bed from Suzette, and set to painting walls and putting down rush matting on the floors. All this took time, and the family was not established in 23 Fitzroy Road until 17 December. Ted drove down to Court Green to collect some red corduroy material Sylvia needed for curtains, together with a few other useful pieces of furniture, and brought this back to London, with apples and potatoes from their garden, that same night. The journey along icy roads took twelve hours. Sylvia was grateful, but continued to keep him at a distance. In her letters to her mother she made no mention of his helpfulness.

She was not yet thirty, and must have been hoping to make a new sexual relationship. She was not inexperienced in such matters. She had had several love affairs before meeting Ted,[12] and was deeply involved in an affair with Richard Sassoon even as she went to bed with Ted the first time in 1955.

Al Alvarez seemed the most attractive possibility. He was a brilliant young writer who had been the lover of several beautiful women. He had not only published Plath's poetry before knowing she was Ted's wife, but also shared her admiration for the poetry of Robert Lowell.[13] When she read her recent poems to Alvarez in October, he told her that she was the first woman poet who had interested him since Emily Dickinson.

In a letter to her mother on 16 October 1962 Plath is elated about her new work. 'I am a genius of a writer; I have it in me. I am writing the best poems of my life; they will make my name' (*LH* 468). Though she often faked euphoria in letters to her mother this sounds genuine and, indeed, has turned out to be true.

There is another context to Sylvia's poems at this point that deserves mention, since many critics – including George Steiner and Seamus Heaney – have questioned her appropriation of imagery from the Nazi death camps in 'Daddy' and 'Lady Lazarus'. It should be remembered that all through 1961, newspapers daily reported testimony from survivors of the Nazi Death Camps at the trial of Adolf Eichmann in Jerusalem. It was the year the whole world found itself forced to confront a reality that had been kept strangely at bay since the opening of the Camps in 1945. Many felt the evidence with a visceral horror analogous to lived experience.

Plath introduced 'Daddy' on the BBC as 'a poem spoken by a girl with an Electra complex' (*CP* 293 *n*). In the poem, she fuses her dead father and Hughes into a single figure dressed in the black of an SS officer's uniform, and done to death as a vampire by a village lynch mob. Yet 'Daddy' cannot be read as autobiography, but is rather, 'perfect craft', as I have pointed out elsewhere.[14]

Sometime in December, soon after her move into Fitzroy Road, she and Ted went out together with Eric White of the Poetry Book Society to a restaurant in Dean Street, W1. After an excellent meal, with much red wine, Ted and Sylvia went off together towards Soho Square. Drafts of a long poem many times corrected and never included in *Birthday Letters* take off from their conversation that night, in which Sylvia's jaunty manner collapsed into uncontrollable tears as she confessed that divorce was the last thing she wanted. They talked until two o'clock in the morning, when he took her back with him to his flat, knowing he could neither assuage her grief nor escape it.[15] Sylvia's weeping broke out again as they argued so noisily through the night that the neighbours banged on the walls in protest. The saddest lines in that unfinished poem recall entering Soho Square long after Sylvia's death. In a phrase that Bate cites directly from the manuscript, Ted felt 'like a murderer listening'[16] for 'the ghost of his victim' (the latter is Bate's phrase).[17]

On Christmas Eve 1962, Sylvia was alone with the children in Fitzroy Road. Ted had invited her to spend Christmas with him and his parents in Yorkshire, but she had refused the invitation. Alvarez arranged to look in on her, but he had another appointment, for dinner with V. S. Pritchett, later that evening.

Alvarez saw that she had lost weight, and that her long hair, usually held in a bun, was loose, which gave the air of a priestess. She read him several poems, including 'Death & Co.', with its reference to 'how sweet / The babies look in their hospital / Icebox' (*CP* 254). For all the mockery in that poem, he must have recognised her dangerous state. When he was preparing to leave, he recalls that she burst into tears and pleaded with him not to go. Alvarez writes:

> She must have felt I was stupid and insensitive. Which I was. But to have been otherwise would have meant accepting responsibilities I didn't want and couldn't, in my own depression, have coped with. When I left about eight o'clock to go on to my dinner-party, I knew I had let her down in some final and unforgivable way. And I knew she knew. I never again saw her alive.[18]

This rejection would have been all the more painful to her if her past relationship with Alvarez had gone further than he has disclosed in print.[19]

Sylvia had nowhere to go for Christmas Day 1962, so Suzette invited her and the children for lunch, and prepared a goose bought in Camden Market for the occasion. Sylvia, for all her disappointment the evening before, kept up a flow of cheerful praise for the food, insisting again how much she was enjoying London. She spent Boxing Day alone writing letters.

In January Ted returned from Yorkshire and began to visit Fitzroy Road to see the children. Sometimes he took them for walks. Sylvia was not without money by this time, since Ted had been able to give her £900 in cash and cheques.

She continued to press the Macedos to introduce her to more people in London. So it was that she met Jillian and Gerry Becker, a South-African Jewish family who became immensely supportive in the last weeks of her life. They were sympathetic and hospitable, often taking her out to eat meals with them. Moreover, they had a nanny, and were happy to let Sylvia leave the children with them when she needed to go out.

On 14 January 1963 Heinemann had a small party to launch *The Bell Jar*, under the pseudonym of Victoria Lucas. Ted came to that party but generally speaking the literary elite did not. Sylvia must have been a little dispirited by the novel's reception, though she had disingenuously described it to her mother as a 'pot-boiler' (*LH* 477).[20]

In 1963, England was enduring its worst winter in 150 years, and London was ill-equipped to handle the extreme weather. Pipes were frozen, and there was no hot water. Electricity failed, as too many people turned on their single-bar heaters. It must have been a nightmare for anyone trying look after small children. Plath had no telephone and no hope of getting a line installed. All calls had to be made with coins from an icy phone box on the street. The Beckers, however, had central heating and were ready to take her in.

The elation Sylvia had felt while writing her poems was beginning to fade. The children were often ill, and her own health was uncertain. She picked up a viral infection, and was often feverish. Yet even when Sylvia had flu, the children were clean and dressed, and there were no piles of dirty dishes.

For all Sylvia's courage, Dr Horder recognised the onset of a serious depression. He prescribed monoamine oxidase inhibitors, which do not take effect immediately, and he was worried enough about her to arrange for an au pair to start work in Fitzroy Road on 11 February.

Ted found the unexpected weather exhilarating. He was still seeing Assia secretly, and casually sent greetings from her to Dido Merwin when writing to Bill. He was not overly bothered that Assia hesitated to commit herself permanently to their affair. There were consolations, notably Susan Alliston, an aspiring poet who was working as a secretary at Faber and Faber.

In the scraps of one of Hughes's unpublished journals, which is held by the British Library[21] and was mined by Jonathan Bate,[22] Hughes writes that on Sunday 3 February Sylvia rang Ted in Cleveland Street and invited him to lunch. He had a recording booked at the BBC, but he agreed. He phoned her when the recording began to run late, and did not arrive until 3 p.m., but they enjoyed a very pleasant lunch and their 'most friendly, open time'[23] since their separation. He thought she was in better shape than she had been in some time. Ted claims that he told her that he wanted to take up their old life but he 'couldn't be a prisoner'.[24] He stayed until 2 a.m. and she promised to visit him on Thursday.

On Monday 4 February Sylvia telephoned Ted at lunchtime sounding completely different. She insisted he had to leave the country altogether within a fortnight, because 'he was "ruining her life" by living in London'. He said 'he could not possibly leave England . . . where would he go?'[25] She complained about gossip she had been hearing, but refused to tell him from whom or what it was about.

There was certainly a network of gossip between Assia and Gerry Becker. On Wednesday Ted learned from Assia that Becker had not only been told by Sylvia about their affair, but had also been told – and quite falsely – that Ted had abandoned Sylvia in Devon without a penny. Ted wrote a curt letter to Sylvia, telling her to stop Becker spreading that particular story or he would take legal action.[26] Ted went round to Fitzroy Road to deliver the letter, but in spite of his anger, and her insistence on him leaving the country, they were soon talking again about going away to Yorkshire together. She told him the good news that she had been invited to be on the radio review panel *The Critics*, and he reassured her she would easily cope with it.[27]

The chronology of events of Sylvia's last week is difficult to pinpoint with absolute certainty, but it seems likely that Plath did indeed make her promised Thursday visit to Cleveland Street.[28] The *Birthday Letters* poem 'The Inscription' turns on Sylvia discovering an edition of Shakespeare that she had destroyed in Court Green and which she sees, as if resurrected, on his Cleveland Street shelves. In 'The Inscription' it is the discovery that the new volume is inscribed by Assia that destroys the mood of reconciliation between them, though Ted's willing submission to the bond he feels with Sylvia survives intact: 'Do as you like with me. I'm your parcel. / I have only our address on me . . .' (*BL*[29] 173).

On Friday 8 February Sylvia posted a farewell letter to Ted saying she was going off into the country and intended never to see him again.[30] She expected it to arrive on Saturday, but it arrived the same day, as was possible in London at that period. Ted rushed to Fitzroy Road, and found Sylvia alone there, tidying the place up. She calmly took the letter in from him and burnt it in an ashtray.

We do not have the letter, therefore. But she had also already sent him a copy of 'Edge', completed three days earlier; a poem that writes terrifyingly of a dead woman as 'perfected' (*CP* 272). He might well have rushed round to her after receiving that, and 'wept with relief'[31] when she opened the door, knowing her history and guessing her trajectory.[32]

Yet there are some problems fitting either version of Friday's events with other accounts. According to Jillian Becker, she collected Sylvia and the children from Fitzroy Road on Thursday 7 February, and brought them back to her flat. She remembers returning later the same day to collect baby equipment, and, more surprisingly, a cocktail dress, cosmetics and curlers, which had been forgotten.[33] According to Ted, Sylvia was calmly sorting the flat out on Friday when he rushed round to deliver his letter. However, there were no children in his memory of that meeting, and that would fit in with them being already at the Beckers.

Jillian thought Sylvia spent most of Friday in bed, apart from a long time in the bathroom, before setting off in the evening 'for a very important appointment'. Ted also remembered seeing her in the early evening on Friday. Did he then visit her twice that day? Evidently she returned to the Beckers in her street clothes that evening. It was Saturday, according to Jillian and Suzette, when she came back elated after 'the most important meeting of her life'.[34]

Memory is fallible and these timings are not likely to be resolved. The suggestion however, that it was in her last meeting with Ted that he told her Assia was pregnant now seems peculiarly unlikely. It would have provoked exactly the hysterical emotion Ted was keen to avoid. And since Assia was then far from committed to a continuing relationship with Ted, even if she was pregnant, she might well have decided on an abortion.

The chronology of Sylvia's movements during that last Saturday are also filled with contradictions. According to Suzette,[35] it was on Saturday morning that Sylvia disappeared from the Beckers' flat without telling anyone where she was going. But Jillian has the disappearance late that day: 'On the Saturday evening Sylvia put on or packed her blue or silver dress, I forget which, and went out. She didn't say where she was going or whom, if anyone, she hoped or intended to meet.'[36] Suzette recalls that Frieda began asking for her Mummy, and she was called in to take Frieda to the zoo while Jillian and the nanny looked after Nick. Olwyn suggested to me[37] that Sylvia's absence was for a meeting with Ted, but he markedly makes no mention of such a meeting on Saturday in his journal notes. It is hard to imagine, however, who else Sylvia could have met who might have made her feel that she had just had the 'most important meeting of her life' and 'that everything was coming out right now'.[38] But was it Friday or Saturday when she spoke those extraordinary words? And can Jillian be correct about Sylvia going out in the evening on Saturday? It seems questionable that Suzette would take a child to the zoo in a freezing February darkness (or even that the zoo was still open then); therefore, if the zoo visit did take place, it is more likely that it happened earlier in the day. In any case, Suzette's recollection[39] is that when she returned from Regents Park, Sylvia was back in the Beckers' flat and the Beckers were going out for dinner.

That is the evening when, according to Sue Alliston's journal, Sylvia telephoned Ted in agitation many times, presumably from the Beckers' flat. On Sunday after lunch, Sylvia slept, but on waking declared that she felt so much better that she wanted to be taken back to Fitzroy Road. The Beckers reluctantly agreed, persuaded by her wish to be there for the au pair arriving on Monday morning. It may be that the pills Dr Horder prescribed had begun to take effect. Notoriously, that is the point when antidepressants remove inertia, and so all barriers to action. Gerry reported that she wept copiously in the car.

Dr Thomas, in the flat below Sylvia's maisonette, was the last person to see her alive. She came down to buy a postage stamp from him and he thought she looked strange.

In a letter to Aurelia at the time *Letters Home* was being edited in 1975, Ted explained Sylvia was busy that weekend. It seems he had other commitments himself. He spent those two days with Sue Alliston, and we know about Ted in these last two days of Sylvia's life because Sue kept a journal of the weekend that they spent together.[40]

On Saturday night they were at his flat in Cleveland Street when Sylvia phoned several times. Ted took all her calls – probably not made from that phone box in the dark on a freezing winter night as he later imagined,[41] but from the Beckers' flat. He was in bed with Sue as he took them. We don't know what Sylvia was saying, but Sue Alliston describes hearing a desperate voice and listening to Ted trying to calm her down, once saying 'Take it easy Sylvie'. When that phone call finished, he 'turned his back' on Sue and said, '"But if I go back, I die"'.[42]

On the Sunday night they avoided Sylvia's calls by using a room in the house in Rugby Street where Ted had once lodged. If Sylvia walked down to phone the Cleveland flat that last night of her life, her calls would only have reached an empty room.

The following day, early on Monday morning, her body was discovered by the au pair Dr Horder had arranged for her. Plath had put her head in the gas oven, after taping up the children's room carefully so the gas would not reach them and putting out milk and bread for when they woke up. Ted's telephone number was on the table, alongside the manuscript of the poems that would go into *Ariel*. She also left Dr Horder's telephone number. Dr Horder thought Sylvia Plath died about 4 a.m. on 11 February and it was he who rang Ted to say, 'Your wife is dead.'

Al Alvarez went with Ted to see Sylvia's dead body. He continues to believe that Plath had intended the suicide to fail. Ted's old college friend,

Lucas Myers, believes Ted and Sylvia would have been back together in days if she had not killed herself.

Notes

1. All interviews conducted by Elaine Feinstein are in the Elaine Feinstein Archive, John Rylands Library, University of Manchester Library, uncatalogued – hereafter *EFA*. www.library.manchester.ac.uk/search-resources/spe cial-collections/guide-to-special-collections/a-to-z/collection/?match=elaine+ feinstein+papers. Accessed 4 May 2019.
2. Miller also edited the *Spectator* that year.
3. Elaine Feinstein interview with Al Alvarez, 22 July 1999, *EFA*.
4. Elaine Feinstein interview with Karl Miller, 22 July 1999, *EFA*.
5. Elaine Feinstein interview with Suzette Macedo, October 1999, *EFA*.
6. Feinstein, *Ted Hughes*, 135.
7. Feinstein/Macedo interview, *EFA*, op. cit.
8. Feinstein/Alvarez interview, *EFA*, op. cit.
9. Feinstein/Macedo interview, *EFA*, op. cit.
10. Feinstein/Macedo interview, *EFA*, op. cit.
11. Sylvia Plath to Aurelia Plath, 19 November 1962.
12. See Wilson, *Mad Girl's Love Song, passim.*
13. Feinstein/Alvarez interview, *EFA*, op. cit.
14. Feinstein, *Ted Hughes*, 132.
15. Bate, *Ted Hughes*, 206–7.
16. Bate, *Ted Hughes*, 207; and 589 note 32, which reads "'Soho Square" (BL Add. MS 88918/1)'.
17. Bate, *Ted Hughes*, 207.
18. Alvarez, *The Savage God*, 48.
19. In the course of my research for *Ted Hughes*, Olwyn Hughes told me in confidence that in Plath's last journal (the one Ted burnt) Sylvia discussed her visits with Alvarez. The no-longer-extant journal entry provided the explicit details that Alvarez omits from his accounts in *The Savage God* and *Where Did It All Go Right?* Olwyn's remark appears in the first draft of my manuscript in the John Rylands archive, with a note in Olwyn's hand saying the information had been told to me in confidence. It was not published in my book, but Olwyn must have repeated verbatim these comments to Jonathan Bate, because they appear in his biography, in the same words Olwyn used to me (Bate, *Ted Hughes*, 599 note 35; and more generally 314–16).
20. Sylvia Plath to Aurelia Plath, 25 October 1962.
21. British Library, Add. MS 88918/129. See Bate, *Ted Hughes*, 589 note 36.
22. Bate, *Ted Hughes*, 208–9.
23. Bate, *Ted Hughes*, 208.
24. Bate, *Ted Hughes*, 209.

25. Bate, *Ted Hughes*, 209.
26. Bate, *Ted Hughes*, 209.
27. Bate, *Ted Hughes*, 209.
28. Bate also mentions this Thursday visit to Cleveland Street (*Ted Hughes*, 209) as well as a previous visit in 'early December' (206, 206–7) that took place during the Soho Square episode I describe above.
29. All citations from *Birthday Letters* refer to the Faber and Faber edition.
30. Bate, *Ted Hughes*, 210.
31. Hughes, 'Last Letter', Facsimile of First Page of Late Draft.
32. Bate, *Ted Hughes*, 210.
33. Stevenson, *Bitter Fame*, Penguin 1989 edition, 292.
34. Feinstein/Macedo interview, *EFA*, op. cit.
35. Feinstein/Macedo interview, *EFA*, op. cit.
36. Becker, *Giving Up*, 9.
37. Over lunch in Belsize Park, 2000.
38. Feinstein/Macedo interview, *EFA*, op. cit.
39. Feinstein/Macedo interview, *EFA*, op. cit.
40. See also Alliston, *Poems and Journals*.
41. Hughes, 'Last Letter'.
42. The comments by Hughes are recorded by Susan Alliston in an unpublished journal entry for 12 February 1963, and cited in Bate, *Ted Hughes*, 211–12 and 589 *n* (notes 38, 39 and 40).

CHAPTER 30

Plath in Devon: Growing Words Out of Isolation

Maeve O'Brien

The positive effects of geographical isolation on intellectual and creative productivity is a recurring feature in traditions of white American literature. Colonists staked their claim on the New World with physical settlements on distant frontiers. They emphasised their individualism and difference from the old order, violently separating their writings from the oral and written traditions of the indigenous peoples whose lands they claimed for themselves. The geographical and physical isolation of new frontiers created a synergy whereby aloneness was invigorated by opportunity and possibility; with writer-settlers like St. John De Crèvecoeur insisting that the literature of the 'new' America must reflect the spatial, emotional and ideological distance between America and the Europe left behind.[1] Later, in the nineteenth century, the political scientist Alexis De Tocqueville – who believed that solitude and silence could be sites of divine inspiration – wrote of the affinity Americans in particular have for solitude. Such philosophising was contemporary to the work of Transcendentalists such as Henry David Thoreau who mused on the primacy of isolation to the creative American brain.[2]

Thoreau's *Walden* emphasised the creative potentiality that can be produced when writers, thinkers and artists make the decision to isolate themselves – living removed from society can strip away non-essential elements that interrupt the creative human spirit.[3] Thoreau's testament that geographical isolation offers the opportunity to live 'deliberately' forms one of the most important statements in the canon of modern American literature and resonates into the writing of twentieth- and twenty-first-century authors, poets and critics. Indeed, with her assertion that artistic techniques of isolation and silence have the potential to offer a creative connection to God or a higher power, Susan Sontag's critique of isolation and silence is clearly indebted to Thoreau. Interpreting silence as a transformative, restorative, freeing and creative force, Sontag argued that physical isolation offered the opportunity for artists to 'sketch out new prescriptions for looking, hearing, etc. – which either promote a more immediate, sensuous experience of art or confront the artwork in a more conscious, conceptual way'.[4] Like her predecessors, Sontag believed that spaces of geographical isolation could be considered sites where writers and thinkers gain the opportunity to examine their existence, environment and artistic objectives with a probing intensity that cannot be sustained outside of solitude.

Given the centring of geographical isolation as a foundational feature of the American literary psyche, for writers like Sylvia Plath who grew up in the state of Massachusetts – home to the Transcendentalist movement – it is understandable that throughout her writing life, she would demonstrate an appreciation for spaces of geographical isolation and repeatedly attempt to live 'deliberately' and write. Indeed, Plath made frequent comments on the potentiality of isolation as a space in which to grow words. As early as 1951 she mused that, 'aloneness and selfness are too important to betray for company' (J 70), and Plath's further appreciation of spaces of isolation is exemplified by the positive experiences she had when spending time in Yorkshire and at the Yaddo Arts colony. The wild barren landscapes of England and the curated isolation of Yaddo produced a temperate climate for Plath's writing process. Poems such as 'Hardcastle Crags' and 'November Graveyard' illustrate how having time and space to reflect on desolate landscapes energised Plath's creativity and the production of work. Indeed, it was at Yaddo in 1959 that Plath broke through her crippling writer's block by setting herself descriptive writing tasks in which she documented the majesty as well as the more ordinary features of the colony. It is perhaps in a 1960 letter to her mother that Plath's appreciation of isolation as a compliment to her creativity is best documented. At this time Plath was living in London, in a cramped and busy apartment with her husband and child. Having been allowed the use of a private study to write, Plath reported that isolation was a conduit to her creativity: 'I have found that the whole clue to my happiness is to have four to five hours perfectly free and uninterrupted to write in the first thing in the morning—no phones, doorbells or baby' (LH 416).

Plath's appreciation of her private study space quite obviously resonates with words from Virginia Woolf in her essay 'A Room of One's Own', where Woolf writes of the need for 'a quiet room or sound-proof room' where women writers can have the opportunity to work on their craft without distraction.[5] But given the tradition of isolation that informs the backbone of the American literary experience, Plath's desire for aloneness extended much further than a simple need to find a room in which to write. Indeed, by 1961 isolation had become more than a few hours a morning working in a study – it had become a way of life for Plath. She and her family made the decision to move from London to the extremely rural town of North Tawton in Devon. Perched on the periphery of Dartmoor, the small village was connected to London by train, but the journey took approximately five hours – being more than 200 miles from the city. Connie Ann Kirk records that 'North Tawton consisted primarily of one main road with a few shops, pubs and a few houses'[6] – but these amenities were dwarfed by the dense loneliness of the rural environ. Having visited Court Green before purchasing the house, Plath was aware of its deeply isolated geographical location. But this seclusion did not deter her; and as letters to her mother illustrate, Plath considered the isolation offered by North Tawton to be a positive feature of the property. Plath wrote to her mother of the, 'wonderful deep-breathing sense of joy at the peaceful, secluded life opening up' in North Tawton, and how the 'utter peace' of her new home led to the expansion of her 'whole spirit' (*LH* 423–8).

From what survives of Plath's *Journals* and in correspondence to friends and family, we know that once she settled in North Tawton, Plath set about making comprehensive notes about her new environment. The isolation of the setting allowed her to examine her existence and surroundings in the minutiae. Indeed, Plath was transparent about her desire to record every aspect of human life that she encountered, treating her subjects as if they were experiments to be watched. A memorable note in her *Journals* can be found when Plath reprimands herself for not annotating every aspect of her interaction with a neighbour: 'I have utterly forgot to describe what she wore: must train myself better, from head to toe' (*JP*[7] 230). We know that Plath considered her rough notes and *Journal* entries to be a form of literary 'training', and the notes she made show that she was using her environment as an important source of inspiration for her writing. Indeed, as we can see in short stories such as 'Mothers', Plath used North Tawton as a setting for her fiction work – the geography of the short story matches exactly the layout of the village. This synchronicity suggests that Plath grew her creative work out of the objects, elements and people she encountered in her remote rural village.

Further, even more striking parallels are found between Plath's notes in her *Journals* and the poems she would go on to write in the summer and autumn of 1962. The following excerpt from Plath's *Journals*, where she documents visiting her neighbours Rose and Percy Key finds another life in her poetry:

> She had brought over two old books (one of which I am sure propped Percy's chin), a pile of buttons, thousands, that they had been going to put on cards and sell, an address stamp, also for home business, and a few notebooks: pitiable relics. I had passed once and seen two women, their hair tied from the dust in the kerchiefs, on their knees in the parlour, sorting miscellaneous objects and walled in by upstanding vividly floral mattresses and bedsteads (*JP* 239).

Reading this *Journals* segment alongside 'Berck-Plage' offers an interesting insight into Plath's creative process when living in Devon. Almost exactly, she used the same words and phrases from her notes in her poem. The two old books propping Percy's chin in *Journals* are seen again in the line: 'They propped his jaw with a book until it stiffened' in 'Berck-Plage' (*CP* 198). Additionally, 'Berck-Plage' is also populated with similar objects and imagery that Plath documented in her notes. The floral 'touched garden-ias', 'livingroom furniture' and mention of objects such as pillowcases, mattresses, pyjamas in 'Berck-Plage' all correspond to the *Journals* observations Plath made of her neighbours in their home (*CP* 198–200).

Another set of connections between notes Plath made and poetry she later produced can be seen when we compare her real-life meeting with Devon locals (entitled 'Charlie Pollard and the Beekeepers') with her poem 'The Bee Meeting'. In her notes, Plath writes the following: 'We felt very new & shy, I hugging my bare arms in the cool of the evening for I had not thought to bring a sweater' (*JP* 204). She also makes an addendum: 'Noticed: a surround of tall white cow-parsley, pursy tallow gorse-bloom, an old Christmas tree, white hawthorn, strong-smelling' (*JP* 244). It is clear in her poem 'The Bee Meeting' that Plath recycled these notes, writing: 'In my sleeveless summery dress I have no protection' (*CP* 211). Additionally, the poem includes the same words Plath added in at the end of her notes – she mentions the hawthorn, 'Is it the hawthorn that smells so sick? / That barren body of hawthorn, etherizing its children', as well as gorse, 'I cannot run, I am rooted, and the gorse hurts me' (*CP* 211) and cow-parsley: 'If I stand very still, they will think I am cow-parsley' (*CP* 212).

'The Bee Meeting' is undoubtedly indebted to the notes Plath made about her real-life experience meeting with beekeepers. While this analysis may lend itself to simplistic biographical interpretations of Plath's work during this time, Lynda K. Bundtzen offers a particularly insightful interpretation of 'The Bee Meeting' when she states that in the poem, 'Plath apprentices herself to a literary tradition and history that has often identified the poet as a bee or beekeeper, the bee's activity as akin to the creative labour of the poet, and the honey produced as song.'[8] Bundtzen's reading of 'The Bee Meeting' aligns Plath's poem with values of Transcendentalism, suggesting that the documentation of her environment and real-life experiences was a generative force that opened up Plath's vocabulary and inspiration to new opportunities – thus broadening her creative horizon and imaginative scope.

Given the centrality of Plath's geographical isolation in North Tawton to her creative work, it is apt to consider the words of Gaston Bachelard who said that, 'an immense cosmic house is a potential of every dream of houses. Winds radiate from its centre and gulls fly from its windows. A house that is as dynamic as this allows the poet to inhabit the universe. Or, to put it differently, the universe comes to inhabit his house.'[9] For Bachelard, the home with its four enclosed walls and chosen seclusion can be the epicentre of creativity – providing artists and writers the space to conjure up new worlds. Within the home, the poet may generate their own private literary traditions and assign importance to objects of their own choosing. This concept resonates in context with Plath's lived experience when writing her poems in North Tawton. The Court Green homeplace and surrounding environment became one of Plath's most prominent creative muses.

Many of the poems Plath wrote, in the autumn of 1962 especially, were situated within the setting of the home – the environment in which Plath was primarily located at this time. In these domestic poems, Plath promoted objects and housework tasks to positions of pivotal importance – plates, knives, domestic accidents, pregnancy, illness, childcare and the everyday work of women took centre stage during this period of her writing, as evidenced in poems such as 'Cut'. In this piece, the event that produces the poem is Plath's speaker slicing her thumb open when carrying out the domestic chore of cutting onions. While such an event may be considered mundane, in Plath's newly-established creative canon made possible by her isolation in the home, the cutting of a thumb was of such importance that a poem had to be born out of it.

Indeed, in poems such as 'Lesbos', the documentation of kitchen items and domestic occurrences at times reads like a stock-take of her home environment. Plath's brutal and truthful depictions of domestic work – 'there's a stink of fat and baby crap' – and the trifling insignificances of interior design – 'I see your cute décor / Close on you like the fist of a baby' (*CP* 227) not only reveal the speaker's rage at her circumstances but also illustrate that Plath's 'Lesbos' literally grew out of the inner walls of her home. In her analysis of Plath's domestic poetry, critic Marcia Bryant agrees that Plath uses her home environment as 'a corpus to be archived', and in doing so, she curates 'an archive of the domestic surreal'.[10] Given that the domestic realm has largely been eschewed by the male-dominated literary canon, Bryant's claim that Plath felt that domestic spaces were important illustrates the revolutionary creative act in which she was engaged. By carefully documenting her domestic environment and producing poetry out of these objects and spaces, Plath reconfigured what could and should serve as inspiration for poetry.

Undeniably, that Plath's homeplace became a site of isolation for her indicates the deep personal price she paid for silence – despite any creative gains she made. The dissolution of Plath's marriage and her subsequent separation meant that Court Green – which was once a place with a bustling hearth and full of visitors – became a space of excruciating isolation. Living hundreds of miles away from London in a ramshackle house with two infant children, Plath felt utterly lost and alone, as demonstrated by the many letters she wrote to her mother and brother during this time. On 9 October 1962, she wrote to her mother in despair: 'I have no one . . . Stuck down here as into a sack, I fight for air and freedom and the culture and the libraries of a city' (LH 465). Certainly, Plath was deeply anguished and lonely in Court Green. We witness these emotions in her creative work: for example, in 'Purdah' – a poem whose title literally translates as 'seclusion' – Plath writes of the violence and terror of forced isolation.

The speaker of 'Purdah' laments her seclusion from the rest of the world – castigating the unidentifiable male figure who has hemmed her into isolation using 'Little nets' and 'silk Screens' (CP 242, 243). The speaker tells us, 'I am his' (CP 243). This statement is punctuated with a full-stop and set in its own line, illustrating the finality and hopelessness of her quarantine. Even when the male figure ceases to physically imprison the speaker, she is still dominated and under his control, 'Priceless and quiet' and forced to exist in a space with the inane chatter of 'parakeets, macaws!' (CP 243). Plath's use of an exclamation mark here suggests that these birds drown out and silence the speaker by talking over her, using idiotic meaningless words.

Yet Plath's speaker slowly gains strength and with the domineering male figure absent, she strategizes a plan, to 'unloose' (CP 243) a note of her voice. The repetition of the word 'unloose' throughout the poem stirs up the momentum of the speaker's plan to shriek and liberate herself. Finally, in the last two stanzas of 'Purdah', the speaker triumphantly shatters her seclusion and transforms into a dangerous, powerful and free woman. The use of words such as 'lioness' and 'shriek' (CP 244) in the poem's final stanza show the liberatory strength the speaker has cultivated while in isolation. Similarly, for Plath as a writer, isolation transformed her craft. The aloneness of Court Green offered her the opportunity to reclaim devalued objects and experiences, and position them as central themes of her creative universe. As Bryant has commented, 'transcendence' in Plath's poetry, 'does not rise *above* domesticity, but *within* it'.[11]

Within the rooms of the home, Plath generated the 'cosmic' potentiality to which Bachelard referred – envisaging her own poetic canon by naming and prioritising domestic objects and experiences, and declaring them important literary inspirations. Plath achieved this confidence and independence because her creativity thrived under circumstances of seclusion and isolation. In agreement, critic Jeannine Dobbs has stated that, 'paradoxically, it is out of her domestic relationships and experiences, which she came to feel were stifling, even killing her that the majority of her most powerful, most successful work was created'.[12] The various strangulating isolations Plath experienced only served to intensify her creativity.

Tracy Brain and Sally Bayley have noted that 'Purdah' provides 'a meaningful alternation between different possibilities, so that the apparently submissive woman is revealed as potentially murderous'.[13] Certainly the transformation of Plath's speaker from victim to survivor – and perhaps even a predator – resonates with the transformative relationship Plath developed with isolation when living in North Tawton. No longer simply a creative aphrodisiac, isolation became a weapon and potential source of strength in Plath's poetry.

In the poem 'Letter in November', we truly understand the multifaceted advantages isolation brought to Plath and how she was creatively energised and empowered by it, despite the adversities of seclusion. In this poem, Plath writes a speaker who proudly walks around her garden, independent and contented. The poem expands and pulses with territorial pride ('This is my property') (*CP* 253), with a resilience that has grown out of geographical isolation. The speaker's use of comforting words that yield softness in conjunction with feelings of love and security show that geographical isolation can be positive – producing an affirming and confidence-giving space. By likening the speaker's environment to the Arctic, Plath sets a scene of barren isolation to which her speaker responds favourably. Indeed, the speaker's declaration of celibacy indicates a decision of aloneness made on her own terms – she wishes to remain physically untouched in her secluded space. It is in this isolation that the speaker feels free to declare her independence: 'Nobody but me' (*CP* 254), she says, remarking with a kind of triumph on the fact that she alone walks the grounds of her land. And when, in the last stanza, the speaker is confronted by the 'mouths of Thermopylae' (*CP* 254) being represented as golden 'balls' of apples among 'thick gray death-soup' (*CP* 253), the security provided by her protective isolation means the speaker is not fearful of these mouths of hell.

The isolated desolation of North Tawton would have been most apparent in the early hours of the morning, before Plath's children woke and the noise of the day began. From letters to her mother, we know that Plath got 'up about five, in my study with coffee, writing like mad' and in the dawn, at that time of silence before the countryside animals and birds began to stir, she found creativity (*LH* 466). Plath would have watched the sun rise over her garden, alone in her empty house but for two small children. It was in this environment of emotional and geographical isolation that she wrote some of her best work. Indeed, it is clear that Plath was aware of the connection between isolation and harnessing her creativity. Upon leaving Devon for London in the winter of 1962, she continued to live by an ethos of isolation. Al Alvarez, who visited Plath in her Fitzroy Road flat, wrote that she decorated her new home in a 'Spartan' fashion.[14] This minimalist style coincided with Plath's development of a new phase of poems separate from the *Ariel* movement that she had written in North Tawton. New pieces written in 1963 relied heavily on the bareness of the page, as well as spaces, pauses and gaps that slowed down the pronunciation of words and asked the reader to rely on what is not said as much as what is being said. It was Plath's experience of isolation in North Tawton that provided the funda-mental impetus for these later creative works. Embracing aloneness, seclusion and isolation in life and on the page not only made Plath an active participant in the American literary traditions she knew so well, it instilled in her a creative confidence and energy that allowed her to confront her artistry in its most naked and ambitious form.

Notes

1. St John De Crèvecoeur, 'From Letter III', 660.
2. Paltieli, 'Solitude de son proper Coeur', 183–206.
3. Thoreau, *Walden*, 143.
4. Sontag, *Styles of Radical Will*, 13.
5. Woolf, *A Room of One's Own*, 61.
6. Kirk, *Sylvia Plath* (2004 edition), 86.
7. All citations from *Johnny Panic* refer to the Faber and Faber 1979 edition.
8. Bundtzen, *The Other Ariel*, 161.
9. Bachelard, *The Poetics of Space*, 51.

10. Bryant, 'Ariel's Kitchen', 232.
11. Bryant, 'Ariel's Kitchen', 231.
12. Dobbs, 'Viciousness in the Kitchen', 11.
13. Brain and Bayley, 'Introduction', 7.
14. Alvarez, *Where Did It All Go Right?*, 231.

PART VIII

The Creative Afterlife

CHAPTER 31

An Alternative Afterlife: Plath's Experimental Poetics

Gareth Farmer

Veronica Forrest-Thomson's argument for the formal sophistication of
Sylvia Plath's poetry in her unpublished 1971 review of Plath's posthumously published collection, *Winter Trees*,[1] may not seem particularly radical to our retrospectively wise eyes. We know, like Forrest-
Thomson, of course, that the voices in Plath's poetry are multiple and
contradictory and cannot be easily traced back to a speaking subject
confessing authentic feelings through pellucid and incorruptible language. We know because it is obvious, but also because what Forrest-
Thomson calls the 'general opinion' of literary-critical conceptualisa-
tions of the speaking subject have – in the main – dispensed with
naïve descriptions of a poet's singular voice, as well as with a belief
that language is transparently representative of particular states of
being. Forrest-Thomson, a young, radical poet and critical theorist
who died at the age of twenty-seven in 1975, knew these things before
many of her contemporary literary critics. And she knew that readings
of Plath's poetry as transcriptions of a tortured person, firstly, ignored
the formal complexities of her poetry and, secondly, operated as
a conceptual jail, confining Plath's poetry into a wing of poetic history
marked 'confessional'. Indeed, in a letter to Paul Buck, the editor of
Curtains, a small, radical poetry magazine in 1972, Forrest-Thomson
was keen to differentiate Plath's poetics from those of Ted Hughes and
other dominant poets.[2]

Forrest-Thomson's unpublished review of *Winter Trees*, as well as her
commentary on Plath's poetry in her posthumously published 1978 book,
Poetic Artifice: A Theory of Twentieth-Century Poetry, represent formal
rescue missions of Plath's poetics from the panoptic, patriarchal gazes
petrifying her work in the confessional wing. According to Forrest-
Thomson, Plath's poems are *fictions* and testing grounds for formal
expressivity. For Forrest-Thomson, the technical complexity of some of
Plath's later poems critiqued both the speaking subject and language itself;

in other words, Plath, for Forrest-Thomson, was extending a range of modernist formal practices and preoccupations.

It took a while for literary-critical history to catch up with Forrest-Thomson's 1971 assessment of Plath's formally intricate poetry, but her conclusions anticipate comparable, subsequent remarks. Christina Britzolakis, for example, associates the 'new rhythmic [. . .] freedom' of many of Plath's later poems with what she calls 'a devastating critique of the postwar formalist lyric and a recovery of the wider cultural resources of modernism as critique'.[3] Britzolakis also argues that 'the location of the "I" in these texts is unstable and duplicitous',[4] while Plath's later poems replace formal consistency and linearity with fragmentation, excessive repetition and mixed registers. It is heartening that the reception of Plath's work now draws on modernist and post-structualist insights into the function of language and its relation to the role of the author and their always-already constructedness within language. But, too often, the formal implications of these insights are left to one side, patiently waiting in vain for formal evidence. In other words, Plath's potential contributions to both neo- or late-modernist, as well as post-structuralist or so-called postmodern, aesthetics are rarely, if ever, explored in any detail.

One obvious reason for this oversight is that she does not seem to be influenced by, or write, in the manner of, for example, Mina Loy, or many of the radical, late-modernist poets writing during her time or now. Another reason is the smothering literary-critical industry that is happy to let Plath be like – but a little different to – say, Seamus Heaney, Ted Hughes or John Hollander, but certainly not content to compare her formal or intellectual radicalism with poets like, say, H. D., Lyn Hejinian or Susan Howe. One last reason is the pernicious pathologisation of Plath's work, even in the hands of subtle and sympathetic critics. For example, despite offering insights into Plath's fractured poetics, Britzolakis supplements another conceptual and spectral myth – the return of the repressed – to cluster her readings around a central message: Plath's language is inconsistent because of an insistent struggle of the repressed that erupts into the otherwise 'consistent' poetics.

Similarly, in *The Haunting of Sylvia Plath*, Jacqueline Rose takes on Plath's estate and its insistence on certain truths attaching themselves to her poetry; she draws on post-structuralism and neo-psychoanalytic frameworks to argue that 'Plath regularly unsettles certainties of language, identity and sexuality, troubling the forms of cohesion on which "civilised" culture systematically and often oppressively relies.'[5] So Rose writes of Plath's creation of fantasy landscapes that enable her to explore multiple personae and to critique contemporary culture. At the end of her opening chapter, Rose writes compellingly that:

> Plath is not consistent. It has been the persistent attempt to impose a consistency on her which has been so damaging [...] But to say that Plath is not consistent is not to say that she doesn't articulate something very precise about some of the most difficult points of contestation in our contemporary and political life. Plath is neither one identity, nor multiple identities simply dispersing themselves. She writes at the point of tension [...] without resolution or dissipation of what produces the clash between the two.[6]

Rose's most powerful conclusion – from 1991 – might have been a watershed in reception and understanding of Plath's formal poetics. But it actually operates, and is used, in a less liberated way: as a stopping point to interpretation itself. Her conclusion acts as the teleological end-point – Plath 'writes at the point of tension [...] without resolution'. In this case, it is accepted that Plath's writing at this point of tension does not require evidence except conceptual affirmations of such irresolution in phrases from the poems.

The problem with such externally imposed interpretation is that every reading leads back to Plath *as writer*, not the ways in which such ideas are articulated formally *in her writing*. In other words, there is a practical failure here to extend these ideas to the detail of Plath's work itself, or extension is only granted where such details complement a comment on Plath's 'multiple identities'. It is not Plath who is inconsistent, we might say, but her work. It is not Plath's identities that are multiple, but the personae presented in the poems in particular language, discourses and forms. This move from Plath-centric to work-centric might seem pedantic but, in terms of writing about poetic form, the sleight of mind makes all the difference. Simply put, when we are discussing Plath's poetry, we might always bear in mind that we are discussing her work, not Plath relocated into her language. Another way of stating this would be to claim that the 'formal' Plath needs a reappraisal, beyond all of the attempts to reconcile fragmentation to a consistent vision of an artist developing towards genius, no matter how dissipated or inconsistent. Perhaps Plath's work needs to be read against, or in resistance to, the type of literary-critical contextualisation that cannot help but smuggle the image of the struggling poet through the back door only to reveal that everything was really *Plath Speaking* after all. As such, the title of this chapter should, perhaps, have been: *the alternative afterlives of Plath's poems, with a view to rethinking the status of her poetic form and its non-relation to questions of her actual identity, against readings that too often locate a centralised zone of interpretation in Plath herself, even while pretending otherwise.* But that would be too long! In what follows, I attempt to reframe the ways in which we might discuss Plath's work to understanding its potential alternative, and formal, afterlives.

Reframing Plath's Aesthetics

Any attempt to discern alternative afterlives for Plath's poetic practice needs to resist the forceful mythologisation of the poet, whether it is her own throughout her journals and letters, or those that have been externally imposed by generations of critics, friends, enemies and cultural commentators. Those commentaries have created so many sculptured goddesses of the tragic poet as 'antique museum-cased lady' ('All the Dead Dears', *CP* 70), or petrified by psychoanalytic peroration – 'rigor mortis come to stiffen / All creation' ('Perseus', *CP* 83). Or one must be selective and focus only on that which relates to the work, whether this is Plath's diary entries charting reading and writing habits, letters outlining drafts, changes, notes outlining burgeoning aesthetics or poems that offer up a full or partial précis of her poetics or aesthetic theory. But we must also resist the attitude that is necessary to create a vision of the unified poet, whose work goes through fixed-term shifts. Lowell's notion of her infuriating (to him) 'checks and courtesies' and the 'maddening docility' of her early work, and his subsequent surprise at the 'appalling and triumphant fulfillment' of *Ariel* is, of course, an absurd characterisation of her work and suffocates in the insufferable grasp of his own projected ego-poetics.[7] Every writer goes through stages of development, but these categories can soon ossify into filters through or around which the individual instances of work can barely be seen.

As Deborah Nelson notes during a discussion about resisting the assumption that Plath was always writing about her suffering: 'In a journal entry from 1956, Plath compiled a 'to do' list that ended with the following: 'Be stoic when necessary and & write – you have seen a lot, felt deeply & your problems are universal enough to be made meaningful ...'[8] Perhaps coincidentally, in a document entitled 'My Attitudes and Beliefs' written at the age of sixteen, Forrest-Thomson called for her own version of stoicism with detachment and disinterest at its central precept.[9] Forrest-Thomson was deliberately channelling Ezra Pound and T. S. Eliot's poetics of objectivity and impersonality where, as Eliot puts it, 'the more perfect the artist, the more completely separate in him will be the man who suffers and the mind which creates'.[10] Forrest-Thomson makes the case for an objective poetics in which form and language respond precisely to a given thing,[11] and this seems to describe what Plath desired. As Nelson notes of Plath's articulation of her ideas in her journals: 'she understood universality to be an effect of writing, that is, an aesthetic effect.'[12] For Plath, writing was not an indulgence in feeling, but an examination of feelings, relationships and ways to describe the world through the activity of writing.

Plath's Restless Artifice and Play

As many critics have noted, Plath was a restless stylist throughout her short life, but outlines and detailed comparisons of the clashes of form in her work, or descriptions of her experimentalism, are usually in the background. For example, while Linda Wagner-Martin may observe that Plath's 'break with traditional subject matter through the use of innovative technique was stunning', there is very little analysis of the characteristics of these stunning innovations, technical or otherwise.[13] Wagner-Martin does trace Plath's influence on subsequent poets' use of, for example, 'quick-moving tercets', or 'run-on sentence constructions', or what she calls 'kind of innovative and surprising diction'.[14] However, most of the influences she outlines impact on themes and registers: 'poems about moons and enigmatic women', for example, or those with 'wryly-voiced persona'.[15] Similarly, while Fleur Adcock admires Plath's 'technical ability to transform her emotions and experience into literature and not just self-expression', she offers no characterisation of what she means by 'literature' here.[16] And, to give a final example, while Steven Gould Axelrod may describe Plath's technique as one that glories in its 'figures and tropes', 'formal innovations' and 'rhetorical flourishes', most of his criticism leaves out extended examination of form, except where this complements an already worked-out theme.[17]

In his introduction to the *Collected Poems*, Ted Hughes describes Plath's attitude to her poetry as 'artisan-like'. '[I]f she couldn't get a table out of the material', he continues, 'she was quite happy to get a chair, or even a toy. The end product was not so much a successful poem, as something that had temporarily exhausted her ingenuity' (*CP*, 13). Perhaps a successful poem *is* one that exhausts a writer's ingenuity; a complete work is the unsatisfying end of a battle. Nevertheless, this notion of the 'artisan' poet returns when Hughes describes her early work, written before 1956 (or when she was twenty-three), as 'intensely artificial'. But, he adds, 'they are always lit with her unique excitement' (*CP*, 16). Many of Plath's poems are intensely artificial, deliberately so, and we need to redeem this sense of artificiality from being a negative thing.

Indeed, we might respond to Hughes: what does a 'natural' poem look like? Hughes's descriptions of the 'sense of deep mathematical inevitability in the sound and texture of her lines' and the 'supercharged system of inner symbols and images' (*CP*, 16) do reveal the complexity of her internal patterning as those features that make her poems emphatically artificial (*CP*, 16). It is perhaps because of her descriptive prowess and incisive commentary on relationships, states of mind and extreme emotion – couched in poised and condensed phraseology – that Plath has been primarily praised for what might be called her realism. She gets to the beating and bleeding heart of states of being in the world with memorable and well-honed bon mots. But, what if we adjusted our perspective on aspects of Plath's verse and discussed the artificial and unreal nature of her poetry; that is to say her 'unrealism'? In other words, instead of focusing on how real, truthful and poignantly located in the everyday her poetry seems to be, we might praise it for its baroque unrealism, or for the ways in which its surreal and cultivated excesses take us away from life into the realm of fantasy and performance.

The alternative afterlife of Plath's work I am suggesting runs counter to Hughes's inherent assumptions that poetry should be 'natural', and is one that embraces the baroque artificiality and unrealism of much of her work. As she notes in an early journal entry, she wants to create a 'pseudo-reality' for her reader; '"Pseudo" of necessity' (*J* 88), she continues in parenthesis. In this artificial realm, language is deliberately stretched beyond mere description into an arena of formal indulgence, which cannot easily be subsumed into a simple semantic reading. In a relatively early poem, 'Channel Crossing', for example, Plath's description of the visceral and imminently mortal waves is burlesquely elaborate: 'Waves wallop, assaulting the stubborn hull.'

The Hopkinsean, forced onomatopoeia of the walloping waves, the strange fury of the thrusting ship, and the blunt simile, 'dark as anger' (*CP* 26), could be taken as youthful overreach, as perhaps Hughes would suggest. And the poem is phonetically excessive as it marvels 'at the smashing nonchalance / Of nature' striking a stance, like the sailors described, 'Most mock-heroic, to cloak our waking awe' of the 'rare rumpus' (*CP* 27). However, these bravura, formal performances lay the blueprints for the dense and pared poetics of her later life. And, crucially, Plath's conscious use of excessive formal patterns, particularly in her early work, articulates a restless and intellectual sensibility that could never let formal processes complacently service a neat image. Form, in other words, never served a presentation of the 'natural', but rather repeatedly draws attention to itself as unnatural.

Plath's early poems are far from representative of a 'sedate early style',[18] as Axelrod has described them. So in 'Family Reunion', for example, Plath exercises her incisiveness on a drawing-room scene. Her textual wit emerges primarily through description and caricature – the slightly grotesque 'greasy smack on every cheek' and the 'pink, please squeak / Of Cousin Jane' who is, of course, a spinster. The rhymes enhance the wit and draw attention to the artifice or performance of the poem; 'cheek' and 'squeak' is neat, and the 'eyes' and 'butterflies' (*CP* 300) rhyme is fun, but descriptively ambiguous. It is at moments like these that the exercise of artifice and style seems more important than content, or at least rhyme generation and wit are in and of themselves worth playing around with. Elsewhere, these young exercises are more explicitly formal and display a hard-edged and logical intellectualism. Witness the stretch to precision and the phonetic internal generation of the poem, 'Insolent Storm Strikes at the Skull', where the title doubles as the first line, so that the storm 'assaults the sleeping citadel, / knocking the warden to his knees / in impotence, to sue for peace' (*CP* 325). These lines are artificial indeed, but the artifice produces the taut and unique imagery; Plath cultivates an insolent insistence of sound patterning against sense.

Similarly, Plath's early work also anticipates her later, short and visually striking later poems. In 'Aquatic Nocturne', for example, the placement of the words – in three-line, funnel-like arrangement – is designed to represent the 'slivers' of light emerging and shifting in an aquarium, where they are 'deep in liquid indigo' (*CP* 305). Plath's sensibility and awareness of the artificial performance of her early poems are articulated and formally registered in 'Note to a Neophyte'. The speaker, seemingly a neophyte poet herself, distils advice to a young writer as to how to turn natural processes into the artifices of poetry, and throws it at a reader with cryptic wit. The poem's opening two stanzas register the strained metaphors of craft, labour and effort. A poet must take the 'general mumble' and 'vague vocabulary' of the everyday and turn this vacant anonymity into significant, structural form. The poem offers an example, by metamorphosing the mollusc and the other stuff of nature into a contorted poetic landscape by a 'structural discipline', which stiffens the ordinary into poetic form. The speaker is aware of the compromises of rendering experience and observation in poetic form, distilled in the contradiction of trying to 'make love and logic mix' (*CP*, 306). The poetic process is what she calls in the final stanza of the poem (describing the production of carbon) a crystallisation of the ordinary, and a place where paradox can function without being rendered sensible by logic. Here, paradox and contradiction are enabled by the artificial constraints and labour of the production of the poem. As she puts it in the following poem in the *Collected Poems*, 'Metamorphoses of the Moon': 'For most exquisite truths are artifice / framed in disciplines of fire and ice / which conceal incongruous / elements like dirty socks and scraps' (*CP*, p. 307).

Many of Plath's poems start with riffs on language, phrases and sounds, which then lead to a flowering form. Two such poems are 'Crossing the Water' and 'Among the Narcissi', in which visual and phonetic patterns generate an internal development of imagery. The myth of a perfecting crafts-person likes to turn moments of developing and unfinished experimentalism into the fallacy of the 'finished product', laboured over until burnished clean; the cracks of effort ironed out. But to view a poem this way is to lessen its impact, by pretending that thought *precedes* language. In other words, the notion that this is finished product implies all the thought happens elsewhere, whereas what we are reading is a poet thinking through and with language. 'Pure? What does it mean?', as Plath writes in 'Fever 103°' (*CP* 231). As such, the formal processes are the traces of cognition working itself out as the poem unfolds. Finished aesthetics is often a pretence to hide real and violent offence; to fence off hurt and dirt in the niceties of clean literature. Plath herself invested in this myth, time and time again; but she was a product of her time. Such an active model of language also allows for something else that dour critics of Plath forget: for moments of levity, play, wit and irony; we cannot kill the wit by semantic and mythopoetic constriction. 'Sliding shut on some quick thing / The constriction killing me also', as she puts it in 'The Rabbit Catcher' (*CP* 194).

Plath's Multiplicity

Forrest-Thomson revelled in the moments of phonic and visual play, of puns and witty internally generated images and words in many of Plath's poems in *Winter Trees*. Plath's virtuosity with poetic form and artifice are abundantly displayed in a range of poems ('The Tour', 'Ariel', 'Purdah', 'Mary's Song' and 'Childless Woman', for example). Indeed, many of these poems resemble those by H. D. or Mina Loy, featuring hard-edged or craggy phrases filtered through a wickedly incisive intellect. The last lines of her poem 'Edge' (the final poem in the main section of *Collected Poems*) illustrates her inhabitation of language and form and how this, before content, generates the process of poetic composition. The last two lines read: 'She is used to this sort of thing. / Her blacks crackle and drag' (*CP* 273). The two-line stanzas of the poem alternate between resigned and often deliberately banal or weary description and summative phrases that inflect the prosy first lines. The lines are reminiscent of Pound's 'In a station of the metro' and Plath's complex, contorted and taut lines of this period certainly attain the sharpness and brevity of so-called imagist poetry. We might read the cryptic last line – 'Her blacks crackle and drag' – as generated purely from the previous assonance patterns – /əː/ /a/ /a/ /a/ /aː/. And the line challenges us to read it this way. We could thus treat it as a phonic transcription of previous poetic pattern; or, to make this meaningful, a record of a resignation into the solace of semi-nonsense. Even if this reading is unconvincing, we must allow for such interpretations in order to appreciate the ways in which Plath inhabits poetic form, without trying to turn these 'blacks' and 'crackles' and 'drag' into obvious and restrictive symbols of decay.

Plath's experimentation with a variety of styles throughout her life amounts to what might be called her 'unique multiplicity'. Such multiplicity lends itself to Rose's and others' characterisation of Plath as 'inconsistent', but it has the added bonus of supplying textual and formal evidence for how those inconsistencies play out in poetic form. In concentrating on her style, we get a picture of a mind working in and through poetry (as well as testing her stylistic mettle against those of other poets), and whose poetic intelligence was restless, often manic but always meticulously worked out. If, as Hughes suggests in his introduction to the 1982 *Journals*, 'Sylvia Plath was a person of many masks', some of which 'were camouflage cliché facades, defensive mechanisms, involuntary', while other were 'deliberate poses, attempts to find the keys to one style or another',[19] we should not just dismiss these poses, as Hughes does, as stages towards her expression of some sort of natural truth. We should embrace the eclecticism, eccentricity and contradictions of these textual masks, and try to get to grips with the linguistic characteristics of each 'pose', the better to understand her styles.

As Plath writes in 'The Colossus' of her attempt to patch together another broken bust: 'I shall never get you put together entirely / Pieced, glued, and properly jointed' (*CP* 129). Similarly, 'Poem for a Birthday', we might remember, is several pieces of experimental pastiche brought together with no discernable unity and ends with the ambiguous image of, 'Ten fingers shape a bowl for shadows. / My mendings itch. There is nothing to do. / I shall be good as new' (*CP* 137). Sutures itch, but stoical tolerance will pay off; the discomfort is evidence that repair, perhaps even regeneration, is taking place. 'What am I to make of these contradictions?', a voice asks in 'An Appearance' (*CP* 189). To which the answer is: nothing, except to observe their formal and dialectical clashes. As Forrest-Thomson puts it after her discussion of Plath's poem 'Purdah' in the concluding section of *Poetic Artifice*: 'The only coherence, finally, is on the level of technique. [...] This means that [a poet] has all the tricks of rhetoric and the skills of language but [they] must not make the mistake of thinking that they solve anything.'[20] If we stay with Plath's technique and try to map and describe its formal contradictions, we stay safely in a textual realm and avoid consolidating and perpetuating bad myths about poetic practice.

Notes

1. Veronica Forrest-Thomson, review of Sylvia Plath's *Winter Trees* (London: Faber and Faber, 1971). Unpublished typescript. In the Veronica Forrest-Thomson Archive, Girton College Library, Cambridge. For a further discussion of Forrest-Thomson's poetic theory, particularly in relation to her reading of Plath's work, see the final chapter of Farmer, *Veronica Forrest-Thomson*, 159–99.
2. Veronica Forrest-Thomson, unpublished letter to Paul Buck, editor of *Curtains* magazine, dated 25 July 1972. In the Veronica Forrest-Thomson Archive, Girton College Library, Cambridge.
3. Britzolakis, '*Ariel* and Other Poems', 107, 108.
4. Britzolakis, '*Ariel* and Other Poems', 108.
5. Rose, *The Haunting*, xvi.
6. Rose, *The Haunting*, 10.
7. Lowell, 'Foreword' to *Ariel*, ix.
8. Nelson, 'Plath, History and Politics', 22. Nelson is citing *J* 569.
9. Veronica Forrest, 'My Attitudes and Beliefs', unpublished. In the Veronica Forrest-Thomson Archive, Girton College Cambridge library.
10. Eliot, 'Tradition and the Individual Talent', 41.
11. Forrest, 'My Attitudes and Beliefs'.
12. Nelson, 'Plath, History and Politics', 22.
13. Wagner-Martin, 'Plath and Contemporary American Poetry', 54.
14. Wagner-Martin, 'Plath and Contemporary American Poetry', 56, 57, 58.
15. Wagner-Martin, 'Plath and Contemporary American Poetry', 57.

16. Adcock, *The Faber Book of Twentieth Century Women's Poetry*, 5.
17. Axelrod, 'The Poetry of Sylvia Plath', 74.
18. Axelrod, 'The Poetry of Sylvia Plath', 73.
19. Hughes, *The Journals of Sylvia Plath* (1982), xiv.
20. Forrest-Thomson, *Poetic Artifice*, 86.

CHAPTER 32

British and American Editions of Ariel and The Bell Jar

Elena Rebollo-Cortés

As material and historical vehicles of meaning, the editions of Sylvia Plath's works are relevant to our understanding of her literary afterlife. Throughout the decades, editions have contributed to the critical framework within which we interpret her texts, and which help to shape her image as a writer. At the intersection of Plath Studies with Material Bibliography, this chapter shifts the focus from the text to the book to explore the material context of the most significant British and US editions of *Ariel* and *The Bell Jar*, perhaps her two best-known books. These key works have had a wider readership and presence in the literary market, and their editions have played a major role in the creation and perpetuation of Plath's identification as a tragic figure. This chapter follows the trail of noted Plath scholars Anita Helle, Susan R. Van Dyne, Lynda K. Bundtzen and Tracy Brain in examining how book design elements such as covers, back covers and other paratexts such as blurbs, descriptions or forewords have defined Plath's posthumous identity and prompted readings that blur the lines between poetry, fiction and biography.[1]

Ariel: British Editions (1965–2010)

As a consequence of its intricate publication history, *Ariel* exists in two different versions. Not until 2004 was Plath's own arrangement and selection of poems made available in print to readers. By then, the version of *Ariel* published in 1965 – resulting from Ted Hughes's editorial changes to her manuscript – had long-turned Plath into one of the most acclaimed poets of the twentieth century, its longer circulation in the literary market weaving a richer paratextual tapestry and a deeper influence on many generations of readers.[2]

The front cover of the first hardback edition of *Ariel* provides a prime example of Berthold Wolpe's distinctive designs for Faber and Faber. Its bold combination of blue, white and red along white lettering binds Plath's work and name to Faber's reputation for literary excellence.[3] Plath's new status is confirmed by the back cover of this edition, as she is included for the first time in the list of Faber Poets featured there, a canon reserved for the authors that epitomise the symbolic capital of this prestigious publishing house.

Plath's death becomes crucial in this edition, mentioned both in her biographical note and in the blurbs in the inside front cover. The first one, by A. E. Dyson, reads: 'Sylvia Plath's poems, written just before her death in 1963, have impressed themselves on many readers with the force of myth.'[4] Taken from his 1964 editorial in *Critical Quarterly*, these words form in readers' minds the long-lasting connection between Plath, death, poetry and myth, later to be perpetuated by Robert Lowell in American editions.[5] In the second blurb Al Alvarez labels Plath's verse 'violent without any deliberate exploitation of horrors' and declares that her poems are 'works of great artistic purity'.[6] This excerpt is taken from Alvarez's 1965 review 'Poetry in Extremis', in which he interprets *Ariel* through a framework that is dominated by the bond between art and violence.[7] Alvarez's ideas were far-reaching and portrayed Plath as the tragic victim of her poetic gift.[8] Dyson and Alvarez had the power and authority to mould Plath's literary reputation and were shapers of opinion in later British and American editions of *Ariel*.

After the 1970s paperback editions, Faber reissued *Ariel* under Pentagram's new design in 1983.[9] The picture of a vase of tulips on its front cover becomes a visual reference to the poem 'Tulips', although it also reflects the convention in book design of using flowers and other natural elements to represent female writers and their works. Interestingly, other symbolic transactions can be unveiled from the paratexts on the back cover. The first one reads: 'The poems in this book, including many of her best known such as "Lady Lazarus", "Daddy" and "Fever 103°" were all written between the publication in 1960 of Sylvia Plath's first book *The Colossus*, and her death in 1963.' In just a few lines, Faber capitalises not only on Plath's death but also on her myth by projecting her image as 'Lady Lazarus' who made dying an art, the Electra who penned 'Daddy' and the poet ravaged by 'Fever 103°', challenging the frontiers between poetry and reality, poet and poetic persona. These associations between poetry and death are echoed in the blurb, another fragment from Alvarez's 'Poetry in Extremis', where he describes the *Ariel* poems as 'despairing, vengeful and destructive' but also 'clever, sardonic, hardminded'.[10]

From a historical perspective, this edition still frames *Ariel* through the unaltered critical perspective of extremism: death and violence as the defining characteristics of these poems. In terms of design, the book's renewed image shows a stark paratextual contrast: the beauty of the tulips featured on the front cover, the ideas of despair, revenge and destruction on the back.[11] Finally, the mention of Plath's death prompts biographical readings, reinforced by a process of mythification deeply entwined with three of her most popular poems. This identification of Plath with the lyrical subject of her poems through the idea of death culminates in the 1999 and 2001 editions of *Ariel*, which feature on their back covers the lines of 'Lady Lazarus': 'Dying / Is an art, like everything else. / I do it exceptionally well.'[12] For readers who think of her as Lady Lazarus, Plath's voice is almost rising from the book itself.

Sarah Young's design for the 2010 edition of *Ariel* is a nocturnal landscape built on key imagery evoked in Plath's poems: the moon, trees, the sea, the night, flowers and bees, among other symbols, are used to translate *Ariel* into images. The result is a mesmerising visual composition as unsettling and fascinating as the poems themselves, and one that celebrates Plath as a poet. On the back cover, the lines from 'Lady Lazarus' have given way to the opening lines of 'Cut', showcasing Plath's wit and humour. Finally, its short book description informs readers that '*Ariel* (1965) contains many of Sylvia Plath's best-known poems, written in an extraordinary burst of creativity just before her death in 1963.'[13] Again, the paratextual elements provide a prism of interpretation, though this time the book highlights Plath's poetic universe rather than her death.

Ariel: American Editions (1966–1999)

Ariel was published in the United States in 1966, only one year after the British edition. A comparative paratextual analysis of these two first editions unveils meaningful parallels. Both feature blurbs by A. E. Dyson and Al Alvarez, indicative of a transatlantic critical discourse rooted in the association between poetry and death. In fact, the quote by Dyson printed in the first British edition has been included in all American editions of *Ariel* from 1966 to the present day, perpetuating this interpretative prism for generations of readers. As for Alvarez, this edition features the closing remarks of his 1963 BBC radio tribute 'Sylvia Plath', in which he established the path of future Plath criticism.[14] The 'poems read as if they were written posthumously', he says. And 'poetry of this order is a murderous art',[15] he concludes, depicting Plath as an ill-fated genius.

George Steiner builds on this idea in his 1965 review of *Ariel*, significantly entitled 'Dying is an Art'.[16] In the fragment of the review printed in this edition he asserts that the *Ariel* poems 'take tremendous risks', and they are 'a bitter triumph' for Plath 'could not return from them'. These quotes by British critics are featured on the back jacket, creating a polyphonic space in which *Ariel* is introduced to American readers under the auspices of the *Times Literary Supplement*, which refers to it as 'one of the most marvellous volumes of poetry published for a long time'.[17]

Regarding the iconic front cover, it is worth noting that it has remained almost unaltered in the US literary market since 1966. Ellen Raskin's design achieves high visual impact through her choice of bold black capitals for the title, while the calculated layout of the textual elements at the bottom of the cover establishes a key association between Sylvia Plath and Robert Lowell. Despite the dividing line and the different colour used, both names are linked typographically and symbolically. Not only is his the leading canonising voice in this edition but he is also a major indicator of the position Plath occupies in the American literary map. That is to say, her connection with Lowell places her in the pantheon of confessional poets.

On the front and inside cover of *Ariel*, the opening lines of Lowell's preface lead readers into the book through one of the most influential thresholds of interpretation for Plath's work. As the most celebrated confessional poet in the US, Lowell's voice is invested with timeless defining power, turning American editions of *Ariel* into pivotal vehicles of her mythification. Such is the importance given to his words that they appear on the cover of this edition: 'In these poems, written in the last month of her life and often rushed out at the rate of two or three a day, Sylvia Plath becomes herself, becomes something imaginary, newly, wildly and subtly created.' On the inside cover, the blurb continues 'hardly a person at all, or a woman, certainly not another "poetess" but one of those super-real, hypnotic, great classical heroines'. During the next fifty years, Plath's poems would remain firmly placed within the double framework of confessionalism and fatalism, and her authorial image shaped as a tragic myth. Tragic because as Lowell states 'these poems are playing Russian roulette with six cartridges in the cylinder . . .' A myth because her poetry is infused with the power to transform her into a: 'Dido, Phaedra or Medea'.[18] The paratexts of this book are thus charged with ominous fatalism, culminating in the photograph of Plath that follows her biography on the inside jacket. Taken in Cambridge in 1957 and featuring a young Plath staring intensely into the camera, it would become one of her most iconic pictures and a visual epitome – almost a stock image – of her myth as a tragic woman writer.[19]

All the paratexts included on the internal covers disappeared in the transition of this edition to paperback, but its design would not be updated until 1999. However, instead of creating a brand-new image for the book, Mark Cohen's proposal preserves most of its original features, like the title lettering and some of the blurbs printed on the front and back cover. The number of blurbs is, nevertheless, reduced and, for the first time, Lowell's words are not printed on the front but on the top of the back cover, their prominence somewhat lessened by the move but still holding a position of importance, which is reinforced by a new use of italics for his words. Lowell, Dyson and Steiner's visions of Plath as a near-mythical figure still resonate with readers, as they continue to perpetuate Plath's tragic image and the interpretation of *Ariel* through the unaltered critical framework connecting poetry and death that originated in the 1960s. Plath's photograph, taken by Rollie McKenna in 1959 (and now in the National Portrait Gallery in London) is placed between the critics' words and her biography, illustrating the fateful narrative woven around her.[20]

The Bell Jar: British Editions (1966–2013)

The Bell Jar was published under Sylvia Plath's name for the first time in 1966, in an edition that is now regarded as one of Faber's most celebrated designs. Shirley Tucker's memorable representation of madness through concentric circles graced the book's cover until the 1980s and would later return to it for 2013 and 2015 editions, in a movement that brings together past and present in *The Bell Jar's* publication history.[21] As for the back cover, the 1966 edition capitalises on the same discourse printed on the inside cover of *Ariel*. Thus, the novel and the poetry collection are paratextually linked, as if both works together – poetry and prose – would help readers understand the dramatic final events in Plath's life.

During the 1970s, Robert Scholes's 1971 review 'Esther Came Back Like a Retreaded Tire', published in the *New York Times Book Review*, would provide the critical coordinates for interpreting *The Bell Jar* in Britain and the US.[22] Early Faber paperbacks feature a lengthy excerpt of his text as its main back-cover blurb, its first line again stressing the connection between the novel and *Ariel*: 'it is a fine novel, as bitter and remorseless as her last poems'. A little further on, the biographical reading is fully revealed, as Scholes pinpoints the parallelisms between Esther's and Plath's life, inviting readers to interpret the book as a biography: 'We follow Esther

Greenwood's personal life from her summer job with "Ladies' Day" magazine, back through her days at New England's largest school for women,
and forward through her attempted suicide, her bad treatment at one
asylum and her good treatment at another, to her final re-entry into the
world like a used tire'.

In 1982, Faber and Faber reissued *The Bell Jar* with a fresh image. In this
edition Donna Muir combines vibrant colouring with Plath's personal
photographs. The book cover features her 1955 Smith College graduation
photo while the back cover shows a collage of Plath against a background of
buildings representing New York. In the original photo, however, Plath
poses outside her home in the spring of 1954, right before her return to
Smith following her suicide attempt and treatment. Both pictures are
included in *Letters Home* (1975), and illustrate the period between summer
1953 and 12 August 1955, roughly the time when the events narrated in the
novel occurred. The presence of this photographic material in the edition
sends a clear message to readers: this is Plath's own story, fiction and
biography symbolically juxtaposed through Muir's colouring of Plath's
black-and-white pictures. On the back cover, a short quote from Stephen
Wall's 1966 review of the novel reads: 'This terse account of an American
girl's breakdown and treatment gains its considerable power from an
objectivity that is extraordinary considering the nature of the material.'[23]
The whole design of the edition portrays Plath as Esther Greenwood,
making it impossible not to identify her as the American girl to whom
he is referring.

More recent editions of *The Bell Jar* reflect transformations in the
packaging of the novel. For instance, Pentagram's design for the cover of
the 1999 edition combines a flower with Mathana Yater's photograph of
a young girl. Yet despite visually establishing a clear distance between
author and narrator and presenting *The Bell Jar* as a coming-of-age
novel, the blurb on the back cover still invites biographical readings, stating
that the novel 'broke existing boundaries between fiction and reality'. It
continues that '[it] helped to make Plath an enduring feminist icon. It was
published under a pseudonym a few weeks before the author's suicide.'[24]

This reference to Plath as a feminist icon is, however, missing from
Pentagram's 2001 design, which features another photograph of Plath
posing with a crystal ball taken in 1955 when she was similar in age to
Esther. On the back cover readers find a quote from Scholes's review used
in 1970s editions, but the text is now shorter as the detailed enumeration of
biographical links between the novel and Plath's life has disappeared.
Instead, the focus seems to be shifted to other aspects of the novel: 'in

looking at the madness of the world and the world of madness it forces us to consider the greatest question posed by all truly realistic fiction: What is reality and how can it be confronted?'

Interestingly, feminist readings have been highlighted again in Faber's 2009 and 2013 editions, both designed by Mark Swan, as their back cover blurbs emphasise how its protagonist 'finds herself spiralling into depression and eventually a suicide attempt, as she grapples with difficult relationships and a society that refuses to take women's aspirations seriously'. Once more, the novel is defined as 'partially based on Plath's own life' and her breakdown and suicide central to its interpretation, however this time going beyond the limits of the personal or the biographical as part of the wider discourse of modern feminism.

Nevertheless, the controversy raging around Swan's cover design for the fiftieth anniversary edition of the novel overshadowed this message. His cover design, a picture of a young 1950s girl powdering her face,[25] was considered to project a frivolous image of Plath's novel, undermining its underlying message by reducing it to chick-lit.[26] Not surprisingly, all the online and media attention generated by this cover helped to boost the book's sales, rekindle contemporary readers' interest and foster the critical conversation around the novel fifty years after its publication.

The Bell Jar: American Editions (1971–2006)

The high demand of readers, along with the pressures and legal realities of the literary market, played a major role in shaping the publication of *The Bell Jar* in the US. Given its immediate success, it is worth considering the extent to which the design choices for its first American edition in 1971 contributed not only to making it a bestseller but also to establishing enduring biographical readings. Regarding marketing strategies, this edition presents an intriguing design in which fiction, biography and Plath's mythification are inextricably entwined. By the 1970s, Plath's image as a tragic poet was already fully blown and *The Bell Jar* regarded as an account of her psychological demise. As advertised in the inside back cover: 'Such deep penetration into the dark and harrowing corners of the psyche is rare in any novel . . . It reveals so much about the sources of Sylvia Plath's own tragedy that its publication must be considered a landmark in literature.'[27]

Amy Isbey Duevell's design for the front and back cover reinforces this idea, seamlessly blending fiction and reality through the combination of Plath's photograph from the August 1953 issue of *Mademoiselle* with the fragment of the novel that reflects Esther's emotional turmoil while having her photo taken: 'I didn't know why I was going to cry, but I knew that if anybody spoke to me or looked at me too closely the tears would fly out of my eyes and the sobs would fly out of my throat and I'd cry for a week.' Plath's portrait holding a paper rose and smiling for the camera mirrors the situation described in the text, thus conveying the powerful illusion of *The Bell Jar* as fully autobiographical.[28] Such reading is perpetuated by another paratextual element present in American editions of the novel since 1971: Lois Ames's biographical note. Illustrated by Plath's drawings, Ames's text underlines that 'the central themes of Sylvia Plath's early life are the basis for *The Bell Jar*'.[29] Such an all-encompassing commodification of Plath's life and image proved remarkably successful in terms of book sales, and set the tone for later editions. Thus, the novel is defined on the covers of the 1970s Bantam Books paperback editions as 'the heartbreaking story of a talented young woman who descends into madness' while the back cover shows the opening lines of Scholes's 1971 review: '*The Bell Jar* is a novel about Sylvia Plath's 20th year: about how she tried to die, and how they stuck her together with glue.' Fiction, biography and poetry converge in the interpretation of the novel, while Scholes's reference to suicide and his citing of 'Daddy' conjure up powerful echoes of Plath's myth in readers' minds.

HarperCollins's 1996 twenty-fifth anniversary edition of *The Bell Jar* displays both new and old elements in terms of book design and paratexts. For example, the book's front and back cover no longer display Plath's photograph, even though the image of the rose and the lettering echo the first edition. Inside the book, a foreword by Frances McCullough offers insight into the context of the novel, its publication history and its reception in the US. As she observes: 'For readers, the posthumous publications were of course seen as messages from the grave, clues to the mystery of what really happened.'[30] She also explains that when the novel was published, 'Confessional literature was in vogue. And there was a new fascination with death (. . .) depression and mental illness were subjects much on people's minds as well.'[31] Such background information sheds a new light on the book description featured on the inside front and back covers of the first American edition, more specifically its emphasis on the mental state of its protagonist: 'Step by careful step, Sylvia Plath takes us with Esther (. . .) eventually into the madness itself. The reader is drawn into her breakdown with such intensity that her insanity becomes completely real and even rational.'[32] Twenty-five years later, the same words are reproduced on the inside front cover and a new paragraph inserted in the book description

perpetuates biographical readings: 'The Bell Jar is a largely autobiographical work about Plath's own summer of 1953, when she was a guest editor at
Mademoiselle and went through a breakdown.'[33]

On the back cover, critics' comments on the novel are printed under the
heading 'Praise for The Bell Jar' and focus on Plath's ability to capture
madness in writing. The first one brings together two nearby lines in
Scholes's 1971 review: 'Esther Greenwood's account of her years in the
bell jar is as clear and readable as it is witty and disturbing . . . [This] is not
a potboiler, nor a series of ungrateful caricatures; it is literature'.[34]
The second one, from another 1971 review, states: 'The first-person narrative fixes us there, in the doctor's office, in the asylum, in the madness.'
And even though readers encountered these blurbs in 1996, they can still be
found in the back cover of later 1999, 2003, 2005 and 2006 editions, thus
maintaining to the present day the critical prism through which the novel
was first read in the 1970s.

From The Colossus to the latest two-volume Letters, every edition has its
own fascinating story to tell, especially when considered in relation to
Plath's publications and her literary afterlife. As this bibliographical
approach to Ariel and The Bell Jar has shown, editions provide much
more than mere physical support for Plath's works. They unravel, in fact,
the marketing and symbolic strategies publishing houses use to create and
perpetuate certain critical frameworks for biographical readings and interpretations of her texts. As historical objects, books preserve a material
context that is crucial to understanding how Plath's authorial identity
has been defined from 1960 to the present: a tragic figure, a confessional
poet, a feminist writer, a myth.

Notes

1. See Helle, 'Reading the Paratexts of Sylvia's Unabridged Journals', 94–106;
   Van Dyne, Revising Life, 7–10; Bundtzen, The Other Ariel, 1–7; and Brain, The
   Other Sylvia Plath, 1–12.
2. For a definition of paratexts, see Genette, Paratexts, 1–2.
3. Connolly, Eighty Years, 122.
4. Ariel, Faber and Faber, 1965.
5. Wagner-Martin, Critical Heritage, 11.
6. Ariel, Faber and Faber, 1965.
7. Wagner-Martin, Critical Heritage, 55.
8. Alvarez, Beyond This Fiddle, 57.
9. Connolly, Eighty Years, 212.
10. Ariel, Faber and Faber, 1983.

11. *Ariel*, Faber and Faber, 1983.
12. *Ariel*, Faber and Faber, 1999, 2001.
13. *Ariel*, Faber and Faber, 2010.
14. Alvarez, *Beyond This Fiddle*, 45–58.
15. *Ariel*, Harper & Row, 1966.
16. Newman (ed.), *Art of Sylvia Plath*, 211–12.
17. *Ariel*, Harper & Row, 1966.
18. *Ariel*, Harper & Row, 1966, xiii.
19. This picture was first used in the October 1963 special issue of *The Review*. Since then, it has been used on the cover of many books by or on Plath, for instance, the 1998 Anchor edition *of The Journals of Sylvia Plath* or Faber and Faber's 2000 edition of *The Journals of Sylvia Plath: 1950–1962*.
20. *Ariel*, Harper & Row, 1999.
21. Shirley Tucker on *The Bell Jar*. Interview recorded April 2012. Available on vimeo.com/55871716.
22. Alexander (ed.), *Ariel Ascending*, 130–3.
23. *BJ*, Faber and Faber, 1982.
24. *BJ*, Faber and Faber, 1999.
25. Swan's two cover designs can be seen here: kid-ethic.com/#the-bell-jar-5.
26. For the controversy about this cover see Grocott, '*The Bell Jar's* New Cover Is Just Perfect' and Jordison, 'Don't Judge *The Bell Jar* by Its Cover'.
27. *BJ*, Harper & Row, 1971.
28. Brain, *The Other Plath*, 8–9.
29. *BJ*, Harper & Row, 1971, 293.
30. *BJ*, HarperCollins, 1996, xviii.
31. *BJ*, HarperCollins, 1996, xv.
32. *BJ*, Harper & Row, 1971.
33. *BJ*, Harper Perennial, 1996.
34. *BJ*, Harper Perennial, 1996.

CHAPTER 33

After Plath: The Legacy of Influence

Fiona Sampson

Sylvia Plath is among the most widely read of twentieth-century poets. Substantial editions of her work have been published in thirty languages, from Arabic to Vietnamese.[1] She has been cited by figures as diverse as Lemony Snicket (there's a 'Plath Pass' in *A Series of Unfortunate Events*)[2] and Lady Gaga (in her 2009 track 'Dance in the Dark'). Among the wider readership that creates cultures – students, media professionals, artists, intellectuals – she is one of the most-read Anglophone poets.

Some of this may have to do with the famous life story, made more famous still by Christine Jeffs's 2003 biopic *Sylvia*. Like Mary Shelley, Sylvia Plath has a literary reputation that has both suffered and benefitted from being linked with that of a poet spouse who, in her lifetime at least, was the more famous figure. Specialist readers could feel the life is the enemy of the work it has sometimes seemed to eclipse. Yet in a world where, even today, readers, and critics, assess writing more harshly when it has a woman's name attached to it,[3] it should come as little surprise if that fascinating hybrid, Hughes-and-Plath – like that earlier and significantly analogous compound, The Shelleys – is what clears discursive space for the work itself.[4]

Whilst Mary Shelley prepared (and on pertinent occasion surreptitiously briefed) the posthumous editions that ensured Percy Bysshe's reputation,[5] it was Ted Hughes who prepared the posthumous editions that made Sylvia Plath's work widely available. He was also able to use his personal poetic reputation as leverage to ensure she would in future be published alongside him, by Faber and Faber, that most reputable of imprints.

The conspiracy theories surrounding Hughes's work of selective literary editorship belong, like complaints that Mary Shelley was insufficiently scholarly in the editions she prepared, with a childish notion that there exists a kind of untouchable artistic identity, a spring of authenticity, which both transcends the thoughtful business of literary genre and is easily and instantly recognisable. As Percy Bysshe Shelley put it, in *A Defence of Poetry*:

> It is impossible to read the compositions of the most celebrated writers of the present day without being startled with the electric life which burns within their words. They measure the circumference and sound the depths of human nature with a comprehensive and all-penetrating spirit, and they are themselves perhaps the most sincerely astonished at its manifestations [. . .] Poets are the hierophants of an unapprehended inspiration.[6]

Shelley's essay was itself first published as part of his wife's careful posthumous curation of his reputation. Nearly two centuries later, this tenacious, Romantic concept is strikingly echoed within Plath reception. Even Seamus Heaney, while acknowledging the technical apprenticeship that led to Plath's 'extreme extension of the imagist mode', can't quite resist. The *Ariel* poems, he writes, 'were written quickly and they transmit to the reader something of the unexpectedness of their own becoming. [. . .] There is nothing *poetically* flawed about Plath's work. What may finally limit it is its dominant theme of self-discovery and self-definition.'[7] This is despite the fact that, as scholars including Helen Vendler, Henry Hart and Toni Saldívar point out, Heaney's own poetry in *North* is directly informed by Plath's imagery, engagement with violence and even specific vocabulary.[8]

The Romanticisation of Plath's literary work as spontaneous creation poses a number of difficulties for the poet's literary legacy. One is that it sets up a feedback loop with the over-emphasis on her life story. A second is that it runs the risk of pathologising the imagination and creative risk-taking of a woman writer. Such literal pathologising can be seen in the work of theorists like Susan Kavaler-Adler, who argues that confessional writing by women is a kind of bad behaviour.[9] Instead of responsible reparation, she says, poets like Plath and Anne Sexton are indulging in mere repetition of the hurts they reiterate. Such a critique understands techniques of transformation – imagery, metaphor and register – not as poetics but as involuntary autosuggestion.

Poets may be expected to 'read past' such hurdles. After all, they understand that poems are made not born. But the Romanticisation of Plath is more thoroughgoing still. It continues in a critical reception that tends to isolate Plath's work, reading it in terms of its differences from that of her peers, rather than its continuities with them. Yet it's clearly contradictory to view Plath as *socially* context-laden while *creatively* a recluse. Contradictory: and inaccurate. Even the most cursory reading of her life makes clear how, from her school days, her approach to writing was outward-turned. She knew early that she wanted to be published, and in the best places, as well as to win awards. This is a leitmotif in her letters. 'If only I can meet all the opportunities! [. . .] I just can't stand the idea of being mediocre' (*LH* 57) the eighteen-year-old writes home, after finding her Smith College scholarship is given by the writer Olive Higgins Prouty, whom she will make into a lifelong mentor. A week before her death, she tells her mother, 'There is nothing like the BBC in America—over there they do not publish my stuff as they do here [. . .] I [. . .] have a chance for three weeks in May to be on the BBC Critics program at about $150 a week, a fantastic break I hope I can make good on' (*LH* 498).

But the real harm a Romantic, isolationist reception of Sylvia Plath does is not to her literary biography but to her creative legacy. It's as if we believe an exceptional mind was at play in such occult, unfathomable ways that there's nothing to learn from it, in technical terms at least: indeed, that no poets writing since Plath *have* learnt anything from her. But Plathian poetics, that set of conscious techniques and consistent strategies, have influenced a number of poets.

Sylvia Plath found teaching creative writing demanding, and – doubtless in part because she died young – left no substantial articulation of her poetics. But, forced to fall back on the primary evidence of her poetry, we can see where her early work paid its own literary debts. For example, we hear Marianne Moore, the possible mentor she courted in 1955, especially in two of the poems Plath read in March of that year for Moore and two other judges at the Irene Glascock Poetry Contest at Mount Holyoke. In 'Danse Macabre' and 'Love is a Parallax', the spikiness is ironised away by a quizzically detached, hyper-intellectual diction. Poems like 'Owl' and 'Whiteness I Remember', written in mid-1958 when Plath had been attending Robert Lowell's creating writing class, echo the older poet's scene-setting strategies as Plath articulates inner worlds in concrete terms. From 1956 a formal kinship of both rhythm and register with Hughes's poetry dawns. 'Pursuit' is a bravura poem with a highly memorable opening: 'One day I'll have my death of him' (*CP* 22) is a line all Plath's own. But the endlessly pacing panther who pursues its speaker is recognisably kin to Hughes's 'Jaguar' in his 1957 debut *The Hawk in the Rain*; and when the burning creature follows her into 'the tower of my fears', and she hears its tread 'Coming up and up the stairs' (*CP* 23), transforms Hughes's 'The Thought-Fox', of the same collection, from a figure of redemptive freedom to a horrifying – and literal – dead-end.[10]

In 1963 the traffic of influence may still have seemed fairly one-way, at least to the young couple themselves. But after Plath's death, once Hughes was preparing her poetry for publication – and perhaps, too, after she had become a figure no longer of daily life but purely of psychic process – tropes begin to travel in the opposite direction. In 1967, Hughes published *Wodwo*, the first collection of his in which landscape, myth and psyche are fiercely inter-fused, and the first in which his characteristic loose-limbed free verse appears, moving across genres between animal poems like 'Gnat-Psalm', and 'Skylarks', monster myths like 'Gog' and 'Song of a Rat', and even appearing in the loving 'Full Moon and Little Frieda'. The noise of this versification, in other words, has got in behind the apparent content. It's the noise of a distinct poetic project, and one we recognise: Sylvia Plath was a psycho-geographer par excellence. Her landscapes glitter with pathetic fallacy, and not only in obvious 'countryside' poems like September 1961's 'Blackberrying' and 'Finisterre'. In the later poems, 'Poppies in July' are 'little hell flames' (*CP* 203), while at night 'the garden / Stiffens and odors bleed' (*CP* 273) in 'Edge'. The interpenetration is physical, too: ovaries become trees in a childless woman's 'womb' where 'The tree of life and the tree of life' release 'their moons, month after month, to no purpose' (*CP* 262–3).

The clenched poetics of *Crow*, Hughes's next, signature collection, are all phrasal line-breaks yet undiscursive, image-led diction: straight out of late Plath poems like 'Child' or 'Paralytic'. The clangour to these poems of psychic exploration, with their hurly-burly of images that aren't carefully extended and matched but unexpectedly juxtaposed, is audibly Plathian. Though metaphors may not be sustained, register is – in fact, it's sustained partly by just this exciting crunching together of apparently dissonant materials – and this, too, is a late Plath technique. 'Balloons' may not be the most profoundly exploratory poem in the Plathian canon, but even it has it subject shape-shift between the various incarnations of the title: 'soul-animals', 'invisible air', 'Yellow cathead, blue fish', 'queer moons' and the heartening 'Globes' (*CP* 271).

Plath's poetic legacy starts early, then, with Hughes – and with the poets who have been influenced in turn by him – something I've discussed elsewhere.[11] However the other poets, most notably the women, of Plath's generation who continued to work in Britain – the country, after all, of her poetic emergence – seem to have absorbed little of its influence. This is as one would expect, given the dates of their own debuts. Fleur Adock (1964), Ruth Fainlight (1966) and Elaine Feinstein (1966) or, among the men, members of The Group including Alan

Brownjohn (1954), Peter Porter (1961) and Peter Redgrove (1959) were already formed by the time *Ariel* appeared in 1965.[12] I've written elsewhere[13] about how the highly approachable style of several of this generation seems forged in the new equality of post-war Britain; Plath, of course, grew up in a United States unthreatened by invasion. But these British poets surrounding her as she came of poetic age were also the successors of The Movement and Philip Larkin, and heirs of the Georgian poets and of Thomas Hardy.[14]

Ariel appeared in 1965. The next year, 1966, saw the first publication of Basil Bunting's *Briggflats*, as well as collections by poets like Charles Tomlinson, Elizabeth Jennings, Norman MacCaig, Jon Silkin, Stevie Smith and R. S. Thomas. There's a nubby, psychologically driven character to all this work, both the modernist and lyric, which makes Plath's exploration of internal worlds seem less exceptional than we might be tempted, looking back out of context, to believe. Seamus Heaney's debut *Death of a Naturalist*, the first sounding of the note that would come to dominate in the 1980s and 1990s, also appeared in this year.

So far, so little apparent influence. But turn to poetry of the next decade and there's a step change in poetic colour and risk. By 1975, ten years after *Ariel*, the recognisable patchwork of contemporary British poetics has emerged: ranging from the pop-inflected Liverpool poets to Eavan Boland's narrative lyrics, and from Linton Kwesi Johnson's *Dread, Beat an' Blood*, also released as a dub album, to J. H. Prynne's high modernist *High Pink on Chrome*. Language has become altogether less well behaved. Increasingly baroque in the work of modernists like Geoffrey Hill, it is decompressing in the hands of the Liverpool poets – who by 1977 will include Carol Ann Duffy – and taking on new music in the hands of Black British poets like Johnson, and of Caribbean poets like James Berry and the soon-to-arrive John Agard and Grace Nichols.

It would be absurd to attribute all this to Plath's influence. Numerous cultural influences, including demographic shifts, brought about the widening of British poetics that occurred in the 1970s and 1980s. State-educated post-war baby boomers gained access to higher education (the number of graduates doubled between 1960 and 1970),[15] the Black British community achieved critical mass (rising from 20,900 to 191,600 between 1951 and 1961)[16] and the rise of youth culture meant chart music emerged as increasingly the cultural context of young poets. What it suggests instead is a poetic climate to which Plath's work was able to contribute, and which ensured its contribution would be valued.

Her influence has if anything intensified in the last two decades. A poet who is so widely read as to become pretty much universally known among Anglophone poets becomes part of the toolbox of contemporary poetics. Ways of writing poetry, once known, cannot be unknown. This most widely read of female poets stands both as a kind of gatekeeper and as a permission giver, particularly for women writing poetry in Britain today: 'a model of how to write from deep within the self while being properly and ruthlessly artful',[17] as the poet Lavinia Greenlaw has it. For them Plath, a consummate technician who nevertheless reaches for risky high notes, enlarges the palette and turns up the volume. Among these female poets, of course, is Plath and Hughes's own daughter, the artist and poet Frieda Hughes. Her *Tatler* poem in defence of her parents' privacy, 'My Mother', is directly Plathian in diction.[18] It's no coincidence that most of the other poets mentioned in this chapter are women.

While Plath's style may not make its wholesale way undigested into large numbers of poets' work, it's more than coincidence that certain ways of writing have become possible *after Plath*. One such is celerity. A poem like 'Lesbos', as it casually disposes of matching line-lengths, creates the music of impatience with its colliding, converging and veering end-rhymes, both full and slant, that create an excess, a kind of vortex. In 'Lesbos', the deepening of the vowel sounds from *ee* through *eh* and *uh* to *aw* that Gerard Manley Hopkins elsewhere called 'vowelling on'[19] extends this feeling of vortex, moving through 'pill', 'hell', 'ill', 'beautiful', 'thrill' 'hill', 'spill', 'million' (*CP* 228), 'jewel', 'valuable', 'Animal' to arrive at 'normal' (*CP* 229). I've written elsewhere about the French writer and philosopher Hélène Cixous's strategic celerity,[20] but Plath isn't engaging with essentialist beliefs about the nature of the eternal feminine.[21] Instead, velocity is part of her portraiture of the individual psyche in process: portraiture that, in so far as it is 'staged' by such techniques, could be termed an auto-*persona*; and which belongs in an older tradition than that of confessional verse, alongside the exploratory portrait of the self in process in that truly Romantic project, Jean-Jacques Rousseau's *The Confessions*. A similar waxing and waning celerity can be heard today in, for example, the similarly intimate portraits from US poet Jorie Graham's middle period: in 1993's *Materialism*, long lines map the mind at work in its conscientious daily life; in *Overlord* (2006), irregular, on-rushing lines map the voice of personal prayer.

Another form of engagement with Plath in contemporary verse is image-led rather than argument-led. Plath doesn't *illustrate* what she's saying; instead, her images direct the poem. This is notable in the bee-keeping poems from early October 1962. 'The Bee Meeting', 'The Arrival of the Bee Box', 'Stings', 'The Swarm' and 'Wintering' are by Plath's standards 'what really happened' pieces that might be expected to privilege realist narrative. But even the most chronologically ordered of the set, 'The Bee Meeting', offers transformation after transformation in place of bare sequential narrative, replacing the conventional 'and then ... and then' with 'now ... now' to make of the whole incident one extended present moment. The great set-piece psychodramas like 'Daddy' and 'Edge' are also image-driven. This makes the images they do use more radically apparent. The 'barb wire' (*CP* 223) in 'Daddy', like the monumental 'dead / Body' (*CP* 272) in 'Edge', arrives bare of context: 'The tongue stuck in my jaw. / It stuck in a barb wire snare' (*CP* 223). But once it's there, it creates an opening and a context for the poem's most dangerous reach, into the speaker's very mind, where she finds 'the language obscene' and 'Chuffing me off like a Jew' (*CP* 223). The image itself builds a conceptual-world and tone-world for itself, and it does so not through logical argument but through accumulation ('tongue', 'jaw', 'language'), congruence ('barb wire' moves on from the 'snare' to become the metonym for a death camp) and translation ('chuffing' is both onomatopoeic representation of spoken German and the transport's locomotive).

In other words, these are not mere metaphors but symbols, the engines of thought and experience. Though frowned upon by certain Anglo-Saxon orthodoxies, some poets today continue to structure their poems on the relations symbols create. The Welsh poet Pascale Petit's portraits of her parents as wild creatures – particularly in her most recent collections, *Fauverie* (2014) and *Mama Amazonica* (2017), which deal respectively with the death of her father and an emotionally abusive relationship with her mother – are constructed this way.

In both Plath and Petit, personal fact and emotion are fiercely transfigured by transposition into symbol. This is a very different technique from the way 'confession' is used by North American women poets like Sharon Olds and Louise Glück. Both were born in the early 1940s, midway through the two decades that separate Petit from Plath, and both employ a great deal more narrative structure. Olds's poems have been famously outspoken and, as she says, 'apparently personal', since her 1980 debut *Satan Says*. But as she herself has commented, 'Although I felt, once I read her, that Plath was a great genius, with an IQ of at least double mine [... her] steps were not steps I wanted to put my feet in.'[22] The Glück of 1975's family portrait *The House on Marshland* adopts a more softly spoken, forensic narrative standpoint; later books, like *The Seven Ages* (2001) and *Averno* (2006), increasingly replace narrative with reflection that's not symbol-driven but discursive. Like Plath's, though, Petit's poems do follow symbolic logic. In 'Ortolan', for example, she imagines her father responding to his terminal diagnosis by choosing to eat a roast ortolan, 'the whole singer / in his mouth', letting him taste, in its roasted entrails, the landscapes of everywhere he's lived, so that 'he's flying' home to death, 'his lungs / burning around the mute songbird of his heart'.[23]

Another contemporary British poet who obeys a symbolic logic is Selima Hill. Perhaps relevantly, though ten years older than Petit, she shares with her a background in visual art,[24] a background that Plath also had. Hill's formally unstitched poems are deliberately naïve in tone; something they share with work by Anne Sexton, who as a fellow pupil of Robert Lowell is most often linked with Plath. It's Hill and Sexton, however, who share a tendency to use list forms and repetition to sustain tone – something that's accentuated by their use of relatively short grammatical units. (Hill's affinity with the Sexton who retells dark fairy tales in *Transformations* should be remarked, too.)

'Never Go to Sleep in a Lake' is the title injunction of a poem from 2014's *The Sparkling Jewel of Naturism*, that raises the banner of myth (Raymond Chandler's *The Lady in the Lake*), charges through a list of zoological injunctions (against keeping company with newts/parrots/ snails in a desert) and – as if it had naturalised these high stakes in doing so – swerves back through myth to sexual abuse. Just as with Plath's late poems, though it in fact obeys an expressionist logic, this succession appears at first surreal. Contributing to this impression of surrealism is the wide-ranging character of Plath's symbolic sources, something we observed already in 'Balloons'.[25] These widely spaced images contribute to a sense of Plath's poetics as spontaneous, even artless: something her use of register intensifies. Plath's characteristic high, intense register – think how intense she makes infant experience and frailty appear in 'Child' – generates a sense of immediacy in some readers even as it produces a resistance in others.

Plath's influence has passed into the vocabulary of the poetically possible: in English but potentially in the many languages into which she is translated. Perhaps the best image for this is Plath's own, in 'Stings'. The creative community of a hive is at work: 'Here is my honey-machine, / It will work without thinking' (*CP* 214–15). In the poem it's the workers who ensure the resurrection of the queen: 'Now she is flying / More terrible than she ever was' (*CP* 215). Contemporary poets are far indeed from being drones. But Plath's poetics remain alive, and aloft, in their work.

Notes

1. Steinberg, 'Translations of Sylvia Plath'.
2. 'The orphans have a hard time getting through this pass, named after the poet who committed suicide by sticking her head in an oven', www.npr.org/2011/07/15/6253438/a-series-of-unfortunate-literary-allusions?t=1556049611952. Accessed 5 May 2019.
3. See for instance Mohdin, 'Women Are Horribly Under-Represented'.
4. Enright, 'Diary', 33–35.
5. Mary Shelley prepared three editions of her late husband's work. 1824's *Posthumous Poems of Percy Bysshe Shelley* was withdrawn because Sir Timothy Shelley, her father-in-law, threatened to cut off an allowance. *The Poetical Works of Percy Bysshe Shelley* (1840) and her edition of the prose were both produced after Sir Timothy's death. However, off the record, she also briefed unofficial editions by A. and W. Galignani (1829) and Stephen Hunt (1830).
6. Shelley, 'A Defence of Poetry', 1–57.
7. Heaney, 'The Indefatigable Hoof-taps', 218, 229. All citations from this essay are from Heaney, *Finders Keepers*.
8. See Vendler, *Seamus Heaney*, 45; Hart, *Seamus Heaney*, 79; and Saldívar, 'Gleaning the Unsaid'.
9. Kavaler-Adler, *The Compulsion to Create*.
10. *The Hawk in the Rain* was published in 1957 but the poems were of course written *before* the book appeared.
11. See Sampson, 'Ted Hughes's Literary Legacy'.
12. Plath's 1960 debut, *The Colossus and Other Poems*, had been published to less effect by William Heinemann.
13. See Sampson *Beyond the Lyric*, 12–35.
14. The New Apocalyptics of the 1930s and 1940s modelled themselves on D. H. Lawrence and embraced Dylan Thomas in reaction to this tradition.
15. Warnock et. al., 'Participation Rates'.
16. Ballard, 'Britain's Visible Minorities', 6.
17. Admittedly she is talking primarily about *The Bell Jar*. Greenlaw, 'Sylvia Plath: Reflections on Her Legacy'.
18. Hughes, 'My Mother', 125.
19. Gardner, 'Introduction', xxxi-xxxii.
20. See *The North*, Issue 45, www.poetrybusiness.co.uk/shop/690/489/north-45.
21. Coincidentally, Percy Bysshe Shelley also tried to capture the moment of change, whether social or biological, with onrushing lines that pile up to create sometimes almost indigestible long forms. But poetic influence – its *readability* – is time-limited.

22. Patterson, 'Sharon Olds'.
23. Petit, *Fauverie*, 48.
24. Hill was born into a family of artists and married an artist; Petit trained as a sculptor at the Royal College of Art.
25. 'Winter Trees' (*CP* 257–8) is another example of a poem that comprises multiple symbolic sources. In fifteen short lines, it crams together ink blotters, growth rings, weddings, abortions, weather, pigeons and allusions to Leda and the Pièta.

CHAPTER 34

P(l)athography: Plath and Her Biographers

Heather Clark

'No biographer is compelled to follow his subject into disintegration', wrote Joyce Carol Oates in her 1988 review of David Roberts's *Jean Stafford: A Biography*. Roberts, Oates argued, could have focused on Stafford's 'more scattered, and less dramatic, periods of accomplishment and well being', but instead he chose to expose her life's 'sensational underside'. This was not biography, Oates wrote, but 'pathography': 'Its motifs are dysfunction and disaster, illnesses and pratfalls, failed marriages and failed careers, alcoholism and breakdowns and outrageous conduct. Its scenes are sensational, wallowing in squalor and foolishness; its dominant images are physical and deflating; its shrill theme is "failed promise" if not outright "tragedy".'[1] In 2009, the Oxford professor Hermione Lee, Virginia Woolf's biographer, noted a similar trend in biographies about women: 'Women writers whose lives involved abuse, mental illness, self-harm, suicide, have often been treated, biographically, as victims or psychological case-histories first and as professional writers second.'[2] More recently, the critic Maggie Nelson has argued that a woman who explores depression in her work isn't perceived as 'a shamanistic voyager to the dark side, but a "madwoman in the attic", an abject spectacle'.[3]

Such observations are especially true of Sylvia Plath, a frequent victim of pathography. Since her suicide in 1963, Plath has become a paradoxical symbol of female power and helplessness whose life has been subsumed by her afterlife. Caught in the limbo between icon and cliché, she has been mythologised, and pathologised, in movies, television and biographies as a high priestess of poetry, obsessed with death. These distortions gained momentum in the 1960s when her seminal collection *Ariel* was published. While some critics, like Al Alvarez, saw the book as a watershed moment in post-war poetry, many reviewers did not know what to make of the burning, pulsating metaphors in poems like 'Lady Lazarus', or the chilly imagery of 'Edge'. *Time* called the book a 'jet of flame from a literary dragon who in the last months of her life breathed a burning river of bale across the literary landscape'.⁴ *The Washington Post* dubbed Plath a 'snake lady of misery' in an article entitled 'The Cult of Plath'.⁵ Robert Lowell, in his introduction to *Ariel*, characterised Plath as Medea, hurtling towards her own destruction. Even Plath's closest reader, her husband Ted Hughes, often portrayed her as a passive vessel through which a dangerous muse spoke.

Such caricatures have calcified into the popular, reductive version of Sylvia Plath we all know: the suicidal writer of *The Bell Jar* whose cultish devotees are young women clad in black and full of angst. Plath has become cultural shorthand for female hysteria; 'to be called the Sylvia Plath of anything is *a bad thing*', Nelson writes.⁶ In the 1980s, a prominent reviewer cracked his favourite Plath joke as he reviewed Plath's Pulitzer Prize-winning *Collected Poems*: 'Why did SP cross the road?' 'To be struck by an oncoming vehicle.'⁷ Male writers who kill themselves are rarely subject to such black humour. (Who would dare joke about David Foster Wallace's suicide?) As the critic Carolyn Heilbrun has noted, 'If you admire Auden, that's good taste. If you admire Sylvia Plath, it's a cult.... It is the usual no-win situation: either a woman author isn't studied, or studying her is reduced to an act of misplaced religious fanaticism.'⁸ Melodramatic portraits of Plath as a crazed poetic priestess do not seem to be going away anytime soon. Her most recent biographer, Andrew Wilson, called her 'a sorceress who had the power to attract men with a flash of her intense eyes, a tortured soul whose only destiny was death by her own hand'. He wrote that she 'aspired to transform herself into a psychotic deity'.⁹ Plath defined herself differently: 'I am a damn good high priestess of the intellect', she wrote to her friend Mel Woody in 1954 (*LV1* 781). That Plath is now identified with the clichés she examined ironically in her poems is part of her tragedy. This chapter will give a brief overview of the role Plath biographies have played in pathologising their subject, and show how their illness-centred narratives diminish Plath's intellectual and creative legacy.

Plath's life makes a tempting case study for psychoanalytically minded biographers. *The Bell Jar* was based on Plath's own breakdown, suicide attempt and recovery at McLean Hospital, while she drew deeply upon her own psychodrama in poems like 'Daddy' and 'The Colossus'. Critics (mis) labelled her poems 'confessional', comparing her work to other poets who explored mental illness, such as Robert Lowell and Anne Sexton. Indeed, Plath blurred the borders between her life and her work in innovative ways that complicate her biographers' task. But what Elizabeth Hardwick once wrote of Lowell is also true of Plath: 'He was not crazy all the time—most of the time he was wonderful. The breakdowns were not the whole story.'[10]

While it is tempting to read Plath's poems and novel as straightforward 'confession', her aesthetic impulse was more surrealist than confessional. Indeed, she treated the 'confessional' impulse ironically in poems like 'Lady Lazarus', where the heroine performs a strip-tease for the 'peanut crunching crowd' who has come to watch her bare all and attempt another suicide. Although Plath looked to female writers like Virginia Woolf, Marianne Moore, Elizabeth Bishop, Sara Teasdale, Edna St Vincent Millay and Anne Sexton for models, her formal education was grounded in male modernism. The psychological and anthropological writings of Carl Jung, Robert Graves and James Frazer, as well as the poetry and prose of W. B. Yeats, Dylan Thomas, Wallace Stevens, James Joyce, T. S. Eliot, W. H. Auden, Robert Lowell and Ted Hughes were the bedrock upon which she built her scaffolding. The psychoanalytic approaches that have dominated previous Plath biographies ignore this 'impersonal' literary tradition in which Plath was steeped and out of which her work grew. Jane Baltzell Kopp, who knew Plath and Ted Hughes well at Cambridge University, spoke of 'the old, High Culture' that permeated their student existence: 'that tradition had everything to do with the way we in those days all saw ourselves, each other, and our lives.' Anyone seriously interested in understanding Plath's poetry, Kopp suggested, would learn more by studying her English Tripos exam at Cambridge than her relationship with her dead father. 'The amount—and range—of reading implied by those questions tells the tale.'[11]

Plath mastered this body of work, from Chaucer to Eliot. Her literary expertise may not be immediately apparent in a poem like 'Daddy', with its stuttering lines and nursery-rhyme cadences. But the poem is the product of a long apprenticeship; it is Picasso on the verge of cubism. Plath had to master her tradition in order to create something new. When biographers read Plath's poems as autobiographical 'confessions', they miss an opportunity to showcase her ironic self-awareness, her literary sophistication and her bookishness. As Plath wrote to her friend Phil McCurdy in 1954, 'My bookcases are overflowing—shelves of novels, poetry, plays, with lots of philosophy, sociology & psych. I am a bibliomaniac ...' (*LV1* 727).

One of the most powerful tropes in Plath biography is Plath as Electra, doomed to follow her dead father into oblivion. Plath wrote metaphorically about the pull of her father, who died when she was eight, in 'Full Fathom Five', 'The Colossus', 'Electra on Azalea Path' and 'Daddy'. Plath's first biographer, Edward Butscher, took her literally. The first

Clark much stronger here

sentence of his 1976 biography, *Sylvia Plath: Method and Madness*, reads, 'For Sylvia Plath, as even the most casual reading of her poetry demonstrates, the central obsession from the beginning to the end of her life and career was her father, Professor Otto Emile Plath.'[12] The word 'obsession' introduces Plath as irrational, traumatised, haunted. Butscher goes on, setting the terms for future representations of Plath: 'A situation was needed, a plot ripe with secret tension and geared towards a climax of destruction, betrayal, a re-enactment of an ancient tragedy to forge the tragic poet.'[13] Already the poet's quest is 'tragic', her writing a 'defense . . . neurotic in nature and intensity . . . a substitute for lost parental love'. She has a 'relentless appetite for success', which increases her 'anxiety-driven narcissism'.[14] Butscher, a high school English teacher with no knowledge of Plath's medical records, diagnoses her as 'schizophrenic' and 'neurotic', and claims that she suffered 'sexual confusion' over her father's death.[15]

Butscher's portrayal of Plath as a Little Girl Lost – suffering the wounds of parental abandonment, writing for survival rather than pleasure, wearing masks to hide her 'true' subversive self – proved surprisingly resilient. In *The Death and Life of Sylvia Plath* (1991), Ronald Hayman began his chapter on Plath's childhood: 'Sylvia Plath was eight when her father died, but the seeds of her neurosis had already been planted.'[16] A few pages later: 'Sometimes, when contemplating suicide, as she often did, Sylvia felt as if her father were trying to drag her down into the grave.'[17] Hayman gives no source here – another common problem in the p(l)athographies, where biographers present episodes they have fictionalised as fact. (Tracy Brain has noted this practice in Paul Alexander's and Ronald Hayman's biographies, which she has called 'ethically compromised'.[18]) In *American Isis* (2013), Carl Rollyson often compared Plath to Marilyn Monroe, an inaccurate parallel that saddles Plath with Monroe's baggage and emphasises her victimhood at the expense of her achievement. Even Linda Wagner-Martin's otherwise sympathetic *Sylvia Plath: A Biography* (1987) lapses into psychoanalysis: 'The sense of dependence and the narcissism that were to mark, and sometimes ruin, Sylvia's relationships in the future clearly originated in her childhood fear of abandonment.'[19] Though Ted Hughes hated Butscher's biography, he, too, blamed Otto for his wife's disintegration in the poems of *Birthday Letters*.

What began in Butscher's biography as Plath's 'obsession' with her dead father became, by Anne Stevenson's *Bitter Fame* (1989), a 'curse'. As Stevenson wrote in her controversial biography, 'Her gift was for romantic self-aggrandizing . . . Sylvia was trapped in her own story, condemned to telling it again and again to whoever would listen. She was indeed cursed.'[20] This is the height of pathography, in which one of the most talented, innovative poets of the twentieth century is reduced to a self-aggrandiser, 'trapped' and 'condemned' by her own story. Stevenson compares Plath to Coleridge's Ancient Mariner, doomed to repeat her burdensome tale to a reluctant audience (which, in reality, comprises millions). Stevenson's Plath writes out of desperation rather than fulfilment. Writing becomes a way to stave off madness: 'Haunted by a fear of her own disintegration, she kept herself together by defining herself, writing constantly about herself, so that everyone could see her there, fighting and conquering an outside world that forever threatened her frail being.'[21] There is more of the same in Andrew Wilson's 2013 biography *Mad Girl's Love Song*. He writes that Plath was 'addicted to achievement in the same way an alcoholic is hooked on booze', while her 'competitive drive' was 'pathological' and stemmed from 'interior hollowness'.[22] She wrote to 'guarantee her mother's love'.[23] Rarely has male ambition and drive been described in such terms. Wagner-Martin also tied Plath's ambition to desperation and her 'need to excel ... From early childhood, she had learned that her parents' love depended on her achievements.'[24] These writers were presumably drawing upon comments Plath made in her journal after her therapy sessions with Dr Ruth Beuscher, who encouraged Plath to hate her mother. But she wrote to others during this time of the self-satisfaction she felt upon publishing her work. In 1959, Plath told her Smith friend Ann Davidow that even if she had once used her writing purely to gain love and admiration, she nonetheless wanted to see it in print.[25] In a 1975 letter to Butscher, Plath's brother Warren rejected the suggestion that Aurelia pushed Plath to succeed.[26]

The very structures of Paul Alexander's 1999 biography *Rough Magic*, and Ronald Hayman's *The Death and Life of Sylvia Plath* pathologise Plath: both begin with a chapter on Plath's suicide. Positioning Plath's suicide as the very first event in her life sets up a false teleology; the authors read her life backwards through her suicide rather than forwards through her development as a writer. Titles, too, matter. Hayman's, Wilson's and Rollyson's titles – *The Death and Life of Sylvia Plath, Mad Girl's Love Song* and *American Isis* – perpetuate the myth of Plath as doomed, neurotic, witchy. Of course, Plath *did* suffer after her father's death, as any daughter would. But Otto's death did not condemn her to suicide, or poetry. Plath endured severe depressions that, according to her mother, afflicted several women in her father's family, including her maternal grandmother. To argue that her writing was a 'curse' brought on by Otto's death – a way to

save herself from 'disintegrating' – trivialises Plath's commitment to her literary vocation.

If we read Plath's life forwards rather than backwards, an alternative picture emerges of a confident, talented young woman determined to nurture her gift. Plath's biographers tend to pass over her early poems, save one: 'I Thought That I Could Not Be Hurt'. In April 1947, aged fifteen, Plath wrote this poem about a pastel drawing her grandmother had accidentally smudged. Plath's art teacher had criticised her drawings for months, but finally praised this composition – a still life of a Chinese jug.[27] Plath was thrilled, but when she took the drawing home to show to her mother, somebody smudged it and the piece couldn't be returned to its pristine condition.[28] Plath consoled herself by transforming pain into art as she produced a substitute 'best' composition, a poem that would make up for the loss of her drawing. In 'I Thought That I Could Not Be Hurt', she writes: 'I thought that I must surely be / impervious to suffering' (LH 33).[29] The poem goes on to describe how the speaker's 'world turned gray' when 'careless hands' destroyed her 'silver web of happiness' (LH 34). The young poet eager for 'experience' exploited the situation for maximum dramatic effect.

Anne Stevenson began her biography with a discussion of this poem – which she noted was occasioned by a 'minor mishap' – as an illustrative example of Plath's volatility.[30] Alexander, too, emphasised the poem's melodrama. 'I Thought That I Could Not Be Hurt,' he argued, 'represents an early window into Plath's potentially extreme emotional states.' He pointed to the narrator's 'solipsism' and the poem's 'peculiar sentiments'.[31] Without any knowledge of Plath's struggles to earn her art teacher's praise, or an understanding of the pleasure she derived from using 'experience' to create poems, 'I Thought That I Could Not Be Hurt' might seem melodramatic. But placed back in its original context and read through the lens of Plath's diary description, it stands out as a creative experiment and an artistic turning point. This was the first surviving poem in which Plath dared to write in the first person about 'mental pain' and 'agony' – risky terrain for a daughter raised in a household that had tried to banish the spectre of tragedy. Plath recognised that the poem was 'new, modern' – an exciting departure from the emotionally safe landscape poetry that dominated her juvenilia. For the first time, her poem's speaker refuses to keep quiet about anger and disappointment.

Most of Plath's adolescent poems display a joyful, precocious delight in complex metres and forms, and are not 'depressed'. Her juvenilia suggests an alternate narrative: that the origins of her art were not rooted in trauma or supplication, but in confidence, pleasure and self-satisfaction. As Plath once remarked in a 1962 BBC interview, writing was as necessary to her as breathing. Other evidence suggests that writing was not just something she did to please others, but to please herself. In 1947, for example, she wrote 'Fireside Reveries', a remarkable manifesto of ambition that was published in her school magazine. A young poet sits by the fire, 'dreaming dreams' with an open book of poems in her lap: 'My thoughts to shining fame aspire / For there is much to do and dare.'[32] Plath construes poetry-writing as a risky act, a 'dare' akin to playing with fire. The public expression of this desire – Plath published 'Fireside Reveries' in her school magazine the *Phillipian* – was courageous at a time when modesty was an essential female virtue. 'Didn't you know I'm going to be the greatest, most entertaining author and artist in the world?' she wrote in her diary in March 1947.[33]

Biographers have used 'I Thought That I Could Not Be Hurt' to pathologise Plath at the beginning of her life, and 'Edge' to do so at the end. Widely believed to be Plath's last poem, 'Edge' has been interpreted as Plath's suicide note. Indeed, with its images of a mother and her children abandoned in an interstellar void, 'Edge' gives the uncanny impression of having been written posthumously. Yet the poem is packed with literary and artistic allusions that belie its 'confession'. As in 'Daddy' and 'Lady Lazarus', Plath uses irony to make a devastating sociopolitical point: only a dead woman is 'perfected'. Not perfect, *perfected* – like a work of art or an experiment; something controlled and without agency.

After the ascents of 'Ariel' and 'Lady Lazarus', 'Edge', like 'Sheep in Fog' and 'Words', is flat and resigned. Its tonal colour is blue, not red. All has stilled, including her 'Feet', which 'seem to be saying: / We have come so far, it is over' (*CP* 272). The surrealist painter Giorgio de Chirico painted several works that featured barefoot women dressed in togas, reclining horizontally on rectangular slabs amidst arched stone buildings, long shadows and distant trains. In one, the woman is called 'Melancholia'. In another, she is Ariadne, the classical heroine who led Theseus out of the labyrinth, away from the Minotaur, only to be abandoned by him. Plath had seen de Chirico's painting 'Ariadne' in New York in March 1958, and wrote about it in her journal: 'The statue, recumbent, of Ariadne, deserted, asleep, in the center of empty, mysteriously-shadowed squares. And the long shadows cast by unseen figures – human or of stone it is impossible to tell' (*J* 359). She had shown interest in the legend years before, when she wrote 'To Ariadne (deserted by Theseus)' in 1949. The atmospherics of 'Edge' strongly suggest the surrealism of de Chirico's 'Ariadne'.

Judith Kroll has noted that Plath's image of children coiled like serpents at their mother's breast under an indifferent moon invokes Shakespeare's *Antony and Cleopatra*. In the play, Cleopatra puts an asp to her breast to commit suicide: 'My resolution's plac'd, and I have nothing / Of woman in me; now from head to foot / I am marble-constant; now the fleeting moon / No planet is of mine.'[34] Robert Graves had identified Cleopatra as a manifestation of the White Goddess, which would have made her an even more potent female symbol for Plath. Plath may also have drawn upon D. H. Lawrence's 'Prayer', which she marked up in her copy of his *Complete Poems*: 'O let my ankles be bathed in moonlight, that I may go / sure and moon-shod, cool and bright-footed towards my goal.'[35]

There are echoes of 'Edge', too, in 'I Shall Not Care' by Sara Teasdale, one of Plath's favourite female poets:

> When I am dead and over me bright April
> Shakes out her rain-drenched hair,
> Tho' you should lean above me broken-hearted,
> I shall not care.
>
> I shall have peace, as leafy trees are peaceful
> When rain bends down the bough,
> And I shall be more silent and cold-hearted
> Than you are now.[36]

Teasdale, who was a formative early influence on Plath, committed suicide in 1933. If in 'Edge' Plath is talking back to Ted Hughes, who embodied the living male poetic tradition in her own life, she is also talking back to her hero Yeats, in whose shadow she stood, and in whose house she chose to die. 'Edge' bitterly complies with Yeats's wish for complete womanly surrender in 'He wishes his Beloved were Dead':

> Were you but lying cold and dead,
> And lights were paling out of the West,
> You would come hither, and bend your head,
> And I would lay my head on your breast;
> And you would murmur tender words,
> Forgiving me, because you were dead:
> Nor would you rise and hasten away,
> Though you have the will of wild birds,

> But know your hair was bound and wound
> About the stars and moon and sun:
> O would, beloved, that you lay
> Under the dock-leaves in the ground,
> While lights were paling one by one.[37]

'Edge' cannot be reduced to 'romantic self-aggrandizing', or, as Elizabeth Hardwick claimed, a last ritual performance: 'when the curtain goes down, it is her own dead body there on the stage, sacrificed to her own plot'.[38]

Anne Stevenson chose to end her Plath biography with Hardwick's quote, followed by 'Edge' itself. Butscher wrote that 'Edge', along with Plath's other February 1963 poems, were 'her extended suicide note', full of 'narcissistic self-absorption, and ultimate failure'.[39] Hayman, too, jumps to conclusions, arguing that the presence of children in 'Edge' means Plath 'had been intending to kill the children when she killed herself'.[40] These biographers ignore the poem's sophisticated use of Shakespeare, Greek myth, Graves, de Chirico, Yeats, Teasdale, Lawrence and others. Plath's allusions suggest that 'Edge' is – among other things – an indictment of a sexist culture and literary tradition that equated 'perfect' womanhood with passivity and compliancy. The connections between the poem and Plath's suicide are tempting to make, but impossible to know.

In 1993, Janet Malcolm cast a cold eye on Plath biography in *The Silent Woman: Sylvia Plath and Ted Hughes*. Malcolm famously argued that the biographical quest was at best a fool's errand, at worst exploitation and thievery. Reviewing *The Silent Woman*, the biographer James Atlas conceded that Malcolm had a point. Yet for every seedy celebrity melodrama, he insisted, there was a finely wrought biography that sought to commemorate, 'To recover and bring forth, to preserve against oblivion the documents that give texture to a life'.[41] Sylvia Plath's life and art will always be tied to her suicide – there is no changing that. But her battles with depression, her exhausting efforts to balance writing and motherhood, and her heartbreak over her ruptured marriage remind us that the most famous woman poet of the twentieth century was neither fragile ingénue nor femme fatale. She was no Medea, no Eurydice, no Electra. Rather, she was a highly disciplined writer whose singular voice helped transform American and British literature, and whose innovative work gave new energy to the burgeoning literary and cultural revolutions of her time. This Sylvia Plath waits to be recovered, and brought forth.

Notes

1. Oates, 'Adventures in Abandonment', BR3.
2. Lee, *Biography*, 128–9.
3. Nelson, *Art of Cruelty*, 260.
4. Anonymous, 'The Blood Jet is Poetry', 118.
5. Schott, 'The Cult of Plath', 3.
6. Nelson, *Art of Cruelty*, 141.
7. Pritchard, 'An Interesting Minor Poet?', 33.
8. Dudar, 'The Virginia Woolf Cult', 33.
9. Wilson, *Mad Girl's Love Song*, 13–14; 80.
10. Lehmann-Haupt, 'Elizabeth Hardwick, Writer, Dies at 91', A29.
11. Email to Heather Clark, 9 October 2016.
12. Butscher, *Method and Madness*, 3.
13. Butscher, *Method and Madness*, 10.
14. Butscher, *Method and Madness*, 25–6.
15. Butscher, *Method and Madness*, 35; 34.
16. Hayman, *Death and Life*, 20.
17. Hayman, *Death and Life*, 22.
18. See Brain, 'Fictionalizing Sylvia Plath', 192–3.
19. Wagner-Martin, *Sylvia Plath*, 41.
20. Stevenson, *Bitter Fame*, 32–3. All references from *Bitter Fame* are from the Penguin edition.
21. Stevenson, *Bitter Fame*, 3. *Bitter Fame* was heavily manipulated by Ted Hughes's sister Olwyn, who disliked Plath. Olwyn used her role as the agent of the Plath estate to control Stevenson's narrative; Stevenson, worn down by Olwyn's interference, eventually listed her as a co-author in the first edition and agreed to Olwyn's request for 40 per cent of the book's royalties. Reviewers widely condemned the biography as Hughes propaganda. Janet Malcolm explored the composition of *Bitter Fame* in *The Silent Woman*.
22. Wilson, *Mad Girl's Love Song*, 39; 89.
23. Wilson, *Mad Girl's Love Song*, 36.
24. Wagner-Martin, *Sylvia Plath*, 45–6.
25. Sylvia Plath to Ann Davidow, 12 June 1959. Series 2, Box 16, MRB.
26. Warren Plath to Edward Butscher, 31 August 1975. Edward Butscher Papers, MRB.
27. Sylvia Plath, Diary, 30 May 1947. Plath MSS II Box 7, f 3, LL.
28. Sylvia Plath, Diary, 30 May 1947. Plath MSS II Box 7, f 3, LL.
29. 'I Thought That I Could Not Be Hurt.' 30 May 1947. Plath MSS, Box 7a, f 12, LL.
30. Stevenson, *Bitter Fame*, 2.
31. Alexander, *Rough Magic*, 52.
32. *The Phillipian*, February 1947, p. 7. Plath MSS II, Box 7a, f 11, LL. Also quoted in Mossberg, 'Sylvia Plath's Baby Book', 191.
33. Diary, 23 Mar. 1947. Plath MSS II, Box 7, f 3, LL.

34. Shakespeare, *Antony and Cleopatra*, V.ii.238–41. Quoted in Kroll, *Chapters*, 153.
35. D. H. Lawrence, *The Complete Poems* (London: Heinemann, 1957), 825P696L, MRB.
36. Teasdale, *Collected Poems*, 85.
37. Yeats, *Collected Poems*, 72.
38. Stevenson, *Bitter Fame*, 298.
39. Butscher, *Method and Madness*, 360.
40. Hayman, *Death and Life*, 192.
41. Atlas, 'The Biographer and the Murderer', 74–5.

Bibliography

Note on References

Please note that multiple editions of key Plath texts have been used by the different contributors. All are listed below, with an endnote or endnotes in the relevant chapter indicating which edition has been used. If SMITH or LILLY or EMORY appears at the end of the entry, it indicates that the edition was from Plath's personal library, and the copy is held in the archives.

Works by Sylvia Plath

Plath, Sylvia. *Ariel* (London: Faber and Faber, 1965).
   Ariel (New York: Harper & Row, 1966).
   Ariel (London: Faber and Faber, 1972).
   Ariel (New York: Harper & Row, 1975).
   Ariel (London: Faber and Faber, 1983).
   Ariel (London: Faber and Faber, 1999).
   Ariel (New York: Harper & Row, 1999).
   Ariel (London: Faber and Faber, 2001).
   Ariel (London: Faber and Faber, 2010).
   Ariel: The Restored Edition; A Facsimile of Plath's Manuscript, Reinstating Her Original Selection and Arrangement. Foreword by Frieda Hughes (London: Faber and Faber, 2004) (New York: HarperCollins, 2004).
   A Winter Ship (Edinburgh: The Tragara Press, 1960).
   The Bed Book (London: Faber and Faber, 1976) (New York: Harper & Row, 1976).
   The Bell Jar (London: Heinemann, 1963).
   The Bell Jar (London: Faber and Faber, 1966).
   The Bell Jar (London: Faber and Faber, 1971).
   The Bell Jar (New York: Perennial Classics, 1971).
   The Bell Jar (New York: Harper & Row, 1971).
   The Bell Jar (New York: Bantam Books, 1972).
   The Bell Jar (London: Faber and Faber, 1983).
   The Bell Jar (London: Faber and Faber, 1986).
   The Bell Jar (New York: HarperCollins, 1996).

The Bell Jar (New York: Harper Perennial Modern Classics, 1999).

The Bell Jar (London: Faber and Faber, 1999).

The Bell Jar (New York: Perennial Classics, 1999).

The Bell Jar (New York: Harper Perennial Modern Classics, 2003).

The Bell Jar (New York: Harper Perennial Modern Classics, 2005).

The Bell Jar (London: Faber and Faber, 2005).

The Bell Jar (New York: Harper Perennial Modern Classics, 2006).

The Bell Jar (London: Faber and Faber, 2009).

The Bell Jar (London: Faber and Faber, 2013).

Collected Children's Stories [*The Bed Book, The It-Doesn't-Matter Suit, Mrs Cherry's Kitchen*] (London: Faber and Faber, 2001).

Collected Poems (London: Faber and Faber, 1981).

Collected Poems (New York: Harper & Row, 1981).

The Colossus and Other Poems (London: William Heinemann, 1960) (New York: Knopf, 1962).

'Context', *London Magazine* 1.11 (1962): 45–6.

Crossing the Water (London: Faber and Faber, 1971),

Crossing the Water (New York: Harper & Row, 1971).

'General Jodpur's Conversion', *New Statesman* (10 November 1961): 696–8.

The It-Doesn't-Matter Suit (London: Faber and Faber, 1996) (New York: St Martin's Press, 1996).

Johnny Panic and the Bible of Dreams (London: Faber and Faber, 1977).

Johnny Panic and the Bible of Dreams (London: Faber and Faber, 1979).

Johnny Panic and the Bible of Dreams (New York: Harper & Row, 1979).

The Journals of Sylvia Plath 1950–1962, edited by Karen V. Kukil (London: Faber and Faber, 2000).

The Journals of Sylvia Plath, edited by Ted Hughes and Frances McCullough (New York: Ballantine Books, 1982).

Letters Home: Correspondence 1950–1963, edited by Aurelia Schober Plath (London: Faber & Faber, 1975) (New York: Harper & Row, 1975).

The Letters of Sylvia Plath, Volume I: 1940–1956, edited by Peter Steinberg and Karen V. Kukil (London: Faber and Faber, 2017) (New York: Harper, 2017).

The Letters of Sylvia Plath, Volume II: 1956–1963, edited by Peter Steinberg and Karen Kukil (London: Faber and Faber, 2018) (New York: Harper, 2018).

The Magic Mirror: A Study of the Double in Two of Dostoevsky's Novels (Powys: Embers Handpress, 1989).

Mrs Cherry's Kitchen (London: Faber and Faber, 2007).

Poems, Everyman's Library Pocket Poets (New York: Knopf, 1998).

The Poet Speaks, edited by Peter Orr (London: Routledge & Kegan Paul, 1966).

Review of The Stones of Troy, *Gemini* 1.2 (1957): 98–103.

Selected Poems (London: Faber and Faber, 1985).

Three Women. London: Turret Books, 1968.

Stings: Original Drafts of the Poem in Facsimile, Reproduced from the Sylvia Plath Collection at Smith College, edited by Susan R. Van Dyne (Northampton: Smith College Library Rare Book Room, 1982).

Sylvia Plath: Drawings, introduced by Frieda Hughes (New York: HarperCollins, 2013; London: Faber and Faber, 2013).

The Unabridged Journals of Sylvia Plath, edited by Karen V. Kukil (New York: Anchor Books, 2000).

Winter Trees (London: Faber and Faber, 1971) (New York: Harper & Row, 1972).

Plath, Sylvia and Ted Hughes. 'Two of a Kind: Poets in Partnership', interviewed by Owen Leeming, recorded by the BBC in 1961, *The Spoken Word: Sylvia Plath* (British Library Publishing, 2010).

Plath, Sylvia and Perry Norton. 'Youth's Plea for World Peace', *Christian Science Monitor* (16 March 1950). *SMITH*.

Literary Sources

Bacon, Francis. *Novum Organum*, edited by James Spedding, Robert Leslie Ellis and Douglas Denon Heath, vol. IV of The *Works of Francis Bacon*, 29-248. (London: Longman & Co., 1858).

Bergman, Ingmar. *A Film Trilogy: Through a Glass Darkly, The Communicants (Winter Light), The Silence*, translated by Paul Britten Austen (New York and London: Marion Boyars, 1989).

Blake, William. *The Paintings and Drawings of William Blake*, vol. II, edited by Martin Butlin (New Haven and London: Paul Mellon Centre, 1981).

Brontë, Charlotte. *Jane Eyre* (1847), edited by Deborah Lutz, Norton Critical Edition, 4th edition (London: W. W. Norton & Company, 2016).

Villette (1853) (London: J. M. Dent & Sons, Everyman's Library, 1909, 1949). *LILLY*.

Chambers, E. K., editor. *The Oxford Book of Sixteenth-Century Verse* (Oxford: Clarendon Press, 1950). *SMITH*.

Dickinson, Emily. *The Poems of Emily Dickinson*, edited by Ralph Franklin (Cambridge, Massachusetts: The Belknap Press of Harvard University Press, 1999).

Eliot, T. S. *The Poems of T.S. Eliot: Collected and Uncollected*, vol. I, edited by Christopher Ricks and Jim McCue (Baltimore: Johns Hopkins Press, 2016).

The Complete Poems and Plays (New York: Harcourt, Brace and Company, 1952). *SMITH*.

Emerson, Ralph Waldo. *Selected Journals 1820–1842*, edited by Lawrence Rosenwald (New York: Library of America, 2010).

Enright, Anne. 'Diary', *London Review of Books* 39.18 (21 September 2017): 33–5.

Glück, Louise. *The House on Marshland* (New York: Ecco Press, 1975).

The Seven Ages (New York: Ecco Press, 2001).

Averno (New York: Farrar, Straus and Giroux, 2006).

Heller, Joseph. Catch-22 (New York: Simon & Schuster, 1961).

Hill, Selima. 'Never Go to Sleep in a Lake' in *The Sparkling Jewel of Naturism* (Northumberland: Bloodaxe, 2014), 46.

Hughes, Frieda. 'My Mother', *Tatler* (March 2003): 125. Reprinted in Frieda Hughes, *The Book of Mirrors* (Northumberland: Bloodaxe Books, 2009), 32–3.

Hughes, Ted. *Birthday Letters* (London: Faber and Faber, 1998).

Birthday Letters (New York: Farrar Straus & Giroux, 1998).

Crow (London: Faber and Faber, 1970).

'Last Letter', facsimiles of draft manuscripts reproduced in 'Exclusive: Ted Hughes's Poem on the Night Sylvia Plath Died', *New Statesman* (6 October 2010), www.newstatesman.com/blogs/cultural-capital/2010/10/hughes-poem-poet-publish. Accessed 22 December 2017.

Letters of Ted Hughes, edited and selected by Christopher Reid (London: Faber and Faber, 2007).

Shakespeare and the Goddess of Complete Being (London: Faber and Faber, 1992).

Tales from Ovid (London: Faber and Faber, 1997).

Winter Pollen: Occasional Prose, edited by William Scammell (London: Faber and Faber, 1994).

Jennings, Elizabeth. *The Collected Poems*, edited by Emma Mason (Manchester: Carcanet, 2012).

Joyce, James. *Dubliners* (New York: Random House, 1926). *SMITH*.

Dubliners (London: Penguin, 1992).

A Portrait of the Artist as a Young Man (1916; New York: New American Library, 1948). *EMORY*.

Kesey, Ken. *One Flew Over the Cuckoo's Nest* (New York: Viking Press, 1962).

Larkin, Philip. *The Complete Poems*, edited by Archie Burnett (London: Faber and Faber, 2012).

Lawrence, D. H. *The Complete Poems of D. H. Lawrence* (Ware: Wordsworth Editions Limited, 2002).

Selected Poems, edited by James Fenton (London: Penguin, 2008).

Marlowe, Christopher. *The Complete Poems and Translations*, edited by Stephen Orgel (London: Penguin, 2007).

Milton, John. *The Complete English Poems* (London: Everyman, 1992).

Moore, Marianne. *New Collected Poems*, edited by Heather Cass White (New York: Farrar, Strauss and Giroux, 2017).

Nichol Smith, David editor. *The Oxford Book of Eighteenth-Century Verse* (Oxford: Clarendon Press, 1951). *SMITH*.

Olds, Sharon. *Satan Says* (Pittsburgh, Pennsylvania: University of Pittsburgh Press, 1980).

Orr, Peter. *Plath Reads Plath*, interview with Peter Orr, recorded 30 October 1962 (Cambridge: Credo Records, 1975).

Orwell, George. *Essays* (London: Penguin, 2000).

Petit, Pascale. *Fauverie* (Bridgend: Seren, 2014).

Mama Amazonica (Northumberland: Bloodaxe, 2017).

Pound, Ezra. *Personae: The Shorter Poems of Ezra Pound* (London: Faber and Faber, 2001).

Ransom, John Crowe. 'Janet Waking', Poetry Foundation, www.poetryfoundation .org/poems/47552/janet-waking. Accessed 30 September 2017.

Sagar, Keith, editor. *The Letters of Ted Hughes and Keith Sagar* (London: The British Library, 2012).

Salinger, J. D. *The Catcher in the Rye* (London: Hamish Hamilton, 1951).

Sasek, Miroslav. *This Is Venice* (London: W. H. Allen, 1961).

Sexton, Anne. *A Self-Portrait in Letters*, edited by Linda Gray Sexton and Lois Ames (New York: Mariner Books, 2004).

Transformations (Boston: Houghton Mifflin, 1971).

Shakespeare, William. *The Tempest*, edited by Sir Arthur Quiller-Couch and John Wilson (Cambridge: Cambridge University Press, 1965).

Shelley, Percy Bysshe. 'A Defence of Poetry' in *Essays, Letters from Abroad, Translations and Fragments, By Percy Bysshe Shelley*, 2 vols., edited by Mary Shelley (London: Edward Moxon, 1840), vol. I, 1–57.

Smith, Stevie. *The Collected Poems and Drawings of Stevie Smith*, edited by William May (London: Faber and Faber, 2015).

Novel on Yellow Paper (London: Virago, 1936/2015).

Me Again: The Uncollected Writings of Stevie Smith, edited by Jack Barbera and William McBrien (London: Virago, 1981).

Snicket, Lemony. *A Series of Unfortunate Events*, 13 vols. (New York: HarperCollins, 1999–2006).

Stevens, Wallace. *The Collected Poems of Wallace Stevens* (New York: Knopf, 1954).

Teasdale, Sara. *The Collected Poems of Sara Teasdale* (Digireads.com Publishing, 2012).

Thomas, Dylan. *Under Milk Wood* (London: J. M. Dent, 1975).

Thoreau, Henry David. *Walden in Two Volumes: Volume 1* (New York: Houghton, Mifflin and Co., 1882).

Virgil. *The Eclogues* and *The Georgics*, translated by C. Day Lewis (Oxford: Oxford University Press, 1983).

Wollstonecraft, Mary. *A Vindication of the Rights of Women. The Works of Mary Wollstonecraft*, edited by Janet Todd and Marilyn Butler, vol. V (London: Chatto & Windus, 1989).

Woolf, Virginia. *A Room of One's Own* (London: Penguin, 2004).

A Writer's Diary: Being Extracts from the Diary of Virginia Woolf, edited by Leonard Woolf (London: Hogarth Press, 1953 and St Albans: Triad Press, 1978).

'The Historian and "The Gibbon"', in *The Death of the Moth and Other Essays* (London: Hogarth, 1937), 55–63.

Jacob's Room (London: Penguin, 1992).

To the Lighthouse (London: Penguin Modern Classics, 2000).

The Voyage Out. Oxford: Oxford University Press, 2009.

Yeats, W. B. *The Collected Poems* (New York: Macmillan, 1952). SMITH.

Film Sources

Bergman, Ingmar. *A Film Trilogy: Through a Glass Darkly, The Communicants (Winter Light), The Silence.* Svenskfilmindustri (1961–3). The Criterion Collection (2019) USA DVD.

Brink of Life. Inter-American Productions (1958).

The Magician. Svenskfilmindustri (1958). The Criterion Collection (2010) USA DVD.

The Seventh Seal. Svenskfilmindustri (1957). The Criterion Collection (2009) USA DVD.

Through a Glass Darkly. Svenskfilmindustri (1961). The Criterion Collection (2003) USA DVD.

Cocteau, Jean. *La Belle et la Bête.* DisCina (1946). The Criterion Collection (2011) USA DVD.

Orphée. Andree Paulve Film (1950). The Criterion Collection (2011) USA DVD.

Dreyer, Carl. *La Passion de Jeanne d'Arc.* Société Générale des Films (1928). The Criterion Collection (1999) USA DVD.

Forman, Miloš. *One Flew Over the Cuckoo's Nest.* United Artists (1965).

Jeffs, Christine. *Sylvia.* BBC Films/Capitol Films (2003).

Kubrick, Stanley. *Dr Strangelove, or: How I Learned to Stop Worrying and Love the Bomb.* Columbia Pictures (1964). Sony Pictures (2002).

Litvak, Anatole. *The Snake Pit.* 20th Century Fox (1948). StudioCanal (2004).

Richter, Hans. *Rêves à Vendre* (Dreams that Money Can Buy). Art of This Century Films (1947). BFI Video (2006) UK DVD.

Truffaut, François. *Jules et Jim.* Sédif Productions (1962). The Criterion Collection (2014) USA DVD.

Wilder, Billy. *Double Indemnity.* Paramount Pictures (1944). Universal Home Pictures Home Entertainment (2012) USA DVD.

Wiene, Robert. *The Cabinet of Dr. Caligari.* Decla-Bioscop (1920). Cinema Classics Collection (2015) USA DVD.

Zemeckis, Robert. *Who Framed Roger Rabbit.* Touchstone Pictures (1988). Touchstone Home Video (1999) USA DVD.

Critical and Other Secondary Sources

Abse, Dannie. *The Hutchinson Book of Post-War British Poets* (London: Hutchinson, 1989).

Adcock, Fleur, editor. *The Faber Book of Twentieth Century Women's Poetry* (London: Faber and Faber, 1987).

Aldrich, Ann. *We, Too, Must Love* (Dee Why West, Australia: Eclipse, no date).

Alexander, Jonathan, Deborah T. Meem and Michelle A. Gibson, editors. *Finding Out: An Introduction to LGBTQ Studies* (Thousand Oaks, California: Sage, 2018).

Alexander, Paul. *Rough Magic: A Biography of Sylvia Plath* (New York: Da Capo Press, 1999).

Alexander, Paul, editor. *Ariel Ascending: Writings about Sylvia Plath* (New York: Harper & Row, 1985).

Alliston, Susan. *Poems and Journals 1960–69* (Nottingham: Richard Hollis [an imprint of Five Leaves Publications], 2010).

Alvarez, Al. 'A Poet's Epitaph', *The Observer* (17 February 1963): 23.

Beyond This Fiddle: Essays 1955–1967 (New York: Random House, 1969).

'The New Poetry or Beyond the Gentility Principle', in *The New Poetry* (London: Penguin, 1966), 21–32.

'Poetry in Extremis' (1965), reprinted in Linda Wagner-Martin, Sylvia Plath: The Critical Heritage (Abingdon: Routledge, 2009), 55–7.

'Prologue: Sylvia Plath', in *The Savage God* (New York: Random House, 1972), 15–58.

The Savage God (New York: Random House, 1972).

The Savage God (London: Weidenfeld and Nicolson, 1972).

'Ted, Sylvia and Me', *The Observer* (24 January 2004), www.theguardian.com /film/2004/jan/04/poetry.highereducation. Accessed 23 April 2019.

Where Did it All Go Right? A Memoir (London: Bloomsbury, 2002).

Ames, Lois. 'Biographical Note', in Sylvia Plath, *The Bell Jar* (New York: Harper Perennial Modern Classics, 2005), 3–15.

Anderson, Linda. 'Gender, Feminism, Poetry: Stevie Smith, Sylvia Plath, Jo Shapcott', in *The Cambridge Companion to Twentieth-Century Poetry*, edited by Neil Corcoran (Cambridge: Cambridge University Press, 2007), 173–86.

Armstrong, Tim. *Modernism, Technology, and the Body: A Cultural Study* (Cambridge: Cambridge University Press, 1998).

Ashe, Marie. '*The Bell Jar* and the Ghost of Ethel Rosenberg', in *Secret Agents: The Rosenberg Case, McCarthyism and 1950s America*, edited by Marjorie Garber and Rebecca L. Walkowitz (New York and London: Routledge, 1995, 2011), 215–31.

Astruc, Alexandre. 'The Birth of a New Avant-Garde: *La Caméra-Stylo*', in *The French New Wave*, edited by Peter Graham with Ginette Vincendeau (London: Palgrave Macmillan for BFI, 1989), 31–6.

Atlas, James. 'The Biographer and the Murderer', *New York Times Magazine* (12 December 1993): 74–5.

Axelrod, Steven Gould. 'Plath and Torture: Cultural Contexts for Plath's Imagery of the Holocaust', in *Representing Sylvia Plath*, edited by Sally Bayley and Tracy Brain (Cambridge: Cambridge University Press, 2011), 67–87.

'The Poetry of Sylvia Plath', in *The Cambridge Companion to Sylvia Plath*, edited by Jo Gill (Cambridge: Cambridge University Press, 2006), 73–89.

Sylvia Plath: The Wound and the Cure of Words (Baltimore: The John Hopkins University Press, 1990).

Bachelard, Gaston. *The Poetics of Space* (Boston: Beacon Press, 1994).

Badia, Janet. '*The Bell Jar* and Other Prose', in *The Cambridge Companion to Sylvia Plath*, edited by Jo Gill (Cambridge: Cambridge University Press, 2006), 124–38.

Balázs, Béla. *Theory of the Film: Character and Growth of a New Art*, translated from the Hungarian by Edith Bone (London: Dennis Dobson, 1952).

Ballard, Roger. 'Britain's Visible Minorities: A Demographic Overview' (1999), crossasia-repository.ub.uni-heidelberg.de/286/1/demography.pdf. Accessed 12 December 2017.

Baldwin, Kate A. *The Racial Imaginary of the Cold War Kitchen* (Lebanon, New Hampshire: Dartmouth College Press, 2016).

Barbera, Jack. 'The Relevance of Stevie Smith's Drawings', *Journal of Modern Literature* 12.2 (1985): 221–36.

Barbera, Jack, and William McBrien. *Stevie: A Biography of Stevie Smith* (London: Macmillan, 1986).

Bartlett Nodelman, Ellen, and Amanda Golden. 'Recollections of Mrs. Hughes's Student', *Plath Profiles*, 5 Supplement (Fall 2012): 125–39, scholarworks.iu.edu/journals/index.php/plath/article/viewFile/4353/3978. Accessed 19 November 2017.

Bate, Jonathan. *Ted Hughes: The Unauthorised Life* (London: William Collins [an imprint of HarperCollins], 2015).

Bayley, Sally. *The Private Life of the Diary: From Pepys to Tweets* (London: Unbound, 2016).

'Sublime Encounters in Sylvia Plath's Tree Poems', in *Representing Sylvia Plath*, edited by Sally Bayley and Tracy Brain (Cambridge: Cambridge University Press, 2011), 91–109.

'Sylvia Plath and the Costume of Femininity', in *Eye Rhymes: Sylvia Plath's Art of the Visual*, edited by Kathleen Connors and Sally Bayley (Oxford: Oxford University Press, 2007), 183–204.

Beauvoir, Simone de. *The Second Sex* (New York: Vintage Books, 2010).

Becker, Jillian. *Giving Up: The Last Days of Sylvia Plath* (London: Ferrington, Bookseller & Publisher, 2002).

Beer, John. *Post-Romantic Consciousness: Dickens to Plath* (Basingstoke: Palgrave, 2003).

Bensing, Robert C. 'A Comparative Study of American Sex Statutes', *The Journal of Criminal Law, Criminology, and Police Science* 42.1 (May–June, 1951): 57–72.

Bergman, Ingmar. *The Ingmar Bergman Archives*, edited by Paul Duncan and Bengt Wanselius (Los Angeles: Taschen America, 2008).

Black, Edwin. *War against the Weak* (New York: Four Walls Eight Windows, 2003).

'The Blood Jet is Poetry', review of *Ariel*, *Time* (10 June 1966): 118–20.

Bluemel, Kristin. *George Orwell and the Radical Eccentrics: Intermodernism in Literary London* (New York: Palgrave Macmillan, 2004).

'Suburbs Are Not So Bad I Think: Stevie Smith's Problem of Place in 1930s and '40s London', *Iowa Journal of Cultural Studies* 3 (Fall 2003): 96–114.

Botkin, Daniel. *Discordant Harmonies: A New Ecology for the Twenty-First Century* (New York: Oxford University Press, 1990).

Brain, Tracy. 'Fictionalizing Sylvia Plath' in *Representing Sylvia Plath*, edited by Sally Bayley and Tracy Brain (Cambridge: Cambridge University Press, 2011), 183–202.

'Medicine in Sylvia Plath's October Poems', *Plath Profiles: An Interdisciplinary Journal for Sylvia Plath Studies* 6 (Summer 2013): 9–26.

The Other Sylvia Plath (London: Longman Studies in Twentieth-Century Literature [Pearson Education], 2001).

'Story, Body and Voice: Dating and Grouping Sylvia Plath's Poems', in *Critical Insights on Sylvia Plath*, edited by William Buckley (Ipswich, Massachusetts: Salem Press, 2013), 70–91.

'Sylvia Plath in the Early Twenty-First Century', in *American Poetry Since 1945*, edited by Eleanor Spencer (London: Palgrave Macmillan [New Casebooks], 2017), 111–30.

'Sylvia Plath's Letters and Journals', in *The Cambridge Companion to Sylvia Plath*, edited by Jo Gill (Cambridge: Cambridge University Press, 2006), 139–55.

'Ted Hughes and Feminism', in *The Cambridge Companion to Ted Hughes*, edited by Terry Gifford (Cambridge: Cambridge University Press, 2011), 94–106.

Brain, Tracy, and Sally Bayley. 'Introduction', in *Representing Sylvia Plath* edited by Tracy Brain and Sally Bayley (Cambridge: Cambridge University Press, 2011), 1–12.

Brain, Tracy and Sally Bayley, editors. *Representing Sylvia Plath* (Cambridge: Cambridge University Press, 2011).

Brans, Jo. 'The Girl Who Wanted to be God', in *Sylvia Plath: the Critical Heritage*, edited by Linda Wagner-Martin (Abingdon: Routledge, 1988), 213–215.

Britzolakis, Christina. '*Ariel* and Other Poems', in *The Cambridge Companion to Sylvia Plath*, edited by Jo Gill (Cambridge: Cambridge University Press, 2006), 107–24.

'Conversation Amongst the Ruins: Plath and de Chirico', in *Eye Rhymes: Sylvia Plath's Art of the Visual*, edited by Kathleen Connors and Sally Bayley (Oxford: Oxford University Press, 2007), 167–82.

Bronstein, Carolyn. *Battling Pornography* (New York: Cambridge University Press, 2011).

Brooks, Cleanth. *The Well Wrought Urn: Studies in the Structure of Poetry* (New York: Harcourt, Brace and World, 1947). *SMITH.*

Brown, Judith. *Glamour in Six Dimensions* (Ithaca, New York: Cornell University Press, 2009).

Brownmiller, Susan. *Against Our Will: Men, Women and Rape* (New York: Fawcett Books, 1975).

Femininity (New York: Linden Press, 1984).

Bruinius, Harry. *Better for All the World* (New York: Vintage Books, 2007).

Bryant, Marsha. 'Ariel's Kitchen: Plath, *Ladies' Home Journal*, and the Domestic Surreal', in *The Unraveling Archive: Essays on Sylvia Plath*, edited by Anita Helle (Ann Arbor: University of Michigan Press, 2007), 211–35.

'Everyday Ariel: Sylvia Plath and the Dream Kitchen', in *Women's Poetry and Popular Culture* (New York: Palgrave, 2011), 121–48.

'Plath, Domesticity, and the Art of Advertising', *College Literature* 39.3 (2002): 17–34.

'Queen Bees: Edith Sitwell and Sylvia Plath', paper given at the Modernist Studies Association Conference, Brighton, United Kingdom, in August 2013.

Women's Poetry and Popular Culture (New York: Palgrave, 2011).

Bundtzen, Lynda K. *The Other Ariel* (Amherst: University of Massachusetts Press, 2001).

Burt, Stephen. *Close Calls with Nonsense: Reading New Poetry* (Minneapolis: Graywolf Press, 2009).

'What Is This Thing Called Lyric?', *Modern Philology: Critical and Historical Studies in Literature, Medieval Through Contemporary* 13.3 (February 2016): 422–40.

Butscher, Edward. *Sylvia Plath: Method and Madness: A Biography* (Tucson: Schaffner, 2003).

Butscher, Edward, editor. *Sylvia Plath: The Woman and the Work* (New York: Dodd, Mead and Company, 1977).

Byrne, Sandie. 'Poetry and Class', in *The Cambridge Companion to British Poetry, 1945–2010*, edited by Edward Larrissy (Cambridge: Cambridge University Press, 2016), 116–29.

'Capsule Trip, Capsule Wardrobe', *Vogue* (1 January 1952): 154–5.

Carmichael, Virginia. *Framing History: The Rosenberg Story and the Cold War* (Minneapolis: University of Minneapolis Press, 1993).

Cheever, Abigail. *Real Phonies: Culture and Authenticity in Post-World War II America* (Athens: University of Georgia Press, 2010).

Chesler, Phyllis. *Women and Madness* (New York: Harcourt Brace Jovanovich, 1972).

Christensen, Danille Elise. 'Look at Us Now!: Scrapbooking, Regimes of Value, and the Risks of (Auto)Ethnography', *Journal of American Folklore* 124.493 (Summer 2011): 175–210.

Clark, Heather. *The Ulster Renaissance: Poetry in Belfast 1962–1972* (Oxford: Oxford University Press, 2006).

Cleverdon, Douglas. 'The History of a Radio Classic', *Radio Times* (28 June 1957): 6–7.

Clinton, Alan Ramòn. *Intuitions in Literature, Technology, and Politics: Parabilities* (New York: Palgrave Macmillan, 2012).

'Sylvia Plath and Electracy', *Iowa Journal of Cultural Studies* 8 (2016): 60–71. ir .uiowa.edu/ijcs/vol8/iss1/6/. Accessed 1 June 2017.

Cocteau, Jean. 'Poésie de Cinema', in *The Art of Cinema*, edited by André Bernard and Claude Gauteur, translated by Robin Buss (New York and London: Marion Boyars, 1994), 131–93.

Colum, Padriac. 'Introduction' to James Joyce, *Dubliners* (New York: Random House, 1926). *Smith*.

Connolly, Joseph. *Faber and Faber: Eighty Years of Book Cover Design* (London: Faber and Faber, 2009).

Connors, Kathleen. 'Living Color: The Interactive Arts of Sylvia Plath', in *Eye Rhymes: Sylvia Plath's Art of the Visual*, edited by Kathleen Connors and Sally Bayley (Oxford: Oxford University Press, 2007), 4–144.

'"Madonna (of the Refrigerator)": Mapping Sylvia Plath's Double in "The Babysitters" Drafts', in *Representing Sylvia Plath*, edited by Sally Bayley and Tracy Brain (Cambridge: Cambridge University Press, 2011), 129–46.

'Visual Art in the Life of Sylvia Plath: Mining Riches in the Lilly and Smith Archives', in *The Unraveling Archive: Essays on Sylvia Plath*, edited by Anita Helle (Ann Arbor: University of Michigan Press, 2007), 65–88.

Connors, Kathleen, and Sally Bayley, editors. *Eye Rhymes: Sylvia Plath's Art of the Visual* (Oxford: Oxford University Press, 2007).

Conquest, Robert. 'Introduction', in *New Lines: An Anthology* (London: Macmillan & Co Ltd, 1957), xi–xviii.

Considine, Bob. *It's All News to Me: A Reporter's Deposition* (New York: Meredith Press, 1967).

Cooke, Rachel. '*The Letters of Sylvia Plath, Volume I: 1940–1956* – Review', *The Guardian* (15 October 2017), www.theguardian.com/books/2017/oct/15/the-letters-of-sylvia-plath-volume-one-1940-1956-review. Accessed 24 April 2019.

Coontz, Stephanie. *A Strange Stirring: The Feminine Mystique and American Women at the Dawn of the 1960s* (New York: Basic Books, 2011).

Corcoran, Neil. *English Poetry since 1940* (Harlow: Longman, 1993).

Costello, Bonnie. 'Effects of an Analogy: Wallace Stevens and Painting', in *Wallace Stevens: The Poetics of Modernism*, edited by Albert Gelpi (Cambridge: Cambridge University Press, 1985), 65–85.

Cox, C. B., and A. R. Jones. 'After the Tranquillized Fifties: Notes on Sylvia Plath and James Baldwin', *Critical Quarterly* 6.2 (Summer 1964): 107–22.

Crowther, Gail. '"The Body Does Not Come Into it at All": Material Culture of the Dead', in *These Ghostly Archives: The Unearthing of Sylvia Plath*, edited by Gail Crowther and Peter K. Steinberg (Stroud: Fonthill Media, 2017), 113–25.

Crowther, Gail, and Peter K. Steinberg, editors. *These Ghostly Archives: The Unearthing of Sylvia Plath* (Stroud: Fonthill Media, 2017).

Culler, Jonathan. 'The Lyric in Theory: A Conversation with Jonathan Culler', *Los Angeles Review of Books* (May 27, 2017), lareviewofbooks.org/article/the-lyric-in-theory-a-conversation-with-jonathan-culler/#!. Accessed 26 October 2017.

Curry, Renée R. 'White: It is a Complexion of the Mind: The Enactment of Whiteness in Sylvia Plath's Poetry', in *White Women Writing White: H. D., Elizabeth Bishop, Sylvia Plath and Whiteness* (Westport, Connecticut: Greenwood, 2000), 123–68.

White Women Writing White: H. D., Elizabeth Bishop, Sylvia Plath and Whiteness (Westport, Connecticut: Greenwood Press, 2000).

Davidson, Michael. *Guys Like Us: Citing Masculinity in Cold War Poetics* (Illinois: University of Chicago Press, 2004).

Davie, Donald. 'John Clare', *New Statesman* (19 June 1964).

Purity of Diction in English Verse [1952] (London: Routledge and Kegan Paul, 1967 [reissue]).

'Reason Reversed', *New Statesman* (4 May 1962).

Dobbs, Jeannine. 'Viciousness in the Kitchen: Sylvia Plath's Domestic Poetry', *Modern Language Studies* 7.2 (Autumn 1977): 11–25.

Douglas, Mary. *Purity and Danger* (Abingdon: Routledge, 2015).

Dowbnia, Renée. 'Consuming Appetites: Food, Sex and Freedom in Sylvia Plath's *The Bell Jar*', *Women's Studies* 43.5 (July 2014): 567–88.

Dowson, Jane, and Alice Entwistle. *A History of Twentieth-Century British Women's Poetry* (Cambridge: Cambridge University Press, 2005).

Drakakis, John. 'Introduction', in *British Radio Drama* (Cambridge: Cambridge University Press, 1981), 1–36.

Drew, Elizabeth. *Poetic Patterns: A Note on Versification* (Northampton, Massachusetts: Kraushar Press, 1956). *LILLY.*

T. S. Eliot: The Design of His Poetry (New York: Scribner, 1949). *SMITH.*

Dudar, Helen. 'The Virginia Woolf Cult', *Saturday Review* (February 1982): 33–5.

Dunham, Lena. 'Sylvia Plath: Reflections on her Legacy', *The Guardian* (8 February 2013), www.theguardian.com/books/2013/feb/08/sylvia-plath-reflections-on-her-legacy. Accessed 24 April 2019.

Dunkle, Iris Jamahl. 'Sylvia Plath's *The Bell Jar:* Understanding Cultural and Historical Context in an Iconic Text', in *Critical Insights: The Bell Jar*, edited by Janet McCann (Pasadena, California: Salem Press, 2012).

Dyer, Geoff. *But Beautiful* (London: Canongate, 2012).

Eliot, T. S. 'Tradition and the Individual Talent', in *Selected Prose of T. S. Eliot*, edited by Frank Kermode (London: Faber and Faber, 1975), 37–44.

Elliott, William Y. 'Introduction', in *Television's Impact on American Culture* (Michigan: Michigan State University Press, 1956), 1–9.

Empson, William. *Some Versions of Pastoral* (London: Penguin, 1995).

Esty, Jed. *A Shrinking Island: Modernism and National Culture in England* (Princeton: Princeton University Press, 2004).

Faas, Ekbert. 'Ted Hughes and Crow' (interview with Ted Hughes), *London Magazine* (January 1971), reprinted in Ekbert Fass, *Ted Hughes: The Unaccommodated Universe* (Santa Barbara: Black Sparrow Press, 1980), 197–208.

Faderman, Lillian. *Odd Girls and Twilight Lovers: A History of Lesbian Life in Twentieth-Century America* (New York: Columbia University Press, 1991).

Farland, Maria. 'Sylvia Plath's Anti-Psychiatry Movement', Minnesota Review 55–57 (Fall 2000 and Spring 2001): 256–76.

Farmer, Gareth. *Veronica Forrest-Thomson: Poet on the Periphery* (New York: Palgrave Macmillan, 2017).

Feinstein, Elaine. *Ted Hughes: The Life of a Poet* (London and New York: W. W. Norton & Company, 2001).

Felstiner, John. *Paul Celan: Poet, Survivor, Jew* (New Haven: Yale University Press, 1997).

Fenichell, Stephen. *Plastic* (New York: HarperBusiness, 1996).

Ferretter, Luke. *Sylvia Plath's Fiction: A Critical Study* (Edinburgh: Edinburgh University Press, 2013).

'"What Girl Ever Flourished in Such Company?" Sylvia Plath's Religion', *The Yearbook of English Studies* 39.1/2, *Literature and Religion* (2009): 101–13.

Finneran, Richard J., editor. *The Collected Poems of W. B. Yeats* (New York: Macmillan, 1983; 1989).

Fogarty, Anne. *Wife Dressing: The Fine Art of Being a Well-Dressed Wife* [1959] (London: V&A Publishing, 2011).

'Fogarty Was Ahead of Dior', *LIFE* (31 August 1953): 76.

Foote, Stephanie. 'Deviant Classics: Pulps and the Making of Lesbian Print Culture', *Signs* 31.1 (2005).

Ford, Karen Jackson. *Gender and the Poetics of Excess: Moments of Brocade* (Jackson: University Press of Mississippi, 1997).

Forrest, Veronica. 'My Attitudes and Beliefs', unpublished document, The Veronica Forrest-Thomson Archive, Girton College Library, Cambridge.

Forrest-Thomson, Veronica. Letter to Paul Buck, dated 25 July 1972, The Veronica Forrest-Thomson Archive, Girton College Library, Cambridge.

Poetic Artifice: A Theory of Twentieth-Century Poetry [1978], edited by Gareth Farmer (Bristol: Shearsman Books, 2016).

Review of Sylvia Plath's *Winter Trees* (London: Faber and Faber, 1971), unpublished typescript, The Veronica Forrest-Thomson Archive, Girton College Library, Cambridge.

'Four BWOC', *Flair* (August 1950): 49–52.

'44lb. Travel Wardrobe for a 17-day Flying Trip', *Vogue* (15 May 1952), 58–61, 106–10.

Foucault, Michel. *Madness and Civilization: A History of Insanity in the Age of Reason*, translated by Richard Howard (New York: Pantheon Books, 1965).

Fournier, Bob. *Trauma and the Golden Lady: The Life and Death of Sylvia Plath* (Victoria, British Columbia: FreisenPress, 2016).

Fox, Renee C. *The Sociology of Medicine: A Participant Observer's View* (New York: Prentice Hall, 1989).

Frayn, Michael. 'An Uncollected Poem by Sylvia Plath', *The Independent* (Saturday 8 October 1994), www.independent.co.uk/arts-entertainment/books-an-uncollected-poem-by-sylvia-plath-1441976.html. Accessed 24 April 2019.

Freud, Sigmund. *The Complete Psychological Works*, vol. XIV, translated by James Strachey (London: Vintage, 2001).

Friedan, Betty. *The Feminine Mystique* (New York: W. W. Norton & Company, 2013).

Gallo, Marcia. 'No Secret Anymore: Lesbian Representations in Cold War America', *OAH Magazine of History* 20.2 (2006).

Garber, Marjorie and Rebecca L. Walkowitz, editors. *Secret Agents: The Rosenberg Case, McCarthyism and 1950s America* (New York and London: Routledge, 1995, 2011).

Gardner, W. H. 'Introduction' in *Gerard Manley Hopkins: Poems and Prose* [1953] (Harmondsworth: Penguin Books, 1984), xiii–xxxvi.

Genette, Gérard. *Paratexts: Thresholds of Interpretation* (Cambridge: Cambridge University Press, 1997).

Gilbert, Sandra. 'In Yeats' House: The Death and Resurrection of Sylvia Plath', in *Critical Essays on Sylvia Plath*, edited by Linda Wagner-Martin (Boston: G. K. Hall & Co., 1984), 204–22.

'On the Beach with Sylvia Plath', in *The Unraveling Archive*, edited by Anita Helle (Ann Arbor: University of Michigan Press, 2007), 121–38.

Gill, Jo. *The Cambridge Introduction to Sylvia Plath* (Cambridge: Cambridge University Press, 2008).

'*The Colossus* and *Crossing the Water*', in *The Cambridge Companion to Sylvia Plath*, edited by Jo Gill (Cambridge: Cambridge University Press, 2006), 90–106.

Modern Confessional Writing: New Critical Essays (Abingdon, Oxford: Routledge, 2006).

Gilmore, Paul. *Aesthetic Materialism: Electricity and American Romanticism* (Stanford: Stanford University Press, 2009).

Gilot, Françoise. *Life with Picasso* (New York: McGraw Hill, 1994).

Gitlin, Todd. *Watching Television* (New York: Pantheon, 1986).

Golden, Amanda. *Annotating Modernism: Marginalia and Pedagogy from Virginia Woolf to the Confessional Poets* (New York: Routledge, forthcoming).

'Sylvia Plath's Teaching Syllabus: A Chronology', *Plath Profiles: An Interdisciplinary Journal of Sylvia Plath Studies* 2 (August 2009): 209–20, sc holarworks.iu.edu/journals/index.php/plath/article/viewFile/4746/4381. Accessed 23 September 2017.

Graham, Jorie. *Materialism* (New York: Ecco Press, 1993).

Overlord (New York: Ecco Press, 2006).

Greenberg, Clement. 'Modernist Painting', in *The Collected Essays: Modernism with a Vengeance 1957–1969*, vol. 4, edited by John O'Brian (Chicago: University of Chicago Press, 1986), 85–93.

'Towards a New Laocoön', in *The Collected Essays and Criticism: Perceptions and Judgements 1939–1944*, vol. 1, edited by John O'Brian (Chicago: University of Chicago Press, 1986), 23–37.

Greenlaw, Lavinia. 'Sylvia Plath: Reflections on her Legacy', *The Guardian* (8 February 2013), www.theguardian.com/books/2013/feb/08/sylvia-plath-reflections-on-her-legacy. Accessed 13 December 2017.

Grocott, Kirsty. '*The Bell Jar's* New Cover Is Just Perfect: No Chick-Lit in Sight', *The Telegraph* (7 February 2013), www.telegraph.co.uk/women/womens-life /9854783/Sylvia-Plaths-The-Bell-Jars-new-cover-is-just-perfect-no-chick-lit-in-sight.html. Accessed 24 April 2019.

Gubar, Susan. 'Afterword: The Sister Arts of Sylvia Plath', in *Eye Rhymes: Sylvia Plath's Art of the Visual*, edited by Kathleen Connors and Sally Bayley (Oxford: Oxford University Press, 2007), 223–33.

Gutterman, Lauren Jae. 'Another Enemy Within: Lesbian Wives, or the Hidden Threat to the Nuclear Family in Post-war America', *Gender and History* 24.2 (2012).

Hacker, Helen Mayer. 'Women as a Minority Group', *Social Forces* 30.1 (October, 1951): 60–9.

Hagood, Amanda. 'Wonders with the Sea: Rachel Carson's Ecological Aesthetic and the Mid-Century Reader', *Environmental Humanities* 2 (2013): 57–77.

Halliwell, Martin. *American Culture in the 1950s* (Edinburgh: Edinburgh University Press, 2007).

Hammer, Langdon. 'Plath at War', in *Eye Rhymes: Sylvia Plath's Art of the Visual*, edited by Kathleen Connors and Sally Bayley (Oxford University Press, 2007), 145–57.

'Plath's Lives: Poetry Professionalism, and the Culture of the School', *Representations* 75.1 (Summer 2001): 61–88.

Hardwick, Elizabeth. 'On Sylvia Plath', in *Ariel Ascending: Writing about Sylvia Plath*, edited by Paul Alexander (New York and London: Harper & Row, 1985), 100–15.

Harris, Dianne Suzette. *Little White Houses* (Minneapolis: University of Minnesota Press, 2013).

Hart, Henry. *Seamus Heaney: Poet of Contrary Progressions* (Syracuse, New York: Syracuse University Press, 1992).

'History, Myth, and Apocalypse in Seamus Heaney's *North*', *Contemporary Literature* 30 (Fall 1989): 387–412.

Hayman, Ronald. *The Death and Life of Sylvia Plath* (New York: Birch Lane Publishing Group, 1991).

Heaney, Seamus. *The Government of the Tongue: The 1986 T. S. Eliot Memorial Lectures and Other Critical Writings* (London: Faber and Faber, 1988).

'The Indefatigable Hoof-taps: Sylvia Plath', in *Finders Keepers: Selected Prose 1971–2001* (London, Faber and Faber, 2002).

'The Indefatigable Hoof-taps: Sylvia Plath', in *The Government of the Tongue: The 1986 T. S. Eliot Memorial Lectures and Other Critical Writings* (London: Faber and Faber, 1988), 148–72.

Hedley, Jane. 'Introduction: The Subject of Ekphrasis', in *In the Frame: Women's Ekphrastic Poetry from Marianne Moore to Susan Wheeler*, edited by Nick Halpern Hedley and Willard Spiegelman (Newark: University of Delaware Press, 2009), 15–40.

'Sylvia Plath's Ekphrastic Impulse', in *'I Made You to Find Me': The Coming of Age of the Woman Poet and the Politics of Poetic Address* (Columbus: Ohio State University Press, 2009), 71–102.

Helfand, Jessica. *Scrapbooks: An American History* (New Haven: Yale University Press, 2008).

Heffernan, James. *Museum of Words: The Poetics of Ekphrasis from Homer to Ashbery* (Chicago: University of Chicago Press, 1993).

Helle, Anita. 'Reading the Paratexts of Sylvia Plath's Unabridged Journals', *Plath Profiles* 3 (2010): 94–106.

Hemmerle, Cheryl A. 'That Still, Blue, Almost Eternal Hour: Touching the Sacred and the Profane in Sylvia Plath's Last Poems', in *Critical Insights: Sylvia Plath*, edited by William K. Buckley (Ipswich, Massachusetts: Salem Press, 2013), 273–95.

'Heyday – and Evening – Of the Knitted Dress', *Vogue* (15 October 1955): 128.

Hibbett, Ryan. 'The Hughes/Larkin Phenomenon: Poetic Authenticity in Postwar English Poetry', *Contemporary Literature* 49.1 (Spring 2008): 111–40.

Highet, Gilbert. *The Art of Teaching* (New York: Vintage Books, 1954). *LILLY* hoogland, renée c. '(Sub)textual Configurations: Sexual Ambivalences in Sylvia Plath's *The Bell Jar*', in *Critical Insights: the Bell Jar*, edited by Janet McCann (Ipswich, Massachusetts: Salem Press, 2012), 280–304.

Hobsbaum, Philip. 'The Group: An Experiment in Criticism', *The Yearbook of English Studies* 17 (1987, British Poetry since 1945 Special Number): 75–88.

Hobsbaum, Philip and Edward Lucie-Smith, editors. *A Group Anthology* (London: Oxford University Press, 1963).

Horowitz, Roger. *Putting Meat on the American Table* (Baltimore: Johns Hopkins University Press, 2006).

Howard, Richard. 'Sylvia Plath: "And I Have No Face, I Have Wanted to Efface Myself"', in *The Art of Sylvia Plath: A Symposium*, edited by Charles Newman (London: Faber and Faber, 1970), 77–88.

Howe, Irving. 'The Plath Celebration: A Partial Dissent', in *Sylvia Plath: The Woman and the Work*, edited by Edward Butscher (New York: Dodd, Mead & Company, 1977), 224–35.

Hughes, Ted, and Daniel Weissbort. 'Editors' Note', *Modern Poetry in Translation* 1 (1965): 1.

Huk, Romana. 'Eccentric Concentrism: Traditional Poetic Forms and Refracted Discourse in Stevie Smith's Poetry', *Contemporary Literature* 34.2 (1993): 240–65.

Hurewitz, Daniel. *Stepping Out: Nine Walks Through NYC's Gay and Lesbian Past* (New York: Henry Holt & Company, 1997).

Innes, Sherrie. *The Lesbian Menace: Ideology, Identity, and Representation of the Lesbian Life* (Amherst: University of Massachusetts Press, 1997).

'In Velvet . . .'. *Vogue* (15 August 1950): 126–7.

Jackson, Virginia. 'Lyric', in *The Princeton Encyclopedia of Poetry and Poetics*, 4th edition (Princeton: Princeton University Press, 2012), 826–34.

Jamison, Kay Redfield. *Robert Lowell, Setting the River on Fire: A Story of Genius, Mania, and Character* (New York: Knopf, 2017).

Jinghua, Fan. 'Sylvia Plath's Visual Poetics', in *Eye Rhymes: Sylvia Plath's Art of the Visual*, edited by Kathleen Connors and Sally Bayley (Oxford: Oxford University Press, 2007), 205–22.

Jong, Erica. 'Letters Focus Exquisite Rage of Sylvia Plath', *The Los Angeles Times* (23 November 1975).

Jordison, Sam. 'Don't Judge *The Bell Jar* by Its Cover', *The Guardian* (1 February 2013), www.theguardian.com/books/booksblog/2013/feb/01/the-bell-jar-cover. Accessed 24 April 2019.

Jung, Carl Gustav. *The Archetypes and the Collective Unconscious (Collected Works of C. G. Jung)*, vol. 9, translated and edited by Gerhard Adler and R. F. C. Hull (Princeton: Princeton University Press, 1981).

Kandinsky, Wassily. *Concerning the Spiritual in Art*, translated by M. T. H. Sadler (New York: Dover Publications, 1977).

Katriel, Tamar, and Thomas Farrell. 'Scrapbooks as Cultural Texts: An American Art of Memory', *Text and Performance Quarterly* 11.1 (1991): 1–17.

Kavaler-Adler, Susan. *The Compulsion to Create: Women Writers and Their Demon Lovers* (London: Routledge, 1993).

Keating, Patrick. 'Film Noir and the Culture of Electric Light', *Film History* 27 (2015): 58–84.

Keats, John. *The Crack in the Picture Window* (New York: Ballantine, 1956).

Kellner, Charles H. 'Electroconvulsive Therapy (ECT) in Literature: Sylvia Plath's *The Bell Jar*', *Progress in Brain Research* 206 (2013).

Kendall, Tim. *Sylvia Plath: A Critical Study* (London: Faber and Faber, 2001).

Keniston, Ann. 'The Holocaust Again: Sylvia Plath, Belatedness, and the Limits of Lyric Figure', in *The Unravelling Archive: Essays on Sylvia Plath*, edited by Anita Helle (Ann Arbor: University of Michigan Press, 2007), 139–58.

Kennedy, Elizabeth. '"But We Would Never Talk About It": The Structures of Lesbian Discretion in South Dakota, 1928–1933' in *Inventing Lesbian Cultures in America*, edited by Ellen Lewin (Boston: Beacon Press, 1996).

Kenner, Hugh. *Dublin's Joyce* (London: Chatto & Windus, 1955).

Kirchwey, Karl. 'Women Look at Women: Prophecy and Retrospect in Six Ekphrastic Poems', in *In the Frame: Women's Ekphrastic Poetry from Marianne Moore to Susan Wheeler*, edited by Jane Hedley, Nick Halpern and Willard Spiegelman (Newark: University of Delaware Press, 2009), 93–106.

Kirk, Connie Ann. *Sylvia Plath: A Biography* (London: Greenwood Press, 2004). *Sylvia Plath: A Biography* (New York: Prometheus Books, 2009).

Klein, Viola. 'The Stereotype of Femininity', *Social Issues* 6.3 (Summer 1950): 3–12.

Kneeland, Timothy, and Carol A. B. Warren. *Pushbutton Psychiatry: A History of Electroshock in America*, 2nd edition (Walnut Creek, California: Left Coast Press, 2003).

Knickerbocker, Scott. *Ecopoetics* (Amherst: University of Massachusetts Press, 2012).

Krauss, Rosalind. 'Grids', *October* 9 (Summer 1979): 51–64.

Kroll, Judith. *Chapters in a Mythology* (New York: Harper & Row, 1976).

Kühl, Stefan. *For the Betterment of the Race* (Basingstoke: Palgrave Macmillan, 2013).

Kukil, Karen V. 'The Hot Steamy Drench of the Day: Plath on Poetry', Cathedral of St John the Divine, in Conjunction with the Induction of Sylvia Plath to Poets' Corner, 4 November 2010. Lecture transcript.

Laing, R. D. *The Divided Self* (London: Tavistock Publications, 1960).

La Rocca, David, editor. *Estimating Emerson: An Anthology of Criticism from Carlyle to Cavell* (New York and London: Bloomsbury, 2013).

Lawrence, D. H. *The Complete Poems* (London: Heinemann, 1957). 825P696 L. *SMITH*.

Lazaro, David E. 'Beautiful Clothes: Violet Angotti, Twentieth-Century Dress Designer', in *Dress: The Journal of the Costume Society of America* 37.1 (2011): 39–56.

Locke, Richard. 'The Last Word: Beside *The Bell Jar*', *The New York Times* (20 June 1971), www.nytimes.com/books/98/03/01/home/plath-last.html. Accessed 24 December 2017.

Lee, Hermione. *Biography: A Very Short Introduction* (Oxford: Oxford University Press, 2009).

Lehmann-Haupt, Christopher. 'Elizabeth Hardwick, Writer, Dies at 91', *The New York Times* (4 December 2007): A29.

Leighton, Angela. *On Form: Poetry, Aestheticism and the Legacy of a Word* (Oxford: Oxford University Press, 2007).

Leonard, Garry M. '"The Woman Is Perfected. Her Dead Body Wears the Smile of Accomplishment": Sylvia Plath and Mademoiselle Magazine', *College Literature* 19.2 (1992): 60–82.

Levine, Jay Arnold. 'The Status of the Verse Epistle before Pope', *Studies in Philology* 59.4 (October 1962): 658–84.

Lieberman, Elias. *Paved Streets* (Boston: Cornhill, 1917).

Lieberman, Jennifer. *Electricity in American Life and Letters, 1882–1952* (Cambridge: The MIT Press, 2017).

Lipsitz, George. *Class and Culture in Cold War America* (New York: Praeger, 1981).

Littauer, Amanda H. '"Someone to Love": Teen Girls' Same-Sex Desire in the 1950s United States' in *Creating a Place for Ourselves: Lesbian, Gay and Bisexual Community Histories*, edited by Brett Beemyn (New York: Routledge, 1997).

Lowell, Robert. 'Foreword' to Sylvia Plath, *Ariel* (New York: Harper & Row, 1966), vii–ix.

Lucas, John. 'Value and Validity in Contemporary Poetry', in *Unity in Diversity Revisited? British Literature and Culture in the 1990s*, edited by Barbara Korte and Klaus Peter Müller (Tübingen: Gunter Narr Verlag, 1998), 249–62.

Lysol advertisement, *American Home* (May 1942): 35.

MacKay, Anne, editor. *Wolf Girls at Vassar: Lesbian and Gay Experiences 1930–1990*, (New York: St. Martin's Press, 1993).

Macpherson, Pat. *Reflecting on* The Bell Jar (London and New York: Routledge, 1991).

Malcolm, Janet. *The Silent Woman: Sylvia Plath and Ted Hughes* (New York: Knopf, 1993).

Marcus, Amit. 'A Contextual View of Narrative Fiction in the First Person Plural', *Narrative* 16.1 (January 2008): 46–64.

Marcus, Eric. *Making History: The Struggle for Gay and Lesbian Equal Rights, 1945–1990 – An Oral History* (New York: HarperCollins, 1992).

Marcus, Sharon. 'Fighting Bodies, Fighting Words: A Theory and Politics of Rape Prevention', in *Feminists Theorize the Political*, edited by Judith Butler and Joan Wallach Scott (New York: Routledge, 1992), 385–403.

Marren, Peter. *The New Naturalists* (London: HarperCollins, 2005).

Marthinsen, Leah. 'Purity', in *Theories of Media: Glossary* (University of Chicago, 2004), lucian.uchicago.edu/blogs/mediatheory/keywords/purity/. Accessed 26 April 2019.

Mathers, Madelyn. 'Memo from the Guest Editor', *Mademoiselle* (August 1953): 52–4.

May, Elaine Tyler. *Homeward Bound: American Families in the Cold War Era* (New York: Basic Books, 1988).

May, William. *Stevie Smith and Authorship* (Oxford: Oxford University Press, 2010).

Meyershon, Rolf B. 'Social Research in Television', in *Mass Culture: The Popular Arts in America*, edited by Bernard Rosenberg and David Manning White (New York: The Free Press, 1957).

McClintock, Anne. *Imperial Leather: Race, Gender, and Sexuality in the Colonial Contest* (Abingdon: Routledge, 1995).

McCullough, Frances. 'Anyone Who Remembers', letter to the *Atlantic Monthly* (August 1976).

McGuire, Danielle L. *At the Dark End of the Street: Black Women, Rape, and Resistance—A New History of the Civil Rights Movement from Rosa Parks to the Rise of Black Power* (New York: Vintage Books, 2010).

McKenna, Rollie. 'Sylvia Plath', 1959. *National Portrait Gallery*, www.npg.org.uk /collections/search/portrait/mw209018/Sylvia-Plath. Accessed 18 November 2017.

Middlebrook, Diane. 'The Poetry of Sylvia Plath and Ted Hughes: Call and Response', in *The Cambridge Companion to Sylvia Plath*, edited by Jo Gill (Cambridge: Cambridge University Press, 2006), 156–71.

Her Husband: Hughes and Plath—A Marriage (New York: Viking, 2003).

Milbank, Caroline. *New York Fashion: The Evolution of American Style* (New York: Harry Abrams, 1989).

Mildorf, Jarmila. 'Studying Writings in the Second Person: A Response to Joshua Parker', *Connotations* 23.1 (January 2013): 63–78.

Miller, Ellen. 'Sylvia Plath and White Ignorance: Race and Gender in "The Arrival of the Bee Box"', *Janus Head: Journal of Interdisciplinary Studies, Literature, Continental Philosophy, Phenomenological Psychology and the Arts* 10.1 (2007): 137–56.

Miller, Meredith. 'Secret Agents and Public Victims: The Implied Lesbian Reader', *Journal of Popular Culture* 35. 1 (2001).

Miller, Neil. *Out of the Past: Gay and Lesbian History from 1869 to the Present* (London: Vintage, 1995).

Millett, Kate. *Sexual Politics* (New York: Ballantine Books, 1988).

Mirabella, Angelina. 'The Other Point of View: A Debut Novelist Takes a Chance and Finds her Voice', *Publishers Weekly* (12 January 2015): 64.

'Missing Smith Girl Worried' (Anon.). *The Boston Post* (26 August 1953): 1, 13.

Mitchell, Christine M. 'The Rhetoric of Celebrity Cookbooks', *Journal of Popular Culture* 43.3 (June 2010): 524–39.

Mitchell, Kaye. 'Who is She? Identities, Intertextuality and Authority in Non-Fiction Lesbian Pulp of the 1950s', in *Queer 1950s: Rethinking Sexuality in the Postwar Years*, edited by Heike Bauer and Matt Cook (Basingstoke: Palgrave Macmillan, 2012).

'Mlle's Last Word on: College, '53', *Mademoiselle* (August 1953): 235.

Mohdin, Aamna. 'Women Are Horribly Under-Represented in the World's Top Literary Awards', *Quartz* (17 November 2016), qz.com/838175/the-national-book-award-and-other-top-literary-prizes-seriously-under-represent-women /. Accessed 19 December 2017.

'More Taste Than Money', *Vogue* (15 February 1950): 76–89.

Morrison, Blake. *The Movement: English Poetry and Fiction of the 1950s* (Oxford: Oxford University Press, 1980).

Morrissette, Bruce. 'Narrative "You" in Contemporary Literature', *Comparative Literature Studies* 2.1 (1965): 1–24, www.jstor.org/stable/40245692. Accessed 28 May 2017.

Mortenson, Erik. 'What the Shadows Know: The Crime-Fighting Hero the Shadow and His Haunting of Late-1950s Literature', *American Studies* 54.4 (2016): 99–117.

Mossberg, Barbara Antonina Clarke. 'Sylvia Plath's Baby Book', in *Coming to Light: American Women Poets in the Twentieth Century*, edited by Diane Ward Middlebrook and Marilyn Yalom (Ann Arbor: University of Michigan Press, 1985), 182–94.

Mulvey, Laura. 'Visual Pleasure and Narrative Cinema', in *Visual and Other Pleasures* (Bloomington and Indianapolis: Indiana University Press, 1989), 14–26.

Myers, Lucas. *Crow Steered Bergs Appeared: A Memoir of Ted Hughes and Sylvia Plath* (Sewanee, Tennessee: Proctor's Hall Press, 2001).

Mynors, Roger, editor. *P. Vergili Maronis Opera* (Oxford: Oxford University Press, 1969).

Nadel, Alan. *Containment Culture: American Narratives, Postmodernism and the Atomic Age* (Durham, North Carolina: Duke University Press, 1995).

Nelson, Deborah. 'Plath, History and Politics', in *The Cambridge Companion to Sylvia Plath*, edited by Jo Gill (Cambridge: Cambridge University Press, 2006), 21–35.

  Pursuing Privacy in Cold War America (New York: Columbia University Press, 2002).

Nelson, Maggie. *The Art of Cruelty* (New York: W. W. Norton & Company, 2011).

de Nervaux-Gavoty, Laure. 'Coming to Terms with Colour: Plath's Visual Aesthetic', in *Representing Sylvia Plath*, edited by Sally Bayley and Tracy Brain (Cambridge: Cambridge University Press, 2011), 110–28.

'The New Charm of Red – Disarming', *Vogue* (1 November 1957): 132–3.

Newman, Charles. 'Candor is the Only Wile: The Art of Sylvia Plath', in *The Art of Sylvia Plath: A Symposium*, edited by Charles Newman (London: Faber and Faber, 1970), 21–55.

Newman, Charles, editor. *The Art of Sylvia Plath: A Symposium* (London: Faber and Faber, 1970).

Newton, Esther. 'The "Fun Gay Ladies": Lesbians in Cherry Grove, 1936-1960' in *Creating a Place for Ourselves: Lesbian, Gay and Bisexual Community Histories* edited by Brett Beemyn (New York: Routledge, 1997).

Nicolson, Nigel. 'Introduction', in *The Letters of Virginia Woolf, Volume II: 1912–1922*, edited by Nigel Nicolson and Joanne Trautmann (London: Harcourt Brace Jovanovich, 1978), xiii–xxiv.

Oates, Joyce Carol. 'Adventures in Abandonment', *The New York Times* (28 August 1988): BR3.

'The Death Throes of Romanticism: The Poems of Sylvia Plath', *Southern Review* IX (July 1973): 501–22.

O'Connor, Frank. 'The Lonely Voice', in *Short Story Theories*, edited by Charles E. May (Columbia: Ohio State University Press, 1976).

Ooms, Julie. '"I'm Willing to Let you Know Me If You'll Do the Same": Sylvia Plath's Redemption of Bill the Veteran in "Brief Encounter"', *Plath Profiles* 7 (2014): 33–40.

Oram, Richard W. 'Introduction', in Collecting, Curating, and Researching Writers' Libraries: A Handbook, edited by Richard W. Oram and Joseph Nicholson (Lanham, Maryland: Rowman & Littlefield, 2014).

Paltieli, Guy. 'Solitude de son Propre Coeur: Tocqueville and the Transformation of Democratic Solitude', *The Tocqueville Review* 37.1, 1 (2016): 183–206.

Park Hong, Cathy. 'Whiteness and the Avant Garde', Lana Turner 7, arcade .stanford.edu/content/delusions-whiteness-avant-garde. Accessed 26 April 2019.

Parker, Joshua. 'In Their Own Words: On Writing in the Second Person', *Connotations* 21.2–3 (2011/2012): 165–76.

Patterson, Christina. 'Sharon Olds: Blood Sweat and Fears', *The Independent* (27 October 2006), www.independent.co.uk/arts-entertainment/books/fea tures/sharon-olds-blood-sweat-and-fears-421691.html. Accessed 12 December 2017.

'Peasant Clothes', *LIFE* (17 July 1944): 88–9.

Paulu, Burton. *British Broadcasting: Radio and Television in the United Kingdom* (Minneapolis: University of Minnesota Press, 1956).

Peel, Robin. *Writing Back: Sylvia Plath and Cold War Politics* (Madison: Fairleigh Dickinson University Press, 2002).

Pelt, April. 'Esther's Sartorial Selves: Fashioning a Feminine Identity in *The Bell Jar*', *Plath Profiles* 8 (2015): 13–24.

Penn, Donna. 'The Meanings of Lesbianism in Post-War America', *Gender and History* 3.2 (1991).

Perloff, Marjorie. 'Icon of the Fifties', *Parnassus* 12–13 (1985): 282–5.

Phillips, Claude. *Titian* (New York: Parkstone Press, 2008).

Pollak, Vivian R. 'Moore, Plath, Hughes, and "The Literary Life"', *American Literary History*, 17.1 (2005): 95–117.

Pope, Ged. *Reading London's Suburbs: From Charles Dickens to Zadie Smith* (London: Palgrave Macmillan, 2015).

Pritchard, William H. 'An Interesting Minor Poet?' *New Republic* (30 December 1981): 32–5.

Quinn, Sister Bernetta, O. S. F. 'The Artist as Armored Animal: Marianne Moore, Randall Jarrell', Modern American Poetry, www.modernamericanpoetry.org /creator/sister-bernetta-quinn. Accessed 25 September 2017.

Ramazani, Jahan. *Poetry of Mourning: The Modern Elegy from Hardy to Heaney* (Chicago and London: University of Chicago Press, 1994).

'Red-Black-White', *Flair* (August 1950): 37–43.

Redmond, John. 'The Influence of Sylvia Plath on Seamus Heaney', in *Poetry and Privacy: Questioning Public Interpretations of Contemporary British and Irish Poetry* (Bridgend: Seren, 2013), 111–29.

Rees-Jones, Deryn. *Consorting with Angels: Essays on Modern Women Poets* (Northumberland: Bloodaxe, 2005).

Rich, Adrienne. *What Is Found There: Notebooks on Poetry and Politics* (New York: W. W. Norton & Company, 1993).

Robertson, Nan. 'To Sylvia Plath's Mother, New Play Contains Words of Love', *The New York Times* (9 October 1979), movies2.nytimes.com/books/98/03/ 01/home/plath-mother.html. Accessed 26 April 2019.

Rollyson, Carl. *American Isis: The Life and Art of Sylvia Plath* (New York: St. Martin's Press, 2013).

American Isis: The Life and Art of Sylvia Plath (New York: Picador, 2014).

Rombauer, Irma S., and Marion Rombauer Becker. *Joy of Cooking* (New York: New American Library, 1964 edition).

Romer, A. S. *Man and the Vertebrates: 1* (Harmondsworth: Penguin, 1954).

Rose, Jacqueline. *The Haunting of Sylvia Plath* (Cambridge: Harvard University Press, 1992).

Rosenbaum, Susan. *Professing Sincerity: Modern Lyric Poetry, Commercial Culture, and the Crisis in Reading* (Charlottesville and London: University of Virginia Press, 2007).

Rosenberg, Ethel, and Julius Rosenberg. *The Rosenberg Letters* (London: Dennis Dobson, 1953).

Death House Letters of Ethel and Julius Rosenberg (New York: Jero, 1953).

Rosenstein, Harriet. 'To the Most Wonderful Mummy . . . A Girl Ever Had', *Ms.* (December 1975): 45–9.

Rosenthal, M. L. *The New Poets: American and British Poetry Since World War II* (New York: Oxford University Press, 1967).

Rylands, Philip. 'Palma Vecchio's "Assumption of the Virgin"', *The Burlington Magazine*, 119 (April 1977): 244–50.

Sagar, Keith. *The Laughter of Foxes: A Study of Ted Hughes*, 2nd edition (Liverpool: Liverpool University Press, 2006).

Saldívar, Toni. '"Gleaning the Unsaid Off the Palpable": Seamus Heaney's Response to Sylvia Plath', *Plath Profiles: An Interdisciplinary Journal for Sylvia Plath Studies* [S.l.] 2 (June 2009): 35–54. scholarworks.iu.edu/jour nals/index.php/plath/article/view/4725/4360>. Accessed 13 December 2017.

Sylvia Plath: Confessing the Fictive Self (New York: Peter Lang, 1992).

Sampson, Fiona. Chapter One, 'The Plain Dealers', in *Beyond the Lyric* (London: Chatto & Windus, 2012), 12–35.

'Ted Hughes's Literary Legacy', in *Ted Hughes in Context*, edited by Terry Gifford (Cambridge: Cambridge University Press, 2018), 33–42.

Sanday, Peggy Reeves. *A Woman Scorned: Acquaintance Rape on Trial* (New York: Doubleday, 1996).

Scheerer, Constance. 'The Deathly Paradise of Sylvia Plath', *The Antioch Review* 34.4 (Summer 1976): 469–80.

Scholes, Robert. 'Esther Came Back Like a Retreaded Tire', *New York Times Books* (11 April 1971): 7.

Schott, Webster. 'The Cult of Plath', *Washington Post Book World* (1 October 1972): 3.

Schulze, Robin G. *The Degenerate Muse* (Oxford: Oxford University Press, 2013).

Scigaj, Leonard. 'The Painterly Plath that Nobody Knows', *The Centennial Review*, 32.3 (1988): 220–49.

Scott, J. D. 'In the Movement', *The Spectator* (1 October 1954): 399–400.

Seajay, Carole. 'Essay: Pulp and Circumstance', *The Women's Review of Books*, 23.1 (2006).

Sedgwick, Eve Kosofsky. *Epistemology of the Closet* (Berkeley: University of California Press, 1990).

Sehgal, Parul. 'Sylvia Plath's Letters Reveal a Writer Split in Two', *New York Times Books* (10 October 2017), www.nytimes.com/2017/10/10/books/revie w-sylvia-plath-letters-volume-one.html. Accessed 24 April 2019.

Showalter, Elaine. 'Sunny Sylvia', *Literary Review* (November 2017), literaryreview .co.uk/sunny-sylvia.

Skea, Ann. 'Ted Hughes: *The Wound*', transcript of the interview with Ted Hughes from the Adelaide Festival, reproduced by permission of Radio National and the ABC (Australia); transcribed by Ann Skea. March 1976. a nn.skea.com/ABC2AF.htm. Accessed 24 April 2019.

Smith, Caroline J. '"The Feeding of Young Women": Sylvia Plath's *The Bell Jar*, *Mademoiselle* Magazine, and the Domestic Ideal', *College Literature*, 37.4 (2010): 1–22.

Smith, Patricia Juliana. *Lesbian Panic: Homoeroticism in Modern British Women's Fiction* (New York: Columbia University Press, 1997).

Sontag, Susan. *Reborn: Early Diaries 1947–1963*, edited by David Reiff (London: Hamish Hamilton, 2009).

Styles of Radical Will (London: Penguin, 2009).

Spalding, Frances. *Stevie Smith: A Critical Biography* (London: Faber and Faber, 1988).

'Spanish Styles', *LIFE* (21 August 1950): 57–61.

Spicer, Andrew, and Helen Hanson, editors. *A Companion to Film Noir* (New York: Wiley-Blackwell, 2013).

Spigel, Lynn. *Make Room for TV: Television and the Family Ideal in Postwar America* (Chicago: University of Chicago Press, 2004).

Welcome to the Dreamhouse: Popular Media and Postwar Suburbs (Durham and London: Duke University Press, 2001).

Stanley, Liz. 'The Death of the Letter? Epistolary Intent, Letterness and the Many Ends of Letter-Writing', *Cultural Sociology* 9.2 (2015): 240–55.

Steele, Valerie. *Fifty Years of Fashion: New Look to Now* (New Haven, Connecticut and London: Yale University Press, 1997).

Steinberg, Peter K. 'Translations of Sylvia Plath', *A Celebration This Is*. sylviaplath .info. www.sylviaplath.info/worksnonenglish.html. Accessed 24 April 2019.

'"What's Been Happening in a Lot of American Poetry": Sylvia Plath as Editor and Reviewer', in *These Ghostly Archives: The Unearthing of Sylvia Plath*, edited by Gail Crowther and Peter K. Steinberg (Stroud: Fonthill Media, 2017), 127–43.

Steiner, George. 'Dying is an Art', in *Language and Silence: Essays 1958–1966* (London: Faber and Faber, 1967), 324–31.

Stern, Barbara B. 'Who Talks Advertising? Literary Theory and Narrative "Point of View"', *Journal of Advertising* 20.3 (September 1991): 9–22.

Stern, Frederick C. *F. O. Matthiessen: Christian Socialist as Critic* (Chapel Hill: University of North Carolina Press, 1981).

Sternlicht, Sanford. 'Introduction' in *In Search of Stevie Smith* (Syracuse: Syracuse University Press, 1991).

Stevenson, Anne, *Bitter Fame: A Life of Sylvia Plath* (Boston: Houghton Mifflin, 1989).

Bitter Fame: A Life of Sylvia Plath (London: Penguin, 1989).

Bitter Fame: A Life of Sylvia Plath (London: Penguin, 1990).

Streitmatter, Rodger. *Unspeakable: The Rise of the Gay and Lesbian Press in America* (London: Faber and Faber, 1995).

St John De Crèvecoeur, J. Hector. 'From Letter III. What is an American', in *The Norton Anthology of American Literature, Volume A*, edited by Nina Baym (New York: W. W. Norton & Company, 2011), 657–67.

'Summer Fashion on a Tricolour Basis: Red White Black', *Vogue* (1 June 1957): 114–19.

'Sylvia Plath Tours the Stores and Forecasts May Week Fashions', *Varsity* (26 May 1956): 6–7.

Tansley, Arthur G. 'The Use and Abuse of Vegetational Concepts and Terms' (1935) in *The Philosophy of Ecology: From Science to Synthesis*, edited by David R. Keller and Frank B. Golley (Athens: University of Georgia Press, 2000), 55–70.

Tarrant, Richard, editor. *P. Ovidi Nasonis Metamorphoses* (Oxford: Oxford University Press, 2004).

Temple, Emily. 'A Fifty-Year Visual History of Plath's *The Bell Jar*', *The Atlantic* (16 January 2013), www.theatlantic.com/entertainment/archive/2013/01/a-50-year-visual-history-of-sylvia-plaths-the-bell-jar/267227/. Accessed 24 April 2019.

Thomas, Carolyn de la Peña. *The Body Electric: How Strange Machines Built the Modern American* (New York and London: New York University Press, 2003).

Trautmann Banks, Joanne. 'Introduction' in *Congenial Spirits: The Selected Letters of Virginia Woolf* (London: The Hogarth Press, 1989), vii–xiv.

Travisano, Thomas. *Midcentury Quartet: Bishop, Lowell, Jarrell, Berryman, and the Making of a Postmodern Aesthetic* (Charlottesville and London: University of Virginia Press, 1999).

Tuite, Rebecca. *Seven Sisters Style: The All-American Preppy Look* (New York: Rizzoli, 2014).

Ulmer, Gregory. *Internet Invention: From Literacy to Electracy* (New York: Longman, 2003).

Van Dyne, Susan R. *Revising Life: Sylvia Plath's 'Ariel' Poems* (Chapel Hill: University of North Caroline Press, 1993).

Vendler, Helen. 'The Contest of Melodrama and Restraint: Sylvia Plath's *Ariel*' in *Last Looks, Last Books: Stevens, Plath, Lowell, Bishop, Merrill* (Princeton: Princeton University Press, 2010), 47–69.

   Seamus Heaney (Cambridge, Massachusetts: Harvard University Press, 2000).

Wagner, Erica. *Ariel's Gift* (London: Faber and Faber, 2000).

   'The Many Selves of Sylvia Plath: The Poet's Early Letters Show a Writer in Training', *New Statesman* (6 October 2017), www.newstatesman.com/culture/books/2017/10/many-selves-sylvia-plath-poet-s-early-letters-show-writer-training. Accessed 24 April 2019.

Wagner-Martin, Linda. *The Bell Jar: A Novel of the Fifties* (New York: Macmillan, 1992).

   'Plath and Contemporary American Poetry', in *The Cambridge Companion to Sylvia Plath*, edited by Jo Gill (Cambridge: Cambridge University Press, 2006), 52–62.

   Sylvia Plath: A Biography (New York, Simon & Schuster, 1987; London, Chatto & Windus, 1988).

Wagner-Martin, Linda, editor. *Critical Essays on Sylvia Plath* (Boston: G. K. Hall & Co., 1984).

   Sylvia Plath: The Critical Heritage (London and New York: Routledge, 1988).

Warnock, Mary, et. al. 'Participation Rates: Now We Are 50', *The Times Higher Education Supplement* (25 July 2013), www.timeshighereducation.com/features/participation-rates-now-we-are-50/2005873.article. Accessed 12 December 2017.

Waugh, Patricia. '1963, London: The Myth of the Artist and the Woman Writer', in *The Edinburgh Companion to Twentieth Century Literatures in English*, edited by Brian McHale and Randall Stevenson (Edinburgh: Edinburgh University Press, 2006), 173–85.

Webb, Ruth. '*Ekphrasis* Ancient and Modern: The Invention of a Genre', *Word and Image: A Journal of Verbal/Visual Enquiry* 15.1 (1999): 7–18.

Wertham, Fredric. *Seduction of the Innocent* (New York: Rinehart, 1953).

White, Gillian. *Lyric Shame: The 'Lyric' Subject of Contemporary American Poetry* (Cambridge, Massachusetts: Harvard University Press, 2014).

'Who Won Vogue's 1955 Prix de Paris', *Vogue* (1 August 1955): 142.

Wilson, Andrew. *Mad Girl's Love Song: Sylvia Plath and Life Before Ted* (New York: Scribner, 2013).

   Mad Girl's Love Song: Sylvia Plath and Life Before Ted (London: Simon & Schuster, 2013).

Wilson, Edmund. *Axel's Castle: A Study in the Imaginative Literature of 1870–1930* (New York: Charles Scribner's Sons, 1950). *SMITH.*

Wimsatt, W. K. *The Verbal Icon: Studies in the Meaning of Poetry* (Kentucky: University of Kentucky Press, 1954).

Winder, Elizabeth. 'On Sylvia Plath's Food and Body Issues', interviewed by Jean Fain, *Huffington Post* (27 March 2013, updated 6 December 2017). www.huffington post.com/jean-fain-licsw-msw/sylvia-plath_b_2944939.html. Accessed 24 April 2019.

  Pain, Parties, Work: Sylvia Plath in New York, Summer 1953 (New York: Harper, 2013).

Worster, Donald, *Nature's Economy: A History of Ecological Ideas* [1977] (Cambridge: Cambridge University Press, 1985).

Wrigley, Amanda. 'Dylan Thomas' *Under Milk Wood*, "a Play for Voices" on Radio, Stage and Television', *Critical Studies in Television* 9.3 (2014): 77–88.

Yohannan, Kohle. *Claire McCardell: Redefining Modernism* (New York: Harry N. Abrams, 1998).

Zimring, Carl A. *Clean and White* (New York: New York University Press, 2017).

Index

Abels, Cyrilly, 47, 134
Abse, Dannie, 28, 29
Adams, Henry, 'The Dynamo and the
    Virgin', 267
Adcock, Fleur, 30, 333, 353
The Adjustment of the Male Overt Homosexual
    (Hooker), 172–3
advertising, 87–8, 127–8, 152, 186–7, 191–2,
    196, 210
Aeneid (Virgil), 39, 40
Against Our Will (Brownmiller), 187
Agard, John, 354
Aldrich, Ann, *We Walk Alone*, 175–6
Alexander, Paul, *Rough Magic*, 363, 364, 365
'Alicante Lullaby' (Plath), 78–9
All that Fall (Beckett), 49
'All the Dead Dears' (Plath), 302, 332
Alliston, Susan, 311, 314
Alvarez, Al
    Ariel editions, 205, 341, 342, 360
    British poetry trends, 2, 23–5, 26–7, 28, 29, 31
    ekphrastic poetry, 162
    The New Poetry, 341
    Plath in London, 306, 307, 309, 310, 314, 324
    'Poetry in Extremis', 2, 23–4, 26–7
    The Savage God, 23
    'Sylvia Plath' radio tribute, 342
'America! America!' (Plath), 20
American cuisine, 4, 119, 122, 123–4
American Isis (Rollyson), 363, 364
American Poetry Now (anthology), 20–1
American poetry scene, 1–2, 13–22
Ames, Lois, 77, 347
Amichai, Yehuda, 29
'Amnesiac' (Plath), 60
'Among the Bumblebees' (Plath), 40
'Among the Narcissi' (Plath), 59, 336
'Ancestral Houses' (Yeats), 95
Anderson, Jane V., 267, 289
Anderson, Linda, 66
'Anecdote of the Jar' (Stevens), 163, 164

Angotti, Violet, 130
animal body, 198
Anouilh, Jean, *Antigone*, 38, 256
anthropomorphism, 223–4
Antigone, 34, 38, 81, 256
anti-pastoral elegy, 108
anti-war activism, 241
Antony and Cleopatra (Shakespeare), 367
'Apparel for April' (Plath), 133
'An Appearance' (Plath), 338
'The Applicant' (Plath), 60, 87, 89–90, 140–1
Apuleius, 34–5
    Metamorphoses, 35
'Aquatic Nocturne' (Plath), 335
The Archetypes and the Collective Unconscious
    (Jung), 272
archives
    Emory University, 258
    Lilly Library, 118, 124, 276, 277, 278
    Smith College, 236, 258
Arendt, Hannah, 193
'Ariadne' (de Chirico), 366–7
Ariel (Plath collection)
    American editions, 9, 340, 342–4
    anti-pastoral, 109
    Auden, 16
    auteur cinema, 139, 140, 142
    bee poems, 39–40, 59, 110–11, 355–6
    British editions, 9, 340–2, 344
    British poetry trends, 23, 31
    criticism of imagery, 205
    death of Plath, 314
    electroshock therapy, 264
    experimental poetics, 332
    isolation in Devon, 324
    the lyric, 3, 95, 96, 98, 99, 100, 101, 103
    the pastoral, 111, 112
    Plath biographers, 360–1
    Plath legacy of influence, 351, 354
    religious contexts, 214
    West Yorkshire poems, 8, 300, 304